'I can wholeheartedly endorse this comprehensive and fresh commentary on Numbers. Altmann and Peres offer other scholars, clergy and laypeople a collaborative, ethical and inclusive approach to Numbers in our increasingly pluralistic and complex world. They clearly appreciate and cite numerous scholars, as their bibliography suggests, who are now accessible in this one commentary. The reader can easily discover engaging intertextual references to other parts of the Hebrew Bible and New Testament, as well as a detailed outline for major sections of Numbers. While explicitly stating their readings as shaped by their Christian faith, the enlightening comments of Altmann and Peres are useful to people of any faith or none.'
Dr Adriane Leveen, Senior Lecturer Emeritus in Hebrew Bible, Hebrew Union College

'Despite containing some of the most memorable texts of the Old Testament – the priestly blessing, the manna, the spies, the bronze serpent, Balaam and his donkey – Numbers is often avoided by modern readers. Altmann and Peres interpret this intriguing and beautiful book with historical and theological sensitivity, explaining its unfamiliar concepts and unravelling its difficulties. Pastors, teachers and missionaries, among others, will find it a sure-footed guide to the contemporary understanding of this text.'
Nathan MacDonald, Professor of the Interpretation of the Old Testament, Divinity faculty, and Fellow of St John's College, University of Cambridge

'Altmann and Peres expertly guide the reader through the challenging wilderness landscape of Numbers. They combine an impressive array of perspectives: engagement with the best and most recent scholarship on Numbers, skilful literary sensitivity to how Numbers works as an ancient "book", generative "readings in concert" between two or more biblical texts, theological and pedagogical insights for faith and life, and a Majority World postcolonial lens around issues of identity, empire and justice. One of the best commentaries on Numbers now available.'
Dennis Olson, Charles Haley Professor of Old Testament Theology Emeritus, Princeton Theological Seminary, New Jersey

'This fine commentary is the happy result of a collaboration between two scholars from diverse backgrounds and lived experiences. As a result, the excellent technical commentary on the text is supplemented by sensitive pastoral reflections, which together will make the book an essential addition to the library of scholars, pastors and preachers. I shall be consulting it repeatedly.'

Helen Paynter, Director of the Centre for the Study of Bible and Violence, and Tutor in Biblical Studies, Bristol Baptist College

'The TOTC commentary is well known and highly regarded, not least for its accessible and manageable treatments of the biblical text. In this commentary, Altmann and Peres have hit those high marks while simultaneously including an immense amount of reflection and up-to-date research – all very well written and supremely crafted. The result is a remarkable achievement, with every page brimming with insight that repeatedly demonstrates the ongoing and contemporary utility of Numbers. I recommend it enthusiastically.'

Brent A. Strawn, D. Moody Smith Distinguished Professor of Old Testament, and Professor of Law, Duke University, North Carolina

Tyndale Old Testament Commentaries

Volume 4

TOTC

Numbers

Tyndale Old Testament Commentaries

Volume 4

Series Editor: David G. Firth
Consulting Editor: Tremper Longman III

Numbers

An Introduction and Commentary

Peter Altmann and Caio Peres

ivp

IVP
Academic
An imprint of InterVarsity Press
Downers Grove, Illinois

InterVarsity Press, USA
P.O. Box 1400 | Downers Grove, IL 60515-1426
ivpress.com | email@ivpress.com

Inter-Varsity Press, England
SPCK Group, Studio 101, The Record Hall, 16–16A Baldwin's Gardens
London EC1N 7RJ, England
ivpbooks.com | ivp@ivpbooks.com

InterVarsity Press® is the publishing division of InterVarsity Christian Fellowship/USA®. For more information, visit intervarsity.org.

Inter-Varsity Press, England, originated within the Inter-Varsity Fellowship, now the Universities and Colleges Christian Fellowship, a student movement connecting Christian Unions in universities and colleges throughout Great Britain, and a member movement of the International Fellowship of Evangelical Students.

Unless otherwise noted, Scripture quotations are taken from the New Revised Standard Version of the Bible, Anglicized Edition, copyright © 1989, 1995 by the Division of Christian Education of the National Council of the Churches of Christ in the USA. Used by permission. All rights reserved.

USA ISBN 978-1-5140-1365-6 (hc print) | USA ISBN 978-0-8308-4290-2 (pb print) |
USA ISBN 978-0-8308-9222-8 (digital)

UK ISBN 978-1-78974-524-5 (print) | UK ISBN 978-1-78974-525-2 (digital)

Typeset by Fakenham Prepress Solutions, Fakenham, Norfolk NR21 8NL

Library of Congress Cataloging-in-Publication Data
A catalog record for this book is available from the Library of Congress.

British Library Cataloguing-in-Publication Data
A catalogue record for this book is available from the British Library.

32   31   30   29   28   27   26   25 | 10   9   8   7   6   5   4   3   2   1

CONTENTS

GENERAL PREFACE

The decision to completely revise the Tyndale Old Testament Commentaries is an indication of the important role that the series has played since its opening volumes were released in the mid 1960s. They represented at that time, and have continued to represent, commentary writing that was committed both to the importance of the text of the Bible as Scripture and a desire to engage with as full a range of interpretative issues as possible without being lost in the minutiae of scholarly debate. The commentaries aimed to explain the biblical text to a generation of readers confronting models of critical scholarship and new discoveries from the Ancient Near East while remembering that the Old Testament is not simply another text from the ancient world. Although no uniform process of exegesis was required, all the original contributors were united in their conviction that the Old Testament remains the word of God for us today. That the original volumes fulfilled this role is evident from the way in which they continue to be used in so many parts of the world.

A crucial element of the original series was that it should offer an up-to-date reading of the text, and it is precisely for this reason that new volumes are required. The questions confronting readers in the first half of the twenty-first century are not necessarily those from the second half of the twentieth. Discoveries from the Ancient Near East continue to shed new light on the Old Testament, while emphases in exegesis have changed markedly. While remaining true to the goals of the initial volumes, the need for contemporary study of the text requires that the series as a whole be updated. This updating is not simply a matter of commissioning new volumes to replace the old. We have also taken the opportunity to update the format of the series to reflect a key emphasis from linguistics, which is that texts communicate in larger blocks rather than in shorter segments such as individual verses. Because of this, the treatment of each section of the text includes three segments. First, a short note on *Context* is offered, placing the passage under consideration in its literary setting within the book as well as noting any historical issues crucial to interpretation. The *Comment* segment then follows the traditional structure of the commentary, offering exegesis of the various components of a passage. Finally, a brief comment is made on *Meaning*, by which is meant the message that the passage seeks to communicate within the book, highlighting its key theological themes. This section brings together the detail of the *Comment* to show how the passage under consideration seeks to communicate as a whole.

Our prayer is that these new volumes will continue the rich heritage of the Tyndale Old Testament Commentaries and that they will continue to witness to the God who is made known in the text.

David G. Firth, Series Editor
Tremper Longman III, Consulting Editor

AUTHORS' PREFACE

Our joint efforts over several years brought this commentary to its final form. Initially, Peter was the single author, but he invited Caio to join him as a co-author. Peter wrote drafts on Numbers 1 – 19; 27 – 29; 31; 36; and Caio wrote on Numbers 20 – 26; 30; 32 – 35. We provided each other with extensive feedback on and suggestions for one another's work. For the Introduction, the writing process for most of the material was more synchronized, with constant shared decision-making and contributions. Some topics, however, were mostly written by one of us. Peter is mostly responsible for the topics on Numbers as a book and its composition, how to read Numbers, and biblical 'law'. Caio is primarily responsible for the topics on Israel's identity, holiness and impurity, and atonement and ritual.

We have sought to create a cohesive and balanced text, and we are proud to present a joint commentary. Still, some differences of opinion, approach and style remain. This is inevitable, given our different social locations, personal experiences and academic formation. We consider it uncontroversial to say that the meaning of the text of the Bible requires interpretation. We, as readers, make interpretive choices according to our conscious and unconscious orientations and presuppositions. Given the importance of the biblical text for how numerous individuals and communities lead their lives – our own included – our interpretation has serious ethical implications. Therefore, we each take responsibility for the end result of our chapters and topics. For this reason, we find it essential to articulate our own identities and commitments that, consciously and unconsciously, affect our engagement with the biblical text.

I (Peter) come to the biblical text and the composition of this commentary with gratitude for the deep instruction I received as a theologian and biblical scholar in the profoundly privileged institutions of the Seattle School of Theology and Psychology, Princeton Theological Seminary, the University of Zurich and now Fuller Theological Seminary. My white, male, able-bodied, socio-economically privileged and cosmopolitan Euro-North American background has afforded me the resources and institutional settings to drink deeply of the classic historical-critical tradition, which leads me to value the specific historical particularity of all texts, including canonical biblical ones like Numbers. However, especially my experiences at the Seattle School, Princeton and Fuller invited me to value and seek out a concert of dialogue partners who would necessarily challenge my limited view of the biblical texts. Coming to terms with the contextually limited approach(es) of the modern West – and with the broader historical Christian tradition – has fruitfully informed my interpretation of the texts of Numbers. It also motivated my invitation to Caio to join as a co-author, bringing both his expertise and life experience with regard to specific themes that are prevalent in Numbers. Interest in writing this commentary grew after translating a number of essays by Christian Frevel (published 2020), which suggested to me that Numbers has much to say for the global church's current challenges surrounding movement away from largely Euro-American to Majority World-led institutions and embodiments of faith. I hope that our interpretive work can play a positive role in this development in enlarging God's reign.

Several characteristics of my (Caio) personal experience and identity make me a part of the privileged status quo of Christian Western biblical scholarship. I am a white male Christian with academic training in continental Europe (Vrije Universiteit Amsterdam). Many other parts of who I am, however, distance me from this position. I am Brazilian, live in Brazil, and work as an independent scholar. My scholarship has grown out of and is intertwined with my own and my wife's long history of Christian missionary ministry among vulnerable children and teenagers in the slums of São Paulo. Last, but not least, as a result of our missionary ministry, we are adoptive parents of two beautiful children.

Most fundamentally, my personal experience and identity have led me to pay attention to the margins and to social ethics when approaching the biblical text. Matters of identity unrelated to biological ties, family and communitarian life, inequality of access to social and material resources, food production and consumption, and political oppression and violence have moved to the centre of my scholarship and interpretation of the biblical text. Even more important is that these issues hold more than merely academic significance for me. They affect my personal faith, missionary ministry and family life. Therefore, one of my main interests concerns the ways these issues permeate and form the theology and the religious experience of ancient Israel, Jesus' ministry and followers, the early church, and contemporary church life and missions.

Recognizing my privilege as a white male Christian scholar, I intentionally and joyfully allow Jewish, non-religious, female, black, indigenous and other minority scholars to challenge and influence my perceptions. My sensitivity to the margins and to ethics also leads me to value dialogical, dynamic, non-violent and cooperative approaches to interpretation that I believe can be best described as postcolonial hermeneutics. For this reason, although I make an effort to recognize honestly the possibility that biblical texts may reflect patriarchal, misogynistic, xenophobic and violent purposes, I deliberately choose not to let this be the last word about the biblical text. I find ways in which the text itself and its context can provide tools to advance the love, justice and peace that allow for human and creational flourishing. One of the most important things I have learned from the book of Numbers in the process of writing this commentary is relevant here: we are invited to engage divine revelation with our own input, in view of the common good, with special consideration and care for the more vulnerable parts of the community. Numbers invites us to engage with it and make interpretive choices that will challenge its conscious or unconscious blind spots, so that it cannot be used for ill but for good, and make God's word a source of blessing, nourishment and hope for all. I hope I am following this model faithfully in this commentary and in my scholarship.

Several brief notes on our use of specific terminology are appropriate. Our Christian conviction informs our choices to capitalize the term 'God', to write out the divine name, Yahweh, except where we refer to an author or modern English translation that uses 'Lord/LORD', and to use the expression 'Old Testament' (OT). While we have generally worked from the Hebrew Masoretic Text (MT) in comparison with the Greek Septuagint (LXX) translation, we primarily use the New Revised Standard Version (NRSV) as a base English text where we offer English renderings of the text.

Finally, many people have served as inspiration and support throughout the process of writing this commentary. First, David Firth and Thomas Creedy have provided encouragement, insight, critique and flexibility throughout the years it has taken to get over the finish line. They warmly embraced our co-authorship, which we think greatly improves the commentary. We are especially appreciative of the access they provided to L. Michael Morales' commentary on Numbers, which we unfortunately received only at the final stages of revising our work, such that we interact with it only on a cursory level.

I (Peter) am grateful for Tremper Longman III's introduction to David Firth, which brought about the invitation to take on this project. Konrad Schmid (Zurich) found many ways to provide me with financial and institutional support that allowed me to continue to work on this project. In particular, the joint universities of Lausanne, Tel Aviv and Zurich Swiss National Science Foundation Sinergia project 'The History of the Pentateuch: Combining Literary and Archaeological Approaches' and the European Research Council project 'How God Became a Lawgiver' (under the European Union's Horizon 2020 research and innovation programme grant agreement No. 833222) deeply enriched my reflections. I am grateful for numerous dialogue partners who have provided their own publications and insights related to Numbers: Anna Angelini, Jordan Davis, Christian Frevel, Jürg Hutzli, Jaeyoung Jeon, Nathan MacDonald, Christophe

Nihan, Katharina Pyschny and Julia Rhyder. My theology book club in Reno, Nevada, agreed to read through Numbers and offer insightful comments from their lay point of view. Finally, my wife Birgit has remained an unflagging North Star through the trials and joys of these years.

As an independent scholar on the margins of biblical scholarship and in a missionary context, my (Caio) participation as a co-author for this commentary was possible only because of the encouragement and generosity of many amazing people. To all of them I owe sincere thanks for being the means of God's grace and love. A project like this is never the result of the authors as individual geniuses, but the fruit of collective efforts.

My family and I have been financially supported by a network of families and friends. In Brazil, special thanks go to Igreja da Fé Cristã, the church where I was a member when I first went into missions, and to my dear aunt 'Tia' Vera. Many brothers and sisters in the Netherlands, my wife's home country, have supported us as well. Special thanks to Peter van der Ster and Karel Remmelink at Stichting Nehemia, a missionary fund of the Vergadering van gelovigen. The support we have received from my wife's home church, Eykpunt Gemeente Utrecht, is beyond generous. Their constant interest, trust and involvement in our lives and ministries have sustained us throughout the years.

My parents, Valdir Peres and Marily Dias Peres, have provided the stable and safe foundation for me to keep walking this uncertain and at times precarious path of missionary and academic life. Dot, my wife, continues to be my main inspiration. She believes in my abilities and capacities more than I do and has encouraged me to push through the hard moments of my academic pursuit, including at various points during the writing of this commentary.

The way my academic life has taken shape does not allow me to claim merit for my achievements or mastery over the subject of my research. Therefore, I would like to thank some female friends and colleagues who have read parts of the commentary that are more sensitive to women: my dear friend Amie Aitken, as well as Dr Alexiana Fry and Dr Helen Paynter. Finally, I cannot thank Peter enough. Co-authoring this commentary is solely due to his incredibly generous invitation, after he had already completed a large part of the project. For several years now, Peter has been a mentor and a friend to whom I owe so many of my academic achievements. He models the kind of life-giving leadership idealized in Numbers that I aspire to imitate.

Peter Altmann and Caio Peres

ABBREVIATIONS

ATANT	Abhandlungen zur Theologie des Alten und Neuen Testaments
BETL	Bibliotheca Ephemeridum Theologicarum Lovaniensium
BZABR	Beihefte zur Zeitschrift für altorientalische und biblische Rechtsgeschichte
BZAW	Beihefte zur Zeitschrift für die alttestamentliche Wissenschaft
COS	W. W. Hallo (ed.), *The Context of Scripture*, 3 vols. (Leiden: Brill, 2003)
esp.	especially
FAT	Forschungen zum Alten Testament
HALOT	L. Koehler and W. Baumgartner, *The Hebrew and Aramaic Lexicon of the Old Testament* (Leiden: Brill, 1994–2000)
JSOTSup	Journal for the Study of the Old Testament Supplement Series
m.	Mishnah
NICOT	New International Commentary on the Old Testament
NT	New Testament
OBO	Orbis Biblicus et Orientalis
OT	Old Testament
par.	parallel (text)
TOTC	Tyndale Old Testament Commentaries

Bible versions

AT	author translation
ESV	The ESV Bible (The Holy Bible, English Standard Version), copyright © 2001 by Crossway, a publishing ministry of Good News Publishers. Used by permission. All rights reserved
KJV	The Authorized Version of the Bible (The King James Bible), the rights in which are vested in the Crown, reproduced by permission of the Crown's Patentee, Cambridge University Press
LXX	Septuagint (pre-Christian Greek version of the Old Testament)
MT	Masoretic Text (the standard Hebrew text of the Old Testament)
NASB	New American Standard Bible®, Copyright © 1960, 1971, 1977, 1995, 2020 by The Lockman Foundation. All rights reserved
NASB 1995	The NEW AMERICAN STANDARD BIBLE®, Copyright © 1960, 1962, 1963, 1968, 1971, 1972, 1973, 1975, 1977, 1995 by The Lockman Foundation. Used by permission
NET	The NET Bible, New English Translation, copyright © 1996 by Biblical Studies Press, LLC. NET Bible is a registered trademark
NIV	The Holy Bible, New International Version (Anglicized edition). Copyright © 1979, 1984, 2011 by Biblica. Used by permission of Hodder & Stoughton Ltd, an Hachette UK company. All rights reserved. 'NIV' is a registered trademark of Biblica. UK trademark number 1448790
NKJV	The New King James Version. Copyright © 1982 by Thomas Nelson, Inc. Used by permission. All rights reserved
NLT	New Living Translation
NRSV	New Revised Standard Version

BIBLIOGRAPHY

Achenbach, R. (2003), *Die Vollendung der Tora: Studien zur Redaktionsgeschichte des Numeribuches im Kontext von Hexateuch und Pentateuch*, BZABR 3 (Wiesbaden: Harrassowitz).

Ackerman, S. (2011), 'Who Is Sacrificing at Shiloh? The Priesthoods of Ancient Israel's Regional Sanctuaries', in M. Leuchter and J. M. Hutton (eds.), *Levites and Priests in Biblical History and Tradition*, Ancient Israel and Its Literature 9 (Atlanta: SBL Press), pp. 25–43.

Adam, K.-P. (2012), 'A Didactic Case Narrative on Homicide Law: 1 Samuel 26', in K.-P. Adam, F. Avemarie and N. Wazana (eds.), *Law and Narrative in the Bible and in Neighboring Ancient Cultures*, FAT II/54 (Tübingen: Mohr Siebeck), pp. 107–113.

Akil, T. (2008), 'Ecos no jardim de YHWH: Seis novas relações intertextuais entre Gn 2–3 e Nm 22–24', *Atualidade Teológica* 28: 71–81.

Altmann, P. (2011), *Festive Meals in Ancient Israel: Deuteronomy's Identity Politics in Their Ancient Near Eastern Context*, BZAW 424 (Berlin: de Gruyter).

—— (2021), 'The Significance of the Divine Torah in Ptolemaic Egypt in Documentary and Literary Sources from the Third and Second Centuries BCE', *Journal for the Study of Judaism* 53: 1–31.

Altmann, P. and A. Spiciarich (2020), 'Chickens, Partridges, and the /Tor/ of Ancient Israel and the Hebrew Bible', *Die Welt des Orients* 50: 2–30.

Alves, R. (1972), *Tomorrow's Child: Imagination, Creativity, and the Rebirth of Culture* (New York: Harper and Row).

—— (1974), 'The Seed of the Future: The Community of Hope', *International Review of Mission* 63.252: 551–569.

Amzallag, N. (2016), 'The Serpent as a Symbol of Primeval Yahwism', *Semitica* 58: 207–236.

Anderson, G. A. (2015), '"Through Those Who Are Near to Me, I Will Show Myself Holy": Nadab and Abihu and Apophatic Theology', *Catholic Biblical Quarterly* 77.1: 1–19.

Angelini, A. and C. Nihan (2016), 'Holiness', in C. M. Furey, P. Gemeinhardt, J. M. LeMon, T. C. Römer, J. Schröter, B. D. Walfish and E. Ziolkowski, *Encyclopedia of the Bible and Its Reception Online* (Berlin: de Gruyter), accessed 23 October 2023, https://doi-org.fuller.idm.oclc.org/10.1515/ebr.holiness.

Armgardt, M., B. Kilchör and M. Zehnder (eds.) (2019), *Paradigm Change in Pentateuchal Research*, BZABR 22 (Wiesbaden: Harrassowitz).

Artuso, V. and F. Zandonadi Catenassi (2012), 'A ambivalência do simbolismo da serpente em Nm 21,4–9', *Horizonte* 10.25: 176–200.

Ashley, T. R. (2022), *The Book of Numbers*, NICOT, 2nd edn (Grand Rapids: Eerdmans; e-book).

Avner, U. (2014), 'Egyptian Timna – Reconsidered', in J. M. Tebes (ed.), *Unearthing the Wilderness: Studies on the History and Archaeology of the Negev and Edom in the Iron Age*, Ancient Near Eastern Studies Supplement 45 (Leuven: Peeters), pp. 103–163.

Awabdy, M. A. (2023), *Numbers: An Exegetical and Theological Bible Commentary*, Baker Commentary on the Old Testament (Grand Rapids: Baker).

Ayali-Darshan, N. (2015), 'The Seventy Bulls Sacrificed at Sukkot (Num 29:12–34) in Light of a Ritual Text from Emar (Emar 6, 373)', *Vetus Testamentum* 65: 9–19.

Bach, A. (1993), 'Good to the Last Drop: Viewing the Sotah (Numbers 5.11–31) as the Glass Half Empty and Wondering How to View It Half Full', in J. C. Exum and D. J. A. Clines (eds.), *The New Literary Criticism and the Hebrew Bible* (Valley Forge, PA: Trinity Press International), pp. 26–54.

Baden, J. S. (2009), *J, E, and the Redaction of the Pentateuch*, FAT 68 (Tübingen: Mohr Siebeck).

—— (2012), *The Composition of the Pentateuch: Renewing the Documentary Hypothesis*, Anchor Yale Bible Reference Library (New Haven: Yale University Press).

—— (2014), 'The Narratives of Numbers 20 – 21', *The Catholic Biblical Quarterly* 76.4: 634–652.

Bailey, C. (2018), *Bedouin Culture in the Bible* (New Haven: Yale University Press).

Bailey, R. C. (1991), 'Beyond Identification: The Use of Africans in Old Testament Poetry and Narratives', in C. H. Felder (ed.), *Stony the Road We Trod: African American Biblical Interpretation* (Minneapolis: Fortress), pp. 165–184.

Balogh, A. L. (2018), *Moses among the Idols: Mediators of the Divine in the Ancient Near East* (Lanham: Lexington Books).

Barmash, P. (2004), 'Blood Feud and State Control: Differing Legal Institutions for the Remedy of Homicide During the Second and First Millennia BCE', *Journal of Near Eastern Studies* 63.3: 183–199.

—— (2005), *Homicide in the Biblical World* (Cambridge: Cambridge University Press).

Bartor, A. (2010), *Reading Law as Narrative: A Study in the Casuistic Laws of the Pentateuch* (Atlanta: SBL Press).

—— (2016), 'Legal Texts', in J. Barton (ed.), *The Hebrew Bible: A Critical Companion* (Princeton: Princeton University Press), pp. 160–182.

Bauks, M. (2012), 'Sacred Trees in the Garden of Eden and Their Ancient Near Eastern Precursors', *Journal of Ancient Judaism* 3.3: 267–301.

Bautch, R. J. (2012), 'The Formulary of Atonement (Lev 16:21) in Penitential Prayers of the Second Temple Period', in T. Hieke and T. Nicklas (eds.), *The Day of Atonement: Its Interpretations in Early Jewish and Christian Traditions* (Leiden: Brill), pp. 33–45.

Begg, C. T. (2012), 'Yom Kippur in Josephus', in T. Hieke and T. Nicklas (eds.), *The Day of Atonement: Its Interpretations in Early Jewish and Christian Traditions* (Leiden: Brill), pp. 97–120.

Bell, C. (1992), *Ritual Theory, Ritual Practice* (Oxford: Oxford University Press).

Ben-Gad HaCohen, D. (2016), 'Biblical Criticism from a Geographer's Perspective: "Transjordan" as a Test Case', in J. C. Gertz, B. M. Levinson, D. Rom-Shiloni and K. Schmid (eds.), *The Formation of the Pentateuch*, FAT 111 (Tübingen: Mohr Siebeck), pp. 687–710.

Ben-Shlomo, D. (2018), 'The Ancient City of Hebron', TheTorah.com, https://www.thetorah.com/article/the-ancient-city-of-hebron, accessed 15 August 2023.

Berman, J. A. (2017), *Inconsistency in the Torah: Ancient Literary Convention and the Limits of Source Criticism* (Oxford: Oxford University Press).

Bietak, M. (2015), 'On the Historicity of the Exodus: What Egyptology Today Can Contribute to Assessing the Biblical Account of the Sojourn in Egypt', in T. E. Levy, T. Schneider and W. H. C. Propp (eds.), *Israel's Exodus in Transdisciplinary Perspective: Text, Archaeology, Culture, and Geoscience* (Cham: Springer), pp. 17–38.

Bloch, Y. (2022), 'Blood Vengeance in Ancient Near Eastern Context', TheTorah.com, https://thetorah.com/article/blood-vengeance-in-ancient-near-eastern-context, accessed 24 July 2023.

Blum, E. (1990), *Studien zur Komposition des Pentateuch*, BZAW 189 (Berlin: de Gruyter).

Borowski, O. (1998), *Every Living Thing: Daily Use of Animals in Ancient Israel* (Walnut Creek: Altamira Press).

Brenner, A. (1982), *Colour Terms in the Old Testament*, JSOTSup 21 (Sheffield: JSOT Press).

Briant, P. (2002), *From Cyrus to Alexander: A History of the Persian Empire*, tr. P. T. Daniels (Winona Lake, IN: Eisenbrauns).

Brown, D. W. (2009), *A New Introduction to Islam* (Malden, MA: Wiley-Blackwell).

Brown, K. (2015), 'Vengeance and Vindication in Numbers 31', *Journal of Biblical Literature* 134: 65–84.

Brubaker, R. and F. Cooper (2000), 'Beyond "Identity"', *Theory and Society* 29.1: 1–47.

Budd, P. J. (1984), *Numbers*, Word Biblical Commentary (Waco: Word).

Burke, A. A. (2023a), 'Amorites and Canaanites: Memory, Tradition, and Legacy in Ancient Israel and Judah', in K.

H. Keimer and G. A. Pierce (eds.), *The Ancient Israelite World* (London: Routledge), pp. 523–536.

—— (2023b), 'New Kingdom Egypt and Early Israel: Entangled Identities', in K. H. Keimer and G. A. Pierce (eds.), *The Ancient Israelite World* (London: Routledge), pp. 537–548.

Calabro, D. (2017), 'A Reexamination of the Ancient Israelite Gesture of Hand Placement', in H. L. Wiley and C. A. Eberhart (eds.), *Sacrifice, Cult, and Atonement in Early Judaism and Christianity: Constituents and Critique* (Atlanta: SBL Press), pp. 99–124.

Calvin, J. (1852–55), *Commentaries on the Last Four Books of Moses Arranged in a Form of a Harmony*, tr. Charles W. Bingham, vols. 1–4 (Edinburgh: Calvin Translation Society).

—— (1960), *Institutes of the Christian Religion*, ed. John T. McNeill and tr. Ford Lewis Battles, 2 vols., Library of Christian Classics (Philadelphia: Westminster Press).

Carsten, J. (2004), 'The Substance of Kinship and the Heat of the Hearth: Feeding, Personhood, and Relatedness among the Malays in Pulau Langkawi', in R. Parkin and L. Stone, *Kinship and the Family: An Anthropological Reader* (Malden, MA: Wiley-Blackwell), pp. 309–327.

Catenassi, F. Z. (2018), 'Reclamando "de barriga cheia": O maná e as codornizes em Qibrot-hatta'awah (Nm 11,4–35)', *Estudos Bíblicos* 35.137: 11–24.

Chapman, C. R. (2023), 'The Field Belonging to Boaz: Creating Kinship through Land, Labor, Food, and Feeding', *Journal of Biblical Literature* 142.3: 431–450.

Chapman, S. B. (2013), 'Martial Memory, Peaceable Vision: Divine War in the Old Testament', in H. Thomas, J. A. Evans and P. Copan, *Holy War in the Bible: Christian Morality and an Old Testament Problem* (Downers Grove, IL: InterVarsity Press), pp. 47–67.

Chavel, S. (2012), 'The Face of God and the Etiquette of Eye-Contact: Visitation, Pilgrimage, and Prophetic Vision in Ancient Israelite and Early Jewish Imagination', *Jewish Studies Quarterly* 19: 1–55.

—— (2014), *Oracular Law and Priestly Historiography in the Torah*, FAT II/71 (Tübingen: Mohr Siebeck).

Christensen, D. L. (1974), 'Num 21:14–15 and the Book of the Wars of Yahweh', *Catholic Biblical Quarterly* 36: 359–360.

Christian, M. A. (2008), 'Openness to the Other Inside and Outside of Numbers', in T. Römer (ed.), *The Books of Leviticus and Numbers* (Leuven: Peeters), pp. 579–608.

Coats, G. W. (1993), *The Moses Tradition*, JSOTSup 161 (Sheffield: JSOT Press).

Cocco, F. (2016), *The Torah as a Place of Refuge: Biblical Criminal Law and the Book of Numbers* (Tübingen: Mohr Siebeck).

—— (2020a), 'El libro de los Números como "quintaesencia de La Torá": Uma nueva clave para estructurar el cuarto libro de Moisés', *Revista Bíblica* 82.3–4: 253–274.

—— (2020b), *Women in the Wilderness*, FAT 138 (Tübingen: Mohr Siebeck).

Cozolino, L. (2014), *The Neuroscience of Human Relationships: Attachment and the Developing Social Brain* (New York: W. W. Norton & Company).

Cross, F. M. (1973), *Canaanite Myth and Hebrew Epic* (Cambridge, MA: Harvard University Press).

Crowell, B. L. (2009), 'Postcolonial Studies and the Hebrew Bible', *Currents in Biblical Research* 7.2: 217–244.

Davies, E. W. (1995a), 'A Mathematical Conundrum: The Problem of the Large Numbers in Numbers i and xxvi', *Vetus Testamentum* 45: 449–469.

—— (1995b), *Numbers*, New Century Bible (Grand Rapids: Eerdmans).

—— (2017), *Numbers: The Road to Freedom* (London: T&T Clark).

Davies, G. I. (1974), 'The Wilderness Itineraries: A Comparative Study', *Tyndale Bulletin* 25: 46–81.

Davis, E. F. (2009), *Scripture, Culture, and Agriculture: An Agrarian Reading of the Bible* (Cambridge: Cambridge University Press).

—— (2019), *Opening Israel's Scriptures* (Oxford: Oxford University Press).

Davis, J. (2022), *The End of the Book of Numbers: On Pentateuchal Models and Compositional Issues*, Archaeology and Bible 6 (Tübingen: Mohr Siebeck).

Davis, S. (2016), 'The Invisible Women: Numbers 30 and the Politics of Singleness in Africana Communities', in G. L.

Byron and V. Lovelace, *Womanist Interpretations of the Bible: Expanding the Discourse* (Atlanta: SBL Press), pp. 21–47.

Dearman, J. A. (1997), 'Roads and Settlements in Moab', *The Biblical Archaeologist* 60.4: 205–213.

Diamant, S. (2009), 'Group Identity in the Hebrew Bible: Moab as a Case of Israelite Self-Identity', PhD dissertation, The Jewish Theological Seminary of America.

Dijkstra, M. (1995), 'Is Balaam Also among the Prophets?', *Journal of Biblical Literature* 114.1: 43–64.

Dobbs-Allsopp, F. W., J. J. M. Roberts, C. L. Seow and C. R. Whittaker (2004), *Hebrew Inscriptions: Texts from the Biblical Period of the Monarchy with Concordance* (New Haven: Yale University Press).

Douglas, M. (1996), 'Sacred Contagion', in J. F. A. Sawyer (ed.), *Reading Leviticus: A Conversation with Mary Douglas* (Sheffield: Sheffield Academic), pp. 86–106.

—— (2001), *In the Wilderness: The Doctrine of Defilement in the Book of Numbers* (Oxford: Oxford University Press).

Dozeman, T. B. (2008), 'The Midianites in the Formation of the Book of Numbers', in T. Römer (ed.), *The Books of Leviticus and Numbers* (Leuven: Peeters), pp. 261–284.

Eberhart, C. A. (2004), 'A Neglected Feature of Sacrifice in the Hebrew Bible: Remarks on the Burning Rite on the Altar', *Harvard Theological Review* 97.4: 485–493.

—— (2017), 'To Atone or Not to Atone: Remarks on the Day of Atonement Rituals According to Leviticus 16 and the Meaning of Atonement', in H. L. Wiley and C. A. Eberhart (eds.), *Sacrifice, Cult, and Atonement in Early Judaism and Christianity: Constituents and Critique* (Atlanta: SBL Press), pp. 97–232.

Eichler, R. (2021), 'A Sin Is Borne: Clearing up the Law of Women's Vows (Numbers 30)', *Vetus Testamentum* 71.3: 317–328.

Erbele-Küster, D. (2017), '"She Shall Remain in (Accordance to) Her Blood-of-Purification": Ritual Dynamics of Defilement and Purification in Leviticus 12', in H. L. Wiley and C. A. Eberhart (eds.), *Sacrifice, Cult, and Atonement in Early Judaism and Christianity: Constituents and Critique* (Atlanta: SBL Press), pp. 59–70.

Faust, A. (2016), 'The Emergence of Israel and Theories of Ethnogenesis', in S. Niditch (ed.), *The Wiley Blackwell Companion to Ancient Israel* (Oxford: Wiley Blackwell), pp. 155–173.

Feder, Y. (2011), *Blood Expiation in Hittite and Biblical Ritual: Origins, Context and Meaning* (Atlanta: SBL Press).

—— (2014), 'The Semantics of Purity in the Ancient Near East: Lexical Meaning as a Projection of Embodied Experience', *Journal of Ancient Near Eastern Religions* 14.1: 87–113.

—— (2021), *Purity and Pollution in the Hebrew Bible: From Embodied Experience to Moral Metaphor* (New York: Cambridge University Press).

Feldman, L. M. (2013), 'The Composition of Numbers 32: A New Proposal', *Vetus Testamentum* 63.3: 408–432.

—— (2020), *The Story of Sacrifice: Ritual and Narrative in the Priestly Source*, FAT 141 (Tübingen: Mohr Siebeck).

Finkelstein, I. (2015), 'The Wilderness Narrative and Itineraries and the Evolution of the Exodus Tradition', in T. E. Levy, T. Schneider and W. H. C. Propp (eds.), *Israel's Exodus in Transdisciplinary Perspective: Text, Archaeology, Culture, and Geoscience* (Cham: Springer), pp. 39–53.

Finkelstein, I., N. Na'aman and T. Römer (2019), 'Restoring Line 31 in the Mesha Stele: The "House of David" or Biblical Balak?', *Tel Aviv* 46.1: 3–11.

Fischer, G. (2019), 'Time for a Change! Why Pentateuchal Research Is in Crisis', in M. Armgardt, B. Kilchör and M. Zehnder (eds.), *Paradigm Change in Pentateuchal Research*, BZABR 22 (Wiesbaden: Harrassowitz), pp. 3–20.

Fleming, D. E. (2016), 'The Amorites', in B. T. Arnold and B. A. Strawn (eds.), *The World around the Old Testament: The Peoples and Places of the Ancient Near East* (Grand Rapids: Baker), pp. 1–30.

Fleurant, J. (2011), 'Phinehas Murdered Moses' Wife: An Analysis of Numbers 25', *Journal for the Study of the Old Testament* 35.3: 285–294.

Foster, B. R. (2005), *Before the Muses: An Anthology of Akkadian Literature* (Bethesda: CDL Press).

Frevel, C. (2012), 'Purity Conceptions in the Book of Numbers in Context', in C. Frevel and C. Nihan (eds.), *Purity and the Forming of Religious Traditions in the Ancient Mediterranean World and Ancient Judaism* (Leiden: Brill), pp. 369–411.

—— (2013), 'The Book of Numbers – Formation, Composition, and Interpretation of a Late Part of the Torah: Some Introductory Remarks', in C. Frevel, T. Pola and A. Schart (eds.), *Torah and the Book of Numbers* (Tübingen: Mohr Siebeck), pp. 1–38.

—— (2016), 'Practicing Rituals in a Textual World: Ritual and Innovation in the Book of Numbers', in N. MacDonald (ed.), *Ritual Innovation in the Hebrew Bible and Early Judaism*, BZAW 468 (Berlin: de Gruyter), pp. 129–50.

—— (2018), 'Leadership and Conflict: Modelling the Charisma of Numbers', in K. Pyschny and S. Schulz (eds.), *Debating Authority: Concepts of Leadership in the Pentateuch and the Former Prophets* (Berlin: de Gruyter), pp. 89–114.

—— (2020), *Desert Transformations: Studies in the Book of Numbers*, FAT 137 (Tübingen: Mohr Siebeck).

—— (2021), 'The Texture of Rituals in the Book of Numbers: A Fresh Approach to Ritual Density, the Role of Tradition, and the Emergence of Diversity in Early Judaism', in C. Nihan and J. Rhyder, *Text and Ritual in the Pentateuch: A Systematic and Comparative Approach* (University Park, PA: Eisenbrauns), pp. 188–214.

Frisch, A. (2015), 'The Story of Balaam's She-Ass (Numbers 22:21–35): A New Literary Insight', *Hebrew Studies* 56: 103–113.

Frymer-Kensky, T. S. (1984), 'The Strange Case of the Suspected *Sotah* (Numbers 5:11–31)', *Vetus Testamentum* 34: 11–26.

Gallese, V. (2008), 'Empathy, Embodied Simulation, and the Brain: Commentary on Aragno and Depf/Hartmann', *Journal of the American Psychoanalytic Association* 56.3: 769–781.

Gane, R. E. (2004), *Leviticus, Numbers*, The NIV Application Commentary (Grand Rapids: Zondervan).

—— (2005), *Cult and Character: Purification Offerings, Day of Atonement, and Theodicy* (Winona Lake, IN: Eisenbrauns).

—— (2017), *Old Testament Law for Christians: Original Context and Enduring Application* (Grand Rapids: Baker).

García-Johnson, O. (2019), *Spirit outside the Gate: Decolonial Pneumatologies of the American Global South* (Downers Grove, IL: InterVarsity Press).

Gelblum, O. (2023), 'Transitive Analogies and the Meaning of Balaam's Origin: A Literary Analysis', *Journal for the Study of the Old Testament* 47.3: 322–342.

Germany, S. (2017), *The Exodus-Conquest Narrative: The Composition of the Non-Priestly Narratives in Exodus–Joshua*, FAT 115 (Tübingen: Mohr Siebeck).

Gilders, W. K. (2004), *Blood Ritual in the Hebrew Bible* (Baltimore: Johns Hopkins University Press).

—— (2012), 'The Day of Atonement in the Dead Sea Scrolls', in T. Hieke and T. Nicklas (eds.), *The Day of Atonement: Its Interpretations in Early Jewish and Christian Traditions* (Leiden: Brill), pp. 63–74.

Glanville, M. R. (2018), *Adopting the Stranger as Kindred in Deuteronomy*, Ancient Israel and Its Literature (Atlanta: SBL Press).

—— (2021), 'חרם (ḥērem) as Israelite Identity Formation: Canaanite Destruction and the Stranger (גר, gēr)', *Catholic Biblical Quarterly* 83: 547–570.

Goedicke, H. (1966), 'Considerations on the Battle of Kadesh', *The Journal of Egyptian Archaeology* 51: 71–80.

Goldstein, A. J. (2012), 'Large Census Numbers in Numbers: An Evaluation of Current Proposals', *Presbyterion* 38.2: 99–108.

Gorman Jr, F. H. (1990), *The Ideology of Ritual: Space, Time and Status in the Priestly Theology*, JSOTSup 91 (Sheffield: Sheffield Academic).

Greenberg, M. (1959), 'The Biblical Conception of Asylum', *Journal of Biblical Literature* 78.2: 125–132.

—— (1968), 'Idealism and Practicality in Numbers 35:4–5 and Ezekiel 48', *Journal of the American Oriental Society* 88.1: 59–66.

Greenstein, E. L. (2017), 'What Was the Book of the Wars of the Lord?', TheTorah.com, https://thetorah.com/article/what-was-the-book-of-the-wars-of-the-lord, accessed 10 September 2022.

Greer, J. S. (2021), 'Strange Fire Indeed: The Cultic Violation of Nadab and Abihu in Leviticus 10 in Light of New Discoveries of Mind-Altering Substances and Paraphernalia in Ancient Near Eastern Sources and Archaeology', paper presented at the American Society of Overseas Research Annual Meeting, Chicago.

—— (2022), 'Feasting and Festivals', in J. Fu, C. Shafer-Elliott and C. Meyers (eds.), *T&T Clark Handbook of Food in the Hebrew Bible and Ancient Israel* (London: T&T Clark), pp. 297–318.

Grimes, R. L. (2004), 'Performance Theory and the Study of Ritual', in P. Antes, A. W. Geertz and R. R. Warne (eds.), *New Approaches to the Study of Religion*, vol. 2: *Textual, Comparative, Sociological, and Cognitive Approaches*, Religion and Reason Series 43 (Berlin: de Gruyter), pp. 109–138.

Grosby, S. (2007), 'The Successor Territory', in A. S. Leoussi and S. Grosby (eds.), *Nationalism and Ethnosymbolism: History, Culture and Ethnicity in the Formation of Nations* (Edinburgh: Edinburgh University Press), pp. 99–112.

Grossman, J. (2007), 'Divine Command and Human Initiative: A Literary View on Numbers 25 – 31', *Biblical Interpretation* 15.1: 54–79.

Gudme, A. K. de Hemmer (2009), 'How Should We Read Hebrew Bible Texts? A Ritualistic Reading of the Law of the Nazirite (Num 6,1–21)', *Scandinavian Journal of the Old Testament* 23.1: 64–84.

—— (2019), 'Liquid Life: Blood, Life, and Conceptual Metaphors in the Hebrew Bible and the Ancient Near East', in R. Nikolsky, I. Czachesz, F. S. Tappenden and T. Biró (eds.), *Language, Cognition, and Biblical Exegesis: Interpreting Minds*, Scientific Studies of Religion: Inquiry and Explanation (London: Bloomsbury Academic), pp. 63–69.

Guimarães, A. K. S. (2022), 'A caracterização de YHWH na narrativa de Balaão', MA thesis, Universidade de São Paulo.

Haber, S. (2008), *'They Shall Purify Themselves': Essays on Purity in Early Judaism* (Atlanta: SBL Press).

Hallo, W. W. (2003), 'Offerings to the Temple Gates at Ur', *COS* 3.275–276.

Hartenstein, F. (2007), 'Cherubim and Seraphim in the Bible and in the Light of Ancient Near Eastern Sources', in F. V. Reiterer, T. Nicklas and K. Schöplin (eds.), *Angels: The Concept of Celestial Beings: Origins, Development and Reception*,

Deuterocanonical and Cognate Literature Yearbook 2007
(Berlin: de Gruyter), pp. 153–188.

Heinskou, M. B. and L. S. Liebst (2016), 'On the Elementary
Neural Forms of Micro-interactional Rituals: Integrating
Autonomic Nervous System Functioning into Interaction
Ritual Theory', *Sociological Forum* 31.2: 354–376.

Hinlicky, P. R. (2021), *Joshua*, Brazos Theological Commentary on
the Bible (Grand Rapids: Brazos).

Hobbs, T. R. (2001), 'Hospitality in the First Testament and the
"Teleological Fallacy"', *Journal for the Study of the Old Testament*
95: 3–30.

Hoffmeier, J. K. (1997), *Israel in Egypt: The Evidence for the
Authenticity of the Exodus Tradition* (New York: Oxford
University Press).

—— (2005), *Ancient Israel in Sinai: The Evidence for the Authenticity of
the Wilderness Tradition* (New York: Oxford University Press).

Horsley, R. A. (1987), *Jesus and the Spiral of Violence: Popular Jewish
Resistance in Roman Palestine* (San Francisco: Harper & Row).

—— (2003), *Jesus and Empire: The Kingdom of God and the New World
Disorder* (Minneapolis: Fortress).

Howard, C. B. R. (2008), 'Animal Speech as Revelation in
Genesis 3 and Numbers 22', in N. C. Habel and P. Trudinger
(eds.), *Exploring Ecological Hermeneutics* (Atlanta: SBL Press),
pp. 21–29.

Hundley, M. B. (2011), *Keeping Heaven on Earth: Safeguarding
the Divine Presence in the Priestly Tabernacle* (Tübingen: Mohr
Siebeck).

Hurowitz, V. A. (2004), 'Healing and Hissing Snakes: Listening
to Numbers 21:4–9', *Scriptura: Journal for Contextual Hermeneutics
in Southern Africa* 87.1: 278–287.

Hutton, J. M. (2009), 'The Levitical Diaspora (I): A Sociological
Comparison with Morocco's Ahansal', in J. D. Schloen (ed.),
Exploring the Longue Durée: Essays in Honor of Lawrence E. Stager
(Winona Lake, IN: Eisenbrauns), pp. 223–234.

—— (2011), 'The Levitical Diaspora (II): Modern Perspectives
on the Levitical City Lists (A Review of Opinions)', in J. M.
Hutton and M. Leuchter (eds.), *Levites and Priests in History and
Tradition* (Atlanta: SBL Press), pp. 45–82.

Hutzli, J. (2007), *Die Erzählung von Hanna und Samuel: Textkritische und literarische Analyse von 1. Samuel 1 – 2 unter Berücksichtigung des Kontextes*, ATANT 89 (Zurich: Theologischer Verlag Zurich).

Imes, C. (2019), *Bearing God's Name: Why Sinai Still Matters* (Downers Grove, IL: IVP Academic).

Janowski, M. (2007), 'Introduction: Feeding the Right Food: The Flow of Life and the Construction of Kinship in Southeast Asia', in M. Janowski and F. Kerlogue (eds.), *Kinship and Food in South East Asia*, NIAS Studies in Asian Topics 38 (Copenhagen: Nordic Institute of Asian Studies), pp. 1–23.

Jastram, N. (2008), 'Numbers, Book of', in L. H. Schiffman and J. C. VanderKam (eds.), *Encyclopedia of the Dead Sea Scrolls* (New York: Oxford), https://www.oxfordreference.com/display/10.1093/acref/9780195084504.001.0001/acref-9780195084504-e-366, accessed 13 September 2023.

Jenson, P. P. (2021), *Leviticus: The Priestly Vision of Holiness* (London: T&T Clark).

Jeon, J. (2022), *From the Reed Sea to Kadesh: A Redactional and Socio-Historical Study of the Pentateuchal Wilderness Narrative*, FAT 159 (Tübingen: Mohr Siebeck).

Johnson, D. R. (2020), *Sovereign Authority and the Elaboration of Law in the Bible and the Ancient Near East*, FAT II/122 (Tübingen: Mohr Siebeck).

—— (2022), 'The Allotment of Canaan in Joshua and Numbers', *Journal of Biblical Literature* 141.3: 427–447.

Kallai, Z. (1997), 'The Patriarchal Boundaries, Canaan and the Land of Israel: Patterns and Application in Biblical Historiography', *Israel Exploration Journal* 47.1/2: 69–82.

Kazen, T. (2017), 'Disgust in Body, Mind, and Language: The Case of Impurity in the Hebrew Bible', in F. S. Spencer (ed.), *Mixed Feelings and Vexed Passions: Exploring Emotions in Biblical Literature* (Atlanta: SBL Press), pp. 97–115.

—— (2018), 'Levels of Explanation for Ideas of Impurity: Why Structuralist and Symbolic Models Often Fail While Evolutionary and Cognitive Models Succeed', *Journal of Ancient Judaism* 9.1: 75–100.

Kedar, B. Z. (2008), 'Rashi's Map of the Land of Canaan, ca. 1100, and Its Cartographic Background', in R. J. A. Talbert and R. W. Under (eds.), *Cartography in Antiquity and the Middle Ages: Fresh Perspectives, New Methods* (Leiden: Brill), pp. 155–168.

Kellermann, D. (1970), *Die Priesterschrift von Numeri 1,1 bis 10,10: Literarkritisch und traditionsgeschichtlich untersucht*, BZAW 120 (Berlin: de Gruyter).

—— (1973), 'Bemerkungen zum Sündopfergesetz in Num 15,22ff', in H. Gese and H. P. Rüger (eds.), *Wort und Geschichte: Festschrift für Karl Elliger zum 70. Geburtstag*, Alter Orient und Altes Testament (Neukirchen-Vluyn: Neukirchener Verlag; Kevelaer: Butzon & Bercker), pp. 107–113.

Kislev, I. (2016), 'The Story of the Gadites and the Reubenites (Numbers 32): A Case Study for an Approach to a Pentateuchal Text', in J. C. Gertz, B. M. Levinson, D. Rom-Shiloni, and K. Schmid (eds.), *The Formation of the Pentateuch: Bridging the Academic Cultures of Europe, Israel, and North America* (Tübingen: Mohr Siebeck), pp. 619–629.

Kitchen, K. A. (2003), *On the Reliability of the Old Testament* (Grand Rapids: Eerdmans).

Kiuchi, N. (1987), *The Purification Offering in the Priestly Literature* (Sheffield: Sheffield Academic).

Klawans, J. (2004), *Impurity and Sin in Ancient Judaism* (Oxford: Oxford University Press).

—— (2006), *Purity, Sacrifice, and the Temple: Symbolism and Supersessionism in the Study of Ancient Judaism* (Oxford: Oxford University Press).

Kletter, R. (2006), 'Weights and Measures', in K. D. Sakenfeld (ed.), *The New Interpreter's Dictionary of the Bible* (Nashville: Abingdon), https://www-ministrymatters-com.fuller.idm. oclc.org/library/#/nidb/eaaa8ae9ed10a3d8adbceec5bfd9bcb6/ weights-and-measures.html, accessed 2 August 2022.

Knierim, R. P. and G. W. Coats (2005), *Numbers*, The Forms of the Old Testament Literature (Grand Rapids: Eerdmans).

Knight, D. A. (2011), *Law, Power, and Justice in Ancient Israel* (Louisville: Westminster John Knox).

Knohl, I. (1995), *The Sanctuary of Silence: The Priestly Torah and the Holiness School* (Minneapolis: Fortress).

—— (2004), 'The Guilt Offering Law of the Holiness School (Num v 5–8)', *Vetus Testamentum* 54: 516–526.

Knoppers, G. N. (2004), 'Establishing the Rule of Law? The Composition Num 33,50–56 and the Relationships among the Pentateuch, the Hexateuch, and the Deuteronomistic History', in E. Otto and R. Achenbach (eds.), *Das Deuteronomium zwischen Pentateuch und Deuteronomistischem Geschichtswerk* (Göttingen: Vandenhoeck & Ruprecht), pp. 135–152.

Koch, U. S. (2010), 'Three Strikes and You're Out! A View on Cognitive Theory and the First-Millennium Extispicy Ritual', in A. Annus, *Divination and Interpretation of Signs in the Ancient World* (Chicago: Oriental Institute of the University of Chicago), pp. 43–59.

Kosior, W. (2018), '"Like a Throne of Glory": The Apotropaic Potential of *Ṣiṣit* in the Hebrew Bible and Early Rabbinic Literature', *The Review of Rabbinic Judaism* 21: 176–201.

Kugler, R. A. (1997), 'Holiness, Purity, the Body, and Society: The Evidence for Theological Conflict in Leviticus', *Journal for the Study of the Old Testament* 22.76: 3–27.

Lakoff, G. and M. Johnson (1980), *Metaphors We Live By* (Chicago: University of Chicago Press).

—— (1999), *Philosophy in the Flesh: The Embodied Mind and Its Challenge to Western Thought* (New York: Basic Books).

Lee, W. W. (2003), *Punishment and Forgiveness in Israel's Migratory Campaign* (Grand Rapids: Eerdmans).

Leuchter, M. (2017), *The Levites and the Boundaries of Israelite Identity* (Oxford: Oxford University Press).

Leveen, A. (2005), 'Reading the Seams', *Journal for the Study of the Old Testament* 29.3: 259–287.

—— (2008), *Memory and Tradition in the Book of Numbers* (New York: Cambridge University Press).

—— (2010), 'Inside Out: Jethro, the Midianites and a Biblical Construction of the Outsider', *Journal for the Study of the Old Testament* 34.4: 395–417.

—— (2017), *Biblical Narratives of Israelites and Their Neighbors: Strangers at the Gate* (Abingdon: Routledge).

Levenson, J. D. (1993), *The Hebrew Bible, the Old Testament, and Historical Criticism* (Louisville: Westminster John Knox).

Levin, Y. (2006), 'Numbers 34:2–12, the Boundaries of the Land of Canaan, and the Empire of Necho', *Journal of the Ancient Near Eastern Society* 30.1: 55–76.

Levine, B. A. (1993), *Numbers 1 – 20: A New Translation with Introduction and Commentary*, The Anchor Bible 4 (New York: Doubleday).

—— (2000), *Numbers 21 – 36: A New Translation with Introduction and Commentary*, The Anchor Bible 4A (New York: Doubleday).

Levy, T. E. (2008), 'Ethnic Identity in Biblical Edom, Israel, and Midian: Some Insights from Mortuary Contexts in the Lowlands of Edom', in J. D. Schloen (ed.), *Exploring the Longue Durée: Essays in Honor of Lawrence E. Stager* (Winona Lake, IN: Eisenbrauns), pp. 251–261.

Levy, T. E., T. Schneider and W. H. C. Propp (eds.) (2015), *Israel's Exodus in Transdisciplinary Perspective: Text, Archaeology, Culture, and Geoscience* (Cham: Springer).

Logan, W. A. (2003), 'Criminal Law Sanctuaries', *Harvard Civil Rights–Civil Liberties Law Review* 38: 321–371.

Lozinskyy, H. (2022), *The Feasts of the Calendar in the Book of Numbers*, FAT II/132 (Tübingen: Mohr Siebeck).

Luhrmann, T. M. (2020), *How God Becomes Real: Kindling the Presence of Invisible Others* (Princeton: Princeton University Press).

Lutzky, H. C. (1997), 'The Name "Cozbi" (Numbers XXV 15, 18)', *Vetus Testamentum* 47.4: 546–549.

Maccoby, H. (1999), *Ritual and Morality: The Ritual Purity System and Its Place in Judaism* (Cambridge: Cambridge University Press).

MacDonald, N. (2008a), 'Gone Astray: Dealing with the Sotah (Num. 5.11–31)', in S. D. Walters (ed.), *Go Figure! Essays on Figuration in Biblical Interpretation*, Princeton Theological Monographs (Eugene, OR: Pickwick), pp. 47–64.

—— (2008b), *Not Bread Alone: The Uses of Food in the Old Testament* (Oxford: Oxford University Press).

—— (2012a), 'The Book of Numbers', in R. S. Briggs and J. N. Lohr (eds.), *A Theological Introduction to the Pentateuch: Interpreting the Torah as Christian Scripture* (Grand Rapids: Baker), pp. 113–144.

—— (2012b), 'Deuteronomy and Numbers: Common Narratives Concerning the Wilderness and Transjordan', *Journal of Ancient Judaism* 3: 141–165.

—— (2012c), 'A Trinitarian Palimpsest: Luther's Reading of the Priestly Blessing (Numbers 6.24–26)', *Pro Ecclesia: A Journal of Catholic and Evangelical Theology* 21: 299–313.

—— (2023), 'Did Balaam Write Second Isaiah?', in A. Marschall and A. Schüle (eds.), *Exodus und Erzeltern in Deuterojesaja* (Leipzig: Evangelische Verlagsanstalt), pp. 63–74.

McEntire, M. and W. Park (2021), 'Ethnic Fission and Fusion in Biblical Genealogies', *Journal of Biblical Literature* 140.1: 31–47.

McNutt, P. M. (2023), 'Kinship and Social Organization in Ancient Palestine', in E. Pfoh (ed.), *T&T Clark Handbook of Anthropology and the Hebrew Bible* (London: T&T Clark), pp. 151–188.

Maiden, B. E. (2020), *Cognitive Science and Ancient Israelite Religion: New Perspectives on Texts, Artifacts, and Culture* (Cambridge: Cambridge University Press).

Martins, L. A. I. (2018), 'Ironia e visão na narrativa de Balaão', *Cadernos de Língua e Literatura Hebraica* 16: 84–97.

Marx, A. (1994), *Les Offrandes végétales dans l'Ancien Testament: du tribut d'hommage au repas eschatologique* (Leiden: Brill).

Masalha, N. (2015), 'Settler-colonialism, Memoricide and Indigenous Toponymic Memory: The Appropriation of Palestinian Place Names by the Israeli State', *Journal of Holy Land and Palestine Studies* 14.1: 3–57.

Matthews, V. H. (1991), 'Hospitality and Hostility in Judges 4', *Biblical Theology Bulletin* 21: 13–21.

Mattison, K. (2018), 'Contrasting Conceptions of Asylum in Deuteronomy 19 and Numbers 35', *Vetus Testamentum* 68.2: 232–251.

Mbuwayesango, D. R. (2021), 'Justice for Rahab and the Gibeonites in the Book of Joshua? The Elusive Communities of Justice in Imperial/Colonial Contexts', in L. J. Claassens, C. M. Maier and F. O. Olojede (eds.), *Transgression and Transformation: Feminist, Postcolonial and Queer Biblical Interpretation as Creative Interventions* (New York: T&T Clark), pp. 128–144.

Meyers, C. L. (1976), *The Tabernacle Menorah: A Synthetic Study of a Symbol from the Biblical Cult* (Missoula, MT: Scholars Press).

—— (1983), 'Procreation, Production, and Protection:

Male–Female Balance in Early Israel', *Journal of the American Academy of Religion* 51.4: 569–593.

—— (2002), 'Having Their Space and Eating There Too: Bread Production and Female Power in Ancient Israelite Households', *Nashim* 5: 14–44.

—— (2013), *Rediscovering Eve: Ancient Israelite Women in Context* (Oxford: Oxford University Press).

—— (2014), 'Was Ancient Israel a Patriarchal Society?', *Journal of Biblical Literature* 133.1: 8–27.

Milgrom, J. (1972), 'The Alleged Wave-Offering in Israel and in the Ancient Near East', *Israel Exploration Journal* 22: 33–38.

—— (1976), 'Israel's Sanctuary: The Priestly "Picture of Dorian Gray"', *Revue Biblique* 83.3: 390–399.

—— (1983), 'Of Hems and Tassels: Rank, Authority and Holiness Were Expressed in Antiquity by Fringes on Garments', *Biblical Archaeology Review* 9.3: 61–65.

—— (1990), *Numbers: The Traditional Hebrew Text with the New JPS Translation*, The JPS Torah Commentary (Philadelphia: Jewish Publication Society).

—— (1991), *Leviticus 1 – 16: A New Translation with Introduction and Commentary*, The Anchor Bible 3 (New York: Doubleday).

—— (1996), 'The Changing Concept of Holiness in the Pentateuchal Codes with Emphasis on Leviticus 19', in J. F. A. Sawyer (ed.), *Reading Leviticus: A Conversation with Mary Douglas* (Sheffield: Sheffield Academic), pp. 65–75.

—— (1997), 'Encroaching on the Sacred: Purity and Polity in Numbers 1 – 10', *Interpretation* 51: 241–253.

—— (2000), *Leviticus 17 – 22: A New Translation with Introduction and Commentary*, The Anchor Bible 3A (New York: Doubleday).

—— (2001), *Leviticus 23 – 27: A New Translation with Introduction and Commentary*, The Anchor Bible 3B (New York: Doubleday).

Miller, P. D. (2009), *The Ten Commandments*, Interpretation: Resources for the Use of Scripture in the Church (Louisville: Westminster John Knox).

Miller II, R. D. (2018), *Yahweh: Origin of a Desert God* (Göttingen: Vandenhoeck & Ruprecht).

Miller, Y. (2019), 'Phinehas' Priestly Zeal and the Violence of Contested Identities', *Jewish Studies Quarterly* 26.2: 117–145.

Moffitt, D. M. (2019), 'Weak and Useless? Purity, the Mosaic Law, and Perfection in Hebrews', in D. Lincicum, R. Sheridan and C. Stang (eds.), *Law and Lawlessness in Early Judaism and Early Christianity*, Wissenschaftliche Untersuchungen zum Neuen Testament 420 (Tübingen: Mohr Siebeck), pp. 89–103.

Monroe, L. A. S. (2012), 'Phinehas' Zeal and the Death of Cozbi: Unearthing a Human Scapegoat Tradition in Numbers 25:1–18', *Vetus Testamentum* 62.2: 211–231.

Montanari, M. (2006), *Food Is Culture*, tr. A. Sonnenfeld (New York: Columbia University Press).

Morales, L. M. (2015), *Who Shall Ascend the Mountain of the Lord? A Biblical Theology of the Book of Leviticus* (Nottingham: Apollos; Downers Grove, IL: InterVarsity Press).

—— (2024a), *Numbers 1 – 19*, Apollos Old Testament Commentary 4a (London: Apollos).

—— (2024b), *Numbers 20 – 36*, Apollos Old Testament Commentary 4b (London: Apollos).

Morgenstern, J. (1942/1943), 'The Ark, the Ephod, and "Tent of Meeting"', *Hebrew Union College Annual* 17: 153–265.

Morrow, W. S. (2023), 'The Laws in the Covenant Code and Deuteronomy as *Dienstanweisungen*', *Scandinavian Journal of the Old Testament* 37.1: 128–147.

Moyer, C. J. (2012), 'Who Is the Prophet, and Who the Ass? Role-reversing Interludes and the Unity of the Balaam Narrative (Numbers 22 – 24)', *Journal for the Study of the Old Testament* 37.2: 167–183.

Mroczek, E. (2016), *The Literary Imagination in Jewish Antiquity* (Oxford: Oxford University Press).

Nardoni, E. (2004), *Rise Up, O Judge: A Study of Justice in the Biblical World*, tr. S. C. Martin (Peabody, MA: Hendrickson).

Newsom, C. A. (1996), 'Bakhtin, the Bible, and Dialogic Truth', *The Journal of Religion* 76.2: 290–306.

Niemann, H. M. (2008), 'A New Look at the Samaria Ostraca: The King–Clan Relationship', *Tel Aviv* 35.2: 249–266.

Nihan, C. (2007), *From Priestly Torah to Pentateuch: A Study in the Composition of the Book of Leviticus*, FAT II/25 (Tübingen: Mohr Siebeck).

—— (2008), 'Israel's Festival Calendars in Leviticus 23, Numbers

28 – 29 and the Formation of "Priestly" Literature', in T.
Römer, *The Books of Leviticus and Numbers*, BETL 215 (Leuven:
Peeters), pp. 177–231.

—— (2015), 'The Templization of Israel in Leviticus', in F.
Landy, L. M. Trevaskis and B. D. Bibb (eds.), *Text, Time, and
Temple: Literary, Historical and Ritual Studies in Leviticus* (Sheffield:
Sheffield Phoenix), pp. 94–130.

Nihan, C. and J. Rhyder (2018), 'Aaron's Vestments in Exodus 28
and Priestly Leadership', in K. Pyschny and S. Schulz (eds.),
*Debating Authority: Concepts of Leadership in the Pentateuch and the
Former Prophets*, BZAW 507 (Berlin: de Gruyter), pp. 45–67.

Noonan, B. J. (2020), 'High-handed Sin and the Promised Land:
The Rhetorical Relationship between Law and Narrative
in Numbers 15', *Journal for the Study of the Old Testament* 45.1:
79–92.

Noth, M. (1968), *Numbers: A Commentary*, Old Testament Library
(Louisville: Westminster John Knox).

Novick, T. (2008), 'Law and Loss: Response to Catastrophe in
Numbers 15', *Harvard Theological Review* 101.1: 1–14.

O'Brien, J. M. (2008), *Challenging Prophetic Metaphor: Theology and
Ideology in the Prophets* (Louisville: Westminster John Knox).

Olson, D. T. (1985), *The Death of the Old and the Birth of the New:
The Framework of the Book of Numbers and the Pentateuch*, Brown
Judaic Studies 71 (Chico, CA: Scholars Press).

—— (2012), *Numbers*, Interpretation: A Bible Commentary for
Teaching and Preaching, reprint edn (Louisville: Westminster
John Knox).

Organ, B. E. (2001), 'Pursuing Phinehas: A Synchronic Reading',
Catholic Biblical Quarterly 63: 203–218.

Origen (2009), *Homilies on Numbers*, tr. T. P. Scheck and ed. C. A.
Hall (Downers Grove, IL: InterVarsity Press).

Pardes, I. (2000), *The Biography of Ancient Israel: National Narratives
in the Bible* (Berkeley: University of California Press).

Peres, C. (2021), 'Bloodless "Atonement": An Exegetical, Ritual,
and Theological Analysis of Leviticus 5:11–13', *Journal of
Hebrew Scriptures* 20.6: 1–36.

Pitkänen, P. (2018), *A Commentary on Numbers: Narrative, Ritual,
and Colonialism* (London: Routledge).

Podany, A. H. (2010), *Brotherhood of Kings: How International Relations Shaped the Ancient Near East* (Oxford: Oxford University Press).

Porter, B. N. (2003), *Trees, Kings, and Politics: Studies in Assyrian Iconography* (Göttingen: Vandenhoeck & Ruprecht).

Porter, B. W. (2023), 'The Invention of Ancient Moab', in K. H. Keimer and G. A. Pierce (eds.), *The Ancient Israelite World* (London: Routledge), pp. 619–638.

Pressler, C. (2017), *Numbers*, Abingdon Old Testament Commentaries (Nashville: Abingdon).

Price, M. (2022), 'Food and Israelite Identity', in J. Fu, C. Shafer-Elliott and C. Meyers (eds.), *T&T Clark Handbook of Food in the Hebrew Bible and Ancient Israel* (London: T&T Clark), pp. 423–441.

Propp, W. H. (1988), 'The Rod of Aaron and the Sin of Moses', *Journal of Biblical Literature* 107.1: 19–26.

Rainey, A. F. (1970), 'The Order of Sacrifices in Old Testament Ritual Texts', *Biblica* 51: 485–498.

Rashi (1999), *The Torah*, vol. 4: *Bamidbar/Numbers*, ed. Y. I. Z. Herczeg in collaboration with Y. Petroff and Y. Kamenetsky, Artscroll Series (Brooklyn: Mesorah).

Rendtorff, R. (2004), *Leviticus 1,1 – 10,20*, Biblisher Kommentar, Altes Testament 3 (Neukirchen-Vluyn: Neukirchener Verlag).

Rhyder, J. (2019), *Centralizing the Cult: The Holiness Legislation in Leviticus 17 – 26*, FAT 134 (Tübingen: Mohr Siebeck).

Robbins, J. (2001), 'Ritual Communication and Linguistic Ideology: A Reading and Partial Reformulation of Rappaport's Theory of Ritual', *Current Anthropology* 42.5: 591–613.

Robker, J. M. (2019), *Balaam in Text and Tradition*, FAT 131 (Tübingen: Mohr Siebeck).

Römer, T. (2008), 'De la Périphérie au centre: les livres du Lévitique et des Nombres dans le débat actuel sur le Pentateuque', in T. Römer (ed.), *The Books of Leviticus and Numbers*, BETL 215 (Leuven: Peeters), pp. 3–34.

Romero, R. C. (2020), *Brown Church: Five Centuries of Latina/o Social Justice, Theology, and Identity* (Downers Grove, IL: InterVarsity Press).

Roskop, A. (2011), *The Wilderness Itineraries: Genre, Geography and the Growth of Torah* (Winona Lake, IN: Eisenbrauns).

Roth, F. A., J. M. Smith, K. S. Oh, A. Yafeh-Deigh and K. H. Smith (2022), *Reading the Bible around the World: A Student's Guide to Global Hermeneutics* (Downers Grove, IL: InterVarsity Press).

Sakenfeld, K. (1988), 'Zelophehad's Daughters', *Perspectives in Religious Studies* 15.4: 37–47.

——— (1995), *Journeying with God: A Commentary on the Book of Numbers*, International Theological Commentary (Grand Rapids: Eerdmans).

——— (2012), 'Numbers', in C. A. Newsom, S. H. Ringe and J. E. Lapsley (eds.), *Women's Bible Commentary* (Louisville: Westminster John Knox), pp. 79–87.

Samuel, H. (2014), *Von Priestern zum Patriarchen: Levi und die Leviten im Alten Testament*, BZAW 448 (Berlin: de Gruyter).

Sanders, J. (2017), *Theology in the Flesh: How Embodiment and Culture Shape the Way We Think about Truth, Morality, and God* (Minneapolis: Fortress).

Sapir-Hen, L. (2019), 'Food, Pork Consumption and Identity in Ancient Israel', *Near Eastern Archaeology* 82.1: 52–59.

Savran, G. (1994), 'Beastly Speech: Intertextuality, Balaam's Ass and the Garden of Eden', *Journal for the Study of the Old Testament* 64: 33–55.

Schart, A. (1990), *Mose und Israel im Konflikt: Eine redaktionsgeschichtliche Studie zu den Wüstenerzählungen*, OBO 98 (Fribourg: Presses Universitaires; Göttingen: Vandenhoeck & Ruprecht).

Schellenberg, A. (2014), 'More Than Spirit: On the Physical Dimension in the Priestly Understanding of Holiness', *Zeitschrift für die alttestamentliche Wissenschaft* 126.2: 163–179.

Schiffman, L. H. (1991), 'The Law of Vows and Oaths ("Num." 20,3–16) in the "Zadokite Fragments" and the "Temple Scroll"', *Revue de Qumrân* 15.1/2: 199–214.

Schipper, B. U. (2011), 'Egyptian Imperialism after the New Kingdom: The 26th Dynasty and the Southern Levant', in S. Bar, D. Kahn and J. J. Shirley (eds.), *Egypt, Canaan and Israel: History, Imperialism, Ideology and Literature; Proceedings of a*

Conference at the University of Haifa, 3–7 May 2009 (Leiden: Brill), pp. 268–290.

Schüler, S. (2012), 'Synchronized Ritual Behavior: Religion, Cognition and the Dynamics of Embodiment', in D. Cave and R. S. Norris (eds.), *Religion and the Body: Modern Science and the Construction of Religious Meaning* (Leiden: Brill), pp. 81–101.

Schwartz, B. J. (1995), 'The Bearing of Sin in the Priestly Literature', in D. P. Wright, D. N. Freedman and A. Hurvitz (eds.), *Pomegranates and Golden Bells: Studies in Biblical, Jewish, and Near Eastern Ritual, Law and Literature in Honor of Jacob Milgrom* (Winona Lake, IN: Eisenbrauns), pp. 3–21.

Seebass, H. (1993), *Numeri*, Biblischer Kommentar 4 (Neukirchen-Vluyn: Neukirchener Verlag).

—— (2006), '"Holy" Land in the Old Testament: Numbers and Joshua', *Vetus Testamentum* 56.1: 92–104.

Ska, J.-L. (2014), 'Old and New in the Book of Numbers', *Biblica* 95: 102–116.

Sklar, J. (2008), 'Sin and Impurity: Atoned or Purified? Yes!', in B. J. Schwartz, D. P. Wright, J. Stackert and N. S. Meshel (eds.), *Perspectives on Purity and Purification in the Bible* (London: T&T Clark), pp. 18–31.

—— (2013), *Leviticus: An Introduction and Commentary*, TOTC 3 (Downers Grove, IL: InterVarsity Press).

—— (2015), *Sin, Impurity, Sacrifice, Atonement: The Priestly Conceptions*, Hebrew Bible Monographs 2 (Sheffield: Sheffield Phoenix).

Smith, M. S. (1997), *The Pilgrimage Pattern in Exodus* (Sheffield: Sheffield Academic).

Smoak, J. D. (2016), *The Priestly Blessing in Inscription and Scripture: The Early History of Numbers 6:24–26* (New York: Oxford University Press).

Sommer, B. D. (2001), 'Conflicting Constructions of Divine Presence in the Priestly Tabernacle', *Biblical Interpretation* 9.1: 41–63.

—— (2009), *The Bodies of God and the World of Ancient Israel* (Cambridge: Cambridge University Press).

Spencer, J. R. (1992), 'Phinehas (Person)', in D. N. Freedman (ed.), *The Anchor Yale Bible Dictionary*, vol. 5 (New York: Doubleday), pp. 346–347.

Stackert, J. (2007), *Rewriting the Torah: Literary Revision in Deuteronomy and the Holiness Legislation*, FAT 52 (Tübingen: Mohr Siebeck).

—— (2014), *A Prophet Like Moses: Prophecy, Law, and Israelite Religion* (Oxford: Oxford University Press).

Staubli, T. (2012), 'Cherubim', in C. M. Furey, J. M. LeMon, B. Matz, T. C. Römer, J. Schröter, B. D. Walfish and E. Ziolkowski (eds.), *Encyclopedia of the Bible and Its Reception Online* (Berlin: de Gruyter), accessed 10 October 2023, https://doi-org.fuller.idm.oclc.org/10.1515/ebr.cherubim.

Stern, C. A. (2000), 'Torah and Murder: The Cities of Refuge and Anglo-American Law', *Valparaiso University Law Review* 35: 461–498.

Stökl Ben Ezra, D. (2003), *The Impact of Yom Kippur on Early Christianity: The Day of Atonement from Second Temple Judaism to the Fifth Century*, Wissenschaftliche Untersuchungen zum Neuen Testament 163 (Tübingen: Mohr Siebeck).

Stone, K. (2014), 'Wittgenstein's Lion and Balaam's Ass: Talking with Others in Numbers 22 – 25', in J. L. Koosed (ed.), *The Bible and Posthumanism* (Atlanta: SBL Press), pp. 75–102.

Strathern, A. J. and P. J. Stewart (2021), 'Ritual, Performance, and Cognition', in P. J. Stewart and A. Strathern (eds.), *The Palgrave Handbook of Anthropological Ritual Studies* (Cham: Palgrave Macmillan), pp. 147–158.

Strawn, B. A. (2005), *What Is Stronger Than a Lion? Leonine Image and Metaphor in the Hebrew Bible and the Ancient Near East*, OBO 212 (Göttingen: Vandenhoeck & Ruprecht).

—— (2017), *The Old Testament Is Dying: A Diagnosis and Recommended Treatment* (Grand Rapids: Baker Academic).

—— (2020), 'Criminal Law in the Old Testament: Homicide, the Problem of *Mens Rea* and God', in M. Hill, N. Doe, R. H. Helholz and J. White Jr (eds.), *Christianity and Criminal Law* (London: Routledge), pp. 13–30.

Stubbs, D. L. (2009), *Numbers*, Brazos Theological Commentary 9 (Grand Rapids: Brazos).

Sutton, D. E. (2001), *Remembrance of Repasts: An Anthropology of Food and Memory* (Oxford: Berg).

Tal, O. (2007), 'Coin Denominations and Weight Standards in

Fourth-Century BCE Palestine', *Israel Numismatic Research* 2: 17–28.

Tebes, J. M. (2017), 'Desert Place-names in Numbers 33:34, Assurbanipal's Arabian Wars and the Historical Geography of the Biblical Wilderness Toponymy', *Journal of Northwest Semitic Languages* 43.2: 65–96.

—— (2021), 'The Archaeology of Cult of Ancient Israel's Southern Neighbors and the Midianite-Kenite Hypothesis', *Entangled Religion* 12.2, https://doi.org/10.46586/er.12.2021.8847.

—— (2023), 'Edom and Southern Jordan in the Iron Age', in K. H. Keimer and G. A. Pierce (eds.), *The Ancient Israelite World* (London: Routledge), pp. 639–657.

Thames Jr, J. T. (2021), 'Writing Ritual and Calendar Together: The Biblical Cultic Calendars in Ancient Near Eastern Context', *Religion Compass* 15.9: 1–15.

Trevaskis, L. M. (2011), *Holiness, Ethics and Ritual in Leviticus*, Hebrew Bible Monographs 29 (Sheffield: Sheffield Phoenix).

Van Wolde, E. (2009), *Reframing Biblical Studies: When Language and Text Meet Culture, Cognition, and Context* (Winona Lake, IN: Eisenbrauns).

Vis, J. M. (2017), 'The Purgation of Persons through the Purification Offering', in H. L. Wiley and C. A. Eberhart (eds.), *Sacrifice, Cult, and Atonement in Early Judaism and Christianity: Constituents and Critique* (Atlanta: SBL Press), pp. 33–57.

Walton, J. H. (2006), *Ancient Near Eastern Thought and the Old Testament: Introducing the Conceptual World of the Hebrew Bible* (Grand Rapids: Baker Academic).

Watts, J. W. (1999), *Reading Law: The Rhetorical Shaping of the Pentateuch*, The Biblical Seminar 59 (Sheffield: Sheffield Academic).

—— (2013), *Leviticus 1 – 10*, Historical Commentary on the Old Testament (Leuven: Peeters).

Way, K. C. (2009), 'Animals in the Prophetic World: Literary Reflections on Numbers 22 and 1 Kings 13', *Journal for the Study of the Old Testament* 34.1: 47–62.

—— (2011), *Donkeys in the Biblical World: Ceremony and Symbol* (Winona Lake, IN: Eisenbrauns).

Wearne, G. J. (2015), 'The Plaster Texts from Kuntillet 'Ajrud and Deir ʿAlla: An Inductive Approach to the Emergence of Northwest Semitic Literary Texts in the First Millennium BCE', PhD dissertation, Macquarie University.

Weinfeld, M. (1995), *Social Justice in Ancient Israel and in the Ancient Near East* (Minneapolis: Fortress).

Wellhausen, J. (1885), *Prolegomena to the History of Israel: With a Reprint of the Article Israel from the 'Encyclopaedia Britannica'*, tr. J. S. Black and A. Menzies (Edinburgh: A. & C. Black).

Welton, R. (2020), *'He Is a Glutton and a Drunkard': Deviant Consumption in the Hebrew Bible*, Biblical Interpretation Series 183 (Leiden: Brill).

—— (2022), 'Ethnography and Biblical Studies: "A Land Flowing with Milk and Honey" as a Case Study for Re-contextualising a Familiar Phrase', *Biblical Interpretation* 30.1: 1–20.

Wenham, G. J. (1981), *Numbers: An Introduction and Commentary*, TOTC 4 (Leicester: Inter-Varsity Press; Downers Grove, IL: InterVarsity Press).

Westbrook, R. and B. Wells (2009), *Everyday Law in Biblical Israel: An Introduction* (Louisville: Westminster John Knox).

Whitehouse, H. (2021), *The Ritual Animal: Imitation and Cohesion in the Evolution of Social Complexity* (Oxford: Oxford University Press).

Whitekettle, R. (2018), 'Life's Labors Lost: Priestly Death and Returning Home from a City of Refuge in Ancient Israel', *Harvard Theological Review* 111.3: 333–356.

Wiggershaus, B. (2021), 'The Man of Opened Eye: Ancient Near Eastern Revelatory Convention and the Balaam Cycle (Numbers 22 – 24)', PhD dissertation, Asbury Theological Seminary.

Winkler, M. (2016), 'Maße / Gewichte (AT)', Deutsche Bibelgesellschaft, https://www.bibelwissenschaft.de/wibilex/das-bibellexikon/lexikon/sachwort/anzeigen/details/masse-gewichte-at/ch/ffb367dcdec08bfda9601bfa2d797f31/, accessed 2 August 2022.

Wolters, A. (1988), 'The Balaamites of Deir ʿAlla as Aramean Deportees', *Hebrew Union College Annual* 59: 101–113.

Wright, D. P. (1991), 'The Spectrum of Priestly Impurity', in S. M. Olyan and G. A. Anderson (eds.), *Priesthood and Cult in Ancient Israel* (Sheffield: Sheffield University Press), pp. 150–182.

—— (1999), 'Holiness in Leviticus and Beyond: Differing
Perspectives', *Interpretation* 53.4: 351–364.

Wright, J. L. (2020), *War, Memory, and National Identity in the Hebrew
Bible* (Cambridge: Cambridge University Press).

Wright, S. C., A. Aron and L. R. Tropp (2002), 'Including Others
(and Groups) in the Self: Self Expansion and Intergroup
Relations', in J. P. Forgas and K. D. Williams (eds.), *The Social
Self: Cognitive, Interpersonal and Intergroup Perspectives* (New York:
Psychology Press), pp. 343–363.

Yahalom-Mack, N. and I. Segal (2018), 'The Origin of the
Copper Used in Canaan During the Late Bronze Age
Transition', in E. Ben-Yosef (ed.), *Mining for Ancient Copper:
Essays in Memory of Beno Rothenberg* (Winona Lake, IN:
Eisenbrauns; Tel Aviv: Tel Aviv University), pp. 313–331.

Younger, K. L. (1990), *Ancient Conquest Accounts: A Study in Ancient
Near Eastern and Biblical History Writing*, JSOTSup 98 (Sheffield:
JSOT Press).

Younker, R. W. (2023), 'Ammonites in the World of Israel', in
K. H. Keimer and G. A. Pierce (eds.), *The Ancient Israelite World*
(London: Routledge), pp. 600–618.

INTRODUCTION

1. Why read Numbers?

Reading Numbers is, to state the obvious, difficult for most modern people of faith to engage with. First off, it bears the rather unattractive title 'Numbers' in English (and many other modern languages) taken over from the Greek *Arithmoi*, rather than the Hebrew 'In the Desert', which is slightly more intriguing. Second, it begins with four chapters of lists. And third, it requires a considerable amount of familiarity with matters of purity and holiness that are discussed in Leviticus (and Exodus). Such concepts are at home in ancient Mediterranean cultures at large, but they are quite alien to much of modern, Western-dominated life. Furthermore, a number of its stories and regulations appear in similar forms elsewhere, for example the spy stories of Numbers 13 – 14 in Deuteronomy 1 – 3, or the regulations on offerings and festivals of Numbers 28 – 29 in Leviticus 23. All of this can lead to the basic question: Why do we *need* Numbers?

There are several important and overlapping answers:

a. Numbers is about God's pilgrim people

In the same way that Numbers concerns the Israelites as redeemed by God and on their way to the Promised Land, the church, too, consists of God's people on the way, between the partial fulfilment of the promise of salvation that came with Jesus' life, death and resurrection and the beginning of one's own journey of faith, and the culmination of the coming of God's kingdom that brings complete fulfilment. In this in-between space, Numbers offers people of faith key insights. One overarching category lies in answering the question of what elements it takes to constitute a congregation of God. Many insights on this theme come throughout Numbers 1 – 10: it takes a people who gather together to journey *with Yahweh*, the God who dwells among them (Num. 1 – 4). In this gathering, there is order. Every person and group has a specific place and responsibilities (chs. 2; 4; 8), and they move together at a pace and direction dictated by God (chs. 9–10). This people undertake considerable efforts to remain holy, honouring God's presence with them, which in turn opens them up for blessing (chs. 5–8).

God's people are not only on the move geographically. Numbers also offers insights about various dynamics significant for their formation. Celebrating their central festival of liberation (Passover) is foundational to belonging to the community, opening up the possibility for outsiders to become insiders, and for God and the community to accommodate those at the margins (9:1–14). In their pilgrimage, God's people will also encounter other peoples. Sometimes these encounters are amicable and cooperative (10:29–32), but most of the time they are not (chs. 20–24; 31). In either case, these encounters are opportunities for God's people to reflect on and better understand themselves through their relationships with God and others. Finally, the main feature in the formation of God's people addressed in Numbers is the transition of generations, from the failure of the exodus generation (chs. 13–14) to the new hope of success in the settling generation (chs. 20–36). Although it appears at first that a direct transition from one generation to another takes place, the second census extends beyond the children of the exodus generation. It works like a genealogy for each tribe and includes several generations. For this reason, when referring to the people after the death of the exodus generation, we prefer to speak of the 'new' or the 'settling' generation. This important feature of Numbers shows that there is no one specific group of people who represent God's people in full or who fulfil God's plan for the world on their own. God is committed to forming a people who are continually renewed by divine forgiveness and instruction, and with whom God dwells.

b. Numbers provides important examples of how to interpret God's word over time

Because God's people are always in the process of being formed afresh, Numbers contains many texts that update commands given by God in the previous biblical texts (and in some that follow it in the order of the Bible). Some texts in Numbers fill in loopholes not addressed in Exodus or Leviticus. One example is found in Numbers 9:1–14, which makes a provision for people who cannot celebrate Passover at its normal time because of ritual uncleanness (they should celebrate it a month later). Other texts change the ways that certain rituals were practised or make legal decisions reflecting new circumstances. An example here is the age at which Levites enter service: Numbers 4 states that they are to serve from age thirty to fifty. According to Numbers 8:23–26, they begin their duties at the tabernacle at age twenty-five. In these and several other passages, Numbers *innovates*, showing how God's directives – which remain true to God's character – address specific circumstances and require changes in concrete application among diverse communities and at different points in time. Many texts in Numbers show interpretation in action. In fact, given that Numbers addresses different generations of the *same* community, it sets a model of how to interpret, adapt and apply God's word to a broader variety of communities throughout time and variable geographies.

c. Numbers offers lessons on leadership

From the first chapter onwards, leaders of each of the twelve tribes join Moses (and Aaron or his son and at times Miriam) in preparing and leading the Israelites through the wilderness. Numbers also provides several narratives on the desire and struggle to obtain the mantle of leadership. As an overall direction, Numbers tells a narrative of the diffusion of leadership. In Exodus, most leadership roles are focused on Moses and Aaron (though see Exod. 18:13–27; 24:9–11).

The organization of the tribes into a camp surrounding the tabernacle in Numbers 1 – 4 begins the process of decentralization. It elevates the leadership of each tribe and promotes Judah as the leading tribe. It also sets up the Levites led by Aaron's family as those immediately responsible for the care of God's sanctuary. The promotion of Aaron's family as priests and the Levites as sanctuary attendants sets in motion a reduction of Moses' priestly duties.

While God still speaks directly to Moses and Aaron (Exod. 12:50; Lev. 11:1; 13:1; 14:33; 15:1; Num. 2:1; 4:1, 17; 19:1; 20:23), Moses recognizes that God's people can follow the leadership of experienced and wise foreigners (Num. 10:29–32) and declares that he (Moses) cannot lead the Israelites alone (11:14). God's provision is seventy leaders who prophesy as a sign of their shouldering the burden with Moses, a development that Moses welcomes (11:29). Thus, Moses' prophetic role is also dispersed.

After the distribution of authority and responsibility from Moses to other individuals, the tension and struggle for leadership drives the narrative for several chapters. It first happens within the core of Israel's leadership, between Miriam, Aaron and Moses (Num. 12). Miriam and Aaron claim authority to speak to Israel in God's name and attempt to diminish Moses before the people because of his foreign wife. Although God's plan for Israel is to elevate their status and distribute authority to all, demanding their individual authority, struggling for leadership in a way that diminishes the authority of others because of their association with outsiders is not the appropriate means to this end. Therefore, God confirms Moses' unique authority and consequently the legitimacy of his marriage with a foreigner, while Miriam and Aaron's attitude is associated with death. From this core struggle, others follow with similar types of actions. In Numbers 13 – 14, there is an insurrection and the people plan to choose their own leaders to return to Egypt. The dispute in

Numbers 16 – 17 touches on the equal status of the whole people and their proximity to the presence of Yahweh, but it specifically addresses how much access Levites and priests have to the sanctuary and its offerings. This episode goes further than the previous ones in its teaching about legitimate and just leadership. Those struggling for leadership are represented by sterile staffs while Aaron's leadership is represented by a lively fruitful staff. The contrast indicates that the purpose of leadership is not concentration of power by limiting access to the divine presence and blessing, but facilitating and distributing these gifts. This dynamic also constitutes Moses and Aaron's failure in 20:2–13. Instead of using their leadership to provide access to what the people needed to live, they used the people's need to affirm their leadership. These episodes show that, although special leadership is confirmed, the final goal is the distribution of authority and the slow process of dissolving hard divides between people and leaders.

This theme develops in the second part of Numbers. Where Moses and Aaron failed, Israel's chieftains and nobles succeed with their own staff (21:17–20). Three occasions highlight the initiative and participation of the people in matters decided by leaders and authorities. In 27:1–11 and 36:1–12, a divine word concerning the important issue of land inheritance is determined through a process of dialogue between a group from the people, Moses and God. In the divine regulations concerning the towns of refuge (35:6–34), one finds instruction for the assembly of the people from each town as the sole arbiter in a matter of life and death. Their decision, closely related to the corruption of the land in which Israel and God dwell together, will determine the possibility of God's continued dwelling and the access to the divine presence and blessing for all the people.

These lessons on leadership and authority in Numbers provide a nuanced and dynamic perspective that challenges understandings of social organization in ancient Israel, in the Bible, and in contemporary local and global geopolitics. For the community of faith, these lessons are central for how God's people organize themselves on their journey towards an existence filled with God's presence and life.

2. Is Numbers a book?

On one level the answer to this question is quite obvious:
Numbers belongs to the 'Pentateuch', which means five books (or
scrolls), and it is the fourth of these five. However, ancient literary
works were not formed and did not function in the same way as
modern books, for several reasons, including different concepts
of authorship, publication, audience and the object itself (see
Mroczek 2016).[1] Some peculiar features of Numbers reflect this
more clearly than other biblical texts. Unlike the other four works
in the Pentateuch, it does not have as clear an identity of its own.
Scholars debate its structure, and it does not really have a clear
beginning or ending apart from the very last verse, which almost
seems 'tacked on'. Thus, one might ask, just what is Numbers? One
way to think about this question is to consider its Hebrew name.
Its English name – 'Numbers' – from the early Greek translation,
the Septuagint (LXX), arises from the census lists in the opening
chapters and Numbers 26. The numbering of the adult males in
these chapters highlights one of the major themes and turning
points in Numbers. The theme articulates that the Israelites have
become a large group of people in need of organization. The
turning point in the second census is that the generation of adults
that left Egypt has given way to a new generation, which will cross
into the land God promised.

On the other hand, the Hebrew name for Numbers, *Bamidbar*,
'In the desert/wilderness', comes from the setting for the events.
As such, it allows for understanding the various texts in it as a
collection or *assemblage* more than as a narrative with a clear plot.
Viewed in this way, Numbers communicates essential factors
about what made *Israel* what it was. It is a kinship-based society
with a hierarchy that accords priests a place of honour. It is oriented
around a centralized though mobile location for the worship of

---

[1]   Unfortunately, the use of the term 'book' to designate ancient literary
      works remains unavoidable. But we ask the reader to be aware of this
      issue and to guard against importing modern definitions into ancient
      contexts.

Yahweh, and it has a special though fraught relationship with a land promised to it by Yahweh.

This does not imply that Numbers is devoid of development from beginning to end, but the narrative development serves as less of a focus than one might expect. As such, this collection of material tends to make it more difficult for modern readers to engage with. We are less clear on *how* to read it because we do not know *what* to expect. We suggest that it is more helpful to think of the experience of Numbers as a literary work as structured like a human life. Our lives take place 'along the way': in the wilderness, so to speak. We *can* speak of them as a narrative with a clear beginning, developing plot, climax and end. In fact, we expend considerable effort in attempting to identify the themes, patterns and developments of our individual and group stories. And such efforts do bear much truth: we are born, and we die, thus providing a clear beginning and ending. However, telling one's life story with such a clear development requires omitting many parts. Numbers instead mixes in some of these parts: actual life experience is less linear than we often recount. As a result, the 'story' of Numbers can be disconcerting if one expects narratives to have a clear point. Numbers instead invites readers on a more circuitous journey with a looser, though at points still identifiable, structure. We will address how this tension fits together in the next two sections.

3. How Numbers fits into the Pentateuch and Hexateuch

When it comes to the development of God's story with Moses and the Israelites from Egypt to the Promised Land, Numbers tells the portion of the story of the journey from Sinai to the plains of Moab across the Jordan River from Jericho, on the cusp of entering the land connected with the promises that God made to Israel's ancestors Abram (Abraham) and Jacob in Genesis 12:6–7; 15:7; and 28:13. Given the general lack of narrative material in the book of Leviticus and the nature of Deuteronomy as Moses' final speeches (which do, however, recall many of the same narratives found in Numbers), Numbers plays a crucial role in the narrative of Israel's exodus from Egypt to its entrance into Canaan. It connects the previous events of the book of Exodus and the later events of the book of Joshua.

As part of the *Pentateuch*, Numbers reaches almost as far as Deuteronomy, though Numbers does not provide a report of Moses' death (cf. Deut. 34) but only announces that he will die (Num. 27:13). These two books together provide an ending to the Pentateuch, which ends *outside* the Promised Land. As such, this fivefold book ends with anticipation.

However, as part of the *Hexateuch* (Genesis–Joshua), Numbers offers several important constellations of commands that Joshua 13 – 21 takes up and implements. For example, Numbers 34 details the boundaries of the land that the Israelites should apportion by lot according to the size of the tribe. The Israelites carry out this division of the land in Joshua 13 – 19. Towns for the Levites to dwell in that function as towns of refuge are prescribed in Numbers 35, and Joshua 20 – 21 reports on the fulfilment of this command. The two-and-a-half tribes desiring to live in the Transjordan make an agreement with Moses that they will fight on behalf of the other tribes to take the land in the Cisjordan (to the west of the Jordan) in Numbers 32. The fulfilment of their duty and return to the Transjordan is narrated in Joshua 22. In addition, Numbers at times includes instructions for more durable institutions that should be established once Israel settles in the land. For example, Numbers 15 outlines a number of offerings that Israelites should bring 'when you come into the land' (15:2, 17). While omitting this clause, Numbers 18 describes the apportioning of offerings between priests and Levites of items available only once Israel farms its own lands, such as firstfruits, wine, oil and grain.

4. The order of the material

Why is *this* material put *here*? This question can easily arise – and it has done so frequently for audiences over the centuries! – with regard to many passages in the book. For example, why does 5:5–10, which treats the restitution plus a 20% penalty of any economic defrauding of another person, not appear right after Leviticus 6:1–7, to which it has a strong thematic connection? Or why do the offerings of the tribal leaders in 7:1–88 (and Moses hearing the voice above the ark in 7:89) not come after Exodus 40, or even Leviticus 9, chapters which narrate events *from the very same day* as Numbers 7? In fact, the events of Numbers 7 take place a month *before* those in Numbers 1 – 4 (Num. 5 – 6 do not indicate when they take place), so why not place Numbers 7 before Numbers 1 – 4? In other words, there is a question of the order of the material as it relates to the chronology, that is, the time when the events take place.

As already mentioned, a different challenge with regard to the order concerns the different genres, or types, of texts. Why do the sections on the ritual practices found in Numbers 5 – 6 come between the ordering of the camp in Numbers 1 – 4 and the tribal heads' gifts for the operation and transportation of the tabernacle in Numbers 7? For Numbers 5 – 6 treat topics that do not immediately seem to relate to that narrative. In order of appearance, they provide God's directives on putting people who have become unclean outside the camp (5:1–4), how to address economic fraud when the wronged party has died without beneficiaries (5:5–10), a jealous husband suspicious that his wife has committed adultery (5:11–31), the Nazirite regulation in which a layperson decides to devote themselves to God in a special way for a period of time (6:1–21) and, finally, how Aaron and the priests should bless the people (6:22–27). Similarly, why does the instruction concerning the lamps (8:1–4) appear between the offering of the tribal leaders (ch. 7) and the consecration of the Levites (8:5–26)? A similar question might be asked about Numbers 15 and Numbers 18, instructions concerning sacrificial offerings and portions that come immediately after rebellions (chs. 13 – 14 and 16 – 17, respectively). And, finally, why do the two chapters that deal with daughters inheriting when a man has no sons appear in Numbers 27 and then Numbers 36, rather than right next to each other?

The question of the order of the different types of material does not resolve easily, or perhaps at all. As mentioned above, perhaps this is simply part of what it means for God's people to travel in the wilderness, on the way to the place that God has for them: it is not linear, even though there are repeating themes and outlines of various structures of meaning.

A third issue is that of repetition. Why repeat, mostly with the same data, the census results of Numbers 1 in the organization of the camp in Numbers 2? This kind of repetition is also something that happens between texts in Numbers and other books of the Pentateuch as well, as addressed in the previous section.

Despite texts whose placements in the book are difficult to understand, some overall structures – there is more than one – do emerge from it and overlap with one another. Some possibilities arise from internal markers, especially the chronological dates (1:1; 7:1; 10:11; 20:21; 33:38) and geographical locations (1:1; 13:3; 22:1). However, these divisions do not correspond well with the content or message of Numbers. For the content, two particular proposals stand out. The first is the change in generations exemplified in the two censuses (chs. 1 and 26; see Olson 1985). The second focuses on the preparation for the journey (1:1 – 9:14 or 10:10), then the journey itself (9:15 or 10:11 – 25:18), and finally the preparation for settlement (26:1 – 36:13; see Budd 1984: xvii–xviii).[2] Both of these approaches emphasize the constitution of the Israelites as the people of God in Numbers 1 – 4, the generally positive outlook before Numbers 11, and the transition to the next generation in Numbers 26. It is striking that the entire first generation (except Caleb and Joshua) dies in the interim (26:63–65), while no death takes place before Numbers 11 or after Numbers 26 (Olson 1985: 89, 125).

However, many scholars doubt whether either of these structures accounts for all the material in the book. One of the concerns is that readers try too hard to make the various texts fit together and thereby dim the message of a particular text. For example, pivotal events take place in both Numbers 13 – 14, when the Israelites fail to enter the land, and Numbers 21, when the Israelites defeat the Amorites led by King Sihon and then Bashan

---

2   The placement of the transition from 'preparation' to 'journey' occurs in the three interlocked sections of Num. 9:15–23; 10:1–10; and 10:11–28, which makes it difficult to name the precise verse for a break from one section to the next.

under King Og. One might, then, propose a narrative structure of
five sections (following Frevel 2020: 57–58):

1 Preparation for the journey (1:1 – 10:10).
2 The journey begins, but ends in the failure to take the land
   (10:11 – 14:45).
3 Return to and punishment in the wilderness (15:1 – 20:29).
4 Hope returns with initial conquest of land and Balaam's
   blessing (21:1 – 25:18).
5 A new generation prepares to enter the land (26:1 – 36:13).

Another possible arrangement proposed by Cocco (2020a) might
be helpful beyond the narrative structure of Numbers:

1 The march of the exodus generation and their failure (1:1
   – 14:45).
2 'Passing the torch': lessons from the old generation to the new
   (15:1 – 25:18).
3 The march of the new generation fulfils the divine promises
   (26:1 – 36:13).

The strength of Cocco's proposal is its elevation of the unique
coexistence of generations in Numbers when compared with
the other books of the Pentateuch or Hexateuch. In contrast
to Leviticus, which concerns only the exodus generation, and
Deuteronomy, which concerns only the settling generation,
Numbers functions between the two as a bridge (see Römer 2008:
23–32). Numbers' canonical position, therefore, forces readers to
pay close attention to the middle section of the book in which the
two generations march together. The fact that the exodus generation is not eradicated completely after their failure in Numbers 13
– 14 but dies during the process of formation of the new settling
generation suggests that this process has a pedagogical purpose.
The formative purpose of this middle section involves negative
examples (chs. 16–17; 20; 25), a strong message of hope and
blessing (chs. 22–24), reminders of how to live before God (chs.
15; 18; 19) and successful events (ch. 21). The middle section, then,
reminds the new generation of the life lived with God dwelling

among them as seen in Leviticus, as well as reminding the older
generation to pass on to their children the covenantal life on
display in Deuteronomy. The pedagogical purpose of the middle
section in the formation of the settling generation is confirmed
in the initial words from God to Moses after the failure of the
exodus generation, 'when you enter the land of your dwelling that
I am giving you' (15:2, AT). Cocco's final remark is that Numbers
is the quintessential reflection of the function of the Torah *as
instruction*, in this case, from one generation to another in the
formation of God's people (Cocco 2020a: 272; see below, 'What is
"biblical law"?').

   The combination of the narrative structure proposed by Frevel
and the more theological-oriented structure proposed by Cocco
results in narrative turning points interspersed with ritual and
sacrificial directives, such as those in chapters 15; 18; 19; and
28–29. These ritual texts might be viewed as reminders of God's
commitment to Israel through instructions on how to be God's
people as immediate responses to pivotal events in the journey,
specifically episodes of decisive rebellion (chs. 13–14; 16–17; 25)
and the definitive change to a new generation (ch. 26). They
therefore provide a density of rituals. Those who practise them are
marked as, and formed into, Israel. However, given the composite
nature of Numbers and the necessity of combining different
structures based on different criteria, we argue that the audience
of Numbers should hold these structures lightly. The book is thus
organized in several overlapping ways.

5. Composition and compilation

Numbers often reports God speaking to Moses, sometimes
including Aaron (e.g. 1:1; 2:1), and it once mentions Moses
writing down the names of stages of the Israelites' journey
through the desert (33:2). Nonetheless, especially since the
seventeenth century in the West, interpreters have held very
divergent views on the authorship and date of writing of
Numbers. These questions are invariably connected with understandings of the nature of biblical authority and veracity,
especially as they relate to questions of the historical nature of

the narratives and persons in the book. Was Moses a historical figure? If so, when did he live, and how is the writing of the Pentateuch connected with him and his times? How do the narratives in Numbers relate to memories and oral traditions that precede their writing?

How one answers such questions often relates closely to one's reaction to discussions of sources and editing in the Pentateuch that arose before but are strongly associated with the positions taken by Julius Wellhausen in what has come to be known as the Documentary Hypothesis (Wellhausen 1885). Building on earlier modern Western interpreters, Wellhausen adduced four main sources in the Pentateuch, which he called the Jahwist (German for Yahwist; who used the proper name Yahweh for God), the Elohist (who used the more general term Elohim for God), the Deuteronomist (whose material was focused in the book of Deuteronomy and the terminology and writing style found there) and the Priestly writer (responsible especially but not solely for much of the ritual material in Exodus–Leviticus–Numbers). This differentiation focused especially on Genesis but also Exodus, and it encountered more difficulty in Numbers (Noth 1968: 4–5). More problematic is that Wellhausen's hypothesis, as well as those of other nineteenth-century Protestant critical scholars, reconstructs Israel's history based on ideological prejudices (see Frevel 2013: 8; Stackert 2014: 1–16). In this reconstruction, legal and ritual expressions are deemed legalistic and institutionalized degenerations of true religion. Unfortunately, within nineteenth-century Germany, these theories functioned as exaltations of Protestantism as the true religion against Judaism (see Levenson 1993: 10–15).

In this commentary, we refer in a number of places to texts that scholars have determined as coming from different traditions and perhaps sources. We limit our determinations to 'Priestly' and 'Non-Priestly'. Priestly literature, which scholars identify especially in Genesis through to Numbers, is unsurprisingly characterized by interest in sanctuary matters, issues related to purity, and rituals. That is not to say that it is limited to such concerns, or that other traditions within the Pentateuch (or the biblical literature as a whole) never reflect such interest. Nonetheless, Priestly literature also displays a high concentration of certain terminology, such as specific terms for inheritance (*'ăḥūzzâ*) or impurity (*ṭāmē'*). This literature also frequently exhibits a divine command ('And God said to Moses . . .') followed by a report of the implementation of this command ('And Moses [and the Israelites] did what God commanded'). Much of the material in Numbers 1:1 – 10:10; 28 – 30 is categorized as Priestly, though it can appear in other places in the book as well. As a further note, this designation does not necessarily indicate that it was written or collected by a single person.

On the other hand, Non-Priestly literature does not demonstrate an emphasis on these same characteristics. As the moniker 'Non-Priestly' indicates, such texts exhibit more diversity. For the specific case of Numbers, considerations of its relation to Deuteronomic traditions are often relevant, while the classic distinction between Yahwist (J) and Elohist (E) traditions provides little insight. Much of the narrative material in Numbers 11 – 15; 16 – 17; 20 – 25 falls into this category. Some of the texts in this category could have arisen before their combination with the Priestly literature (pre-Priestly), and some of them later (post-Priestly), in which case they may even incorporate Priestly material and points of view for their own purposes.

It should be noted that our treatment comes in the context of more recent Western scholarly approaches, many of which ascribe to one of two trends: (1) attempts to delineate the sources identified by Wellhausen in Numbers more persuasively (cf. Baden 2009; 2012) or (2) the abandonment of the traditional sources of J and E, along with the ascription of increasingly more material from Numbers to editors with the entire Pentateuch in view in the Persian period (fifth and fourth centuries BC; see, e.g., Achenbach 2003; Germany 2017; J. Davis 2022; Jeon 2022).

Especially relevant, considering the Priestly and Non-Priestly division, as well as these two recent approaches, is that Numbers has become a central point of dispute for understanding the formation of the Pentateuch (Ska 2014: 105). The combination of Priestly and Non-Priestly materials in Numbers can be understood from its function as a bridge between Leviticus and Deuteronomy, as mentioned above. This proposal fits the nature of the growth of the Pentateuch as a literary corpus as seen happening around two main poles – Priestly and Deuteronomic material – that gather new materials around them and eventually converge upon one another to become one (MacDonald 2012a: 120). Numbers works to combine these two poles and bring them together. This is not to say that Numbers completely harmonizes them and does not offer its own view on matters shared with these other bodies of literature. A good example that can be seen in this commentary is how the material on the towns of refuge in Numbers 35 works with that from Exodus 21:12–14 and Deuteronomy 19:1–13, entangling them with the role of the high priest in the Day of Atonement (Lev. 16) and Priestly concepts of impurity already modified by new insights from Numbers 19. More generally, Numbers integrates Priestly narratives with legislation in creative ways, so that distinguishing between them as means to separate sources from different dates becomes highly speculative (see Frevel 2013: 19). We see, therefore, that the composition of many parts of Numbers does have the arc of the entire Pentateuch in view, as proposed by approach 2 above. But the form of composition of the whole Pentateuch might also reflect the intricate composition of Numbers, holding together diverse materials, in what we might call a divergent unity that complicates attempts at discerning discrete sources and specific forms of the higher level of composition such as redactions (see Fischer 2019).

The disagreements between these groups, including more conservative scholars who challenge source and redaction hypotheses (see Armgardt et al. 2019), are deep, but they agree on the composite character of the Pentateuch and all see very little or none of the material in Numbers emanating from Moses himself or from a historical journey of the Israelites from Egypt to the Promised Land, as described in the biblical text, in either the fifteenth or thirteenth century BC, which is when they would be dated according to the internal biblical timeline (see 1 Kgs 6:1). Even when some historical elements of the exodus are affirmed, especially the close relationship between the biblical material with ancient Egypt (see especially Levy et al. 2015; Berman 2017), their understanding of past memories emphasizes the *theological* and *political* import of the narratives, rituals and other types of writing intended to help explain and answer challenges encountered by the Israelites and Judeans at later points in their history as a people. While the arguments put forward in discussions of historical contexts remain speculative, they do highlight that any evidence for Israel's journey in the wilderness from Egypt under Moses remains circumstantial, for the earliest manuscripts of fragments from Numbers come from the Dead Sea Scrolls. While some scrolls date to the third century BC, those containing texts of Numbers are dated to 150 BC at the earliest (Jastram 2008). Scholars also generally conclude that the translation of the Pentateuch into Greek (Septuagint/LXX) took place a century earlier in Egypt, so the text of the book stabilized at that time, for there are few pronounced differences between the Greek texts of Numbers and the oldest Hebrew texts. Therefore, one can firmly conclude that Numbers was written before the third century, but this says little about *how much earlier* the traditions that the texts contain arose and came together in written form.

Some correspondences with traditions from the Late Bronze Age (1500–1200 BC) when Moses and the Israelites leave Egypt according to the calculations in the biblical books can be noted. For example, the layout of the camp in Numbers 2 bears similarities to the arrangement of Pharaoh Rameses II's military camp in the thirteenth century BC. However, the earliest inscriptions in the Hebrew language date no earlier than the time of David (tenth century BC), centuries after the Israelites settle in Israel according to the biblical narrative. Thus, oral traditions played an integral role in any transmission of stories, rituals, prophecies, songs or other material from earlier generations. Early literary traditions are also important. The text of Numbers itself notes some of these as sources for its composition. *The Book of the Wars of [Yahweh]* is probably the literary origin not only of the divine itinerary poem of Numbers 21:14–15 but also of two songs, the Well Song in Numbers 21:17–19 and the Heshbon Song in Numbers 21:27–30. Even without mentioning its sources, the geographical, religious and literary proximity between the Balaam tradition of Numbers 22 – 24 and that of the Deir ʿAlla Inscription from *c.*800 BC is more evidence of early literary sources that contain traditions used in the composition of Numbers. Nonetheless, no known evidence ensures that the narratives and other literary traditions in Numbers did not arise at a later date.

The overall picture of Israel in Numbers fits fairly well for Judah during the Persian period after the Babylonian exile (530–300 BC). But that does not mean this historical context is the only one relevant to consider for the composition and meaning of every text in Numbers. The sociopolitical and economic system envisioned in Numbers reflects tribal organization and ethics, or a kinship-based society, and the absence or omission of a royal-dominated system. This conception fits different contexts in Israel's history for different groups of people, from pre-monarchic period to the Persian period. Two specific cases in Numbers might be illustrative of the importance of managing different historical contexts when considering the composition and meaning of Numbers. The depiction of Canaan in Numbers 34 reflects the historical relationship with Egypt in the thirteenth and seventh centuries. The notion of Israelite presence in the Transjordan in Numbers 22 – 36 corresponds well with the political realities of the ninth and eighth centuries between Israel, Moab and Aram (Syria). Therefore, even if the Persian period is more relevant for Numbers, other historical contexts should not be disregarded for specific parts, given the use of early traditions, oral or literary, in its composition. The integration of traditions from different contexts opens up possibilities of investigations beyond the notion of an 'original' context.

An important *philosophical* question that emerges in the discussion of such historical issues is the relationship between *fact* and *truth*. For readers belonging to communities of faith who wish to ascribe authority to the biblical text of Numbers, the question becomes *what kind* of authority, and whether this authority must have a specific kind of relationship with historical facts. In other words, are there ways that stories, even fiction and myths, constructed within literary conventions different from ours, can communicate divine truth? If so, is there a limit to the 'truth of fiction'? Without attempting to provide a resolution to these enquiries, we do note that the close equation of 'truth' with 'fact', especially in relation to historical questions, took on increased importance during the Euro-North American Enlightenment, which, with regard to history, conflated truth with its reconstruction of the 'facts' of the way things actually happened. The biblical text, emerging from a very different era and culture, does not share this form of perception of reality.

We understand the Pentateuch instead as *theological* and *remembered* history, following ancient forms of doing history and literary conventions, that emphasizes the formation of God's people in the light of God's providential and personal interaction and guidance. Instead of weakening the veracity and authority of the biblical text, such a view reinforces God's incarnational character, which consists of God's interaction with creation and revelation to humanity (and to a jenny, a female donkey!) in all its particular times, cultures and locations. As such, it can be important to reconstruct (though speculative) the various socio-historical settings of the human groups responsible for the composition and compilation of Numbers. While historically contingent, and taking place for various political, economic, religious and other motivations, the faith communities of Yahweh-worshippers within early Judaism (including Samaritans!) and Christ-followers affirm that such writing and editing endeavours come together to take on authority when seeking to understand the nature of God's presence in and interaction with the world. Such a perspective does not answer all questions, but rather opens the door to investigation of the historical and theological processes involved in the composition, compilation, reception and interpretation of biblical texts like Numbers with regard to their meanings both in the communities of their earliest audiences and in modern communities of faith.

6. How to read Numbers

If the previous comments consider *why* read Numbers and *what* it is, the next question concerns *how* we might most profitably read it. Some parts of the book are quite familiar to us: most communities of faith – ancient and contemporary – are more or less acquainted with stories such as those found in Numbers 13 – 14 (the spy narratives), Numbers 16 – 17 (Korah, Dathan and Abiram swallowed up by the earth) and Numbers 22 (Balaam's talking jenny). However, mixed in with these narratives are other, less familiar types of texts: census lists, sanctuary and ritual instructions, and topics such as impurity and holiness that appear to have little to do with life in some modern cultures. This mixture raises specific questions about the way that the various texts and chapters fit together (or if they do!).

a. Reading sequentially
First of all, its location as the fourth book or scroll of the Pentateuch calls for Numbers to be read as part of a narrative (Watts 1999: 29). Furthermore, this narrative extends (first) through the so-called Primary Narrative that reaches from the creation of the world in Genesis to the hopeful sign of restoration for a descendant of David in 2 Kings (retold in the books of Chronicles, Ezra and Nehemiah that likewise begin with the creation of the world but end later, with a partial return and restoration of God's people around a second Jerusalem temple in the land under Persian imperial rule). For Christians, this narrative naturally reaches all the way from Genesis to the complete establishment of God's kingdom on earth at the end of Revelation.

b. Reading in concert
However, the mix of the different genres in Numbers at a minimum calls the sufficiency of a 'sequential' reading (Num. 1, then 2, then 3, and so on) *by itself* into question: why do stipulations on purification after contact with a dead body appear in Numbers 19, just after rules for the Levites' and priests' receipt of the tithes and offerings in Numbers 18, and before a long sequence of narratives and oracles in Numbers 20 – 25? These difficulties may suggest that other reading strategies can prove profitable. Instead of a linear reading, based on progression of arguments typical of Western propositional logic, we suggest that Numbers is better appreciated when also read in concert.

First, reading in concert takes place within the book itself. Even when the arrangement of the material, as demonstrated above, does not seem to follow a single logic, readers are still invited to consider how different narratives and instructions addressing related issues are combined in Numbers and illuminate one another. This reading might consider literary structures or thematic concerns. Literarily, for example, the donations from the Israelite leaders for the inauguration of worship in Numbers 7 are framed by the priestly blessing in 6:22–27 and the arrangement of the lamps in 8:1–4. This structure suggests that the two outer sections are connected to and inform the meaning of the middle part, and vice versa. A similar though more complex structural function that is better read in concert occurs between Numbers 20 – 21, then Numbers 22 – 24, and Numbers 25. Related to this last example, one thematic concern is how Numbers presents foreigners in relation to Israel. A certain dynamic develops between inclusiveness and exclusiveness, sometimes leading to full integration or full aggression. For instance, the hospitality and cooperation between Israel and Midian, reflected in the relationship of Moses and his father-in-law in 10:29–32, is questioned in Miriam and Aaron's challenge to Moses' authority in Numbers 12, becomes the reason for Israel's corruption in Numbers 25, and turns into mutual hostility and war in Numbers 31. Read sequentially, it seems as if the argument and final word on the issue is complete exclusion and estrangement. A reading in concert, however, offers possibilities of contrasting positive and open relationships between Israelites and Midianites while maintaining tension in how they interact as two different peoples (see below, 'Israel's identity and its neighbours').

Second, considering the function of the composition of Numbers within the Pentateuch presented above, one can read in concert with texts addressing the same or similar issues in Exodus, Leviticus and Deuteronomy. In the Protestant tradition, this manner of reading goes back at least to John Calvin's *Harmony of the Law* from the sixteenth century, though Calvin organizes the legal material of these books mostly according to the Ten Commandments, which can prove helpful but also squeeze some of the material into unhelpful categories. However, what we propose here does introduce a different way of approaching such an inner-biblical comparison. The versions in Numbers often update, or 'riff' on, the other discussions (Römer 2008: 24–25). For example, one might compare the instructions for the tithe in Numbers with those in Deuteronomy (esp. Deut. 14:22–29) and Leviticus 27:30–33. The goal of such reading, much like with the telling of the story of Jesus in the four Gospels of the New Testament, is not to iron out any differences. It does not seek to *conflate* the different sets of instructions and narratives to arrive at the one complete way to practise (or understand) them. Rather, the different perspectives on this example concerning contributions given to the Levites and priests in the different texts in the Pentateuch intend to provide us with (1) a multifaceted view on what the tithes could be, and (2) *how they could change in different situations.* This second aspect goes beyond the analogy with the Gospels in that the instructions of the Torah (or the Pentateuch) *change over time.* Drawing on a core Christian doctrine, God's guidance for people of faith becomes *embodied* (like the incarnation of Jesus) in the particular places and times.

There are several important results from seeing God's revelation in this manner. First, God is and remains 'Immanuel' (Hebrew for 'God with us'). There is a profound manner in which God 'dwells' with the people wherever they go. This sharing of life with God is on display in Numbers in the image of God travelling with the Israelites in the desert in the tabernacle. Second, and perhaps less familiar but central for the application of the biblical text to modern lives of faith because the instructions change over time, the Bible inherently provides *guidelines for interpretation.* Through the study of Numbers in conjunction with other biblical passages on the same topics, readers can observe the canonical interpretations of earlier texts. These inspired interpretations can teach readers to become more attuned to the ways in which the Holy Spirit may lead communities to interpret and apply Scripture to their lives and situations.

Excursus: comparative texts for interpreting Numbers
In order to support these approaches to reading, Table I.1 provides a number of relevant texts. Some of them, like Genesis 12, operate along the lines of promise and fulfilment, with the fulfilment of the promise of many descendants on display in Numbers 1. Similarly, God commands the Israelites to divide the land up between the tribes in Numbers 34, and the report of their

execution of this command appears in Joshua 13 – 19. However, most of the texts listed in the table contain treatments of the same or similar topics, such as purity regulations in Numbers 5:1–4 in relation to those in Leviticus 13 – 15; 22:4. The texts do not provide readers with an explanation of the exact relationship between these regulations: interpreters are left to bring them together as they see fit. Similarly, the chart simply offers a range of other texts, especially from the Pentateuch, that we find relevant for understanding and interpreting the specific import of the material in Numbers. It serves as an index in support of our view that interpretation of Numbers benefits from 'reading in concert' with other texts in both Numbers and the Pentateuch. When texts outside this range appear, they are often as clear fulfilments or thematically and terminologically related. Thus, the list serves as an intertextual guide.

Table I.1: Comparative texts for interpreting Numbers

Chapter/verse in Numbers	Important comparative texts
1	Gen. 12:2; 13:16; 15:5; 17:2; 46:3; Num. 26 Exod. 30:12; Num. 26; Josh. 8:10; 2 Sam. 24; 1 Chr. 21:1–17; 2 Chr. 2:17
1:47–53	Gen. 34; Exod. 32:25–29; Num. 18:3
2	Num. 10:11–28, Ezek. 45:1–6; 47:13 – 48:35
3 – 4	Deut. 18:1–8; Ezek. 44:10–16
3:1	Gen. 6:9; 10:1; 11:10, 27; 25:12, 19; 36:1, 9; Exod. 6:16
3:1–4	Exod. 6:20, 23; Lev. 10:1–3
3:11–13	Exod. 11; 12:29–32; 13:11–16; 22:29–30; 34:19; Deut. 15:19–23
3:14–39	Exod. 25 – 27; 30
3:47–48	Lev. 27:6; Num. 18:16
4	Exod. 25 – 27; 30:1–10; 35:11–18; Num. 3:25–37; Num. 7:6–9; 8:24
5:1–4	Lev. 13 – 14; 15:2–31; 22:4
5:5–10	Lev. 6:1–7
5:11–31	Lev. 20:10; Deut. 22:13–29

Chapter/verse in Numbers	Important comparative texts
6:1–21	Lev. 10:9; 21:11; Judg. 13 – 16; Ezek. 44:20–25; Amos 2:11–12
6:22–27	Ps. 121
6:27	Exod. 28:9–12
7:1	Exod. 40:9–10; Lev. 8 – 9
7:89	Exod. 25:22; Num. 9:15
8:1–4	Exod. 25:31–40; 27:20–21; 37:14–24; Lev. 24:1–4
8:5–26	Lev. 8 – 9
8:16–17	Exod. 13:2; 34:19–20; Deut. 15:19–23
8:23–26	Num. 4:3, 46–47; 1 Chr. 23:27; 2 Chr. 31:17
9:1–14	Exod. 12; Lev. 23; Deut. 16:1–8
9:15–23	Exod. 40:16, 34–38
10:1–10	Lev. 25:9; Ps. 98:6
10:11–28	Num. 2
10:29–32	Exod. 3:1; 18:1; Num. 25; 31; Judg. 1:16; 4:11
11:1–3	Deut. 9:22
11:4–35	Exod. 16
11:16–30	Exod. 18:13–27; Deut. 1:9–15
12	Exod. 2:15–22; 18:2
12:4–5	Exod. 16:10; 19:9; 24:15–18; 33:9–10; Num. 11:25
12:6–8	Exod. 33:20; 34:29–35; Deut. 34:10–12
13:1	Deut. 1:22
13:2–15	Deut. 1:23
13:17, 23, 26	Deut. 1:24–25
13:22, 28, 32–33	Deut. 1:29
13:29	Gen. 36:12; Exod. 17:7–16; Num. 24:20; Deut. 25:17–18
14:1–2	Deut. 1:27
14:11	Exod. 3 – 4
14:12–25	Exod. 32:7–14
14:18	Exod. 34:6–7
14:22–23, 24, 25	Deut. 1:35–36, 40
14:39–45	Deut. 1:41–45
15:3–16	Lev. 1; 3; 23:12–14; Ezek. 46:5–7, 11, 14
15:22–31	Lev. 4:13–21, 27–35

Chapter/verse in Numbers	Important comparative texts
15:32–36	Exod. 20:8–11; 31:14–16; 35:1–3; Deut. 5:12–15
15:38–41	Deut. 22:12
15:40, 16:3	Exod. 19:6; Lev. 19:2; Deut. 7:6; 14:2, 21
16	Deut. 11:6; Ezek. 8:7–13; 44:6–16
16 – 17	Deut. 10:6–9; 18:1–8
16:4–7 (17–19, 35)	Lev. 10:1–3
16:8–10	Num. 3; 4:19–20; 8:11, 15, 19
16:47	Num. 8:19
18:1–7	Lev. 22:1–9; Num. 1:47–54; 3 – 4; Ezek. 40:46
18:8–10	Lev. 6:11, 22; 7:6; Deut. 18:4; Ezek. 44:29–30
18:11–19	Exod. 13:1–2, 11–16; 34:19–20; Lev. 22:1–16; 27:26–27; Deut. 15:19–23; 18:4; Ezek. 44:30
18:20	Deut. 18:2; Ezek. 44:28
18:21–24	Lev. 27:30–33; Num. 3:11–13; Deut. 14:22–29; Ezek. 44:10–13, 30
19	Lev. 21:1–4, 11; Deut. 21:1–9
20:1	Num. 13:26; 27:14; 32:8; 33:36; Deut. 1:19, 46; 32:51
20:1–13	Exod. 15:22–27; 17:1–7
20:14–21	Num. 22 – 24; Deut. 2:1–8
20:22–29	Num. 33:38
21:1–3	Judg. 1:16–17; Num. 14:39–45
21:4–9	Gen. 3; 2 Kgs 18:14
21:10–20	Num. 33:41–47; Deut. 2:1, 13, 24
21:21–25	Num. 22 – 24; Deut. 2:26–37; 3:12–17; Judg. 11:19–22
21:27–30	Jer. 48:45–46
21:33–35	Deut. 3:1–3
22 – 24	Num. 20:14–21; 21:21–24; Num. 31:16; Deut. 23:4–6; Josh. 13:21–22; 24:9–10; Neh. 13:1–3
22:5	Gen. 36:32; Num. 24:3, 15
22:6	Num. 24:9; Gen. 12:1–3
22:21–35	Gen. 3:24; Num. 20:14–21; 31:8
23:23	Gen. 3; Num. 21:4–9

Chapter/verse in Numbers	Important comparative texts
23:28	Num. 25:3
24:3	Gen. 36:32; Num. 22:5; 24:15
24:5–6	Gen. 2:8–10
24:7	Gen. 36:12; 1 Sam. 15:1–9
24:9	Num. 22:6
24:15	Gen. 36:32; Num. 22:5; 24:3
24:15–19	Gen. 27
24:17	Gen. 4:25
24:20	Gen. 36:12; Exod. 17:7–16; Num. 13:29; Deut. 25:17–18
24:22	Gen. 4:1
24:23	Num. 21:33–35
24:24	Gen. 10:1–4, 21; 11:16–25
25	Num. 31:8; Deut. 4:3–4; 23:4–5; Ps. 106:28–31; Hos. 9:10
25:1–2	Exod. 34:15–16
25:3	Num. 23:28
26	Num. 1
27:1–11	Lev. 25:44–46; Deut. 21:15–17; 25:5–10; Ruth
27:12–23	Deut. 31:7–8, 14–15, 23; 32:48–52; 34:1–3, 9
28 – 29	Exod. 23:14–19; 29:38–41; 34:18–25; Lev. 23; Deut. 16; Ezek. 46:13–15
30	Lev. 5:4; Deut. 23:21–23
31:1–12	Num. 10:29–32; 24:25; 25
31:8	Num. 22 – 24
31:14–16	Num. 25
31:19–24	Num. 19
32:1–32	Num. 21:24, 35; Deut. 3:18–20; Josh. 13:8–12
32:20–32	Deut. 3:18–20
32:33–42	Deut. 3:12–17
33	Num. 21:10–13
33:3–4	Exod. 12 – 13
33:5–8	Exod. 12:37; 13:20; 14:2; 15:22–26
33:9–15	Exod. 15:27; 16:1; 17:1–2; 19:1–2
33:16–17	Num. 11:34–35

Chapter/verse in Numbers	Important comparative texts
33:30–33	Deut. 10:6–7
33:35–36	Deut. 2:8
33:38–39	Num. 20:22–39
33:42–49	Num. 27:12; Deut. 32:49
33:50–56	Exod. 23:33; 34:12; Num. 26:52–56; Deut. 7:2–6, 16; 12:2–3
34:1–12	Gen. 17:8; Num. 13:3, 21–26; Josh. 13:2–6; 15:1–4, 12; Judg. 20:1; 1 Sam. 3:20
34:16–29	Josh. 14:1–2
35:1–8	Josh. 21
35:9–14	Exod. 21:12–14; Deut. 4:41–43; 19:1–13; Josh. 20:1–9
36	Num. 27:1–11

c. Interpreting different genres

Bank statements may not provide for tantalizing bedtime reading, but their contents can prove very important for everyday life! And, to understand their significance, the reader must be equipped with the skills (mathematics) and relevance (the importance of money for purchasing items) of their line items. Such skills differ from those necessary for grasping the application of a court decision on one hand or a science fiction novel on the other. Each kind of writing presupposes a level of cultural and educational competency for understanding its meanings and significance for a variety of audiences. Such presuppositions also come into play when modern-day audiences interact with the book of Numbers, which includes, or rather subsumes, a variety of genres. A sampling, which could continue in great detail, includes the following major types:

- Census (Num. 1; 26): in biblical literature, this genre focuses on the counting especially of men at an appropriate age for military service or with raising taxes in either labour or goods.
- Purity regulations (5:1–10; 6:9–12; 35:9–34): appearing more

frequently in Leviticus 11 – 15, such regulations provide instructional elements that the text finds central for how the people or their belongings could move from an impure towards a pure state, which was necessary for maintaining God's presence among them during their journey and after settling in the land.

- Ritual regulations (5:11–31; 6; 15; 18; 19): similar to purity regulations, *ritual* regulations provided guidance on focal elements for how the Israelites or their leaders, often Levites or priests, could carry out duties that should bring them into closer proximity to Yahweh.
- Offering report (ch. 7; 31:21–54): coming in response to divergent situations, this genre depicts administrative records of the amounts and kinds of physical materials given by leaders and/or members of the people as offerings to God and those responsible for the sanctuary.
- Narratives (chs. 11–14; 16–17; 20–21; 25): a fairly general category, these theologically defined stories or tales narrate events always from a particular point of view, communicating their perspective through their choice of actors and actions.
- Rescripts (9:1–14; 15:32–35; 27:1–11; 36:1–12): these texts begin with a specific enquiry of God, their sovereign judge. God's response to their specific situation, in the course of the text, becomes generalized to apply to the broader people of God.
- Death/burial report (20:1, 22–29): a short note for Miriam but an extended report for Aaron, this genre uses the death of key characters to mark narrative transitions and often notes the location, significant events of the character's life, and the grieving of those close with the person.
- Battle reports (14:40–45; 21:21–35; 31:1–12): the texts in this genre recount with very different amounts of detail the preparations and results of military conflict. In Numbers they minimize details extraneous to demonstrating God's military superiority over both Israel and their enemies, such that the outcome follows God's will.
- Oracles (chs. 23–24): in biblical literature these texts are associated most closely with the prophetic books. In Numbers they consist primarily of blessings towards Israel and

condemnations of other peoples, a feature also found in, for example, Isaiah 13 – 23; Amos 1 – 2.

- Songs/poems (10:35–36; 21:17–20, 27–30): while it sometimes remains unclear whether intended to be spoken or sung, the texts in this genre in Numbers contain short lines with classic features of ancient Hebrew poetry such as parallel lines.
- Festival calendar (chs. 28–29): while these chapters adopt the ritual regulations for offerings found in Leviticus 1 – 7, they organize the offerings into a daily, weekly, monthly and yearly calendar.
- Itineraries (21:10–20; 33:1–49): recording places where Israel camped and set out from, the lists of geographical locations intend the designation of the places and people in them as under God's authority.

As a whole, the variety of genres brought together in Numbers indicates the *awareness of genre* required for engaging with the biblical texts. While one may come to the book for spiritual insight, acknowledging and respecting the ancient forms of communication gathered enhances that process. By paying attention to the genre, one can set expectations for what that section of text may offer.

7. Key concepts

a. What is 'biblical law'?

The books of Genesis–Deuteronomy have been known since their translation into Greek in third-century BC Egypt as 'law' (Greek: *nomos*). At least since the rise of the Romans as the rulers of the Mediterranean, including the southern Levant where most of the events of the Old and New Testaments take place, 'law' has come to be understood as a codified set of legislated regulations enforced by a ruler and serving as the basis for court decisions by judges. However, both the Greek term *nomos* and the underlining Hebrew term *torah* contain considerable latitude in meaning that differs from the Roman-dominated understanding. First, the Hebrew term *torah*, which came to serve as a title for the Pentateuch, more precisely means 'instruction' rather than 'law'. Second, even the Greek term *nomos* can include unwritten custom and cultural habits. Third, the most widely accepted notion of law in the modern world conceives of law as a code containing a complete and non-contradicting set of regulations. However, comparison with Ancient Near Eastern legal treatises and the lack of use of the Pentateuch as the direct basis for legal judgments in early Judean communities (Altmann 2021) point in a different direction. Fourth, the multiple and unsystematic treatments of the same topics in different places in the Pentateuch also suggest that these legal declarations had a different function, which indicates that a different interpretive methodology is required. As a whole, the assumption that law in Numbers and the Pentateuch functioned like modern-day law requires adjustment.

Legal treatises and vast numbers of judicial documents from across the Ancient Near East have been investigated since the discovery of Hammurabi's Laws in 1901. While these laws, dating to the 1700s BC, were widely copied throughout Mesopotamia and similar laws also appear in the Pentateuch (especially in Exod. 21 – 22), they do not appear as the basis for judicial decisions. Rather than functioning as 'law' in a modern sense, these legal treatises instead serve as a kind of social wisdom intended to provide instruction for the formation of a well-ordered society (Westbrook and Wells 2009: 26).

As a result, they can contain contrary points of view (much like one also sees in the book of Proverbs) that offer contradictory implementations of important values. To offer one example, Proverbs 26:4 reads, 'Do not answer fools according to their folly', while verse 5 reads, 'Answer fools according to their folly.' Resolution of these opposing imperatives calls for reflection and innovative application. Similarly, the legal provisions are not meant for implementation according to their 'letter', but require interpretation for particular concrete situations. For example, differences in the conception of the provision of towns of refuge in Deuteronomy 19 and Numbers 35, or between the festival calendars in Leviticus 23; Numbers 28 – 29; and Deuteronomy 16, do not require harmonization, but rather appreciation in order to understand the important values and motivations that materialize in their diverging conceptions. One can then evaluate how the different formulations reflect distinct temporal or geographic contexts. In part, this simply follows the Pentateuch's own way of distinguishing between rules: roughly partitioned between those from Sinai (Exodus – Num. 9), those along the way (Num. 10 – 19), and those intended for implementation in the land (Num. 27 – Deut. 31).

In their relation to the functioning of a judicial system, the biblical laws, including those of Numbers, intend to help judges become wise in assessing and deciding in each case, rather than providing them with a list of rules directly applicable in any and every context.

A completely different issue related to the understanding of law concerns the interweaving of various types of legal concerns with the regulation of sanctuary and broader religious practices. In contrast to most legal texts of Mesopotamia, Egypt and other cultures of antiquity, the Pentateuch brings together regulations on adjudicating cases of homicide (Num. 19; 35) with regular offerings brought to sanctuaries (Num. 18). However, Hittite royal instructions from Anatolia (modern-day Türkiye) could also include a variety of material including troop management, fortification-building, administration of justice, and sanctuary administration (Morrow 2023: 138). Numbers goes one step further in that it also embeds these regulations into the complex pilgrimage of the Israelites' travel in the wilderness. As a whole, Numbers melds together the various types of regulations into a depiction of how Israel becomes a people, more specifically God's people. For this reason, the people are included in a dialogue with their leaders, especially Moses in Numbers, participating in the assessment and decision-making of public affairs (27:1–12; 32; 35:16–34; 36).

In a way, the use of legal material here correlates with every modern constitution in that they all have a conception of how the people under the influence of that vision should live together. However, unlike the judicial means envisioned to implement that conception through the powers invested in a government, biblical law influences its audiences through wisdom and the spiritually compelling nature of its vision.

In other words, no records exist of economic transactions following the laws against charging interest in, for example, Deuteronomy 23:19–20, and animal bones from some creatures declared unclean in Leviticus 11/Deuteronomy 14 are found in relative abundance in Israel in the periods of Israel and Judah's existence. These data do not necessarily mean that the practices legislated in Numbers and the rest of the Pentateuch never took place: rather, it is probable that some of the ritual regulations and instructions about societal practices emerged from and matched concrete customs in some communities at some times in ancient Israel and Judah. However, the connection between legal instructions and actual practice can vary significantly from imagined and counter-factual, to a sacred ordinance practised by a small minority, to a custom taken for granted among a widespread majority, even to one extending beyond those who might have some affiliation with Israel and Judah.

To summarize, there are ways in which the laws in Numbers and the Pentateuch more broadly participate in ancient Mediterranean, Near Eastern or human cultural patterns. There are also ways in which the biblical laws distinguish themselves from other traditions. And all along this continuum, the degree to which laws were implemented can vary. However, in all cases there is rarely evidence that the laws served as something like a 'law of the land' that was backed by a political authority which decided guilt or innocence by analysing the text as some kind of codified law as one envisions for modern legal systems.

b. Israel's identity and its neighbours

The identity of Israel as a people is a central theme in Numbers. Israel's identity in Numbers, as with other forms of human identity, is relational, both individually and collectively; it is bound and bonded. Therefore, the formation of Israel's peculiar identity depends on boundaries and differentiation, as well as permeability and porosity that recognize and allow the participation of others in the formulation of who they are.

What is unique in Numbers is how instructions and narratives are subservient to the organization of the camp and the formation of a new generation, both in preparation for a movement in which Israel encounters a diversity of other peoples in the Promised Land. Connected to the question of Israel's identity in Numbers, therefore, is how it relates to God, to itself and to others.

Thus, consideration of some critical concepts concerning identity and the history of Israel's origins provides elucidation for the biblical texts. Identity itself is a general term for a combination of distinctive characteristics that conceptualize forms of self-understanding, relatedness and social cohesion (see Brubaker and Cooper 2000). Place of origin or settlement, language, nationality, ancestry, gender, religion, profession and so on, are characteristics that might be used to establish identity. Individuals and groups might elevate one or more of these over others to form their identities depending on particular contexts or purposes. Social and neuropsychologists use the term 'self-expansion' (Wright et al. 2002) with regard to such negotiation of identities to enhance efficacy in preserving themselves.

A good example of self-expansion is the formation of kinship and ethnicity. Like almost every other form of identity, kinship and ethnicity are relational, fluid and porous. Both are mistakenly considered a biological identity (see Carsten 2004). Kinship, biological or otherwise, is formed by close relationships of sharedness and mutuality. In traditional cultures kinship is formed by shared dynamics in the production and consumption of food, especially sharing the core starch produced by a specific group or culture in their land, prepared and consumed in a specific household (see Janowski 2007; cf. C. R. Chapman 2023: 435–436). Food, like blood and breast milk, is considered a form of 'life-force', so that sharing it forms kinship bonds (Carsten 2004: 310–314).

When it comes to the early history of Israel and its neighbours, Egyptian sources from the New Kingdom Period (c.1539–1075 BC) provide information about different groups of people in the southern Levant, such as Israel, Edom and Moab. It remains unclear whether these different identities are self-designations or external perceptions and impositions. But Egyptians designate these groups 'Shasu', an identity that points to social class and way of life (mobile or semi-mobile agro-pastoralists). This term marks a sociopolitical differentiation between them and the Egyptian personnel and vassals who composed the elite and ruling class in the region (see Levy 2008: 251; B. W. Porter 2023: 622; cf. Burke 2023b: 542). The genesis of local chiefdoms structured by the coalescence of tribal organizations, such as Israel, Edom,

Ammon and Moab (see Tebes 2023: 641; Younker 2023: 601), after the demise of Egyptian rule in southern Levant still carried more contrast between them and Egypt than among themselves. The best form in which to consider these peoples' identities is to see them in a continuum (cf. Carsten 2004: 314). From a cognitive perspective, identities are categories often defined by prototypical exemplars that exist in gradations (see Sanders 2017: 30–34).

Historically, then, some observable traces might characterize prototypical Israelites in a continuum with their closest neighbours in the early Iron Age: simple pottery, undecorated and not imported, complete lack of or low consumption of pork, and four-room-house architecture. These traces suggest an ethos of egalitarian simplicity in a less stratified society in contrast to the imperial organization of Egyptian regional domination and its palace economies (see Faust 2016: 165–170). These traits are not exclusively Israelite, however. The case of pork consumption, for example, marks some class distinction between urban and rural lifestyles even among Philistines (see Sapir-Hen 2019; Price 2022). However, it does have an important function throughout Israel and Judah's history. For example, the urban elite lifestyle in eighth-century Samaria – with ivory inlays, hierarchical and oppressive production and consumption of food – is denounced by Israelite prophets as incompatible with Israel's identity (see Amos 6:4–6). Even clear identity markers such as statehood, territory and language are not enough to imagine a homogeneous and rigid identity. Therefore, for a more detailed sense of Israelite identity, one must consider the biblical witness, including Numbers, as political and intellectual forces attempting to define who belongs to Israel in a context of close proximity between different peoples, in relation to contexts ranging from the early Iron Age to at least the Persian period (1200–330 BC).

Numbers does not present Israel's identity from a typical monarchic perspective, using state, language or territory as crucial markers. Four particular characteristics of Israelite identity in Numbers deserve special attention. The first concerns belonging to an Israelite tribe. The book's first four chapters structure the community by tribal position and following tribal leadership, which imply that belonging to Israel means being part of one of its tribes.

The second characteristic concerns living as a people around the presence of Yahweh. The presence of God appears structurally attached to the community and moves with the people (10:35–36). To be Israel is to move with and at the pace of the divine presence, which incidentally follows the needs of those in more vulnerable conditions (9:6–14; 12:15–16).

The third characteristic concerns living as a people formed by the wisdom of Torah. After decisive episodes of rebellion, when Israel is at risk of losing its identity, God reminds Israel of foundational instructions (chs. 15; 18–19; 28–29). It is striking that these chapters are almost entirely dedicated to instructions concerning festivals and offerings. Therefore, crucial to the Torah's role in the formation of Israel's identity is Israel's relationship with the land and its produce. They must be considered and treated as God's good gifts (see Num. 13), and Israel must serve God by working the land and consecrating its produce through the offering of part of it in communal religious feasts and festivals. To be part of Israel, individuals and communities must participate in its religious festivals (9:13) and dedicate its food to God by distributing it to the community (6:13–21; 7), sharing the same food in a fairly equal manner with Israel's leaders, the whole community, and even God.

The fourth characteristic of Israelite identity in Numbers is a shared destiny (cf. Leveen 2017: 48) as established by Numbers 32. The Transjordan tribes confirm their Israelite identity by kinship (*your brothers*, 32:6) in their commitment to subordinate their settlement in the land to the settlement of all Israelites in their land (32:17–18). Israelite identity attaches the well-being of particular individuals and communities to the well-being of the whole people.

Numbers establishes these four characteristics as the basis of Israel's unity and identity. They align with the ethos of egalitarian simplicity seen in the historical identity of prototypical Israel mentioned above.

In the same way that Israel's identity as God's people in Numbers is advanced by internal events, encounters with other peoples are also used to establish, negotiate and deconstruct boundaries between them. When Israel is preparing to move from Sinai, issues concerning foreigners start to emerge (9:14; 10:29–32; 12:1). They find their apex at the centre of the narrative in Numbers 20 – 25, when Israel approaches and settles on the plains of Moab. As a general statement for the whole Bible and for Numbers in particular, Israel's encounter with other peoples might result in peace or violence, cooperation or competition, conquest or coexistence, and integration or expulsion.

The prominence of the Moabites and Midianites in Numbers serves as a kind of theme to explore the closeness and distance between Israel and other peoples (see Diamant 2009: 61; Leveen 2010: 412). The presentation of Moses' Midianite father-in-law is so positive that he is included in Israel (10:29–32). In contrast, Numbers 25 and especially Numbers 31 present the Midianites negatively: both texts describing gruesome violence with divine approval.

In addition to considering these as two divergent traditions about Israel's relations to other peoples, it is possible to see them as a complex picture of identity formation. Actions of violence, conquest and expulsion are directed towards ways of life that threaten Israel's identity. Integration and cooperation between groups are typically easier on the level of individuals and families, and more difficult on the level of complex structures such as tribes, villages and nations (see McNutt 2023: 158). Unsurprisingly, the negative encounters on the level of complex structures are significantly reduced when members of each group have personal connections with members of the other group (Wright et al. 2002: 354). Social fusion or integration is more focused on peaceful rather than violent outcomes and on rituals of shared intense experiences (Whitehouse 2021: 100, 106). It is important, then, that the biblical tradition in general and Numbers in particular personalize encounters between Israel and other peoples, such as Jethro and Zelophehad's daughters, as models of positive relationships that might even lead to integration and kinship formation. However, the institutionalizing of identities, in the person of a king or of whole peoples, as found in Numbers 25 and 31, in negative encounters serves as models of what (not whom) Israel stands against. The positive encounters suggest how Israel should live their everyday lives with other peoples (see B. W. Porter 2023:

629) in such a way that would reduce the possibility of actual negative encounters fomented by prejudice against stereotyped foreign identities (see Leveen 2010: 417).

The main purpose of these encounters in Numbers, therefore, is not to chastise specific groups of people, but to highlight identity markers that impede the formation of Israel's identity as God's people (see Dozeman 2008: 283). The whole picture drawn in Numbers is a complex one that prioritizes cooperation, coexistence and even kinship integration as alternatives to competition and violence. This is true for the historical emergence of Israel in a context of plurality, diversity and porosity between different peoples under the shadow of Egypt's imperial domination, as well as for the context of the composition of Numbers in the exile and the post-exilic period, when Israel and Judah were strangers from the perspective of their powerful masters (cf. Leveen 2017: 197).

Historically and ethically important, this proposal for Israel's identity in relation to its neighbours is also theologically foundational. In the main extended episode in Numbers that addresses Israel's relationship with other peoples, Numbers 22 – 24, the prototypical other, Balaam, is caught between cursing violence and blessing integration. The Balaam Pericope demonstrates how the bound and bonded dynamic between Israel and other peoples has profound implications for the relationship of humans with God. Even when Israel and other peoples are set apart as different identities, the possibility and effort to negotiate permeability, to cross boundaries and to produce integration between the two is a foundation for how God and humans can also cross the ultimate boundary between humanity and divinity. If humans, in their differences, cannot cross boundaries and integrate their identities, what hope is there for us to ever meet with God? It is not just an intriguing detail, then, that the genealogy of Jesus' Israelite identity expands to include Moabites and Canaanites in Matthew, and goes all the way back to humanity's common origins in Luke. The human crossing of boundaries is resonant with God crossing boundaries to become one of us in the incarnation; the expansion of Israelite identity is the foundation for all humanity to be integrated into God's people.

c. From impurity to holiness

The biblical texts draw upon the concepts of holiness, purity and impurity to address the tension that exists in the relationship between God and creation. This is a concern for several ancient and contemporary cultures and religions. Proximity to God's presence requires human awareness and carefulness (cf. Exod. 3:3–5). No wonder Leviticus, after God takes up his residence in the tabernacle, so thoroughly treats the conditions and behaviours qualified as impure, profane, pure and holy. These issues are less frequent in Numbers, but they are no less central. New information, clarification and expansion occur that provide a better grasp of the logic and function of these concepts in life and theology.

The role of Israel's camp in Numbers makes clearer and more explicit how conditions from holiness to impurity are conceptualized. The camp is imagined as a structure with concentric borders based on the holy divine presence in its middle (cf. Frevel 2012: 378–408). In this scheme, there is a gradation from holiness to impurity that follows the logic of proximity and distance from the divine presence (see van Wolde 2009: 255–256). This spatial conceptualization, therefore, informs the relationship between God and Israel reflected in the condition of purity or impurity of the land, the camp and the tabernacle (see below, 'Atonement and ritual').

Levites are consecrated or enter a state of holiness in the initiation of their service (Num. 8). More extraordinarily, the Nazirite vow (Num. 6) provides attainable high-priestly consecration to every member of the community, a condition reinforced in the intriguing command for each Israelite to wear priestly-like tassels to be holy for their God (15:37–41). In relation to the camp, we see a subtle positive implication of its purity in the instruction for the purification of those involved in the Midianite war, including foreign war prisoners, and of their objects as well as spoils of war, before everyone and everything can enter the camp (31:13–24). A positive implication of the land's holiness can be seen in the instruction for the towns of refuge that is based on the strong attachment between God and the land where the divine presence dwells (35:34).

Because of the potential for holiness, people and land can also be profaned, polluted or contaminated. In Numbers, impurity – and similar concepts such as pollution and contamination – is more clearly associated with death (cf. Lev. 21:1; see Frevel 2012: 387). Although there are some intricately implicit correspondences between the condition of skin defilement and death in Leviticus (see Trevaskis 2011: 125–160), in Numbers 12 it is explicit: 'like a stillborn, with half flesh eaten away when he comes out of his mother's womb' (12:12, AT). Similarly, the manufacturing of special purifying water and a whole purification ritual procedure for impurity caused by corpses is presented in Numbers 19. Homicide is a cause of pollution and contamination of the land in 35:33–34.

In Numbers 5, many of the peculiarities described so far converge. Numbers 5:1–4 mentions the three typical forms of impurity – skin defilement, bodily discharges and contact with corpses – and imposes a distance between impurity and the camp. It follows that sin committed against fellow members of the community must be dealt with through compensation to the cult in God's dwelling place (5:5–10). A relational conflict between husband and wife in which impurity might be a cause of separation, a possible analogy of the relationship between God and Israel, closes the chapter (5:11–31).

One might be tempted to think that the main purpose of this scheme is to keep Israel distant from God, but the opposite is true. One basic definition is that holiness is intrinsically a divine attribute and impurity is a typical human condition. In this dichotomy between holiness and impurity, purity plays a liminal function of recognition of the separation between them and the condition necessary to encounter God, be consecrated and be in a condition of holiness (see Milgrom 1996: 72; D. P. Wright 1999: 353; Frevel 2012: 380, 384; Jenson 2021: 53). In Numbers, as demonstrated above, the possibility for consecration and the divine presence are expanded. The concentric borders exist, but they are permeable and there is a demonstrable impulse for expansion of the centre to the borders (cf. Milgrom 1996: 67, 70–72).

This impulse raises questions of responsibility and morality in relation to holiness, purity and impurity. For didactic purposes differentiating types of impurity can be useful. There are those caused by morally neutral human experiences, such as body fluids (Lev. 12 – 15) and human corpses (Num. 19), and those caused by sinful behaviour, such as idolatry (Lev. 18 and Num. 25) and homicide (Num. 35). The aspect of gradation from holiness to impurity offers a better conceptual framework that avoids dichotomies such as ritual and moral (Klawans 2004) or tolerated and prohibited (D. P. Wright 1991) types of impurity. Cognitive studies, an interdisciplinary field that studies the human mind, is of great help here. First, and quite simply, it defines categories as gradient and without rigid boundaries, aligning well with the notion of gradation seen in Leviticus and Numbers (see Sanders 2017: 32–34). Second, and extremely relevant, is the contribution of cognitive studies for the understanding of conceptual metaphors.

Language and reason are built from embodied experiences so that our conceptual world is pervasively formed by metaphors. For the topic at hand, purity or cleanness lies behind our notions of morality through the conceptual metaphor *morality is health* (Sanders 2017: 142–143). An embodied, even biological, experience informs this conceptualization, as human disgust plays a role in avoiding infection and disease by physically keeping away from or scraping off slimy, rotting and decaying materials (Kazen 2018: 93–94). This is reflected in language. In Hebrew and cognate languages, words for impurity have the basic meaning of 'dirt' or 'mud', while words for purity, also used in the sense of holiness, have the basic meaning of 'shiny' or 'clear' (Feder 2014: 94–95, 100; Kazen 2017: 104). The human ideal of well-being is the cognitive connection between physical experiences of dirt and decay and the conceptual meaning of moral purity and impurity. Individual and communal well-being depend on physical health and moral values, while their lack is a cause of decay (see Lakoff and Johnson 1980: 250; 1999: 307–309). Cognitive studies help debunk dichotomies in favour of a continuum from body to concept, from ritual to morality, from physical to spiritual. From a cognitive perspective, the two ends of the spectrum are defined as life and well-being at one pole and death and decay at the other. Using the theological construction of Leviticus and Numbers, life and well-being are defined by holiness and integrity, and death and decay are defined by impurity and mortality.

From the most innocent and even positive types of impurity, such as giving birth, care for a deceased family member or participating in certain ritual procedures, to the most sinful and harmful types, such as child sacrifice and homicide, they are largely marks of our mortal and transient human condition that distance us from who God is (cf. Maccoby 1999: 49–50; Jenson 2021: 19). For this reason, impurity demands and causes distance from God's dwelling, and most forms have resulting negative effects. Most cases of impurity are replicated as stains in the tabernacle that need removal; otherwise, they cause God's presence to leave (see Milgrom 1976). However, the most serious cases even affect the land as God's dwelling and result in expulsion and death of individuals and communities (35:33–34). One way Leviticus and Numbers depict these sinful conditions and effects of impurity is to be 'cut off' (e.g. Lev. 18:29; 20:3; 22:3; 23:29; Num. 15:30–31; 19:13; see D. P. Wright 1991: 161; Feder 2021: 54). Therefore, the gradation of the human mortal and transient condition of impurity is a theological interpretation of our separateness from God that includes the neutral and the sinful, the unavoidable and the reproachable, the non-harmful and the destructive. As a separation from God, the life-giving force, impurity is a consequence of the forces of death or mortality in human existence.

To a certain degree, this definition of impurity establishes a contrast between God and humanity to the point of incompatibility between the two. God is immortal and whole; God does not undergo the human experiences of birth, sex, sin and death. Therefore, purification as a condition to draw near to God must be interpreted as a process of becoming more similar to who God is while still human (Klawans 2006: 55–66). This process might involve one or several of these elements: abstinence from sex and avoidance of corpses, passing of time, bathing, repentance, material compensation, offerings, rituals and periods of exclusion. The possibility of purification as a God-like condition establishes its relation to holiness that justifies the most basic and fundamental of divine requirements to Israel: 'be holy, for I am holy'. It also reveals that divinity and humanity are not utterly opposite, incompatible and distinct forms of being (contra Gudme 2009: 71–72).

There are two important implications for this theological construction of impurity associated with the mortal and transient human condition (cf. Douglas 1996). The first is that it removes guilt and sinfulness from being attached to every aspect of human existence. People with impurities associated with illnesses, such as skin defilement and abnormal and debilitating bodily discharges, cannot be held responsible for their own conditions. The second implication is that impurity becomes controllable and reversible. In this case, embodied mortal humans can still interact with divine holiness and be associated with it (cf. Schellenberg 2014: 174–175). The high priest and the Nazirites are good examples. One reflection of the consecration of Nazirites is the qualification of their hair/head as holy (6:5, 8, 11, 19–20). The association of holiness with the high priest's body is more complex. In Leviticus, animal body integrity – 'without blemish' (*tāmîm*) – is a qualification for their use in offerings (e.g. Lev. 1:3). These animals must be the best representatives of their species (see Mal. 1:8–14). In the Bible, *tāmîm* can also be a moral qualification ('blameless'; e.g. Gen. 17:1; Deut. 18:13; Ps. 15:2). Animal body integrity is combined with the integrity of the high priest's body (cf. Lev. 21:16–24 and 22:17–25; see Trevaskis 2011: 208–229). From a cognitive perspective, it is possible to discern a move from bodily experience to the conceptual metaphor of morality and religion: *to be holy is to be whole*. The high priest's holiness is an expression of the ideal human, a prototype that represents the best specimen of humanity. This is not a merely static and ritual form of holiness. In their state of holiness in intimate proximity to God, the life-giving force, they serve as a means of communion with God and access to divine blessing for the whole community. They distribute consecrated material resources that sustain the lives of individuals and of the community in the form of offerings presented in the tabernacle, the dwelling place of God (see *Comment* on 6:13–21 and 6:22–27 below). Holiness, then, is the ideal human condition of wholeness in proximity to and imitation of God as the life-giving force that sustains our individual and communal existence and well-being.

The process of purification and expression of holiness as a God-like condition and experience cannot remove human mortality. However, the theological construction of impurity, purity and holiness in Leviticus and Numbers is used in the epistle to the Hebrews to interpret Jesus' life and ministry. Among many correspondences (see Moffitt 2019), Hebrews presents the resurrection of Jesus as God's final solution for human mortality and its subjection to impurity. Jesus' resurrected body is the prototype of the human God-like condition that subdues mortality and death and fully unites humans to God. In the theology of Hebrews, Jesus fulfils to the maximum the ideals of purity, integrity and holiness proposed in Leviticus and Numbers. For this reason, such theological connections remain bulwarks against the elevation of mind over body or the spiritual over the material. There are still theologies that castigate human bodies as obstacles to our relationship with God. Even worse, there are still theologies that consider certain bodies and human conditions as closer to God than others, limiting other bodies from sources of life. Jesus' resurrection with a tortured and wounded body challenges these theologies in the light of the theology of holiness, purity and impurity. Impurity, sin, death and mortality are not intrinsic to our bodily existence or specific bodily conditions. Purification is possible; holiness is achievable; intimacy with God and access to the sources of life, integrity and well-being are our destiny as embodied humans.

d. Atonement and ritual

In several cases of sin and conditions of impurity, individuals and the community are required to make offerings and practise certain rituals that effect atonement (*kipper*; e.g. Lev. 4:1 – 5:13; 12 – 16; Num. 5:5–8; 6:9–12; 15:22–29). If sin and impurity are in opposition to holiness, reflecting and causing distance between humanity and God, atonement relates to a process of drawing closer to God and consecration or becoming holy.

The few references to atonement in Numbers provide particular perspectives that present a broad and diverse picture. In Numbers 5:5–8, atonement is a process of reconciliation with a neighbour, involving confession of the sin, restitution of losses, and a purification offering called a 'ram of atonement'. Related to sin, but described as a deviation from divine instructions, Numbers 15:22–29 prescribes offerings to make atonement. Here, it is clear that it is not only the purification offering but also the burnt offering with the tribute and libation offerings that effect atonement (cf. 8:12). In two cases, atonement is effected to avert divine wrath, hence a form of propitiation. Phinehas makes atonement for the Israelites (25:13) by killing two people, and Aaron effects atonement by burning incense with the fire of the altar while standing in the middle of the people (16:46–47). In both cases there is no animal sacrifice or blood manipulation (cf. Lev. 5:11–13). Another intriguing case of atonement appears in Numbers 31. Soldiers involved in the battle with the Midianites go through a process of purification along with prisoners and spoils of war (31:19–24). But their atonement is effected by their offering of valuable jewellery (31:50), which is purified by fire (see 31:22–23) and turned into a memorial in the presence of Yahweh (31:54; see Awabdy 2023: 24).

In Numbers 35 one learns that the impurity of land cannot be dealt with ritually, but only by means of the blood of the murderer (35:33). While the complexity of the case in Numbers 35 is addressed in the *Comment* on the chapter, here atonement is associated with 'ransom' (*kōper*, 35:31–32) as a form of substitution, commonly for someone who is guilty (cf. Exod. 21:28–32; 30:11–16; Ps. 49:7–8 [8–9]; Isa. 43:3–4; see Sklar 2015: 48–67). The death of the high priest also has an atoning effect for one who has committed manslaughter (35:28). Finally, Numbers presents cases of atonement that are directly related to the process of consecration or becoming holy. Atonement is needed in cases of impurity caused by corpses and is a form of renewing the consecrated state of the Nazirite (6:11). The consecration of the Levites in Numbers 8 is qualified as a form of purification (8:21), and it prepares the Levites to make atonement for the Israelites (8:19). The proximity to the divine presence, at a holy place (28:7) and in answer to a holy calling (28:18, 25, 26; 29:1, 7, 12), explains the requirement of atonement for participation in the Israelite annual festivals even without any mention of sin and impurity (see 28:22, 30; 29:5).

The broad and diverse use of atonement language in Numbers makes it clear that limiting its effect and meaning to *just* purification, expiation, ransom or forgiveness of sins is inadequate. The Hebrew *kipper* is a hypernym, a type of umbrella term that encompasses a conceptual process that moves from impurity to holiness (see Gilders 2004: 137; Eberhart 2017: 226). The atonement process might include several steps described by other important priestly ritual terms, such as purification, cleansing, bearing of sin, forgiveness, ransom and consecration (see Kiuchi 1987: 97–98, 109).

Some important clarifications and implications require comment. First, the overall purpose of Israel's experience as the people of God in the Priestly tradition material, especially in the cultic environment, is defined by atonement. For this reason, the term *kipper* first appears at the beginning of the cultic instruction, in Leviticus 1:4 (see Watts 2013: 326). Second, each of these steps, even when they occur in isolation and without reference to the term *kipper*, has the overall purpose of the process in view. Third, to understand atonement as a process helps solve an important conundrum in scholarship about the effect of *kipper* in relation to people and in relation to the sanctuary and its objects (see Milgrom 1991: 253–258; cf. Gane 2005: 106–143; Vis 2017). In cases of impurity or sin, offerings – including the purification offering – are brought only after a declaration of purification (e.g. Lev. 15:13–15) or after repentance that encompasses remorse, restitution and contrition (e.g. Lev. 5:1–3; 6:1–7 [5:20–26]; 16:29–34; see Feder 2011: 80). However, because the sanctuary reflects the conditions of the community in relation to God, the sins and impurities attached to it also need removal to reflect the new purified or forgiven status of offerors (see Milgrom 1976; Schwartz 1995: 20–21; Schellenberg 2014: 170–171; Nihan 2015: 96, 125–126). As part of the atonement process, the purification offering attunes community and sanctuary and makes it possible for the sanctuary to continue as a place of encounter between the community and Yahweh (cf. Nihan 2015: 127). The *kipper* process is a ritual recognition and overcoming of the distance between divinity and humanity so that they experience symbiosis, a shared life in a shared space. For this reason, the rendering of *kipper* as 'atonement', following its original meaning as resuming a relationship by bonding two or more parts, seems the most appropriate.

Lastly, the process of atonement presented in the biblical text qualifies both how this encounter is possible and its results. The encounter results in the consecration that occurs through ritual offering and consumption of animals and vegetables. What is offered by Israel is the produce of the land through the constant intervention of humans to adapt and modify nature to best supply their needs and sustain their lives. Animals and vegetables offered are the representative specimens resulting from this long history of breeding, selecting, separating and sharing to the point that they carry in themselves the life and identity of the offeror. The religious self-giving and self-sharing is the basis to establish an environment of encounter with God and with one another by sharing the table and eating the same representative specimen of animals and vegetables, especially the most basic of foods, Israel's core starch: bread (see Marx 1994: 70–167). As mentioned above in the discussion of 'Israel's identity and its neighbours', sharing the core starch is the basis for forming kinship relations, because the core starch is a life-force like blood. Therefore, God and Israel are kin, sharing the same life-force through the consumption of portions of offering. By doing so, the offeror and Israel as a community are imitating God's involvement with the world (see Klawans 2006: 62–66). God creates, selects, separates and provides in order to establish an environment where encounters with creation and humanity can take place. God's holy and life-giving force imbues each of these resources that sustain the life of the world. God's consumption of the offering by the altar's fire, specifically blood, the portion of fat and semolina (flour), is a return of the life-force to its original source (cf. Gudme 2019) at the same time that the offeror's life, imbued in the offering, is consecrated by entering into contact with divine holiness (see Peres 2021; cf. Eberhart 2004: 491; Morales 2015: 139). The result of the *kipper* process, then, is the formation of individuals and a community who are kin representatives of the divine holiness.

This is a highly theological definition of atonement derived from the biblical texts, and it raises the question about the efficacy of ritual practices to accomplish such profound religious experience and constructions. Despite some modern and Protestant ideas that true meaning and belief come from verbal propositions while rituals are empty and meaningless, there are many indications that the latter are quite significant for human development, and religious experience and belief.

Ritual as practice is derived from and reinforces our biological human ability to learn by imitation and our social need for belonging. These two aspects are actually intertwined (see Cozolino 2014: 205–257). We have a biological tendency to mirror the body movements of others with whom we interact, creating bodily synchrony that promotes neurological and emotional attunement. Part of this process depends on and produces internalized representations of others, including their motivations, intentions and feelings, in our own minds. Humans understand, connect and empathize with others through this kind of embodied simulation of others in their minds (see Gallese 2008; cf. Cozolino 2014: 216). Our attunement to others is the basis for human cooperation, sympathy, empathy, solidarity and group identity (see Schüler 2012: 99–100; Heinskou and Liebst 2016; Whitehouse 2021: 48, 99).

The above discussion concerns the embodied experiences of ritual practices, so one may ask how it transfers to theology, the biblical text and, most importantly, to one's relationship with God? Concerning theology and the biblical text, it is relevant that humans' conceptual world is constructed by embodied experience in the world, as mentioned under the previous topic. Ritual practices, therefore, are a central foundation for the biblical text and theological exploration. Highly relevant is the fact that our tendency to imitate others and engage in ritual practices as a form of learning and communication is probably the foundation for human language skills (Gallese 2008: 770–771; Cozolino 2014: 208–209). Ritual, then, as specific combinations of bodily movements and gestures, is a form of human communication that the participant or observer must be able to 'read' by the actions themselves (see Bell 1992; cf. Grimes 2004). This is the reason why, for example, ritual texts, including those in the Bible, do not offer explanations, because explaining ritual practice with verbal propositions is not explaining ritual at all. There are two paradoxical implications here. First, because ritual is a bodily form of communication, it produces meaning more concretely than symbols as in verbal and written language (see Robbins

2001). Second, rituals have the potential to promote a diversity of meanings for different participants and for the practice of rituals in different contexts (see Strathern and Stewart 2021).

These two implications provide a foundation for consideration of ritual texts in the Bible. The rituals in the Bible, even ritual instructions, are not ritual scripts for ritual performances. They are constructed from actual ritual practices and are intended to inform actual ritual practices, but they are not identical to ritual practices. There is selectivity, emphasis, glossing, dismissal, and so on, according to determined purposes (Hundley 2011: 20). And it is possible to say that the purpose of ritual texts in the Bible, many of them in Numbers (5:11–21; 6:9–12, 13–20, 23–27; 9:9–14; 15:1–21, 22–29; 16:17–19, 36–50, 46–48; 19; 25:7–8; 28 – 29; 30), is to create an ideal textual world to which the real world, including ancient and modern addressees, can be related (Frevel 2021). In connection with what was argued for the meaning of atonement, we can use the priestly blessing (6:22–27) as the textual ideal to which ritual practices might connect. The priestly blessing is recontextualized from oral and ritual practices in ancient Israel to the textual ritual ideal of Yahweh worship. The blessing is textually connected all the way back to Leviticus 9 as the culmination of the inauguration of the tabernacle and its worship, as well as to the immediate context of the Nazirite vow (Num. 6:1–21), the offering of the tribes (Num. 7), and the arrangement of lamps in relation to the bread of presence in the tabernacle (8:1–4). The priestly blessing is a representation of consecration because the priest declares it from the top of the altar where the offerings are lying and will be consumed by the divine holy presence in the form of fire. In this image, consecration happens by self-offering for the benefit of others, through distribution of material resources as divine gifts that bless and sustain the life of the community. The divine blessing, therefore, is the result of imitating and becoming kin with God.

For this meaning to have any significance, one needs practices that will train one's body to create mind representations of such experience. For the biblical ritual texts to actually inform religious experience, just as with the ancient addressees, one needs to practise it (see Maiden 2020: 229). That does not mean repeating the same practices, but engaging in practices that will create internal representations that connect to the texts when they are read or while they are recalled in ritual practices. Religious ritual is a human technique that creates spaces, times, relations and practices in which God becomes real in embodied experiences. Taking seriously the mind representation of others, religious rituals, including Bible reading, is a technique of including God in one's social relationships by training the body and mind to pay attention to and experience God in one's life (see Schüler 2012; Luhrmann 2020). In the end, given how human bodies and minds work, atonement, attunement and kinship with God in a perceived imitation of God will necessarily involve practices that promote attunement, cooperation, solidarity and kinship with other people in sharing oneself in several forms of resources that sustain the life of the world, which is the divine holy presence.

e. The different types of offerings

The book of Numbers includes an array of offerings or sacrifices, which English translations usually render as burnt offering, sin offering, guilt offering, peace (or fellowship) offering, grain offering and drink offering. This diversity bewilders the modern reader, who is often familiar only with a single type of sacrifice by Jesus in the New Testament, namely as an expiation by his blood for sin (Rom. 3:25; Heb. 2:17; 9:26; 1 John 2:2; 4:10), though the New Testament also presents more diversity than just this with regard to both Christian practice and pagan worship.

When attempting to understand the purposes of each offering, it is helpful to keep several things in mind. First, the Old Testament nowhere sets out to give readers a treatise on the meaning or purpose of each type of offering. Second, and related, this omission likely has (at least) two consequences: (1) The *meaning* of each offering is not necessarily the most important thing about it. Rather, the *action* of the offering is primary. One might say that the *body* takes precedence over the *mind* in such cases. People share practices more than meanings. (2) The meaning attributed by the writers of the texts and by those carrying out the offerings could vary from person to person and in different times and places. This is not to say that the meanings are endless, but some degree of divergence would be expected.

Offerings and sacrifices were a very important means of communication between the divine and human worlds in the ancient world of Israel and the surrounding cultures. Literally every culture from Babylon to Egypt to Greece and Rome worshipped through the offering of agricultural and animal goods (along with other valuable items). Thus, it made *sense* to ancient Israelites to conceive of worship in the same categories.

Besides the discussion on atonement above, applying the category of *order* to the offerings provides several insights, which can be related to the affirmation, restoration or celebration of God's order in the human community and in creation as a whole. However – and this is a very important disclaimer – *order* is not the *only* category or lens through which one can or should consider these offerings. As mentioned earlier, they are actions that could and likely did mean different things at different times and places to different people. Thus, while there remains some kind of boundary between acceptable and inacceptable meanings, there is considerable variation within the canon of Scripture about what certain events or practices 'mean', and the offerings are no different in this regard. One might argue for more or less convincing or persuasive points of view *for a particular book or author*, but, while God's character does not change, God's interaction with humans takes on different hues because human cultures and understandings of the world do change. Therefore, the brief descriptions that follow should be taken as a 'rule of thumb' for the meaning of each type of offering.

Understanding the nature of ancient Israelite and Judean offerings also requires a grasp of the nature of its (mostly) agricultural way of life. The offerings consisted primarily of the basic foodstuffs, either in their natural or in processed forms: grains, flour, bread, olive oil, grape wine and meat. One small but expensive addition was incense (and frankincense) that came from the Arab peninsula.

What is often translated *burnt offering* (*ʿōlâ*) derives from the root meaning 'go up, ascend'. One might also understand it as the 'whole' offering, in that the entirety of this (usually animal) offering is burnt on the altar; no human receives any part of it to eat, although the priests receive the skin of the animal (leather) according to Leviticus 7:8. Similar offerings appeared throughout the broader Levant, Anatolia and Greece (Milgrom 1991: 173–175). Its regulations in the sanctuary setting are laid out in Leviticus 1; 6:8–13. In this commentary, we opt for the rendering 'burnt offering' because in this offering most parts are actually burned.

The *tribute offering* (*minḥâ*), according to Leviticus 2, consists mainly of fine flour (semolina) mixed with olive oil and frankincense or flat bread or toasted grains. Furthermore, the tribute offering could be barley and unaccompanied by oil or frankincense for some specific purpose, such as a husband jealous of his wife (Num. 5:15). Outside of the Priestly material, the term *minḥâ* does not indicate the materials used for the offering, so it can be used for vegetable and animal offerings as in Genesis 4:3–4. Apart from its religious uses, *minḥâ* can appear in a wide variety of settings, including those more concerned with giving tribute to a king (Judg. 3:15; 2 Kgs 20:12) or friendship (Gen. 32:13). Grains, and in their processed forms as flour and eventually bread, formed the basic foodstuff in ancient Israel. Therefore, bringing a grain offering meant passing on to God and the sanctuary personnel (priests and Levites) some of one's basic sustenance.

Together with the burnt offering, the *shared offering feast* (*zebaḥ šĕlāmîm*) formed the core of ancient Israel's worship sacrifices (see Exod. 24:5; Josh. 22:23; 1 Sam. 6:15). It is commonly rendered in English as 'peace' or 'fellowship' offering. In several biblical texts, this offering appears only as *zebaḥ*, from the common verb for sacred slaughter (*z-b-ḥ*; e.g. 1 Sam. 1:3–5; 2:12–17; 9:12–24). The sacrificial altar itself is defined by this offering, being called *mizbēaḥ*, literally 'the place of slaughter'. The most important characteristic of this offering is that its meat and other foods are shared between God, the priests and the offeror along with their household and guests. It constitutes a festive occasion with abundant food to celebrate, confirm and establish close relationships between its participants. In Numbers, the best image of this offering appears in the conclusion for the Nazirite vow in Numbers 6. Although several other offerings are combined, the Nazirite's hair, which represents her or his dedication, is associated

with the shared feast offering (6:18) that culminates with the final
encouragement towards extreme generosity with their resources
(6:21). This offering, therefore, provided the community of Israel
with an experience of feasting among all participants, including
God. Probably for this reason it gained the qualification of *šĕlāmîm*
in the Priestly regulation (Lev. 3). From the root *š-l-m*, this qualification points to an experience of wholeness and well-being that
results from a shared offering feast.

The *purification offering* (*ḥaṭṭat*, from the root 'sin') was often
focused on purifying the sanctuary, or in dealing with inadvertent
sin (Levine 1993: 275; Nihan 2007: 173–174), and receives extended
discussion in Leviticus 4 – 5. In other words, there was more than
one type of purification offering: those addressing the community
and its representatives and those of individual Israelites. In some
texts (Hos. 4:8), it addresses moral failing. The problem with
understanding it only as a 'sin' offering, though this would fit
the literal meaning of the root, is that it mostly appears when
no sin has taken place (Lev. 12:6–7; 14:10–31; 15:14–15, 29–30;
Ezek. 43:18ff.; 45:18–25). For this reason, we have opted for the
rendering 'purification offering'. With regard to the sanctuary, this
offering often served to make the sanctuary 'ready' for subsequent
offerings: it got rid of the impurity (including that caused by sin)
that had accumulated there or that the person had experienced.
Sometimes parts of the animals brought for this ritual were given
to the priests to eat (Lev. 6:17–23), but in other situations the
animal was burned outside the camp (Lev. 4:3–21).

In contrast, the *reparation offering* (*ʾāšām*, often translated 'guilt
offering') has several characteristics missing from both the purification offering and all the others as well. Prominent texts featuring
this offering are Leviticus 7:1–7 and Numbers 5:5–10. This offering
addresses misappropriation of resources from others, especially
sacrificial portions belonging to God and the priests. It therefore
requires material compensation. For this reason, this offering,
unlike any others, could be changed into a silver payment and
concerns the restoration of community.

Numbers presents a particular emphasis on the *drink offering*
(*nesek*, or 'libation'). The most complete instructions for offerings
in Leviticus 1 – 7 omit the drink offering. Wine and 'strong

drink' (*šēkār*), the two possible ingredients for the drink offering, receive no mention there; they do make a single appearance in the worship instruction of Deuteronomy 14:26, but without the technical term for 'drink offering'. In contrast, Numbers follows the indication of Exodus 25:29//37:16; 29:40–41 and Leviticus 23:13, 18, 37 and expands on the relevance of the drink offering as a constituent element in Israel's sacrificial regulations. In Numbers 6; 15; and 28 – 29, the drink offering appears as an indispensable accompaniment to several other offerings, and even plays a role in effecting atonement in 15:22–26. The use of wine, specified in Exodus 29:40; Leviticus 23:13; and Numbers 15:5, 7, 10; 28:14, is often paired with the high status of meat offerings (e.g. Num. 28:10, 15, 24, 31), associating the drink offering with elite festive banquets, especially those in royal contexts (see Welton 2020: 132–134; Greer 2022: 306). However, the lists of offerings almost always pair the drink with the tribute or bread offerings (e.g. Exod. 29:41; Lev. 23:12–13; Num. 6:13–15; 15:1–5; 28:8, 9; 29:11, 16; cf. Joel 1:9, 13; 2:14). Such cases may imply that the drink offering probably consisted of 'strong drink', specified in Numbers 28:7, a more common and less expensive ingredient like grape schnapps/ grappa, with a higher percentage of alcohol than wine. It may also have consisted of either beer made of wheat or barley with a lower percentage of alcohol than wine, around 2–4%. Given how the pairing of bread and beer was more common for ancient Israelites' religious experience in the household and sanctuary (Welton 2020: 117–118), the emphasis on the drink offering in Numbers brings the sacrificial regulations closer to this experience.

For the offering traditionally rendered as 'wave offering' (*tĕnûpâ*), evidence from other languages closely related to Hebrew (Ugaritic, Arabic and Akkadian; see *HALOT* 1762) suggests two promising alternatives: either 'elevation offering' (related to Arabic *nāfa*, 'to be high') or 'supplemental offering' (related to Akkadian *nūptu*, 'addition', and Arabic *nauf*, 'excess, surplus'). An Egyptian ritual with a person raising an offering from Karnak is accompanied by the text 'Come, O King, elevate offerings before the face (of the god)' (Milgrom 1972: 35), which supports that understanding for the rite. The rite appears especially (but not only) in conjunction with the dedication of items for one-time

events: materials for the ark (Exod. 35:22; 38:24, 29) and the
initiation rites of the priests (Exod. 29; Lev. 8) and Levites (Num.
8). Except for the materials for the ark, the items tend to come
from parts of other offerings, such as from a tribute offering and
shared offering feast in Numbers 6:20, and from a shared offering
feast in Leviticus 7:30, 34. However, if the action was a physical
raising of the offering, it could only be figurative in Numbers 8:11,
where it refers to Aaron presenting the Levites to God as part of
their commissioning. The striking nature of this elevation offering
is that it depicts the only time that *people* function in the role of
the object. The function of this ceremony, therefore, seems to be
related to the witness of those participating in the service with
the priests. Given that the priests are the main beneficiary of the
portions 'elevated', participants can attest that they have appro-
priated the correct portion from the offering.

Excursus: weights and measures used in the offering descriptions
The weights and measures used in the Old Testament as a whole
and in the book of Numbers in particular present readers with
difficulty in determining their amounts in modern terms (see
Kletter 2006; Winkler 2016). One reason for the challenge lies in
the fact that the measures grew out of everyday experiences that
contained some level of variation. For example, for dry measures
(such as amounts of flour), the base measurement was a *homer* (see
Ezek. 45:11), a derivation from the Hebrew term for donkey: *hamor*.
Thus, a *homer* consisted of the amount that a donkey could bear.
It is more difficult to determine the exact amount, by modern
standards, of the number of quarts/litres because there is little
record of a standard to which one could compare. In any case,
important for Numbers (esp. Num. 15; 28 – 29) is that, from
Ezekiel 45:11, one homer is said to be ten ephahs. Further information in Exodus 16:36 reports that one omer is one-tenth of an
ephah, which corresponds to the daily portion of flour/bread
for each individual adult (Exod. 16:16), which was around 1.8 l
/ 1.9 quarts. Furthermore, a *bath* (a jug) – which consisted of the
same amount according to Ezekiel 45:11 – could be divided into
six hins. Based on standardized jugs from the pre-exilic period
(eighth–seventh centuries BC), at that time *one* bath equalled 22 l

/ 5.8 US gallons, which means that a hin equalled approximately 3.7 l / 1 US gallon. However, if calculating backwards from the Jewish Mishnah (c. AD 200–400), at that time a hin was understood to equal one-quarter bath (5.5 l / 1.5 US gallons).

8. Christian application of the book of Numbers

Numbers is not an easy book to read, whether in the context of academia or devotionally in the context of our faith communities. It is no wonder that it has long been neglected by Christians (see Strawn 2017: 28–38). As far back as the time of the early Church Father Origen (third century), Christians had trouble finding anything helpful in its teachings. Talking about Numbers 33, a long itinerary, Origen says that his contemporary Christians would 'immediately reject it and spit it out, as heavy and burdensome foods and as those that are not suitable to a sick and weak soul' (Origen 2009: 168).

Part of the problem is the complex structure of Numbers that does not follow our literary conventions of progressive linearity. Although a final word about Numbers' structure was not established above, when considering a Christian reading it is helpful to take its basic narrative form into consideration. Numbers concerns the people of God on a journey to the place God has chosen for them to fulfil their destiny as a people and individuals in union with God. The wilderness has been a common way of depicting God's people's journey, from Numbers to Isaiah to John the Baptist to the Desert Fathers (early Christian hermits of the third century who gave rise to Christian monasticism), from Jewish to Christian communities. Understood in this way, as a shared journey of all God's people, Numbers can profitably address the movement of the Christian community or communities (church or churches) and of individual believers from the point of formation by God's redeeming actions in Jesus' first coming and continual office to our final destiny in his second. The question of how and which specific topics hold the most promise, however, can prove more difficult to identify.

One may begin with the consideration of the ways in which Israel's wilderness journey appears in other texts of the Old

Testament. Most texts view this time negatively, highlighting Israel's waywardness from God and the death of an entire generation (e.g. Pss 78:17–41; 95:8–11; 106:13–33). However, several prophetic texts note God's tender care for Israel during this time, which set it apart (Hos. 13:5–6; Jer. 2:2, 6), and the hopeful image of anticipation of God's action (Isa. 41:18–19; 43:19). The combination of these perspectives invites audiences to reflect on their journeys of faith in terms of both God's provision and proximity, and the generally unflattering human response.

Turning to the New Testament's interaction with themes from Numbers, it is important to note that these texts generally employ Numbers for their own purposes, which yields an answer with some complexity. However, much like our recourse to the theme of the journey, Paul in 1 Corinthians 10:1–11 typologically applies episodes from the journey to the Corinthian Christians' own lives. Some allusions recall episodes from the book of Exodus, though the cloud (1 Cor. 10:1 – Exod. 13:21–22; Num. 9:15–23), the water from the rock (1 Cor. 10:4 – Exod. 17; Num. 20), twenty-three thousand dying in one day (1 Cor. 10:8 – Num. 25:9 [24,000]), Israelites killed by snakes (1 Cor. 10:9 – Num. 21:4–9) and the death in the wilderness (1 Cor. 10:5 – Num. 11 – 25) have references in Numbers. Paul takes these traditions (vv. 11–13) as pertinent lessons for the Corinthian Christians on behaviours to avoid, but even more as warnings against complacency in their status as recipients of divine favour.

Closely related, the wilderness plays a special role in Jesus' formation as well as Paul's as a place where the relationship with the Father takes a significant step forward. Jesus' forty days in the wilderness recapitulate Israel's forty years (Matt. 4; Luke 4), with Jesus succeeding in maintaining trust in God's provision in ways in which Israel failed (cf. Olson 2012: 1–2). One of the key challenges for the Israelites (and Jesus) lies in the people's willingness to trust in God's provision in all the difficult situations they encounter. While God might not condemn the people for crying out for provision (Num. 20:1–8), every new situation demands trust that God will somehow provide, and that returning to Egypt – the way of apparent safety (but really of oppression and death) – must be rejected at all costs. To give in and return to the Egyptian way of life is to negate the identity and vocation of God's people.

The image of the wilderness therefore opens into several profound theological themes. Some of them will be explored in what follows. First, however, it is relevant to note how the wilderness works as a middle ground between Egypt and the Promised Land. It is the book of Numbers that capitalizes on this image of the wilderness as a geographical middle ground to create a conceptual space of liminality (in-betweenness) that is used in these theological appropriations of the wilderness to characterize the faith journey as one of formation and hope. In Numbers, the wilderness serves as a liminal space to discern and negotiate boundaries between two opposite poles in several issues relevant for the formation of God's people. Some of them have been presented in the Introduction already, but a good list of examples would be boundaries between God's holy presence and Israel's camp, Israel and other peoples, leaders of the people and the people themselves, old generation and new generation, tradition and innovation, Promised Land and other lands, Canaan and Transjordan, liturgical and common time, purity and impurity, blessings and curses, God's judgment and God's forgiveness. The dynamic between discernment and negotiation of these boundaries in Numbers, Dennis T. Olson states, presents us with a 'dialogical theology, an ongoing and unsettled dialogue of varied voices' (Olson 2012: 8; for the concept of dialogue applied to the interpretation of the Bible, see Newsom 1996).

The appreciation of this particular character of Numbers is important both for understanding it historically and for modelling several aspects of Christian life today. Navigating internal and external diversity, Christians have a profound responsibility to discern and negotiate boundaries of all sorts. We will present some of these in what follows, but one general principle here is that much of what we deem absolute and rigid is more provisional and flexible than we typically expect. At a certain level, Numbers shows that in the wilderness, in between the starting point and the destination, the formation of God's people requires wisdom to adapt, accommodate and innovate. Holding tight to traditions, authorities, places, times and people of the past can hinder God's people's movement towards their future (see E. W. Davies 2017: 79). This is not to say that the past has no importance in Numbers or in Christian life. Rather, the dialogical theology depends on our present negotiation with our past with the intention to move forward. Each generation has a responsibility to create and nurture the seed of the future, instead of preserving itself. As Rubem Alves, an important Brazilian theologian, has said: 'one hopes for the future because one has already seen the creative event taking place in the past' (Alves 1974: 562). Such hope and commitment to the future require an important acknowledgment from each generation, which we can see in Numbers and in the history of the church: 'one moves toward the future in the certainty that the present has not said all that is to be said' (Alves 1974: 561).

A major theme for Christian communities to ponder concerns Numbers' many-sided approach to the formation of those coming out of Egypt *into a structured community*. Most important in this formation is the maintenance of the divine presence as a focal point. Numbers 1 – 4 does this by describing the *spatial centrality* of God's tent in the midst of the camp. Issues of purity, holiness, authority and ritual play significant roles in how Numbers depicts this structure. The book also accomplishes this focus by contrasting alternative attempts to find safety that include comingling with other deities and their ways of producing provision (ch. 25). Considering the wilderness context and the purpose of order in creation narratives such as Genesis 1 and other Ancient Near Eastern traditions, Israel as God's structured community envisions an environment that can bring forth and sustain life (see Awabdy 2023: 2). Such image and purpose, of course, imply several features of human experience in the world, from religion to ecology to economy to politics. New Testament authors can use different metaphors for God's structured community, such as body (1 Cor. 12), house and sanctuary (1 Pet. 2:4–5), to describe God's collective people from other angles. The centrality of God and abundant life, and how to secure it, in all these images is foundational for the identity and vocation of God's people. One central element here is leadership and its relationship with the people at large. The distribution of the Spirit in Numbers 11 is God's answer to Moses' overwhelming responsibility to care for the people that is compared to God's maternal care and nourishment of infant Israel. A similar distribution of the Spirit appears in Joel 2, where God's care and nourishment to reform the elect people (Joel 2:26–27) is followed by the pouring out of the Spirit on all (Joel 2:28–29). When the Spirit is distributed among the followers of Jesus in Acts 2, explained in the light of Joel 2, the result is also God's care and nourishment of the newly formed community of faith through the actions of care of its members (Acts 2:41–47). Numbers paints a vision for how God's people are formed and must live in the world in allegiance, faithfulness and obedience to God in very concrete ways.

More generally, reading Numbers as the transition from the first, exodus, generation to subsequent generations that will settle in the Promised Land speaks to transitions of generations in Christian communities. Numbers 13 – 14 shows how a dim picture of a once-promising generation can give way to hope for those who follow. Even the pattern mostly operative for the exodus generation (chs. 11–25) – complaint and rebellion, followed by God's anger and punishment, intercession and blessing from Moses and Aaron, and God's forgiveness – is not centred on individuals and the present generation. This pattern points to God's commitment to Israel beyond specific groups and even generations. The reworking of various types of regulations – Passover (ch. 9), tithes (ch. 18), an annual calendar centred on worship (chs. 28–29) or towns of refuge (ch. 35) – provides suggestions for the ways in which central practices and familiar teachings of Christian communities may require revision by a later constellation of the same community in the light of past mistakes, new demands in new contexts, and the present and future life of this community.

The formation of God's people in Numbers includes negotiation not only between generations within the community, but also with outsiders. Numbers' manifold narratives about interactions with surrounding peoples helps Christian communities navigate the complex boundaries necessary for these relationships. Narratives of openness, cooperation and even inclusion of outsiders as part of God's people are interspersed with narratives of exclusiveness, competition and open aggression. This dynamic invites readers to consider and discern the purpose of each of these episodes and how they teach about life in a plural and diverse world.

The memory of the complex character of Balaam illustrates well how this dynamic was used in the history of reception of the story and invites further engagement with this discussion in present communities. Balaam served as a type for several New Testament authors in naming problematic characters in their own contexts. Jude associates Balaam with Cain and Korah (Jude 11) and links the motivation for financial gain to Balaam. The notion of money leading Balaam astray intensifies in 2 Peter 2:15–16, which also recalls his jenny's rebuke. While Revelation 2:14 highlights the accusation already found in Numbers 31:16 that the invitation to false worship by the Midianites in Numbers 25 arose from Balaam's advice, all three of these New Testament texts associate Balaam with inappropriate transgression of the boundaries separating God's people from paths leading to death. However, in the Balaam Pericope itself, the foreign diviner goes through a process of entering into a trusting and intimate relationship with God and understanding the relationship between Israel and other peoples. Even if the biblical text never explicitly speaks of Balaam's integration into Israel as part of God's people, he does enter into the mutual blessing dynamic that God envisions for Abraham's family as God's elect (Gen. 12:1–3). By making Balaam, and many other outsiders, part of the story of God's people, the book of Numbers fosters a sense of interdependence and belonging between these groups that is typical of family stories (cf. Pressler 2017: 1, 4). In the complex history of the world and Christianity, interaction between insiders and outsiders concerns more than just tension, dispute and opposition. Christians can learn from Numbers about the dynamics of cooperation and integration by creating narratives of complex encounters that, ideally, lead to relationships of mutual blessing for all.

Further, Numbers offers Christian communities a handbook on the challenges of leadership. The book offers a variety of leadership structures. There can be one especially inspired leader (Moses), or a dyad or triumvirate (with Aaron and Miriam). Both structures come with particular difficulties. When alone, Moses calls for an expansion of leaders among the people so that the community can be cared for and nourished appropriately (ch. 11). Miriam and Aaron challenge Moses' privileged relationship with God and demand recognition of their privilege as well (ch. 12). As a response to the failure of the ten spies in Numbers 13 – 14, and their attempt to form a new group of leaders to go back to Egypt, God instructs all Israelites to wear a piece of clothing that grants them royal or priestly status (15:37–41). Then, in Numbers 16 – 17, the narratives delve into the tension between *all* of God's people having access to God, but God still choosing some specific individuals (Moses, Aaron and Aaron's sons) to have the authority to fulfil particular responsibilities. This authority, however, should be exercised to foster life for the community, which the flowering of Aaron's staff (17:8) indicates. Although affirming of special responsibilities for certain leaders, Numbers also shows their ultimate failure. Exemplifying similar traits to those who challenge their position, Moses and Aaron affirm their own authority instead of using it for the well-being of the people (ch. 20). Thus, the book must also address questions surrounding the transfer of leadership to subsequent generations. Moses is succeeded in part by Joshua, and Eleazar takes over the priesthood from Aaron. The literary construction that combines negotiation of the distinctions between leaders and the people intends to provide new generations of God's people with information on how and why leaders must be evaluated and that they can be critiqued. Several narratives speak of the necessity and gift of continuing discernment processes for new forms of issues confronting the community (chs. 9; 27; 36), many times in the light of discussions concerning leadership (chs. 15; 18).

Besides addressing the purpose of the leadership and exemplifying the people's appropriate critique of it, Numbers also offers an intriguing possibility for Christian views and practices of leadership. The combination of Moses' desire that all God's people might become prophets (11:29) and the possibility for laypeople to gain similar status and function to priests, even of the high priest, through the Nazirite vow (ch. 6) and by wearing tassels (15:37–41) shows the possibility that the designations of boundaries and special functions and responsibilities were likely intended, in the end, to dissolve into obsolescence. One may broaden this trajectory to many of the other boundaries discerned and negotiated in Numbers, such as between Israel and other people, the tabernacle and the Israelite camp, the Promised Land and other lands, special liturgical dates and common dates, and so on. If the special and distinct element functions in the way it should function, it is able to expand to all others and becomes useless. This is similar to how New Testament authors interpret the Torah in the light of the Christ event, as its ultimate fulfilment, so that, for example, Sabbath, temple, Israel and high priesthood converge in Christ and can be expanded to all times, all places, all peoples and all individuals. This is not a substitution, much less a critique of these boundaries and special functions discerned and negotiated in Numbers. Rather, it is the highest appraisal of their importance in leading God's people to their destination in and with God.

Finally, Numbers can teach Christians about how to relate to biblical authority and our need for plural perspectives in our interpretation of the text as well as in our journey of faith as individuals and communities. We see in Numbers a strong dialogical dynamic in the combination of different voices that form the text, even if they are not always complementary and harmonized. Numbers helps Christians see one way in which authority is established through the negotiation of diverse voices in internal dialogue, but also by the invitation of later voices of new generations of God's people to interact with the text and participate in this negotiation. The repetition of instructions for both generations in Numbers 15 and 18 and for the new generation in Numbers 28 – 29 reveals this interplay between texts. These repetitions never rise to the level of quotations of previous instructions because they are responding to new developments and contexts in the story of God's people. The best example of how Numbers includes new voices in the formation of divine revelation appears in the dynamic of Numbers 27 and 36. At the initiative of the people addressed in previous divine instructions, God and Moses consider from different perspectives an issue that embodies the concerns of those who are vulnerable to the misuse of previous legislative provisions.

This is an invitation for contemporary audiences of Numbers to engage in these continuing elucidations of God's Word. In one sense, contemporary engagement with the text is part of the process of divine revelation. Faith communities are not passive recipients. Of course, the invitation is extended to include diverse faith communities in the history of interpretation of the biblical text as those who preserved it and acknowledge it as imbued with authority. Therefore, in our contemporary experience of biblical interpreters, among scholars or in faith communities, there is the demand to reconsider what we know in the light of input from those in more vulnerable positions. While white-male Euro-North American views dominated biblical interpretation for several centuries, new voices coming from marginal and marginalized places have shed so much new light in recent decades, such that ignoring them is detrimental with regard to learning and receiving God's word for us (cf. E. W. Davies 2017: 17–28). This is true for biblical interpretation in general, but several specific issues presented in Numbers especially highlight the importance of the voices of women and postcolonial critics, especially from marginalized cultures. The transition of the bulk of Christian communities from the Global North to the South makes this even more necessary for the future of the church's identity and vocation in the world in response to God's word for us today and tomorrow (see Roth et al. 2022; cf. García-Johnson 2019; Romero 2020).

One overall point of Numbers' importance for Christians is that there is no 'pure' generation of Christians or 'pure' confession, denomination and local church that represents God's people in full, that understands the fullness of God's revelation in the biblical text, or that fulfils God's plan for the world on its own. All communities participate in something far greater than themselves and need not only to dialogue with different members of Christ's body in history and globally, but also to work for the present and future well-being of the whole body. For that to happen, consideration of the transition of the exodus to the settling generations in Numbers indicates the importance of giving prominence to those in more vulnerable positions, for it seems that they, and not those in privileged and powerful positions, are the ones who can contribute the most to the formation of the future of God's people (see Alves 1974: 565; cf. 1 Cor. 12:22–25).

ANALYSIS

The compositional character of Numbers helps explain the complexity of its literary structure as well as justify our attempt to discern some structure. As presented in the Introduction ('The order of the material'), it is often difficult, sometimes even impossible, to understand why some passages appear in their present locations or why certain themes reappear in a different literary and narrative context. However, different criteria for determining a literary structure for Numbers emerge from the text itself. There are clear geographical and chronological markers that help with some divisions, while discernible changes in the content indicate the movement of the narrative. Because these criteria can be used in a variety of ways to establish the structure of Numbers, commentators will present different structures. Our proposed outline, delineated below, combines two forms of narrative structure, one with five divisions and another with three divisions. The five divisions are mainly based on the movement of the camp towards the Promised Land (preparation, march, failure and punishment, hope and conquest of the land, renewed preparation), while the

three divisions are mainly based on the transition of generations
(the exodus generation, transition, the settling generation). Given
the importance of the geographic movement for the flow of the
narrative, we also include a visual marker (in bold) to indicate the
three main places where the Israelite camp is located in Numbers.

THE EXODUS GENERATION

Desert of Sinai

I. **PREPARATION FOR THE JOURNEY** (1:1 – 10:10)
- A. Preface with chronological (first day, second month, second year) and geographic (desert of Sinai) markers (1:1)
- B. Census of the tribes (1:2–46)
- C. The exemption of the Levites (1:47–54)
- D. Census of groups according to the marching and settling order of the tribes (2:1–34)
  - i. Group headed by Judah on the east side of the tabernacle (2:1–9)
  - ii. Group headed by Reuben on the south side of the tabernacle (2:10–16)
  - iii. The Levites (2:17)
  - iv. Group headed by Ephraim on the west side of the tabernacle (2:18–24)
  - v. Group headed by Dan on the north side of the tabernacle (2:25–31)
  - vi. Summary (2:32–34)
- E. Census and responsibilities of the Levites (3:1 – 4:49)
  - i. Aaron's son and the succession of the priesthood (3:1–4)
  - ii. Levites as Aaron's assistants to substitute for Israel's firstborn (3:5–13)
  - iii. Census of the Levites and their clans, their order and their responsibilities in the camp (3:14–39)
  - iv. Levites as substitutes for Israel's firstborn (3:40–51)
  - v. Responsibilities of the Kohathites (4:1–20)
  - vi. Responsibilities of the Gershonites (4:21–28)
  - vii. Responsibilities of the Merarites (4:29–33)
  - viii. Census of the three levitical clans (4:34–49)

F. Cultic preparation of the camp (5:1 – 10:10)
   i. Excluding cases of impurity (5:1–4)
   ii. Rectifying misappropriation of resources (5:5–10)
   iii. The ritual of the jealous husband and the wife suspected of adultery (5:11–31)
   iv. Nazirite vow of extraordinary consecration (6:1–21)
   v. The priestly blessing on the camp (6:22–27)
   vi. Gifts and offerings from the tribes' chieftains for the dedication of the altar and the inauguration of the tabernacle's cultic service (7:1–89)
   vii. Arrangement of the lampstand and the direction of its light (8:1–4)
   viii. Purification and consecration of the Levites (8:5–22)
   ix. Working age of the Levites (8:23–26)
   x. Instruction for the celebration of the Passover with accommodation for a second date (9:1–14)
   xi. Divine guidance for the marching and settling of the camp through the divine theophany of cloud and fire (9:15–23)
   xii. Divine royal sign for marching: the silver trumpets (10:1–10)

2. MARCHING TOWARDS AND FAILING TO ENTER THE PROMISED LAND (10:11 – 14:45)

A. Departure from Sinai in marching order (10:11–28)
B. Human and divine guidance (10:29–36)
   i. Moses invites his Midianite father-in-law to guide Israel (10:29–32)
   ii. Divine theophany and the presence of the ark to guide Israel (10:33–36)
C. Rebellion and failure (11:1 – 14:45)
   i. The pattern of rebellion (11:1–3)
   ii. Manna and Moses are not enough (11:4–33)
     a. The people's complaint about the manna (11:4–6)
     b. Description of the manna (11:7–9)
     c. Moses' complaint to God about his leadership role (11:10–15)

      d. God's answer to Moses and to the people (11:16–20)

      e. Moses and God discuss (11:21–23)

      f. God resolves the people's and Moses' complaint (11:24–33)

  iii. Geographic location (11:34–35)

  iv. Miriam and Aaron rebel against Moses' leadership (12:1–16)

Desert of Paran

  v. The great rebellion and failure to enter the Promised Land (13:1 – 14:45)

      a. Divine instruction to survey the land and the choice of leaders (13:1–24)

      b. Return and report of the scouts with positive and negative features (13:25–33)

      c. The rebellious decision of the people to choose leaders to return to Egypt (14:1–4)

      d. Joshua and Caleb give a positive report and encourage the people (14:5–10)

      e. God's condemnation and Moses' intercession (14:11–19)

      f. God's forgiveness of Israel, but judgment against the exodus generation (14:20–35)

      g. Death of the ten spies who slandered the Promised Land (14:36–38)

      h. Attempt and failure to enter the land without the divine presence (14:39–45)

THE TRANSITION FROM THE EXODUS TO THE SETTLING GENERATION

3. RETURN TO AND PUNISHMENT IN THE WILDERNESS (15:1 – 20:29)

  A. Revising instructions of consecration of the people in the Promised Land (15:1–41)

    i. Instructions for offerings with emphasis on proportions of offerings and accompaniments (15:1–16)

4. FLASHES OF HOPE FOR THE NEW GENERATION (21:1 – 25:18)

A. The pattern of success (21:1–3)

B. Remedy for failure through the copper snake (21:4–9)

C. Successfully arriving at the plains of Moab (21:10–20)

D. Victory over King Sihon and King Og (21:21–35)

Plains of Moab

E. Balaam's oracles/divinations (22:1 – 24:25)

   i. Balak's perspective on Israel (22:1–4)

   ii. First set of three divinations to decide whether Balaam should go with Balak's messengers (22:5–35)

      a. First divination: denial (22:5–13)

      b. Second divination: approval (22:14–20)

      c. Third divination: qualified approval (22:21–35)

   iii. Balak requires Balaam to see Israel as he does and curse it (22:36–41)

   iv. Second set of three divinations to decide if Israel is cursed or blessed (23:1 – 24:24)

      a. First divination/oracle: Israel is blessed (23:1–12)

      b. Second divination/oracle: Israel is blessed (23:13–24)

      c. Third divination/oracle: Israel is blessed (23:25 – 24:24)

   v. Balak and Balaam part ways (24:25)

F. Faithfulness amid unfaithfulness (25:1–18)

   i. The daughters of Moab and submission to Baal (25:1–5)

   ii. Phinehas's demonstration of faithfulness to Yahweh (25:6–18)

THE SETTLING GENERATION

5. A NEW GENERATION PREPARES TO ENTER THE LAND (26:1 – 36:13)

A. Organizing the camp of the settling generation (26:1–65)

   i. Second census (26:1–51)

   ii. Logic of land distribution among the tribes (26:52–56)

G. Transjordan and the unity of the tribes (32:1–42)
    i. Reuben, Gad and half of Manasseh's request to settle in Transjordan (32:1–5)
    ii. Moses reprimands the request (32:6–15)
    iii. Explaining the intention of the request and their commitment to unity (32:16–19)
    iv. Moses' proposal of a covenant (32:20–24)
    v. Agreement with the terms of the covenant and confirmation of its future validity (32:25–33)
    vi. The land given to Reubenites, Gadites and Manassites in Transjordan (32:34–42)
H. Mapping Israel's itinerary from Egypt to the plains of Moab (33:1–56)
    i. Stages of the itinerary (33:1–49)
    ii. Divine instruction for Israel's entrance into Canaan and the consequences of failure (33:50–56)
I. Mapping the territory of Canaan (34:1–29)
    i. The boundaries of Canaan (34:1–15)
    ii. Leaders assigned by God to distribute the land among the tribes (34:16–29)
J. Special issues concerning the Promised Land (35:1–34)
    i. Levitical towns (35:1–8)
    ii. Towns of refuge (35:9–15)
    iii. Homicide and the corruption of the land (35:16–30)
    iv. Homicide, 'ransom', and the corruption of the land (35:31–34)
K. Renegotiating land distribution and inheritance outside tribal patrilineage (36:1–12)
    i. Concerns for land inherited by Zelophehad's daughters (36:1–6a)
    ii. Concerns for land inherited by daughters in the future (36:6b–9)
    iii. Enactment of God's decision in the case (36:10–12)
L. Conclusion for Numbers (36:13)

COMMENTARY

1. PREPARATION FOR THE JOURNEY (1:1 – 10:10)

Context

The book of Leviticus ends in 27:34 with the summarizing statement 'These are the commandments that the LORD gave to [lit. 'commanded'] Moses for the people of Israel on Mount Sinai.' Almost the entire book of Leviticus provides laws, many of which concern ritual practice at the sanctuary, though some societal and family ordinances appear as well. Except for Leviticus 8 – 10, hardly any narrative appears in the book. Therefore, with regard to the narrative, Numbers 1 picks up from Leviticus 10; 16:1; and, going back further, even from Exodus 40. The Israelites have continued to camp at Sinai, though, until this point, only God's tent (the tabernacle) has been properly constructed and ordered. On the other hand, in Exodus 12:37–38, both the Israelites (about six hundred thousand men – see Additional note below) and 'a great mixture' (AT) had left Egypt together. The focus now turns increasingly to them.

The major question for modern readers, however, concerns justifying the need for such a detailed description here of the numbering of the tribes. The short answer comes in the promises from the larger narrative reaching back to God's promises to Abraham in the book of Genesis.

A census takes place at several other points in the Bible (e.g. Exod. 30:12; Josh. 8:10; 2 Sam. 24; 1 Chr. 21:1–17; 2 Chr. 2:17). They occur in connection either with military campaigns or with the raising of taxes or a labour force – often for a building project. In this case, the repetition of the phrase 'everyone able to go to war' in 1:3, 20, 22, and so on, indicates the nature of the Israelites' camp: they will travel as a sacred army on campaign. Therefore, only the men aged twenty and above are counted.

Comment
A. Preface with chronological (first day, second month, second year) and geographic (desert of Sinai) markers (1:1)

1. Numbers begins by noting the location and time of God speaking to Moses in relation to the exodus from Egypt. God's speaking no longer takes place on Mount Sinai, as in Leviticus. This setting *in* the wilderness (or 'Desert', NIV) rather than *on* the mountain of Sinai may indicate a *qualitative* difference between the types of revelation. Furthermore, God no longer speaks from the mountain, but rather in the tent of meeting (Römer 2008: 23). It has been one month since Moses and the Israelites set up the 'tabernacle' or *tent of meeting* and the Lord has filled it (Exod. 40:17–35). This implies that the divine presence has moved from the mountain to the tabernacle.

This interpretation is supported by the nature of time: the Israelites have already journeyed for more than a year, so the events and commands found in Numbers take place *along the way*. God's instructions and interactions in this book thus concern the people's pilgrimage with their God.

There are two censuses in the book of Numbers: here in chapter 1 and in chapter 26. As discussed in the Introduction ('Is Numbers a book?' and 'The order of the material'), they serve an important structural and theological role in the book. This census counts the generation that exited Egypt and was at Sinai. The second census will have close to the same number of people, but those included are descendants of the exodus generation, those born along the way. The generation counted in chapter 1 dies in the desert as a result of their disobedience, especially in the matter of the initial refusal to take the land (chs. 13–14). In other words, what is found in chapter 1 is not a new beginning because it offers a counting of those who have been part of the story since Exodus 4. Therefore, those included in the census in Numbers 1 were those able to speak of their first-hand experience of the liberation from Egypt (Exod. 7 – 13) and deliverance at the Sea (Exod. 14 – 15).

However, this is not to say that nothing new takes place with the census in chapter 1. In fact, this chapter presents the transformation of the community. 'Before Sinai, Israel migrated as the liberated community. Now, it is organized and supposed to march as a sacral congregation' (Knierim and Coats 2005: 17). As an overall statement, the Israelites are organized in these chapters as a sacred army on pilgrimage with the divine royal tent in their midst (see at 2:17 below).

Census-taking was an explosive matter in the Old Testament: it required a half-shekel tax in Exodus 30, while David's census in 2 Samuel 24 (par. 1 Chr. 21) brought dire consequences (a plague). The human counting of one's people (or army) may indicate transgressing God's authority and knowledge (Stubbs 2009: 30–31).

B. Census of the tribes (1:2–46)

2–4. God gives the overarching command for administering the census, which, as noted above, focuses on the men capable of military service. The tribes are even counted according to 'their military units' (*lĕṣib'ōtām*). Not only Moses and Aaron, but verse 4 states that a representative from each tribe should help with the census. Both here and, for example, in Numbers 7, the tribal heads play an important role as the leaders and perhaps the embodiment of their tribes as a whole.

5–16. The naming of a leader from each tribe to help Moses and Aaron with the census marks one of the key themes of the book of Numbers: who is qualified to lead the people of God, and how are such leaders to be designated? (See Introduction, 'Christian application of the book of Numbers'.) This opening chapter provides several insights: they are representative in some way (one from each of the twelve tribes); they are leaders of their respective tribes; they cooperate with Moses and Aaron (v. 4); and they are chosen by God (v. 5). By the end of the book, tribal leaders have taken on further significance, while Aaron has been replaced by his son and Moses is partially replaced by Joshua (20:22–29; 27:12–23; 34:16–29).

17–19. These verses provide continuity with Exodus 25 – 31; 35 – 40: the Israelites act in obedience to God's commands to Moses. The organization of the camp matches the building of the tabernacle, as will become clear in the next chapter, given that both are intended to preserve God's presence among Israel.

20–46. The census is divided into twelve parts, beginning with the eldest son of Jacob, Reuben (cf. Gen. 29:32). However, the largest tribe is Judah, which shows God's favour towards it, confirmed in Numbers 10:14. Furthermore, Judah also camps on the same side of the tent as Aaron and the priests (3:38). One might connect this prominence with Judah's willingness to suffer on behalf of his brother Benjamin in Genesis 44. It also foreshadows the story's progression – King David (and therefore Jesus) descends from Judah.

One surprise in the order of the tribes, in comparison with the order of the chieftains in 1:5–16, is Gad placed third (in the LXX, the early Greek version of the Bible, it comes between Benjamin and Dan). Perhaps the reason is that the Gadites come to be located in the Transjordan (east of the Jordan River; 32:1; Josh. 13:15–31) along with the Reubenites (Achenbach 2003: 454) or because it reflects the order of the encampment (Morales 2024a: 87). Genesis recounts that Reuben and Simeon are Jacob's two eldest children by his wife Leah, while Gad's mother was Zilpah, Leah's servant.

C. The exemption of the Levites (1:47–54)

47. Lastly, there is a note that the Levites are not counted with the Israelite army – they are set apart. Instead, to reach the important number of twelve, the two sons of Joseph, Ephraim and Manasseh, are counted as separate tribes (cf. Gen. 48 – 49).

Table 1.1: Israel's first census

Reuben	46,500
Simeon	59,300
Gad	45,650
Judah	74,600
Issachar	54,400
Zebulun	57,400
Ephraim	40,500
Manasseh	32,200
Benjamin	35,400
Dan	62,700
Asher	41,500
Naphtali	53,400
Total	**603,550**

Thus, in some ways there are thirteen tribes that can be counted as twelve in various ways. There is more importance in the *symbolism* of the number twelve than in how one concretely gets to that number.

What can one make of the inclusion of the repetitive detail in this chapter? First, each of the twelve sections is structured the same way. Second, all tribes (however one counts them, given the reference to the Levites in vv. 48–53) are included, which is important given the division of Israel into Northern and Southern Kingdoms after Solomon, and the scattering of the tribes by their later conquerors (722 BC for the North; 586 BC for the South). In sum, the repetition communicates that each tribe counts in the formation of Israel as a people.

Additional note: the large numbers in the census

This census represents the first time (other than the seventy members of Jacob's family named in Gen. 46) that the Israelites are ordered by tribe. Therefore, it represents a transition from a *family* to a *people*. Thus, the central question raised here (and in many places in the OT) is *who belongs to God's people?* Numbers 1 arranges its answer in terms of being counted as part of a tribe – as kin.

But how was one counted? Westerners largely understand kinship as established by blood relations and therefore unchanging; this is not the case in other societies (Glanville 2018: 20–26). As discussed below in relation to the Passover in Numbers 9, shared food can function as the foundation for kinship (see Introduction, 'Israel's identity and its neighbours'). Given the appearance of the mix of perhaps Egyptians or other foreigners leaving Egypt with the Israelites (Exod. 12:38), this census serves to solidify the group as one people. This will become even more explicit in the second census in Numbers 26 with several individual names representing non-Israelite groups. A comparative example from early Islam is the adaptation of tribal genealogy: non-Arab converts became adopted members of an Arab tribe (D. W. Brown 2009: 30–31). According to this logic, to become part of God's people, one needed to become part of a tribe that belonged to God. Taking on Yahweh as God *necessarily* meant taking on one of the Israelite tribes as one's human community.

A related issue concerns the omission of women, children, as well as slaves from the list (Cocco 2020b: 1), for the census consists only of military-able men. This number would then indicate that the entire group numbered several million people (Hoffmeier 2005: 153), which raises a historical question for the interpretation of the text. First, however, it should be noted that six hundred thousand is a multiple of twelve, so symbolic significance again emerges.

Second, in Genesis 12:2; 13:16; 15:5; 17:2, God promises to give Abraham a multitude of descendants. In Genesis 46:3, God similarly promises to make Jacob into a great nation *while* his family is in Egypt. The subsequent verses (Gen. 46:4–27) name the seventy people belonging to Jacob's family at that time, which provides the amazing contrast with Numbers 1 (E. W. Davies 1995a: 468). The first steps towards this multiplication take place in Exodus 1:7, 12, though no numbers appear there. Therefore, the census in this chapter celebrates God's great work, though only partially fulfilled at this point because the Israelites have not yet entered the Promised Land.

The same number is also found in Exodus 12:37 and Numbers 11:21 as a round number, and more exactly in Exodus 38:25–26, which refers to a similar census (see Exod. 30:11–16) taken in order to tax the people half a shekel for materials for the construction of the tabernacle. This duplication raises the question as to *why the people need to be counted again*, if they were counted just a month before? While of course taking two censuses is historically possible (Ashley 2022: 58), this represents a strained harmonization, though it aptly underlines the question of timing. It makes more sense to see it as a repetition with a different emphasis, taking a cue from the repeated narration of the completion of the tabernacle in Exodus 40; Leviticus 9; and Numbers 7 (also Milgrom 1990: 338).

This army would have been massive – especially by the standards of the large empires of the Ancient Near East! At its height, Egypt's army numbered twenty thousand (Hoffmeier 2005: 154). A number of attempts to explain the numbers as they stand have appeared; none have managed to convince a majority of interpreters (for a summary of theories, see E. W. Davies 1995a):

- They represent the literal, actual numbers, an approach which follows the calculations of the text of Numbers in adding them together to reach 603,550. However, in addition to such large numbers being out of place in the Ancient Near East and numbers often being hyperbolic, this approach also falters on the number of firstborn (22,273) given in Numbers 3:43. If both numbers are taken as literal, then it would suggest a 27:1 ratio, meaning that each firstborn male would have twenty-six brothers, not to mention numerous sisters.
- The numbers are retrojected from another time in Israel's history. While this approach accords with figures from 2 Samuel 24:9 (800,000 men in Israel's army and 500,000 in Judah's; cf. 1,100,000 for Israel and 470,000 for Judah in 1 Chr. 21:5) for David's time, archaeological and comparative Ancient Near Eastern evidence suggests that Israel never came close to this size in ancient times.
- Some kind of numerical symbolism (gematria) contains a hidden meaning, perhaps adding the values of the Hebrew letters together (Hebrew letters also functioned as numbers). However, no such suggestion explains more than a couple of the amounts.

- Understanding the Hebrew word for 'thousand' (*'elep*) alternatively as 'group' or 'tribal unit' (Hoffmeier 2005: 159) or as 'captain' (Wenham 1981: 62–64). This theory flounders on the counting of the Levites in Numbers 3:21–34 (E. W. Davies 1995b: 16), because the Levites were not a fighting force, and their numbers were meant to serve as a replacement for the exact number of Israelite firstborn sons (Num. 3:39–43).
- Extrapolating from the amount of silver needed for the tabernacle, which Budd calculates as 100 talents and 1,775 shekels, which equals 301,775 shekels. Given the half-shekel tax in Exodus 38:26, one reaches the number of 603,550 (Budd 1984: 8). This ingenious calculation only pushes back the question one step: the number is still very high.
- Similarly, if one views the total number as a reference to the whole people and not only to military-aged men (Morales 2024a: 106–108), the number is historically high and now rejects the focus on able-bodied men in verses 45–46.

Therefore, the number is best understood within its ancient historical context, where hyperbole comes into play. In other words, the numbers intend to show the magnanimous nature of God's blessing. Indeed, the people have become very numerous. Furthermore, ancient narratives – including historical narratives – show little interest in the kinds of accuracies found in many modern societies (Goldstein 2012: 106).

48–54. This section provides a small footnote explaining Levi's omission. The separation of the tribe of Levi hints at its purpose within the book, which will receive more attention in the next few chapters. Most clearly, Yahweh calls for Moses to dedicate the Levites to the care of God's residence in the midst of the Israelites – the *tabernacle* (*miškān*), which in Hebrew literally means 'dwelling place' or 'tent, abode', as can be demonstrated through its use for people's tents in Numbers 16 (for Korah). The Levites' duties laid out in this text consist primarily of the work of breaking down and setting up Yahweh's portable residence. They are, in this sense, God's porters with a religious rather than a military character.

However, verses 50 and 53 point to another responsibility: the Levites keep guard over (Milgrom 1997: 243–244) or do the service of Yahweh's residence (Levine 1993: 141–142) so that no outsiders draw near. The former fits with the Levites' warlike role in Genesis 34 and Exodus 32:25–29, while the latter fits more with Numbers 18:3 (also Ezek. 44:8–15). If outsiders do come too close, then they shall be killed, though it is unclear from the text just who carries out the execution – whether it is by the hands of the Levites, the Israelites or Yahweh. It may depend on the interpretation of the Levites' work, which remains unclear (see 3:7 below).

Regardless, the underlying point is that God's presence among the Israelites, or any non-sanctioned people, represented a threat to them. God expresses this danger after the Golden Calf incident in Exodus 33:5: 'if for a single moment I should go up among you, I would consume you.' God's holiness and glory mark the radical distinction between God and humanity, which intends to induce respect and honour in the Israelites, comparable with the attitude and course of action one should take towards a king (similarly, though only on this point, see Esth. 4).

Meaning
What is the importance of such a military mustering? One might think here more broadly of the 'book of life' (Exod. 32:32; Dan. 7:10; Phil. 4:3; Rev. 20:12) and the importance of inclusion among those whose names are mentioned. Similar is the phrase 'I want to be in their number' from the song 'O When the Saints Go Marching In'. Both Numbers 1 and the song display the human desire for participation in God's movement. They therefore address those times and situations when one wonders, 'Do I belong?' And, in this case, 'belong' also means inclusion in a particular human family (or tribe). Belonging to God means being part of, or even grafted into, the Israelites as God's people. It obliquely reduces the hurdles to bringing outsiders *into* the human families or communities who follow God. Communities following God are invited to welcome outsiders stepping across to join their number.

Second, if one can conclude that God knew the numbers of the Israelites, then the purpose for the census would lie primarily in demonstrating to the Israelites themselves (and the readers of the text) the immense size of the nation. God in essence commands them to 'count their blessings'. This detailed counting – a look back at the miraculous work of God (the same number already appears in Exod. 38:26) – also can provide the Israelites with confidence that God will continue to care for them in the wilderness. They belong to God and to one another, which awakens hope for their shared future.

Finally, the short note on the Levites and their role among the Israelites points to a religious qualification of the military language that characterizes the census and the ordering of the camp. It also indicates an enduring tension for God's people. For God to remain among them requires a level of honour and respect, rather than taking that presence for granted. Furthermore, it is up to *God*, not the people, to set the boundaries for *how* and *when* the people can draw near.

D. Census of groups according to the marching and settling order of the tribes (2:1–34)

Context

Chapter 2 continues – or rather recapitulates – the census of chapter 1. However, it describes the organization of the tribes into an ordered camp expanding the brief mention in 1:52. Understanding this portrayal requires visualization of something like an architectural floor-plan, especially in relation to the tabernacle, inviting consideration on how spatial relationships indicate focal points. The organization of the camp and of the marching order in this chapter provides insight into a prominent way of viewing the human world as a whole in the Old Testament. One camp is located on each side (east, south, west, north) of the tent of meeting where the divine king camps and which commands the audience's attention. The camps on each side function to separate God's sanctuary from the rest of the nations.

There is a clear hierarchy in the constellation of the twelve tribes in this chapter. Judah, as the most important – from which will come the Davidic line of kings and in whose future territory the temple will be built (Jerusalem) – sets out first with the largest military unit. Second is Reuben, the firstborn of the eponymous tribes, having been demoted from his position as firstborn. Third – after the tent of meeting – comes Ephraim, which will become the largest tribe of the Northern Kingdom of Israel. Last comes the group led by Dan, which will dwell in the northernmost corner of the land. These four tribes may also represent different portions of the future land: Judah represents the south, Reuben the Transjordan (east of the Jordan River), Ephraim the central Northern Kingdom, and Dan the far north.

Comment
i. Group headed by Judah on the east side of the tabernacle (2:1–9)
1. All the numbers and the leaders of the tribes in this chapter agree with the material presented in Numbers 1. Thus, the question arises – as it will frequently – why repeat this information in the very next chapter? While Numbers 1 focuses on the number of the Israelites, and thus, in the larger Pentateuchal narrative, on the partial fulfilment of God's promise to the patriarchs Abraham, Isaac and Jacob in terms of the growth of their descendants, Numbers 2 sets its sights on the future, on the journey to and settlement of the land in fulfilment of the promise to these same patriarchs to give their descendants the land (Gen. 15:7; 17:8; 28:13). However, more specifically, Numbers 2 and Numbers 7 describe the formation of the people into a sacred military camp. The focus here lies on how God dwells in the midst of the Israelites on their present journey, which was briefly mentioned in 1:52. The description of the camp in Numbers 2 shares much with Ezekiel's vision of the resettlement of the land in Ezekiel 45:1–6; 47:13 – 48:35, which places all the tribes surrounding the temple city. Both portrayals imagine a configuration of all the tribes of Israel around God's sanctuary. However, among other differences, in Ezekiel the tribes are settled, while in Numbers 2, they and God are on the way (Seebass 1993: 50). Neither takes any topographical obstacles (e.g. mountains or bodies of water) into consideration and, therefore, depicts a specific theological ideal.

It is surprising that Aaron is also addressed, given that he does not reappear at the end of the chapter (v. 34). Both Moses and Aaron are addressed together only in Numbers 2:1; 4:1, 17; 14:26; 16:20; 19:1, while God addresses Moses alone thirty times. Aaron's role here may hint at the Levites' central location around the tabernacle (in v. 17) and the particular importance of the priests in line with the spatial focal point of the entrance to the tent of meeting or the tabernacle (the two often appear as interchangeable; see, e.g., Exod. 40:2, 6, 22, 29, 34–35; Num. 3:7–8, 38). According to Numbers 3:38, the families of Moses and Aaron camp in this location.

2. The tribes camp either 'some distance' from (NIV) or *facing* (NRSV) the tent of meeting. The Hebrew term here, *minneged*, may point to both meanings simultaneously: the former in order to respect the danger inherent in God's presence as king in their midst, and the latter so that each household tent concentrates their attention towards God. This verse, and the chapter as a whole, assumes that the reader has some familiarity with the tabernacle. In Exodus 25 – 31, God tells Moses how to construct a moveable dwelling (a tent surrounded by a wall) so that God can travel with Israel as it moves to the Promised Land. Then, Exodus 35 – 40 reports that Moses and the Israelites built it according to God's commands, much like the tone of Numbers 2, where God now instructs them to lay out the camp in a particular way and they do it (see v. 34). This command–fulfilment structure marks many of the texts accorded to the Priestly material in the Pentateuch.

Perhaps the most significant – and easily overlooked! – insight from this chapter is that it prescribes an *ordered* structure as the way in which God's people can set up a camp that honours God and invites God to travel with them. God's place in the tent of meeting lies at the centre when camped and travels in the middle with the Levites when on the way. The banners or markers indicate to each tribal regiment where they should camp and what their place in the marching order should be. It resembles God's creative act in Genesis 1 that brings order out of a chaotic context so that God can dwell within the creation.

3–4. Unlike in Numbers 1, this constellation of tribes begins with Judah, according it, as mentioned above (1:20–46), pride of place at the front of the travelling army (see Rhyder 2019: 124–128, 163–166). Judah's encampment on the east also aligns with that of the Aaronide priests and the opening of the tent of meeting that will be discussed in detail in Numbers 3 – 4.

5–9. On each side of Judah are Issachar and Zebulun, who are part of the Judah-led regiment. Their camp is the largest of the four, and all three tribes descend from Jacob's wife Leah (Gen. 29 – 30).

For these three, as well as the other nine tribes, their leaders are the same men named in 1:5–16 to help Moses and Aaron with the census. Their role as census administrators coincides with their continuing leadership of the tribe.

ii. Group headed by Reuben on the south side of the tabernacle (2:10–16)

10–16. After the Judah-led tribes to the east follow the three tribes led by Reuben that should camp south of the tabernacle. The principle binding these three tribes together is less obvious: Reuben and Simeon descend from Leah, while Gad descends from Leah's servant Zilpah (cf. Gen. 29 – 30). Arguments have been made that this position represents a less prestigious location than either that of Judah to the east or Ephraim to the west. Reuben and Simeon, both sons of Leah, did things viewed as disgraceful (Reuben: Gen. 35:22; 49:4; Simeon: Gen. 34; 49:5–7). As the son of a servant mother, Gad did not occupy a place of honour.

iii. The Levites (2:17)

17. The location of the tabernacle is in the middle of the Israelite camp. An alternative tradition places the tent of meeting *outside* the camp (Exod. 33:7–11; perhaps Num. 11:26–30), so some posit there being two different tents. However, two traditions with similar theological messages seems preferable. In both cases God's presence threatens the Israelites. In Numbers 1:53; 2:2, 17; 3:23–38, this danger is mitigated by the *Levites* camping next to God's tent as a layer of protective separation from their fellow Israelites. The Exodus 33 tradition instead locates the tent of meeting at a distance from the camp, which similarly insulates common Israelites.

The central location of God's tent coincides with the location of the royal tents of both the Egyptian pharaoh Rameses II in a relief from Luxor, Egypt, from the thirteenth century BC (Hoffmeier 2005: 208) and the Persian emperor from the sixth and fifth centuries BC (Achenbach 2003: 478). Both concern military camps. The Persian camp faced east, with the most trusted followers placed in front of the opening of the emperor's tent (Briant 2002: 188; Jeon 2022: 185). The Judah regiment camps at this location in Numbers 2. In other words, the centre represents the concentration of authority. As a sign of the importance of the royal tent, after the battle the conquering army would enter the tent of the enemy's ruler and place the crown upon the conquering ruler's head. However, in contrast to the textual and iconographic depictions of these camps in comparative cultures, the pack animals and other supports do not appear in Numbers 1 – 2. As is the case in Numbers 1, no mention of the women and children appears here.

Therefore, Yahweh functions as the divine *king* in ordering that the tabernacle be set up in the middle of the camp. However, as the *divine* king, Yahweh's presence there can also be understood to provide the Israelites with protection and prosperity.

The Levites surround the tent of meeting, and they constitute the middle of the caravan as they carry its pieces (according to v. 17). This directive also comes in the middle of the chapter. This constellation presents a different view from that of Joshua 3:3–4 and 4:10, which place the ark of the covenant at the *front* of the convoy. These are marginally different in that Joshua discusses only the ark, which is a centrally important part of the tent's furniture.

iv. Group headed by Ephraim on the west side of the tabernacle (2:18–24)

18–24. Following the Levites come the tribes led by Ephraim, which include Manasseh and Benjamin. These three descend from Jacob's wife Rachel. Their shared genealogical roots from Rachel suggest that their location to the west may also be one of honour. This conclusion may also receive support from the rise of Joshua, an Ephraimite, to become Moses' successor later in the book (27:18–22), though the order of the Levite clans in Numbers 3 disputes this claim.

v. Group headed by Dan on the north side of the tabernacle (2:25–31)

25–31. The final camp is led by Dan and includes the tribes of Asher and Naphtali. Each tribe in this camp to the north traces its heritage back to Bilhah and Zilpah, the servants of Leah and Rachel (cf. Gen. 30:5–13). The make-up of each camp generally follows the same genealogical principle, with Reuben's camp diverging the most in the case of Gad. Still, the Reuben group is aligned with Leah, while the Dan group diverges in that all three come from the servants of Leah and Rachel (for a clear graphic display and discussion, see Douglas 2001: 176–178). Dan and Naphtali descend from Bilhah, while Asher descends from Zilpah. These details become important when considering the later story of the Israelites, when the choice of Judah as the leader (cf. Gen. 49:8–12) becomes concrete for the first time in the biblical story. Judah's election also points forward beyond the time of the judges and the reign of King Saul to David's ascension to the throne. And, while Saul, David and Solomon rule over the entirety of these tribes, this kingdom quickly devolves into an Ephraim-led Israel in the north and a Judah-led kingdom of Judah (including Simeon and Benjamin) in the south. Israel's hold over Dan in the north and the Transjordan lands allotted to Reuben and others is tenuous. Therefore, this unified image of the tribes memorializes a lost and idealized past, and a call to return to a structured and hierarchical unity. The depiction concerns the entirety of the people of God (at that time) on display.

vi. Summary (2:32–34)

32–34. The conclusion of this main part of the census gives the final and total number: 603,550. There is an emphasis on how everything was done according to what Yahweh had commanded (cf. 1:19, 54), which is relevant considering that taking a census could be an act of rebellion against God (see 2 Sam. 24). The purpose of the census, however, is given here and it is not about the numbers per se, but the organization and order of the camp as they settle and march.

Meaning

One of the repeated themes in the book of Numbers, and in the Bible as a whole, revolves around when, where, how and for

Figure 1.1: The order of Israel's camp

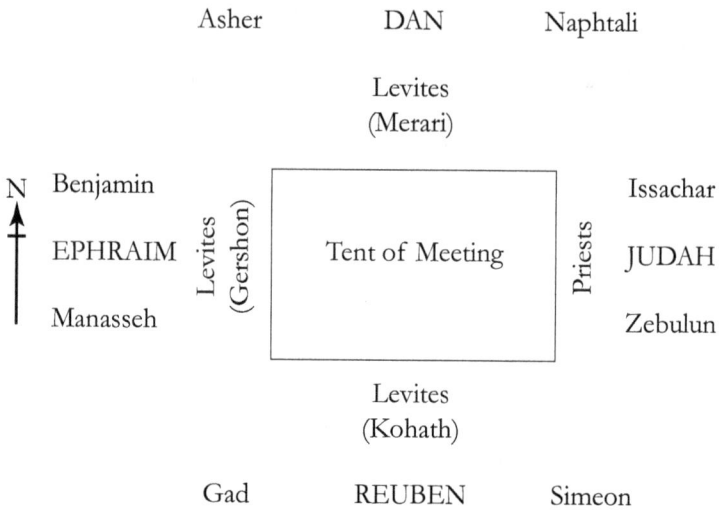

Asher   DAN   Naphtali

Levites
(Merari)

N   Benjamin   Issachar

↑   EPHRAIM   Levites (Gershon)   Tent of Meeting   Priests   JUDAH

    Manasseh   Zebulun

Levites
(Kohath)

Gad   REUBEN   Simeon

what purpose God will be present among humans. Numbers
2 provides some insight into the questions *for what purpose* and
where. The Israelites in this chapter take on the form of a sacred
army on a God-directed mission to travel to the land promised
to their ancestors. In other words, when a group of God's people
moves towards a destination that God has ordained for them,
God travels in their midst. Second, God travels with them when
they respect the tension of God being *with* them but also *separate
from* them. The disorderly masses that include foreigners become
orderly family units that mediate God's presence to the wider
world. Numbers 2 challenges God's people to balance the gift of
God's presence among them with respectful and grateful action
in response to that presence. This tension continues to receive
attention in subsequent chapters, especially those that address
issues surrounding leadership of the community such as the
narratives in Numbers 12, where Moses' siblings question his
authority, and Numbers 16, where Korah and associates challenge
the unique closeness to God's inner sanctuary accorded to Aaron
and his sons, the priests.

In the New Testament, John 1:14 and Revelation 21:3 speak of God dwelling in the midst of humans in another way at different times: as Jesus at his first coming, and in the New Jerusalem as part of the remaking of heaven and earth at the end of history. However, there are also ways in which God retreats from or abandons humanity, and even God's people. One of the most powerful displays comes in Ezekiel 8 – 11, where God's glory leaves the Jerusalem temple around the time of Jerusalem's fall to the Babylonians and the destruction of that temple, only to return in Ezekiel 43. Jesus, similarly, speaks of the destruction of 'this temple' which he will restore in three days (Mark 14:58; 15:29; cf. Matt. 26:61; 27:40; John 2:19–22). Those contexts play on the different understandings among first-century Jews of the Jerusalem temple on one hand, and Jesus and later the disciples of Jesus' own body on the other. In these texts as well, God in Jesus retreats from humanity, which causes turmoil among his followers.

E. Census and responsibilities of the Levites (3:1 – 4:49)

Context
After setting up the Israelites as a camp around the tabernacle, Numbers 3 turns its attention nearer to the tabernacle. This chapter and the next form a single unit that expands on the short remarks about the Levites in 1:47–53 and 2:33 to provide more detail on how God commanded and Moses and the Israelites obeyed in completing the organization of the camp. The prominence of the Levites in the census and the organization of the Israelite camp, having a separate and extended section dedicated to them, points to the religious nature of the camp.

Numbers 3 splits into a number of related sections: it begins in verses 1–4 by setting the stage of the beginning of the priesthood of Aaron and his sons, which took place on Mount Sinai, and then the initial transgression of God's holy space, recalling the events of Leviticus 10. The rest of the chapter takes place under the cloud of the danger of encroaching on God's holy space. The sections 3:5–13, 14–20 and 21–39 explore and expand on the in-between and thus protective role of the Levites as helpers for the priests, which requires organizing the Levites by taking a census of them, identifying their leaders, assigning them their tasks for the journey and designating their camp location. Two sections, 3:11–13 and 3:40–51, take up a different question: the choice of the Levites as replacements for the firstborn sons of Israel.

Comment
i. Aaron's son and the succession of the priesthood (3:1–4)

1–4. The first section begins in a rather surprising manner (v. 1): 'These are the generations of . . .' (ESV). Genealogies are well known from the book of Genesis, especially the Priestly material, both for the world itself (Gen. 2:4) and for the families and nations that formulate or initiate significant events in the history of God's people after episodes of rupture in God's plans for the world (Gen. 6:9; 10:1; 11:10, 27; 25:12, 19; 36:1, 9; Exod. 6:16; Num. 1; Matt. 1; see Achenbach 2003: 489–490; E. F. Davis 2019: 57–58). Thus, this verse marks an important development – the beginning of the priesthood, its responsibilities and its privileges – after the rupture that occurred in Leviticus 10. This all belongs to Moses and Aaron, and then only to Aaron's descendants, which is why no genealogy appears for Moses' children, indicating the transmission of Moses' office to the priesthood. This verse also marks the importance of the separation of Aaron and his sons to the priesthood by noting that it took place *on Mount Sinai* (Pressler 2017: 27), differing from most of the events in Numbers 1 – 10:10 which occur *in the wilderness of Sinai*. Aaron's priestly leadership will repeatedly be disputed later in the book (esp. Num. 16 – 17).

These verses recall the brief genealogy of Aaron's family in Exodus 6:20, 23 and bring up the events of Leviticus 10:1–3. Much debate remains over the nature of the 'strange fire' (AT) that these two sons brought and why God struck them down for their action: was the problem burning the wrong thing (e.g. not incense: for this possibility see Exod. 30:9 and Greer 2021)? Did they bring it at the wrong time? Were they the wrong people to bring it (instead of Aaron; cf. Nihan 2007: 580)? Did they bring it without being appropriately purified? Had they been involved in worshipping a different deity (E. W. Davies 1995b: 27)? Or is the text intentionally vague to account for God's otherness and freedom from any human constraining structure (Anderson 2015)? Given the lack of detail about the nature of their offence, the verses instead invite reflection on the only detail added here to what is known from Leviticus 10: it is explicitly stated that Nadab and Abihu had no children – in other words, the *consequence* of their action. As such it points to the tragedy and thus extreme danger of the priestly office.

ii. Levites as Aaron's assistants to substitute for Israel's firstborn (3:5–13)

5–6. A new section (vv. 5–10) and a new topic begin in verse 5, as often in Numbers, through Yahweh speaking to Moses. It is unclear whether this section returns to the time of Numbers 1 – 2, in the *second* month (cf. 1:1), in which case it would pick up on 1:48–51, which discusses the roles of the Levites. Attention here turns from Aaron and the priesthood to the male members of the tribe of Levi as a whole *in their relationship to Aaron and the priests*. The Levites standing before Aaron the priest and serving him indicates a clearly hierarchical relationship (v. 6): the Levites serve the priest. This aspect is also highlighted in verse 9 by the expression *unreservedly given*, which translates the repeated Hebrew passive participle 'be given, be given'.

7–8. In connection with 1:50, 53, these verses name two responsibilities for the Levites: to *perform duties* and [*do*] *service at the tabernacle*. As mentioned in the comment on 1:50, 53, the exact nature of these tasks is debated. Both concern a verb + object construction in Hebrew: the first is *šāmar* + *mišmeret*, which come from the root *š-m-r*, meaning 'guard, observe'. As a result, many interpreters understand this responsibility as guard duty. However, this terminology, specifically the noun *mišmeret*, appears quite frequently in this chapter (vv. 7, 8, 25, 28, 31, 32, 36, 38), which is concerned with all living male Levites, not just those of an age appropriate for guard duty. Also, it would make little sense for the tiny group of priests to camp at the opening to the tent, while the Levite clans camped on the other sides, if guard duty was a primary task (Seebass 1993: 70–71; Knierim and Coats 2005: 62). Therefore, this type of responsibility is more broadly conceived. Given the limitations on priestly powers in the next verses, it might imply a levitical role of observing the correct ritual duties by the priests, following a system of mutual surveillance among all parts of Israel as a cultic community (cf. Rhyder 2019: 140). Still, it is directly concerned with keeping the articles in question safe and separate from uncleanness. Likewise, the second formulation, in Hebrew *ābad* + *ăbōdâ*, concerns terms meaning do/work + work/service. This terminology appears far more frequently in Numbers 4.

9. There is a disagreement among the early witness to the Hebrew (and Greek) texts as to whether the Levites belong to Aaron/the priests or to Yahweh (cf. 8:16). While they are clearly given *to Aaron*, the text may still be making a point that they *belong* to God, and not to Aaron/the priests, which limits the powers of the hierarchically superior priests over the Levites.

10. This verse registers the priests, the results of which actually appeared in verses 2–4 (Samuel 2014: 162). It then emphasizes the danger of the wrong people approaching the sanctuary (repeating 1:51; also 3:38; 18:7), reusing the term *zār* ('foreign, strange') found in verse 4 for the nature of the fire that Nadab and Abihu brought.

11–13. This next short section provides the first justification for God's choice of the Levites in the book of Numbers, relating it to God's destruction of Egypt's firstborn as the final (tenth) plague that led to Israel's deliverance from Egypt (Exod. 11; 12:29–32). The Levites take the place of the firstborn, whom God has claimed (see also Exod. 4:22–23; 13:11–16; 22:29–30; 34:19; Deut. 15:19–23 for the expression of similar claims by God to the firstborn). Exodus 13:15 sets out the principle of the redemption (for discussion, see below on vv. 44–51) of the firstborn Israelite son as a continuing practice. In line with Exodus 4:22–23, there is a principle of symmetry: God views *Israel* as his firstborn, and now God makes a claim on the *firstborn of the firstborn*. Their position of honour also accords in part with the tradition in Exodus 32:25–29, where the Levites kill three thousand fellow Israelites who are engaged in worship of the golden calf. However, this latter story (Exod. 32:29) states that the Levites (lit.) 'filled their hands for Yahweh' ('you have ordained yourselves for the service of the LORD', NRSV), which bears similarities to the expression describing the priests above in verse 3, whose 'hand' 'he filled . . . for priestly action' (*whom he ordained to minister as priests*, NRSV).

iii. Census of the Levites and their clans, their order and their responsibilities in the camp (3:14–39)

14–20. The bulk of the chapter consists of two different lists that count the tribe of Levi. They begin in verse 14 not only with the typical report of Yahweh speaking, but also explicitly returning the location to the wilderness, followed by the command and fulfilment (vv. 15–16). Moses' task is to count the Levite males older than one month. This age limit differs from the twenty years and up for the other tribes in 1:18, but also from the registration of Levite males between the ages of thirty and fifty in Numbers 4. Why? Given the high levels of infant mortality in antiquity, it appears that a child was seen as viable after surviving for one month. Furthermore, this determination aligns with the lack of an age distinction given in the plague narrative in Exodus. The first list (vv. 17–20) simply separates the various clans and ancestral houses of the Levites. It seems to function as a way to group the eight clans into three groups, which will allow them to be assigned specific tasks and a specific location in which to camp.

21–37. A second list includes the counts of these various clans as well as their camp locations and specific tasks. These verses recall and expand on 1:51, 53. Just like the camps set up in Numbers 2, the Levites are also split into four groups, each with a named leader and with a particular side of the tabernacle designated for their camp location. The Gershonites, camping to the west of the tabernacle, receive the responsibility of carrying the outer, structural parts of the tabernacle complex (v. 25; cf. Exod. 25 − 27; 30). The Kohathites, who camp to the south, take care of the most holy material, such as the ark (v. 31; cf. Exod. 25 − 26); and the Merarites, camping to the north, are responsible for the structural parts of the inner sanctuary and the instruments in the courtyard (vv. 36–37; cf. Exod. 26). More details on how the items should be packed and carried appear in Numbers 4.

38–39. Once again the place of honour is to the east of the tabernacle, the direction of its opening, which is where Moses and Aaron camp. A key, if obvious, limitation on the priests' (Aaron's family's) service comes in this verse: it is (lit.) 'for the service of the Israelites'. They perform their duties not for themselves, but rather for the community as a whole.

It is repeated that a foreigner coming near (or encroaching; see Milgrom 1997: 243) shall be put to death. As in 1:51, it remains unstated whether God would strike the person down (as in Lev. 10:2) or whether the priests or Levites should do this (as in Exod. 32:25–28). The grammatical construction is a passive 'He shall be killed' or 'Let him be killed'.

As often noted, the three numbers in the Hebrew text of verse 22 (7,500), verse 28 (8,600) and verse 34 (6,200) add up to more than the *twenty-two thousand* given in verse 39. The omission of a single letter in verse 28 has led to the change from 'three' in 8,300 to the 'six' of 8,600; the ancient Greek version, the Septuagint, reads '8,300'. Such small copyist mistakes frequently take place when a scribe makes a new copy of an older manuscript.

iv. Levites as substitutes for Israel's firstborn (3:40–51)

40. The final section of the chapter returns the focus to the substitution of the Levite males for the firstborn Israelites that entered the discussion above in verses 11–13. The text assumes a logic of a one-for-one substitution: one Levite male for one non-Levite male.

41–42. It is striking that God commands Moses to count the firstborn animals in addition to the humans given the focus of the chapter on the Levites functioning as substitutes for the firstborn Israelite males. The inclusion of the firstborn animals may be necessary for the way in which the Levites will be consecrated as cultic representatives of Israel. The animals used for this consecration are representatives of the Levites (see 8:5–26, esp. 8:10–13). No number is given for the count of the animals, neither for those in the Levites' possession nor the firstborn animals belonging to the remaining Israelite tribes. However, the inclusion of the animals amplifies the connection with the tenth plague upon Egypt in Exodus 12:29; 13:12–16.

Three times in this chapter (vv. 13, 41, 45) the reason provided for God's command or statement that the Levites be set aside for himself is simply, *I am the LORD* [Yahweh]. This formula appears frequently, especially in Leviticus 19, but also more generally in Leviticus 11; 18 – 26. In Numbers 10:10 and 15:41 it is appended with the phrase *your God*, thus 'I am Yahweh, your God' or 'I, Yahweh, am your God'. The formulation also appears in Exodus and Ezekiel, where the focus is on Israel or others *knowing* that 'I am Yahweh', but that is different in Leviticus and Numbers 3. At least in the Leviticus contexts, a close relationship emerges between God's holiness and the formula itself (see Lev. 20:7–8, and Milgrom 2000: 1607, 1740), which should motivate Israel to action. It also appears in Isaiah 42 – 45 to emphasize God's unique nature as both the only God and Israel's saviour/redeemer. Yahweh's prior deliverance of the Israelites serves as a key motivator in the use of the formula in Numbers 3.

43. The count of the non-Levite, firstborn Israelite males comes to 22,273, which proves quite problematic in relation to the census numbers given in Numbers 1 (roughly six hundred thousand men; see further comment in the Additional note 'The large numbers in the census' above), which would mean that each firstborn male would have twenty-six brothers (Ashley 2022: 66).

44–51. The focus of this narrative turns to the problem that arises with regard to the registration of the Levite males that establishes a shortfall of 273 Levites in comparison to the firstborn Israelites. Because a Levite male cannot be substituted, the extra 273 firstborn males must be *redeemed*. Unlike in Exodus 13:13–16, which commands a practice of continuing redemption for each Israelite firstborn male, this chapter deals with a *one-time* redemption of all firstborn males at that point in time. The amount of five shekels in verse 47 equals the amount for redeeming a vow of a boy aged one month to five years in Leviticus 27:6; Numbers 18:16. A shekel was a unit of weight, in this case for silver, but the exact weight was not standardized throughout the Ancient Near East or even in the region of the southern Levant, consisting of Israel and its neighbours. However, the shekel was somewhere around 0.01 kg = 0.35 oz (Tal 2007; often equated with the Babylonian shekel of 0.011 kg = 0.4 oz; see Winkler 2016).

This notion of redemption appears frequently in these verses in the repetition of the Hebrew root *p-d-h* in this section. The basic notion here comes from the judicial sphere, where a debt-slave,

war captive or someone liable for harm is redeemed through a
payment in silver (e.g. Exod. 21:8, 30). In the Old Testament, the
foundational story of redemption often called upon is that of
Yahweh *redeeming* Israel from Egypt as recounted in Exodus 1 –
15 but recalled in other texts (e.g. Deut. 15:15; Ps. 77:15; Mic. 6:4),
including this one here. However, the exodus context is not always
in view when this terminology appears for God saving Israel.

Meaning

Chapter 3 of Numbers, like many other chapters, sets out an
ordered hierarchy for the roles that different groups should
assume for worship to take place appropriately. The chapter takes
place under the spectre of the consequences of failing to do so
in the example of Nadab and Abihu. As such, it strafes against
modern Western notions of identity, which begin with and equate
individual equality of roles with a person's value in society.
Numbers 3 has a different starting point and view of the *different*
roles assigned by God, which are intended to create a balance of
power among the people, and some of the limits, responsibilities
and dangers that go along with either (1) improperly carrying them
out, like Nadab and Abihu, or (2) transgressing the boundaries of
one's role, such as the wrong person approaching the sanctuary
or forgetting the purpose of their role for the common good (vv.
10, 38). Numbers indicates that God's approval lies in *successfully
carrying out one's given role* (rather than in the levelling of all roles),
which is common in societies outside of the modern West. Part of
the message here resides in respecting divine–human boundaries
(cf. Gen. 11:1–9) and the particular way in which God has made
and placed each person in their specific time and place, though it
does not mean that God's people forfeit the responsibility to work
towards the introduction of God's justice into human societies.

As insightfully noted by Olson (2012: 28), the substitution
of the Levites for the firstborn sons of Israel and their animals
provides a living reminder of God's work of redemption on their
behalf in the past, in Egypt (cf. the child's question in Exod.
13:14: 'What does this mean?'). This visual reminder recalls the
firstborn's traditional responsibility of service to Yahweh, now
adopted by the Levites. A danger arises in that God's people

might forget God's work, thus leading to the frequent reminder in Deuteronomy to 'remember that you were slaves in Israel', redeemed to become God's family, much like the New Testament call to remember God's salvation through Jesus (Eph. 2:11–13).

v. Responsibilities of the Kohathites (4:1–20)
Context
Numbers 4 largely builds on the material in Numbers 3 (especially vv. 25–26, 31, 36–37). It answers the question, 'How can God move with us?', and the basic answer is, 'Very carefully.' The chapter provides detail on how the packing of God's tent complex should proceed before transport. However, in contrast to the enrolment of all viable Levite males who substitute for firstborn Israelite males from the other tribes, here the focus shifts to those Levite males between the ages of thirty and fifty, who receive the task of moving the sanctuary and its furnishings.

As with the previous three chapters, the question arises here as well as to why this material is included in the book: understanding its significance requires addressing the different types of objects, which determine the order of mention of the different Levite clans in this chapter, in contrast to the arrangement by birth order in Numbers 3.

Some commentaries treat Numbers 3 and 4 together, reading over the modern chapter breaks (which were only devised in thirteenth-century England), and there is some justification for reading them together: they both address the number and role of the Levites in transporting the tabernacle. The Jewish reading tradition (going back to the Talmudic era, AD 200–600), on the other hand, makes its first big break in the sections of the book at Numbers 4:21 (each section contains the reading portion for a single Sabbath, with the first section extending from 1:1 to 4:20, and the second from 4:21 to 7:89).

Chapter 4 generally divides into God's commands concerning the Levites' enrolment and the objects apportioned to each clan for transport – to the Kohathites (vv. 1–20), the Gershonites (vv. 21–28) and the Merarites (vv. 29–33). However, as each of those sections begins with a divine command to enrol the male Levites between the ages of thirty and fifty, there is a hesitation in the report of the results of the census, which only comes later in the report of the census of each clan (vv. 34–45). The implementation of the taking down of the camp and transport takes place much later in 10:17–21. An overall summary (vv. 46–49) ends the chapter.

Important comparative texts for reading Numbers 4 include Exodus 25 – 27; 30:1–10; 35:11–18; Numbers 7:6–9; 8:24 (for discussion on comparative reading, see Introduction, 'How to read Numbers').

Comment

1–2. The detailed description of the various elements of the moveable sanctuary in Exodus 25 – 27; 30:1–11 reveal the intricacies of the tent complex. The materials were substantial and required considerable organization to move. Figure 1.2 provides an overview of the responsibilities of each clan.

A striking element of chapter 4 appears in the limitation of the Levite males enrolled for the tasks in this chapter to those between the ages of thirty and fifty (vv. 3, 23, 30). This contrasts with the census in the previous chapter, and with the expansion to age twenty-five in 8:24. Given that many teenagers and men in their twenties have more physical strength than those in their late forties (especially in antiquity, with a shorter life expectancy), physical strength alone does not explain the criterion (Calvin 1852–55: 3.505). It remains unclear why different ages appear in chapters 4 and 8, merely four chapters apart from each other.

Figure 1.2: The responsibilities of each levitical clan

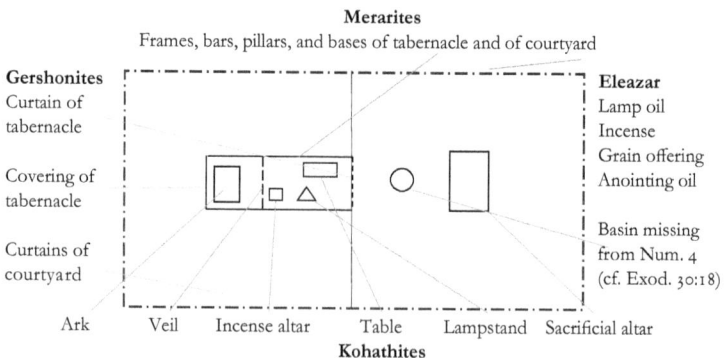

3. It is surprising that the initial term used for the Levites' service, *ṣābā'*, usually refers to military service, making the age requirement even stranger, but this is immediately focused on the tent of meeting. The use of this term for sanctuary service indicates the camp's religious character even within a military framework in which the importance of the Levites' transport work equals that of the military service of the other tribes (Budd 1984: 48).

4. Verses 4–20 form the longest section and concern the tasks of the Kohathites. They should transport, according to verse 4, the *most holy things*, but these items, according to verses 7–15, also include those that come from the outer room, and not just the Holy of Holies (the inner room) of the sanctuary, where only the ark of the covenant was found.

While this section concerns what the Kohathites carry, in fact much of it commands the priests (v. 5: *Aaron and his sons*) to dismantle the sanctuary and cover up the furnishings such as the ark, table and incense altar (*golden altar* in v. 11) with covers of various colours *before* the Kohathites enter to touch (v. 15) or even see (vv. 17–19) the items. This concern arises only with the objects apportioned to the Kohathites, given that these objects are positioned closer to the divine presence, not with those for the other clans. One item that Exodus 30:17–21 places in the courtyard that is missing from the furnishings of the Hebrew text here in Numbers 4 is the bronze basin for priestly washing. The early Greek version (LXX) includes it in verse 14.

The importance of the coverings and colours proceeds in descending order from inner sanctuary to the courtyard. Both the *blue* (vv. 6, 7, 9, 11, 12) and *purple* or 'red' (v. 13) represent hues of violet dye coming from snails found near and exported by the Phoenician cities on the modern-day Syrian coast that were highly valued throughout the ancient world, typically being reserved for royalty and the elite (cf. 2 Chr. 2:7; Esth. 1:6; Prov. 31:22; Jer. 10:9). The snails produced a very permanent dye, but a large number of them was required for even a small amount. The Hebrew terms for colours do not align perfectly with modern ones (Brenner 1982: 143–148).

A translation difficulty arises in verses 6, 8, 10, 11, 12, 14 for the type of covering put over several tabernacle furnishings.

The Hebrew term is *taḥaš*, classically translated skin of 'badger' (KJV) or 'porpoise' (NASB, 1995 edn), but also as 'goatskin' (ESV), or 'durable' (NIV) or *fine* (NRSV) leather. The early Greek version (LXX) translated it to mean 'blue', and more recent scholarship has posited 'yellow-orange'. In addition to its use for the coverings of the tabernacle (also in Exod. 26:14; 36:19; 39:34), the term appears in Ezekiel 16:10 as apparently expensive material used for sandals.

5–6. The list begins with the ark, the only item found in the inner sanctuary (the 'Holy of Holies' or 'Most Holy Place'), and thus the most holy piece. For this reason, it is covered in three layers (the curtain to the inner sanctuary consisting of blue-violet, red-violet and crimson tapestry [see Exod. 26:31–33], then the *taḥaš* leather, and finally a blue-violet cover). The outer layer was a different colour from the coverings on the other items, so it was identifiable by colour while in transit. There is a tension in verse 6, which ends with the command to put the ark's carrying poles in place, with Exodus 25:15, which commands that the poles be left in place.

7–12. The list then moves to the furnishings in the outer room of the sanctuary: the table (three layers: blue-violet, crimson, *taḥaš* leather), the lampstand (two layers: blue-violet, *taḥaš* leather), the incense altar (two layers: blue-violet, *taḥaš* leather), and all the utensils used for the rituals that take place there (two layers: blue-violet, *taḥaš* leather).

13–15. Finally, the list moves to the altar in the courtyard designated for burning meat and grain sacrifices and their accompanying utensils (two layers: red-violet, *taḥaš* leather). The point of all these coverings was certainly to provide protection for the items and those who were carrying such holy objects, but also to highlight their extreme importance.

16. A brief aside addresses the supplies in the tabernacle that the priest Eleazar rather than the Levites should transport, indicating their extreme holy nature. This theme also provides the place to remark that Eleazar has the overall responsibility for the transportation of the tabernacle as a whole. Eleazar later becomes high priest (20:25–28), which is foreshadowed here by the responsibility given to him in contrast to his brother Ithamar, who oversees the Gershonites and Merarites below (vv. 28, 33).

17–20. The concern that follows is that the Kohathites do not perish as a result of improper handling of the holy furnishings. The responsibility for their well-being lies upon the priests (v. 19). In other words, the dangerous nature of the items most closely connected with God is reiterated. This concern for the Kohathites foreshadows the tragic result of the narrative in Numbers 16, where Korah, a Kohathite, along with several others, challenges Aaron's exclusive claim to the priesthood (see esp. 16:9–10).

vi. Responsibilities of the Gershonites (4:21–28)

21–28. Next is the command to take a census of the Gershonites and the description of their transport responsibilities. This section mirrors the outline for the framework of the Kohathites above. However, there are no asides noting the danger in handling their items. The reason for this is that they have the task of transporting the coverings and curtains. In other words, once all the furnishings accorded to the Kohathites have been dealt with, now the soft items of the walls and ceiling can be dismantled.

vii. Responsibilities of the Merarites (4:29–33)

29–33. The tasks for the Merarites follow. They move the wooden structural pieces of the tabernacle and the larger courtyard. That is, their responsibility is for the heavier items. These pieces must logically be dismantled last (and set up first).

viii. Census of the three levitical clans (4:34–49)

34–48. The actual results of the census commanded first in verses 1–3 are reported here in verses 34–49. The Kohathites and Gershonites contain relatively close to the same number of men aged thirty to fifty, which could correspond to their tasks. The Merarites have a larger number, which matches their heavier burdens.

The inclusion of the community leaders in the counting (v. 34) comes as something of a surprise, given that they did not appear earlier in the chapter, though it matches the help they provide Moses and Aaron with the census of the other tribes in 1:4–17.

49. The report closes with two important notes. First (in the first and final clauses of the verse), the tasks of enrolling the

Levites and assigning them their duties were done according to
Yahweh's command. The Israelites listen closely to what God
commands them to do and carry it out. Second, *each man* receives
a specific assignment. They do not all have the same task. As with
Numbers 1 – 3, however, the Levite women receive no mention
in the chapter.

Additional note: the Levites

Considerable attention has been paid to the relationships between
the Levites and the priests in modern biblical scholarship as
a result of the different statuses and hierarchical relationships
between them in Numbers 3 – 4 in comparison with Deuteronomy
18:1–8 (and elsewhere in Deuteronomy) and Ezekiel 44:10–16,
among other texts. In short, Deuteronomy 18:6–8 allows *all
Levites* (males) to function as priests at God's central sanctuary
established in the land. In contrast, Ezekiel 44:10–16 demotes *most
Levites* (males) from serving as priests. Numbers 4 sets out a clear
hierarchy between the priestly family of Aaron and the rest of
the Levites, though it does not indicate at all that this distinction
represents a loss of standing for the Levites. The question arises
as to how to understand these texts in relation to one another.
Do they represent different viewpoints in disagreement with one
another, that is, different sides of a discussion? Do they represent
the realities of practice at different historical times? And, as a
related question, in which historical period: before the establishment of the Israelite state (1200–1000 BC), the pre-exilic period
from David to Jehoiachin (1000–586 BC), or after the Babylonian
exile until around the conquest of Alexander the Great (586–*c.*300
BC)?

Some interpreters (the classic statement is Wellhausen 1885:
121–151) reconstruct a historical progression for the Israelites that
follows this trajectory: all Levites as priests (Deut. 18:6–7) > a
struggle among Levite groups leads to the sole priesthood for the
Zadokites (Ezek. 44:15: 'But the levitical priests, the descendants
of Zadok . . .') > an established system where only Aaron's
Zadokite descendants function as priests and the Levites are their
helpers (Num. 3 – 4; see also 1 Chr. 15; 16; 23 – 26).

Support for this reconstruction is derived from the overwhelming presence of Levites in helper roles in the book of 1 Chronicles in comparison with 1–2 Samuel. Both books narrate the events of David and Solomon, but Samuel, which is typically viewed as composed much earlier than 1 Chronicles (placed in the Persian or Hellenistic period, that is, 500–300 BC), mentions Levites only in connection with the ark (1 Sam. 6:15 and 2 Sam. 15:24). These data are understood as indicating the growing importance of Levites as sanctuary helpers in later times, but not earlier. A pertinent example appears in the parallel stories of 1 Chronicles 15 v. 2 Samuel 6, where David brings the ark into Jerusalem. The Chronicles version highlights Levite involvement, while Levites do not appear at all in the Samuel version. Furthermore, contrary to Numbers 4:5–20, in 1 Samuel 6:15 it is the Levites who see and touch the ark of the covenant.

Another group of interpreters (e.g. Cross 1973: 195–215; Ackerman 2011; Leuchter 2017) views the texts as representing realities in the pre-exilic period, but at different sanctuaries, for example at Jerusalem for some texts (Num. 3 – 4), at Shiloh for others (1 Sam. 1), and at local sanctuaries for still others (e.g. in the city of Dan: see Judg. 17 – 18).

What is striking, regardless of how one brings together the divergent texts, is that they are allowed to stand together in one canonical collection. This fact indicates that the compilers of the biblical canon (and this carries through into the tradition of the four canonical Gospels) did not view non-contradiction in historical narratives, or in this case divine commands for the hierarchical structure of the sanctuary personnel, as being of fundamental importance. Historical development and/or simultaneous disagreement can exist within the Scriptures.

Meaning

The overarching message from Numbers 4 is the care with which God's dwelling place should be treated, and the fact that God moves about with the people. The requirement for the priests to cover and pack all the furnishings before the Kohathites touched or even saw them, or else they would die (v. 20), demonstrates that one should not trifle with things from God's intimate sphere.

Given that we no longer conceive of God taking up residence in
a particular tent or more fixed structure in the same way (cf. John
4:20–24), the *physical* spaces that are intimate to God can no longer
be defined in the same way. In some ways, even in the Priestly
theology of creation in Genesis 1, the whole physical universe
is a place for the divine presence and of worship, but there are
still levels of sacrality attached to specific spaces that must be
maintained and respected, even if such spaces can change locations
from time to time, following the locomotive character of the tabernacle (see Sommer 2001). However, one might instead conceive of
the people of God, the church, *as* the holy 'place', which must be
treated with inordinate respect, as on display in the death sentence
experienced by Ananias and Sapphira in Acts 5:1–11.

Similarly, Paul writes of the Corinthians who receive the letter
of 1 Corinthians as themselves the holy temple of God, such that
'If anyone destroys God's temple, God will destroy that person.
For God's temple is holy, and you are that temple' (1 Cor. 3:17; see
also 2 Cor. 6:16; Eph. 2:21). In this verse, Paul proclaims a similar
penalty to Numbers 4:20.

A larger implication from Numbers 4, which was also the case
in Numbers 1 – 3, is that individuals receive different responsibilities from God the King. Yahweh is envisioned as the King on
the move in this chapter, and each Levite male receives a specific
task (v. 49) in order for the tent to be dismantled and transported.
Paul likewise conceives of the church as a body with many
different parts that should take special care to honour those parts
that usually receive less acclaim (1 Cor. 12:4–26) – perhaps like the
Merarites and Gershonites, rather than the priests.

F. Cultic preparation of the camp (5:1 – 10:10)

Context
Chapters 5–6 fit very loosely within the context of Numbers 1 –
10:10, which as a whole prepares the Israelites for their journey
away from Sinai towards the land. The genealogies and ordering
of the camp in Numbers 1 – 2 and the ordering of the Levites for
taking down and setting up God's tent in their midst in Numbers 3
– 4 are followed in an abrupt change in Numbers 5 by instructions

about (1) removing people with specific impurities to outside the camp, (2) paying restitution for defrauding someone when that person and their relatives have died, and (3) a ritual to deal with a wife's suspected adultery. The latter two address actions in the tent to prevent or eradicate defilement. Then Numbers 6 offers movements more concerned with direct contact with the holy sphere: the Nazirite vow and Aaronic blessing. While the first four chapters set out the necessary structure of the community for God to travel among the Israelites, chapter 5 begins to address challenges of both a physical and a social nature that could confront the Israelites and threaten God's presence with them, which would endanger the people's very existence. Beginning in chapter 5 and carrying through most of the rest of Numbers, one of the keys for understanding the texts of Numbers comes in their dialogue with other texts in the Pentateuch (see Introduction, 'Excursus: comparative texts for interpreting Numbers').

The first section of chapter 5 is based on a conception of God's presence that requires death and uncleanness to remain at a distance. The most difficult passage for modern interpreters is the ritual ordeal of a wife whose husband suspects her of adultery. Achenbach (2003: 499) insightfully notes that the type of impurity moves from the external (skin disease) inwards, first with unfaithfulness with goods and finally to jealousy. Ritually and theologically, external and internal forms of impurity are conceptually intertwined (see Introduction, 'From impurity to holiness').

Comment
i. Excluding cases of impurity (5:1–4)
1–4. Understanding of this section requires noting both its placement after the layout of the camp in Numbers 1 – 4 around the tent of meeting and also the statement here in verse 3 that *they must not defile their camp, where I dwell among them*. God's radical desire to dwell with humans in the midst of creation (see also Gen. 2:2; 3:8; 5:22, 24; 6:9) here encounters human limitations: skin defilement, bodily discharges and death. The first two serve as external markers of death or of the breaching of boundaries (genital fluids moving from *inside* to *outside* a body). These verses build on the discussion in Leviticus 13 – 14; 15:2–31; 22:4 which provide

more details about skin defilement and kinds of genital fluids that make a person unclean and the length of their uncleanness. However, Numbers 5:2–3 adds the *location* for persons during their impurity (*outside the camp*), extending the exclusion in place for skin defilement already in Leviticus 13:46; 14:8.

This promise of shared space between God and the Israelites on earth appears earlier in Exodus 29:42–46. However, the stark differences between divine and human call for limitations on the times, places and personal state that one must be in to encounter God safely that signify the fundamental differences between humanity and God – God's holiness, incomparability and immortality (cf. Klawans 2006: 57–58; Angelini and Nihan 2016). In these verses, the named impurities, which do not indicate sinfulness, call for a spatial distance from God's place of residence in the tent of meeting. They also share the ability to transmit impurity from one person to another (or to a surface) through touch. Thus, when impure, a person was removed to outside the camp so that they would not be within contamination range of the sanctuary.

While classically translated 'leprosy' (e.g. NRSV, ESV), the Hebrew term (*ṣârûaʿ*) in verse 2 comprises several skin conditions as indicated by the descriptions in Leviticus 13, where it can also include fungus on clothing or walls. It does not mean Hansen's disease, commonly known as leprosy (see *HALOT* 1057 and discussion in Levine 1993: 184–185).

The Hebrew term rendered *corpse* (*nepeš*, 'person') is not the normal one (*nĕbēlâ*), though it is also used in this manner in Leviticus 19:28; 22:4; Numbers 6:11; 9:6, 7, 10; Haggai 2:13. A person's corpse still represents their 'personality'; it is diminished but not extinguished by death (Frevel 2012: 389–391; Feder 2021: 153–157). This category of defilement is often associated only with priests (Lev. 10:4–7; 21:2; Ezek. 44:25, 27) and the Nazirite (Num. 6:6–7), but here and in Numbers 19; 31:19–34 it is extended to Israelites as a whole. The passage also connects with one other section, Numbers 12, which narrates Miriam's skin condition as a form of divine punishment.

Finally, in contrast to what will appear in many places in Numbers 11 – 25, verse 4 (and typical for Num. 1 – 10) comments that the Israelites carried out Yahweh's command to Moses.

ii. Rectifying misappropriation of resources (5:5–10)

5–10. The precepts extended here are found elsewhere, in this case in Leviticus 6:1–7, which addresses what a person should do when they realize (or acknowledge) a wrong they have done to another person, especially when uttering a sworn oath (Knohl 2004). In this case, the main extension is what to do when the victim has died or emigrated and left no survivors.

There are several smaller additions to the regulations in Leviticus 6 as well: (1) verse 6 includes both men and women as possible perpetrators, rather than men only. (2) Verse 6 also describes the offence as sin by a person (against a neighbour, according to Lev. 6:3) *and betrayal/disloyalty* to Yahweh (NRSV, *breaking faith with the LORD*). This phraseology clearly connects treatment of others with loyalty to God, rendering it impossible to act unethically, especially in the realm of economics and business according to the underlying description in Leviticus 6, and appropriately honour God (cf. Lev. 6:5–6). (3) Verse 7 adds to the basic scenario the step of confessing one's sin (though it does not indicate *to whom* one should confess), which solidifies that the offence is against both the human victim and God.

Then verse 8 states that, if the man who had been wronged has no survivors (literally, no redeemer), then the restoration should still take place. As in the basic scenario (though only stated in Lev. 6 for that situation), the guilty party should bring a guilt offering of a ram to the sanctuary for atonement. In this circumstance, however, the priest performing the sacrifice also receives the restitution plus one-fifth required to alleviate the wrong committed, as well as the meat from the ram, assuming the animal parts are dealt with as a reparation offering (cf. Lev. 7:1–10). Verse 9 makes the specific rule about the priest performing the ritual receiving the restitution into a general principle: the officiating priest is the one who receives the 'payment'. As a limiting remark, verse 10 regulates offerings in general, though it would be especially important for the festive fellowship meat offerings: whoever brings an offering, that offering belongs to them, while (repeating the principle of v. 9) what they give to the priest belongs to the priest.

Exodus 22:1–4, 7, 9 lays a heavier punishment on the wrongs than Leviticus 6 and Numbers 5 (double rather than 120%). This difference suggests that the legal precepts are instantiations of divine justice for different times and/or places.

iii. The ritual of the jealous husband and the wife suspected of adultery (5:11–31)

11–30. These verses deal with a very specific scenario adding to the ordinances in Deuteronomy 22:13–39; Leviticus 20:10. It concerns the situation when a husband suspects his wife of adultery, though there are no witnesses or proof. As a result, the problem cannot be solved judicially, which would require witnesses (two or more according to Num. 35:30; Deut. 17:6; 19:15). This is the only trial by ordeal for a secret sin in the Bible. There is a verbal connection in the 'unfaithfulness' (*m-ʿ-l*) of verses 6 and 12 pointing to a shared theme with the previous section; it predominately describes Israel's behaviour towards God, and concerns a marriage only in this passage. A further reason for the placement of this section here is the repeated mention of impurity, linking it with 5:1–4 in which impurity by genital fluids, including those emitted in sexual intercourse, is implicit (cf. Lev. 15:18).

The framing of the issue is from the perspective of the husband who suspects his wife's infidelity (vv. 12–13) and only considers the possibility though uncertainty of her innocence (v. 14). Thus, the text begins by seeing the situation skewed through the eyes of the husband, which are themselves mentioned in verse 13 (see, e.g., ESV; Calvin 1852–55: 3.110).

In order to resolve the situation, a complex series of ritual actions takes place before Yahweh under the guidance of the priest. The description here bears some similarities to ordeals in the surrounding cultures, though they all differ in some ways (Levine 1993: 204–205). The section is quite repetitive in comparison with the earlier sections of the chapter, but the order of actions – introduced in verses 11–14 and concluded with a summary in verses 29–31 – is as follows:

- A husband suspects his wife has been unfaithful, so he brings her and the appropriate offering to the sanctuary (vv. 15–16a).
- The priest, carrying water mixed with dust, brings the

woman, who carries the offering, before the altar. He unbinds her hair and has her swear an oath that she has not committed adultery, but if she has, then she will experience physical consequences (vv. 16b–22).
- The priest writes these curses on a scroll and then scrapes off the writing into the water. He then makes her drink the water (vv. 23–24).
- The priest takes the offering from her and puts some of it on the altar, where it burns and goes up in smoke (vv. 25–26).
- The curse from verse 22 – accepted by the woman in verse 24 – is proclaimed for a guilty woman, while innocence is declared for a woman who does not exhibit the effects of the curse (vv. 27–28).

What triggers the process (v. 14) is that the husband has a jealous spirit towards his wife, and an intervention at the sanctuary is required to put the matter to rest, one way or another. Nowhere else in the Bible does a *spirit of jealousy* appear, and no indication of the *cause* of this spirit appears in the text. While the phraseology is that this spirit comes upon him, this need not indicate that this 'spirit' represents something demonic.

The jealous husband (v. 15), if he is to have his wife undergo the ordeal, must furnish the necessary offering (¹⁄₁₀ ephah of barley flour – *c*.1.8 l / 1.9 quarts; see Kletter 2006),[1] so it comes at a minimal economic cost to him (cf. Lev. 5:11–13). The preparation of this offering (without oil or frankincense) and the flour from barley rather than the more valuable wheat shows that it is a different kind of ritual from a typical grain offering (like those in Lev. 2). This ritual seeks to identify innocence or guilt, like a judicial case, rather than being an offering that celebrates the connection between God and the Israelites.

---

[1] One-tenth of an ephah is compared to one omer in Exod. 16:36, which is explicitly the daily portion of bread (*leḥem*) for each individual Israelite (Exod. 16:15–16, 32). The estimated amount of flour necessary for the intake of bread per capita in traditional cultures similar to ancient Israel is about 0.5 kg = 1 lb. See Meyers 2002: 21–22.

Nowhere else does dust of the sanctuary (v. 17) play a ritual role, though dust itself is often connected to mourning rites (Isa. 47:1; Lam. 2:10), which is also a possibility for the verb for dishevelling the woman's hair (v. 18: *p-r-*'; see Lev. 10:6; 21:10; or impurity in Lev. 13:45).

Unlike Leviticus 20:10, which prescribes the death penalty for adultery, this text has in mind a somatic curse and shame before the community (vv. 21, 27). It has been suggested (Budd 1984: 65) that the punishment in verses 21–22 (lit: 'your thigh drop and your belly swell') entails a miscarriage, in which case her pregnant belly likely brought on suspicion. However, more compelling is that the envisioned punishment was reproductive failure and therefore sterility (Frymer-Kensky 1984: 20–21), which is reflected in the NRSV contra the NIV. Regardless, the result is childlessness, an undesirable status for a woman in a society so focused on progeny (cf. Gen. 15:2; 16:1–6; 21:6–7; Hos. 9:11).

The reason for the writing of the curse and scraping off of the ink into the water (v. 23) along with dust of the sanctuary remains unstated, so readers of the text are left to speculate about the way it should become activated against a guilty wife. Written letters conveyed a symbolic power in themselves in the ancient world, where few were literate. There is little support for a naturalistic illness resulting from the mixture of dust, ink and water; rather, the decision concerning punishment lies in God's hands (Sakenfeld 1995: 37). What is clear is that, by drinking the words, the woman assumes the responsibility for the curse should the curse come to fruition (underscored in her repeated *Amen. Amen* in v. 22). The words become a part of her, something elsewhere found in prophets embodying oracles from God (Ezek. 3:1–3; Rev. 10:9–10).

Still, this section raises an even bigger question about justice: why does it mention only the *woman* suspected of adultery and not her supposed partner? And what about a situation in which a wife suspects that her *husband* has been unfaithful? The text does not speak of any recourse for her. Nor does it note the trauma of a false accusation by her husband. On the flip side, given the patriarchal nature of ancient Israelite society, this ritual opened the male head of household up to an authority beyond his own for his household's internal matters, thereby leading to all but the most extreme cases of jealousy dissipating before the potential shame of having misjudged one's wife. Perhaps, by analogy with Deuteronomy 24:4, the husband having sexual relations with a wife who has been unfaithful brings impurity into the community, thus opening the community up to the dangerous clash of God's holy presence and impurity. Nonetheless, despite the protection – economic, social and otherwise – that male household heads could provide for women in ancient settings, this does not alleviate the unevenness between genders. From Genesis 4:19 onwards, men could have multiple female sexual partners, but the reverse was not the case. The patrilineal transmission of inheritance might explain the gravity of a woman's alleged adultery, which could lead to the possibility of inheritance confusion. In this sense, female sexuality posed a considerable threat (Bach 1993: 32; Pressler 2017: 48).

The whole ordeal rests upon and enacts a number of contradictions: there is dust, but it is from a sacred location. Rather than speaking words, they are ingested. An offering is brought, but it comes from low-quality flour and it is not presented to God. These elements highlight the bitterness of the entire scenario of possible infidelity on the part of a wife and a husband's jealousy. Each one represents a perversion of marriage. This ritual action provides a stop-gap measure to restore community for imperfect people rather than an ideal. Nonetheless, the unfolding of the section points to the significance of the spousal relationship and the paternity of the children born to the wife (vv. 27–28).

31. *The woman shall bear her iniquity.* This clause should be understood to mean that there will be no *human* punishment that should be added to the woman in this situation. The results lie with God, who will either allow her to bear children or not (cf. vv. 28–29).

Meaning

The juxtaposition of these three sections in chapter 5, which include both physical and social offences against God's order (God's holiness), indicates several ways in which God is distinct from humanity. Humans are subject both to natural perdition and to social offences. Modern Western Protestantism, through a certain way of understanding New Testament discussions of purity, now struggles with their placement in the Christian Bible. If nothing more, verses 1–4 call Christians to pay attention to the physical world as also a sphere for which God cares. Yet they also call for the continuing respect for the radical difference between God and humanity, even in the light of God joining with humanity in Jesus' incarnation.

The second section, verses 5–10, solidifies the importance of social relationships as part of a person's connection with God. There is a need for economic restitution before one can approach God, much like Jesus' teaching in the Sermon on the Mount (Matt. 5:23–34).

An intriguing interpretation of the suspected adulterous wife / jealous husband is that it should be read more as a commentary on the relationship between God and the Israelites and by extension the church (MacDonald 2008a). This theme returns in the polemic of the Baal-peor incident in Numbers 25. In this approach, God is jealous of wayward Israel and Judah (cf. Ezek. 16; 23; Hos. 1 – 3). Israel's participation in the cultic rituals will reveal if they are innocent or guilty of adultery. That explains the use of the dust of the sanctuary, pointing to the effect of impurity in the sanctuary, and the written letter, pointing to the commandments that result from the covenant between God and Israel. The final result will be evidenced by Israel's ability to be fertile and multiply or, alternatively, if it becomes sterile and just dies out as a people.

In Hosea 1 – 3, God commands the prophet Hosea to marry a promiscuous woman and then, *contrary to biblical law* in Deuteronomy 24:1–4, to take her back after she has been unfaithful and divorcing her as an example of the way God will act towards Israel. However, this analogy does not undo the harm done through the way the matter is conceptualized to a *wrongly accused* woman in Numbers 5:11–31. Nevertheless, it does demonstrate that, if the punishment is left to God, divine mercy will win out in the long run, something that will be proven repeatedly in Israel's journey in the wilderness. Thus, the chapter leaves the reader with a tension between God's holiness and human impurity – an impurity that permeates all spheres of human existence. In the end, the text leaves the pain of the faithful wife unarticulated and without relief, calling for a more perfect resolution, perhaps like Jesus' treatment of the Samaritan (shunned) woman at the well in John 4 (Olson 2012: 38–39) or the woman caught in adultery in John 8:1–11. The challenge to modern readers with regard to marriage is how to imagine and act so that *both* partners belong to the other and are honoured by the other.

iv. Nazirite vow of extraordinary consecration (6:1–21)
Context

Most of chapter 6 deals with the vow, presumably by a non-priest or Levite – and significantly by a man or a woman – to draw especially close to Yahweh for a designated period. Following through on such a vow entails several ritual actions that were generally unnecessary for Israelites. The key point of this special time is that the woman or man emulates the behaviours of the priests (Ezek. 44:20–21, 25; Calvin 1852–55: 1.467), even the high priest (Lev. 10:9; 21:11).

The final verses of chapter 6, verses 22–27, include a specific priestly blessing that bears remarkable similarity to the message on two silver amulets from a burial cave near Jerusalem from around 600 BC (Smoak 2016). It is the oldest known material evidence of a text so similar to the Bible.

As a compilation, the sections of Numbers 5 – 6 highlight ways that all members of the community can hinder (5:1–31) or welcome (6:1–27) God's presence. There is also the continuity of oaths between 5:11–31 and 6:2–21, the repeated reference to 'man or woman' (5:3, 6; 6:2), and focus on hair in 5:11–31 and 6:2–21. These shared features show that the connections from one section to the next in biblical law texts may in some places be such practical or linguistic associations more than indicating logical or theological progression. Read after Numbers 1 – 4, these sections also unpack the relationships between the community as a whole and the priests. They both share the responsibility to maintain or recover the state of blessing on display in Numbers 1 – 4, sometimes even with the possibility of lay Israelites incorporating specifically priestly features. For, as Frevel (2016: 142) writes, 'The camp is not the perfect world which it appears to be in Numbers 1 – 4. It is threatened by everyday situations and its holiness is endangered by humans.'

Comment

Nazirites are also encountered in Amos 2:11–12, as well as in the character of Samson (Judg. 13:5, 7; and possibly Samuel)[2] in the Old Testament. Refraining from wine appears in Amos, and not cutting one's hair also plays an important role in Judges. However, the understanding of 'Nazirite' in especially the texts about Samson is hard to reconcile with that of Numbers 6 in that Judges tells us that the divine messenger commands Samson's mother to abstain from wine *and unclean food* for Samson's Nazirite status. There is no mention of Samson taking this step, nor of him *choosing* to take a Nazirite vow. The specific contrast is that Samson (and Samuel) should be Nazirites for life, which contrasts with the limited time of such a commitment in Numbers 6. The characters in these stories appear unaware of or unconcerned with the regulations in Numbers 6, especially avoidance of contact with corpses. In the case of Samson, his complete lack of care for impurity seems intentionally highlighted in the construction of his character and the narrative. It is possible that these different biblical traditions on the Nazirite vow reflect different stages in the formulation of the vow. Also possible is that 'Nazirite', which literally means 'consecrate' or 'separate', could take on different connotations in different settings. This final option takes seriously the *wisdom* rather than *legal* nature of the biblical 'law' corpus (see Introduction, 'What is "biblical law"?'). Some similar-type rituals also appear in Acts 18:18; 21:23–26 (and the early Jewish book of 1 Macc. 3:49 from the second to first century BC).

1–2. This section (vv. 1–21) assumes that there was a practice of a vow of (self-) consecration already known to the Israelites receiving this instruction, and now this text attempts to regulate that practice. It *does not* provide information on *why* one might make such a vow.

The inclusion of both *men* and *women* in verse 2 makes this ritual practice the highest action that a woman or layman could take to dedicate themselves to Yahweh. The regulations mirror

---

those placed on priests, and even the high priest, though the time period is limited. Neither do the regulations admit the Nazirite to the sacred spaces of the sanctuary typically reserved for priests.

3–8. The nature of the *strong* or 'fermented' (NIV) drink (*šēkār*) remains uncertain. It may concern something like grappa or a grape-based liquor on one hand, or beer and grain-based alcohol on the other (a third possibility is mead, which comes from honey). The focus on grapes in this verse suggests that here it remains within the sphere of grape-based alcohol, though this may not be the case elsewhere. The abstinence from grape products stands out, given the location of these regulations in the wilderness narrative of Numbers. Grapes fit better in the sedentary agricultural environment of life in and on the land.

The emphasis on the hair (v. 5; cf. vv. 9, 18) may indicate a wordplay in Hebrew: *nezer* means crown, and this term is (often) written only with the same letters as the term 'Nazirite': n-z-r (vowels were not written in ancient Hebrew). The free-flowing hair (crown) was an important sign of the Nazirite's vow to be 'holy to Yahweh'. The Nazirite's hair may operate on an analogy to the high priest's golden plate (*ṣiṣ*), worn as a crown on his forehead and engraved with the expression 'holy to Yahweh' (Exod. 28:36, AT).

Not shaving one's head accords with, and emphasizes, the avoidance of defilement for the dead (Lev. 21:5). Thus, along with verses 6–12, this text emphasizes the importance of avoiding human corpses and the related mourning rituals. The defiling nature of a dead corpse appeared earlier in 5:2, which requires a person to dwell outside the camp for a week in order to avoid defiling the place where God dwells. The heightened sanctity of the consecrated (Nazirite) makes this issue more significant.

9–11. There is a mitigation ritual for when something goes wrong – when a Nazirite does happen (the Hebrew text emphasizes the unintentionality) to encounter a corpse. As Milgrom (1990: 46) notes, it is striking that the Nazirite must only come near (*nearby*; ESV: 'beside him') rather than *touch* a corpse to defile her- or himself, which sets them apart from other clean Israelites (19:11–12, 16).

The importance of the hair is underscored by the requirement to shave one's head at the end of the purification period (presumably the seventh day; cf. 19:11–12). Then a series of three types of offerings must take place in order for the Nazirite to restart their period of devotion: a purification offering, a burnt offering and a reparation offering. Instructions for performing these offerings appear in Leviticus 1 – 7, which one must have in mind to understand the regulations here. The offerings of the two birds follows Leviticus 14:30–31 (cf. 5:7–10),[3] and require a much smaller outlay than the de-consecration rites in verses 13–21 that follow. The purification offering in this case concerns the encroachment of death upon a consecrated person rather than some type of moral offence (Seebass 1993: 163). Like impurities caused by skin defilement, for example, it indicates that the contact with – or in this case, nearness to – a corpse defiles the sanctuary. It thus serves to purify the sanctuary from this opposition between death and God. The burnt bird offering may express the possibility of approaching God after the cleansing of the sanctuary. These two offerings together appear to reflect what counted as a major defilement (Nihan 2007: 170) and effect atonement for the person (for the meaning of atonement, see Introduction, 'Atonement and ritual').

12. Finally, there is the reparation offering (always offered for a private individual), which may function as the restoration to God of the loss of the consecrated person (Levine 1993: 223), with Leviticus 5:14–16 as the model, though the animal differs, perhaps indicating the special situation of the Nazirite (or a different temporal or geographic setting for the writing of Num. 6 from Lev. 5). At this point the person begins the period of their Nazirite vow again from the beginning.

13–21. Much like the similarity to the priests in the purity regulations during one's time as a Nazirite, the final section bears a number of similarities to some offerings related to priestly consecration, specifically the dedication of the first priests (Aaron and his sons) in Exodus 29 and Leviticus 8 – 9. It is striking, however, that these rituals have opposing ends: the priests are

---

3 While typically translated 'turtle-doves or pigeons', *tôr* more likely represents wild partridges (Altmann and Spiciarich 2020).

consecrated while the Nazirite ends their period of consecration. The fulfilment of this vow precipitates an expensive worship celebration. After the offerings that recognize the distinctions between God and humanity and stabilize that relationship (the burnt and purification offerings), a larger animal – a ram – constitutes the main dish of the offering shared between God, priest and Nazirite, and presumably other worshippers present at the sanctuary. Cakes and flatbread grain offerings, which also appear in Exodus 29 and Leviticus 8, show up here as an accompaniment along with a drink offering (see v. 3 above). These offerings are all presented to Yahweh (vv. 16–17), after which the preeminent sign of the Nazirite vow to be holy to Yahweh, the free-flowing hair, is shaved off and burned (v. 18). It serves as the concluding ritual of the vow.

The Nazirite then makes a bodily connection with the parts of the meat and grain of the shared offering feast that will become the holy portions belonging to the priest administrating the ritual – this time a shoulder after boiling (v. 19). This represents a larger portion than normal (cf. v. 20 and Lev. 7:30–32), indicating again the special nature of the Nazirite vow, which God and the community now celebrate together.

As discussed in the Introduction ('The different types of offerings'), the nature of the 'wave' or 'elevation' offering remains debated. In this context (v. 20), it clearly has something to do with presenting chosen elements to participants at the sanctuary before enjoying them. Drinking wine (v. 20) represents a major sign that the Nazirite has transitioned back to their normal state. The final regulation, *apart from what else they can afford*, in verse 21 highlights that the Nazirite puts on a succulent feast for the sanctuary personnel (priests and presumably Levites), and other worshippers present. As such, the concluding rites for the Nazirite vow of extraordinary consecration to Yahweh culminate in community enjoyment of the presence and blessing of Yahweh, who receives the presentation of various elements of the feast in verse 20.

v. The priestly blessing on the camp (6:22–27)

22–23. The section extending through Numbers 5 – 6 concludes here with the so-called Aaronic blessing, which is well known throughout Protestant churches due to its inclusion in the church liturgy by Luther (MacDonald 2012c). Interpreters have long questioned the positioning of this blessing at the end of Numbers 5 – 6. It connects closely with the association between the Nazirite vow and priestly features, as well as with the culmination of the Nazirite vow at the sanctuary by the offering altar, from where Aaron declares the blessing (Lev. 9:22).

Generally, the priests performed blessings (Lev. 9:22; Ps. 118:26), though in several instances kings (2 Sam. 6:18; 1 Kgs 8:14, 55) took on this role. However, there was overlap with common greetings as well (Ruth 2:4).

24–26. The text of the blessing itself contains three poetic lines of increasing length that repeat the divine name (Yahweh) for emphasis in each line. This repetition underscores that blessing comes from Yahweh, not somewhere else.

The opening line of verse 24 provides the two aspects of the trajectory – blessing and guarding – that are intertwined: there can be no continued blessing without protection from enemies. The subsequent two lines (vv. 25–26) expand these elements. There are numerous related texts throughout the Bible, especially in Psalms. Psalm 121 explores the ways that God 'keeps' or 'guards': from the sun, from evil and while on the way, while Psalm 67:1 combines God's graciousness, blessing and shining countenance in a different order. The importance of safety while travelling ('on the way') is one important aspect for the blessing's placement within Numbers, as part of preparation for the journey to Canaan (to begin in Num. 11).

The statement *make his face to shine upon you* in verse 25 (cf. Pss 31:16; 67:1; 80:3, 7, 19; 119:135) draws on solar imagery: Yahweh is (like) the sun, a metaphor also found in earlier Ancient Near Eastern cultures for a king denoting favour, which could also suggest protection (as in Ps. 119:132–135). The relation between light imagery and divine blessing towards Israel has a ritual sign in Numbers 8:1–3. Thus, the blessing fits the situation for when Israelites come as pilgrims before their divine king at the sanctuary (Chavel 2012: 19).

Lift up his countenance [or *face*] does not appear elsewhere, but its opposite ('hiding his face', e.g. Deut. 31:17) demonstrates that the expression here means showing favour or support.

As often discussed, *peace*, *šalôm* (v. 26), conveys more than merely absence of conflict, but rather wholeness, health and well-being. Its broad meaning makes it fitting as the summation of the blessing (Sakenfeld 1995: 45).

27. The expression *put my name on* is unique in the Old Testament for a person or people; it usually appears in relation to a sanctuary (e.g. Deut. 12:5) that Yahweh designates as the single chosen place for a temple. Given the fact that a very similar blessing appears on ancient amulets that people wore, the command *So they shall put my name on the Israelites* was understood as literally to *wear* the blessing. A similar command appears in Exodus 28:9–12, where the names of the Israelites are engraved on stones to be set into the garment Aaron puts on when entering the sanctuary (Smoak 2016: 76). However, no mention of an engraved stone (or amulet) appears in Numbers 6:27. Nevertheless, in this interpretation, just as the priests carried the Israelites' names before Yahweh, now Yahweh commands that they bear the name of God out into the world as his representatives (see Imes 2019).

In this way, this verse provides a climactic closing for the material in Numbers 5 – 6 and the spatial concerns about who can approach God's presence and what the divine presence intends to confer on them. The concluding clause of verse 27 therefore emphasizes, like the triple repetition of Yahweh in the blessing itself, that *Yahweh*, here *I*, does the blessing, and it takes place through the priests at the sanctuary (other texts in Numbers will indicate that it is borne by every Israelite as they live in the world). Divine blessing can be received and then dispersed if the Israelites deal appropriately with the natural (5:1–4; 6:9–12), economic (5:5–10) and marital (5:11–31) impurities that defile them, as well as when they commit themselves to holiness to Yahweh for which the priests, the high priest and the Nazirite are extraordinary models.

Meaning

As demonstrated through the overall structure of chapter 6, the zeal for separation to God exemplified in the Nazirite's special vow on top of guarding the personal and societal parameters for God's presence in Numbers 5 leads to the experience of

God's fruitful blessing and protection. These culminate in divine protection and the well-being of the community (*šalôm*).

The Nazirite regulations highlight the opportunity for *anyone* among God's people to take the initiative to dedicate themselves to God for a specific time or purpose. No-one is barred from worshipping (serving) Yahweh. Throughout the history of the church, this passage has served as a warrant for setting oneself aside for specific service, such as that of a nun or monk.

The rituals performed at the conclusion of the Nazirite's period of service show how the Nazirite's service should bring her or his community into enjoyable connection with God. While the vow is carried out individually, its benefits do not remain with the individual. Everyone present participates in a feast to God's honour.

The fact that a small amulet could contain a quite similar blessing to that of Numbers 6:24–26 around 600 BC indicates the treasured nature of these written words. Likewise, stepping back from the message *in* the text, the fact that the text in Numbers *writes* the words of the blessing itself (this is the only place where the OT contains the words that the priests used to bless) gives Numbers a link to this divine blessing. That is, Yahweh's blessing is *placed* (like God's name in v. 27) in the text. This fact renders reading Numbers itself an action infused with God's blessing. One no longer needs to go to a physical sanctuary to receive Yahweh's blessing through the mediation of a priest; instead, one can encounter it through reading. However, the fact that it is commanded that the priests bless the Israelites suggests an important role in the communal (rather than individual) conferring of blessing as it is recapitulated (rather than replaced) by Christian practice. The invitation that arises for us, given that all Christ's followers have priestly status, is to speak and distribute God's blessing in the world.

vi. Gifts and offerings from the tribes' chieftains for the dedication of the altar and the inauguration of the tabernacle's cultic service (7:1–89)

Context

Numbers 7 is the second longest chapter in the Old Testament after Psalm 119: but why? It returns the narrative to the moment in

Exodus 40:9–10, 17–33 (and perhaps preceding or coinciding with the events of Lev. 8 – 9) when Moses has finished God's earthly house, a passage which does not, however, report the commanded anointing of the tabernacle found here in Numbers 7:1. In response the tribal leaders demonstrate their loyalty to the divine ruler by bringing gifts. Furthermore, a number of these gifts have the express purpose of rendering it possible for God's presence to remain among them as they travel through the wilderness. In other words, the long list of offerings in this chapter underscores loyalty and gratitude overflowing into concrete gifts allied with the importance of having 'God with us' for the Israelites wherever they go, similar to the culmination of the Nazirite vow with a feast in the previous chapter.

This report does not comment on Yahweh's overwhelming glory filling the tabernacle on that day (Exod. 40:34–35), but rather the appropriate human response to God taking up residence among humans.

The chapter splits into two sections: verses 1–9 report the gift of the wagons and oxen, while the bulk of the chapter (vv. 10–88) recounts the gifts from each leader. The concluding verse (v. 89) changes to the successful result of Moses hearing from God in the tabernacle. The long, virtually identical lists of what each leader offered constitute an administrative record, quite similar to others found in temples from the Ancient Near East.

Comment

1–5. The date given even precedes the events of 1:1, 18. Thus, these events take place *after* the first day of the first month of the second year after leaving Egypt. However, the census or enrolment mentioned in verse 2 (along with the allotment of wagons to specific groups of Levites in vv. 7–9) presupposes – or perhaps better, correlates with – the events that take place in Numbers 1 – 4.

In contrast to Exodus 40, which emphasizes *Moses'* obedience to the divine command to build the tabernacle, and to Leviticus 8 – 9, which focuses on the *priestly* initiation, this chapter retells the events with the spotlight on the *tribal leaders'* contribution, creating 'an envelope structure around the entire discussion of the tent of meeting' (Feldman 2020: 133). Reading these sections together offers a richly overlaid description of the multiple important parts that make up the divine–human interaction in worship and the sociopolitical organization of the cultic community. Impressionistic overlaying takes priority over logical consistency. The return to the glorious day of God's indwelling of the tabernacle takes the Israelites back to what needs to be the focus when they head out on their journey through the wilderness: God's presence with them.

In both sections (vv. 2–9 and vv. 10–88) the leaders contribute the exact same amounts regardless of their tribes' size or standing within the overall community. They bring their gifts in the same order in which they will march (cf. 10:11–28). Thus, the support and benefit of the sanctuary belong equally to each tribe. It shows the difference in the understanding of the community in that only the tribal leaders rather than every family or even every individual bring an offering. The community is not conceived as a collection of individuals, but rather as a collection of tribes (consisting of other smaller groupings). The significance (and thus the length) of this provision for the basic needs that enable transport and the implementation of sanctuary worship emerges when seen in comparison with the means of provision for other sanctuaries in the Ancient Near East. Especially central sanctuaries were provided for by the kings (cf. 1 Kgs 8:62–65; Ezra 7:14–22). More like the continuing instructions of Deuteronomy 12:13–19, though in this case it is tribal leaders rather than heads of households, the responsibility falls to a somewhat larger group that takes a royal function here.

No divine command appears (v. 2) to bring either the wagons and oxen on the one hand, or the various dishes and edible products on the other (v. 10). The initiative for these offerings apparently lies in the observation of the leaders of a need for these gifts and their desire to meet that need – a so-called free-will offering, similar to the voluntary character of the Nazirite vow, though the text does not identify it as such. They provide the concrete means for transporting God's home with them.

Also important in the narrative progression, as the medieval French Jewish commentator Rashi (1999: 69) highlights, these leaders are likely the same ones who underwent beatings by Pharaoh's foremen (Exod. 5:14) and thus embody the move from slavery and oppression to liberation and royalty.

In verse 3, a philological difficulty arises with the term *ṣāb*, translated *covered* (NRSV, NASB 1995, NIV), following the Greek Septuagint for describing the wagons or carts. It otherwise appears only in Isaiah 66:20, where various English versions correctly translate 'wagons' or 'litters'. Perhaps the term became unclear, so a scribe glossed with *'eglôt*, another term for 'wagons'.

6–9. The apportionment of the wagons coincides with the tasks of transporting the different elements of the tabernacle assigned to the three Levite clans in Numbers 4. The Merarites are tasked with the heaviest portions, the structure of the tent itself, so they receive four carts (and four pairs of oxen). The Gershonites should transport the curtains, screens and coverings, for which they will have two carts. As a result, while the gifts are brought equally by the twelve tribes in spite of their different sizes (cf. Num. 1), the Levite clans are apportioned them primarily according to the weight or bulkiness of the items they are tasked to transport.

In contrast, the Kohathites must carry the especially holy items by hand (v. 9). Thus, what marks the difference for their task is not (necessarily) the size of the items, but rather their distinctive status. While not explicitly stated, the need to carry, for example, the ark may provide a partial explanation for God striking Uzzah for stabilizing the ark when it was carried on a wagon in 2 Samuel 6:6 (other factors, such as Uzzah not being a Levite, may also have played a role).

10–11. A new section begins with the leaders again initiating the bringing of gifts, but this time for the dedication specifically of the altar. Unlike in the previous section, Yahweh commands a modification to their offerings, expanding the time period to twelve days, with each day reserved for the presentation of the offering by one tribal leader. Such accounting lists of offerings (or taxes, tribute or the like) are well known from every period of Ancient Near Eastern history, especially from Mesopotamia (cf. Hallo 2003 for one example). They are also found in Ugarit (northern Syria; fifteenth to thirteenth centuries BC).

12–83. Given that the events of the chapter last for twelve days, how do they overlap with the Sabbath? Bound up with this is the question of the general purpose of each type of offering (purification, burnt, shared feast; see Introduction, 'The different types of offerings') and the striking order in which they appear in the leaders' presentations. It is uncommon for the *burnt* offering to precede the *purification* offering (contra Stubbs 2009: 86) – that is, if the offerings are listed in the order they are sacrificed (cf. Lev. 8 – 9). One possibility is that the special initiatory nature of this event called for a different order. A second interpretation is that the order of the offerings changed over time, and the order was different at the time of the composition of Numbers 7 from that of other biblical texts (e.g. 6:16–17; Lev. 8 – 9). This explanation draws on the support that this chapter could very well fit after Exodus 40, but instead appears here. Finally, perhaps the list accords with temple archive accounts from the broader Ancient Near East that may not have the order of offerings in mind, and, therefore, the offerings did not necessarily take place during these twelve days (there is no report of their slaughter, etc.). Instead, the dishes, basins, flour, incense and animals are transferred into the ownership of the temple personnel for *later* public sacrifice. As noted by Milgrom (1990: 363), this explains the absence of the reparation offering (see 5:5–10), which was a *private* offering rather than for the community at large. Rainey (1970: 491) insightfully argues that the list here instead presents an administrative order '(1) to credit the offerers and (2) to keep track of the treasures and supplies coming in'.

With hardly any variation, verses 12–83 report that each tribal leader brings the same gifts (see the presentation in the Good News Translation, which summarizes these verses similarly):

- a silver dish (1.5 kg = 3.3 lb) filled with high-quality flour and oil;
- a silver basin filled with high-quality flour and oil (0.8 kg = 1.75 lb; these two are the grain offering);
- a gold bowl or ladle filled with incense (0.11 kg = 4 oz);
- animals for the burnt offering;
- 1 animal for the purification offering;
- 17 animals for the shared offering feast.

84–88. A summary of all gifts is presented. The section as a whole presents something akin to an accountant's spreadsheet, complete with the total sums. As with the materials necessary for the construction of the tabernacle as a whole, the narrative shows no interest in the *source* of these riches for a group of former slaves. One possible answer lies in the plundering of the Egyptians by their former captives in Exodus 12:35–36.

In one small change from the list of gifts from each day, the totals count the flour of the grain offering as belonging to the burnt offerings, which is in line with the requirement found in 15:3–12 (cf. Ezek. 45), though it does not include the same regulation for the shared offering feast (it should be noted that 15:2 states that these regulations become operative *in the land*).

89. This final verse is somewhat awkward in that the account of the offerings seems to close in verse 88. Considerable unclarity remains on a couple of points in this verse: (1) how it relates to the prior and following sections, and (2) whether it concerns a one-time or a repeated action.

With regard to the first question, the inclusion of this material here recapitulates the events of Exodus 40 (also Num. 9:15), but not with an emphasis on the overwhelming divine glory that kept Moses from entering the tabernacle. Rather, in relation to question 2, the verse serves as the report of a narrative consequence of the tribal leaders' generous and voluntary gifts: Moses entering and hearing God's voice (here literally *the voice*). The text places emphasis on the origin of the voice from above the covering of the ark between the cherubim (functioning as a partial fulfilment of Exod. 25:22). This is a sure sign that God accepts the gifts and dwells with the Israelites.

As often noted, the cherubim represent powerful gatekeepers or doormen (like bouncers at a nightclub) that protect the Holy of Holies from unacceptable intrusion. The Old Testament understanding of these figures is based on the imposing Mesopotamian *lamassu* or Egyptian sphinx – hybrid lions or bulls with wings – who guard the entrances to palaces, throne rooms and the boundaries between earth and heaven (Gen. 3:24; 1 Kgs 6:29, 32, 35; Ps. 99:1; Ezek. 28:14, 16; see Staubli 2012). Sphinxes also form the design of royal thrones in Canaan, like the one illustrated on a slip of ivory found in Late Bronze Age Megiddo, c.1200 BC.

The question of the one-time versus repeated revelation rests on the translation of the verb 'he heard' (e.g. NIV), which, grammatically speaking, represents a singular event. However, given its reference back to Exodus 25:22, which concerns repeated action, here it indicates the *first* instance of the fulfilment of Moses receiving new revelation. The Hebrew text 'and he heard [the voice] converse to/with him' only otherwise appears in Ezekiel 2:2; 43:6 and concerns God commissioning Ezekiel to speak the divine word. Thus, the sanctuary intends not only to function as a place of sacrifices and offerings to honour, restore and enjoy the holy order that makes God's presence possible; it also points forward to future possibilities of God's guidance (Sakenfeld 1995: 49).

The mention of the voice also points away from Moses and the elders *seeing* God in Exodus 24:9–11 (cf. Num. 12:8 for God speaking *face to face* with Moses, which is vaguer) and is more in line with the emphasis of Deuteronomy 4:12–19 (though these verses concern the Israelites hearing God's voice from the fire on Sinai) that they should not make an image of God.

Meaning

The return to the glorious day of God's indwelling, as the date in 7:1 sets out, suggests that there are reasons for followers of God to remember – and to remember divergent aspects at different times – the foundational events of God's appearances in the biblical story (e.g. the exodus in Exodus 1 – 15 and many psalms, Jesus' incarnation in the Gospels, and the beginnings of the church in Acts 2; 4). While not 'anything goes', God's theophanies or 'special manifestations' have a variety of impacts. In this case, 7:2–9 concentrates on the leaders' concern to provide for the practical means to move God's tent with them on the way towards Canaan.

The chapter presents a challenge to modern Westerners and others who tend to identify themselves as individuals. In this section, the community *as a whole* is represented by the actions of its tribal leaders. This perspective invites individuals to commit to a community and allow the group and its contribution to take on a more important role as reflected in the notion of the corporate nature of Christ's body described by Paul (e.g. Rom. 12; 1 Cor. 12), which also draws on the language of sacrifice in Romans 12:1.

The major question coming from this chapter for modern readers is *why include such repetitive detail?* The short answer is to show the consistent and thoroughgoing generosity of *every* tribal leader in *equal* manner in Israel at this time (Wenham 1981: 93). The chapter intends to call forth similar patterns of provision from God's people in which worship and community well-being are intertwined as a whole experience and not as two separate domains. As Matthew records Jesus stating in the Sermon on the Mount, 'For where your treasure is, there your heart will be also' (Matt. 6:21). Second, when considering that these were Israelite leaders who had suffered and experienced deliverance in and from Egypt, their gratitude at relief from that situation overflows in their practical support of the sanctuary to guarantee God taking up residence with them. The challenge today lies in considering one's (or one's community's) practical, financial response to God's act of taking up residence among us (individually and collectively). The character of this community, of course, goes way beyond our local churches and envisions our broader communal life in different contexts. The multifaceted (Exod. 40; Lev. 8 – 9; Num. 7) event of God's indwelling has space for active participation for God, the community, its representative leaders, and individuals.

And as the wagons and other gifts, as well as the initial speaking of God to Moses in 7:89, indicate, the great experiences of God taking up residence with us are not meant to simply remain past memories: God intends to 'move with us' through our lives (our wilderness), continue speaking and dispense blessings.

vii. Arrangement of the lampstand and the direction of its light (8:1–4)

Context

Numbers 8 begins where 7:89 leaves off: in the tabernacle. However, rather than concern with the *voice* of God over the ark, located in the Holy of Holies, verses 1–4 address the light shining forth from the lampstand – the Menorah. Its location in the tabernacle is one step removed from the ark, outside the curtain in the holy place (see Figure 1.2 above, p. 96). It was discussed earlier in Exodus 25:31–40, so new here is the execution of God's instruction to put it to use.

Verses 5–26 move out a step further. These verses pick up on Numbers 3 – 4 (esp. 3:5–13), which describe the separation of the Levites, and from them the Aaronides as priests. Mostly what is new here, just as in verses 1–4, is the enactment of the previously given instructions. Both sections thus pick up on divine instructions that, being fulfilled here, prepare the Israelites to set out on their journey to the Promised Land (Olson 2012: 48).

There is also a connection to the narrative material in Numbers 16, which narrates the challenge of Korah, a Levite from the Kohathite clan (along with non-Levites), to Aaron's leadership (and that of Moses as well). As a result, it is clear that the book as a whole shows considerable concern for questions of leadership and hierarchy.

Comment

1–4. An understanding of these verses requires familiarity with Exodus 25:31–40 together with 37:17–24, and with Exodus 27:20–21 together with Leviticus 24:1–4. The first two texts describe the form and materials of the lampstand while the second set addresses its lighting. In each case, the first text contains God's commands and the second the human fulfilment. Several foundational details can be gleaned from these texts: the lampstand takes the form of a 'tree of light'. A number of the terms used to describe its various parts in Exodus 25 come from the world of plants, such as branch/cane, calyx, almond blossom, flower/lily and (thickened) shaft (Meyers 1976: 19–26). Thus, as with so many of the texts in this book, it is only through reading cross-sectionally, so to speak, that the meaning can emerge.

The repeated interest in the lampstand in the Pentateuch points to its importance as part of the tabernacle furniture. Only for the lampstand and its appurtenances, among all the furnishings in the tabernacle, is Moses twice instructed to make it *according to the pattern that [Yahweh] had shown* (v. 4; cf. Exod. 25:40). This significance begins on the practical level: it provides the light necessary to perform other tasks in the tent (Exod. 27:20–21 and Lev. 24:1–4 have the lamps lit all night). There should never be a time when there is no light in the tabernacle: natural light by day, and the lamplight by night. Furthermore, the tree-form of the lampstand also draws on a long history of religious symbolism from the Ancient Near East of a tree as a symbol of divine abundance and permanence (cf. Gen. 3:22, 24). This symbolism gained a specific ideology as a form of the 'cosmic tree' represented in New-Assyrian royal gardens and iconography (see Bauks 2012; Porter 2003). In a number of instances in other cultures, the tree is combined with solar significance (Meyers 1976: 120–121). As a stylized tree, the menorah does not embody one particular type of tree, but rather indicates divine presence. God and divine messengers often appear by trees (Gen. 18:1; Judg. 6:11), and in Zechariah's dream, the lamps are interpreted as God's eyes (Zech. 4:2, 10).

Besides providing light, the main concern is the *direction* of the light coming from the lamps (vv. 2–3) and that *Aaron* carried out the instruction (v. 3). This recalls the Aaronic blessing (6:22–27). The action is carried out by Aaron, and God *make[s] his face to shine* (6:25): in this case, the light shines on the twelve loaves of bread on the offering table corresponding to the twelve tribes of Israel (Exod. 40:22–25; Lev. 24:5). While speculative, this provides an explanation for the inclusion of this text here: God's presence and abundance shine forth towards the bread (offering) of the twelve tribes, which are represented by their tribal leaders in Numbers 7.

viii. Purification and consecration of the Levites (8:5–22)

5–19. A new section narrates the purification and separation of the Levites for service at the tabernacle sanctuary. As such, it picks up on Numbers 3 – 4, which is now coming into practice, and it contrasts with the initiation rites for the priests in Leviticus 8 – 9. After the introduction in verse 5, instructions are given in verses 6–19, while they are carried out in verses 20–22, with an appendix in verses 23–26.

The instructions describe a complex commissioning rite with actions carried out by Moses, Aaron, the Israelite congregation and the Levites themselves. Part of the intertwining of actors (especially between Moses, Aaron and Aaron's sons) may result from the fact that while the chapter reports a *one-time* event in the narrative of the book, it was probably envisioned as, or grew to become, a continuing guide for practice in later years, when other Levite men reached the age of service.

First, in preparation, *Moses* sprinkles them with the water of purification, and the *Levites* shave their entire bodies and wash their clothes. Shaving all one's hair as a rite of purification appears in Leviticus 13:33–34; 14:8–9 alongside washing clothes, though in those cases it relates to skin defilement. Shaving alone as a sign of consecration, thus more akin to what takes place here, is found for the Nazirite in Numbers 6:18–19, but only of one's head. Washing one's clothes is more widespread (Lev. 11:25, 28, 40; 13:6; 15:5–13, 21–22, 27). However, a specific 'water of purification' appears elsewhere only in Numbers 19, though the underlying Hebrew term is different, and there it is sprinkled on people who have had contact with a corpse as part of their purification process. Therefore, the two should be differentiated (Levine 1993: 274). In contrast, Leviticus 8 reports the priests being anointed with oil, sprinkled with blood and receiving special clothing. In Leviticus 8:12, the priest (Aaron) is 'consecrated', while in Numbers 8:6–7 the Levites are 'cleansed' or 'purified', and in verse 11 they are 'presented' or 'brought near', as an offering.

Second, after the preparation, the *Levites* prepare a bull for a burnt offering and its accompanying grain and oil, and *Moses* prepares a second one for their purification offering (v. 8). The purification offering in this case clearly has little to do with sin that has been committed (for more discussion of the offering types, see Introduction, 'The different types of offerings').

The *third* phase of their initiation consists of *Moses* bringing them near or 'presenting' them (vv. 9–10, NLT and NASB 1995) – the language suggests that the Levites are an offering – before the tabernacle and gathering the entire Israelite congregation there. The *Israelites* place their hands upon the Levites.

The practice of laying on of hands appears twice in this section, in verses 10, 12: the Israelites lay hands on the Levites in the fifth phase, then the Levites lay hands on the bulls' heads after Aaron has presented them as an *elevation* or 'wave' offering (v. 11; see below for comment). With regard to the laying on of the hand, it is fundamentally important to note that a symbolic gesture need not always communicate the same meaning. A gesture can (1) mean different things to different people practising it at the same time, (2) change in its meaning over time or (3) indicate different meanings in different rituals or different parts of rituals. And more than one of these factors can be at play at any one time – it can be complicated!

Such caution is necessary even in this section. Interpreters frequently turn to Leviticus 16:21–22, where Aaron lays both his hands on a goat sent out into the wilderness, to explain the meaning of this gesture, throughout the Old Testament, as signifying the transfer of sin to the animal. While such an explanation fits well for Leviticus 16, this ritual practice differs significantly from other offering settings (e.g. Exod. 29:10; Lev. 1:4; 3:2; 4:4; 8:14). It especially cannot account for the settings where the gesture takes place for a shared festive offering (Lev. 3; see Rendtorff 2004: 40, 43). A more appropriate generalized meaning is that it stands for the appointing to a specific role or status the object on which the hands are laid (see Calabro 2017). Within this general meaning, it is possible to consider the gesture as necessary to affirm the ownership of the animal (Milgrom 1991: 122; Rendtorff 2004: 44), which fits best for verse 12.

It can also signal a transfer of authority in some cases (Num. 27:18; Deut. 34:9), which is likely the case here in verse 10 (Rendtorff 2004: 34). The Levites have the authority to act on behalf of the people as a whole as commissioned sanctuary personnel. In any case, one should not lose the analogy between the Levites and the sacrificial offering that is established in the way the text constructs the ritual.

The *fourth* phase takes place in verse 11 (cf. v. 13), which uses a seemingly odd action: '*Aaron* is to present the Levites before the LORD as a wave offering' (NIV), which calls into question just what a 'wave offering' might be. First, one might understand it more properly as an *elevation* offering; that is, the priest lifts up the offering, making it visible to the witnesses that this specific portion is being consecrated and it becomes God's (Milgrom 1972: 35–36). As noted by many interpreters, Aaron could not literally have carried out this action with the thousands of Levite men, but the whole ritual is made public so that the consecration of the Levites is witnessed by the community. This impracticality seems to be addressed in verse 13, whereby the Levites stand before Aaron and his sons (the priests), which could also point to the way the commissioning was conceived as taking place with subsequent Levites as well. This is the only place where humans are the elevation offering.

In the *fifth* phase (v. 12), the *Levites* make their ownership of the bulls known through laying on a hand, and then the two are offered. The verse states that the two offerings (burnt and purification) together *make atonement* (NIV, NRSV; *lĕkappēr*) for the Levites. In this case, the atonement focuses on an action at the altar, rendering the space pure so that God's presence can be manifest and encountered there. However, the effect of atonement here also results in the Levites belonging to Yahweh in a special way (v. 14), *separate . . . from among the other Israelites*, which returns to the overarching instruction in verse 6. Their separation related specifically to sanctuary service (vv. 15, 17, 19), and the instructions are further summarized in verse 15. In this ritual, atonement can be envisioned as a form of attunement between God, the sanctuary and all participants who make up the cultic community.

According to verses 16–17, Yahweh emphatically claims the right to the Levites as a special possession based on their replacement for *all* firstborn males (cf. Exod. 13:2; 34:19–20; Deut. 15:19–23): human and animal among the Israelites as a result of God's striking of all the firstborn males of Egypt. In a related explanation, the purpose of the separation of the Levites in verse 19 is *to make atonement for* them (*lĕkappēr*), which is better rendered here as to 'ransom' them, so that no plague will break out against the Israelites when they approach the sanctuary. A similar connection between a form of the root *k-p-r* 'atonement' or 'ransom' restraining a plague appears in Exodus 30:11–16. The firstborn of the other tribes are 'redeemed' or 'ransomed' through the separation of the Levite men (Milgrom 1990: 370; Levine 1993: 277; Sklar 2015: 52–53).

The mention of *plague* here just after recalling the plague against the firstborn of Egypt explains how the Levites function as a buffer like the blood on the doorways before the first Passover in Exodus 11:4–5; 12:7, 12–13, which keeps God from striking. (The same literal wording appears in Exod. 12:13 except for 'you' rather than 'the Israelites': 'and a plague will not be among *you*' / Num. 8:20: 'and there will not be a plague among *the Israelites*'.) However, here the goal is for the Israelites to be able to come near the sanctuary – in other words, for God and the people to reside in close proximity to one another without death breaking out among the people. Furthermore, as noted by Stubbs (2009: 98), the Levites thereby act as a continuing reminder of God's deliverance of them from Egypt.

In contrast to the depiction of the Levites in Deuteronomy, where priests are all described as 'levitical priests' (18:1: NRSV, NIV, ESV, etc.), Numbers makes a stark distinction between Aaron and his sons as priests, and the Levites as a whole (Num. 3 – 4). In verse 19, a hierarchical relationship comes into force, whereby the Levites are given to Aaron as servants. The contrast in their positions also becomes evident through a comparison of their respective initiation rites: the priests receive special clothing and are anointed with oil (Lev. 8:7–13).

20–22. Moses, Aaron, the Levites and the congregation carry out the instructions. The text does not report their shaving nor the two offerings specifically, though it states that they did all that Yahweh commanded (v. 20). Moses, Aaron and the congregation are the subjects in verse 20, emphasizing their action and the Levites' role as the object, while the Levites themselves become actors (and thus representatives of the congregation) in verses 21–22. This enactment is essential within the story because it brings the Israelites one step closer to setting out on their journey (the celebration of Passover in 9:1–14 and making of the trumpets in 10:1–10 remain).

ix. Working age of the Levites (8:23–26)

23–26. The final verses of the chapter provide a supplement defining the age limits for Levites performing the work in the sanctuary: they start at age twenty-five and finish at fifty. The intent of verse 26 is ambiguous. It is unclear whether it concerns Levites over fifty, who may help out their fellow Levites, not by doing the work but by keeping watch (or guard), or if it is a summary statement of the role of the Levites in relation to the priests: that is, they assist their *priestly* brothers and guard the area (Seebass 1993: 220), but they do not carry out *priestly* service (Olson 2012: 50).

In any case, the starting age of twenty-five represents a change from the starting age of thirty that appears in 4:46–47 (note also their starting age of twenty in 1 Chr. 23:27; 2 Chr. 31:17; Ezra 3:8 for service in the Jerusalem temple). It appears that the editors of Numbers felt it more important to include traditions from different times or places in ancient Israel than to follow a logic of noncontradiction on this minor point.

Meaning

How does one articulate the meaning of rituals and symbols with words? This challenge arises in the discussion of the specific placement of the lamps on the lampstand. If anything, it points to the *power* of physical objects that contain a significance eluding description. Calvin seems to indicate this idea by placing this section in the exposition of the second commandment ('make no image'), yet a tree-like lampstand could communicate God's presence in an acceptable manner, for 'God is light and in him there is no darkness at all' (1 John 1:5). The divine light explicitly intends to point to a very specific manifestation of the divine presence in the twelve loaves of bread as representations of God's material blessing to nourish the life of Israel. Thus, some physical signs of God's presence *are* commendable, as long as they do not usurp humanity's role as God's image (Gen. 1:26–28), ultimately fulfilled by the perfect image of God in human form: Jesus (Col. 1:15).

The initiation of the Levites describes a necessary step for those dedicated for a special kind of service. One can make a New Testament parallel with the roles of deacons, separated by the community through the apostles' laying hands on them so that they could 'wait at tables' (Acts 6:1–7; 1 Tim. 3:8–13). Both for Israel and the early churches, such dedication of specific individuals or a specific group envisions a larger community that trusts and submits to those dedicated taking on the assigned role.

Furthermore, the differences between the priests and the Levites conceive of a hierarchy that contrasts with the idealized flat and democratic organizational models in the West. It can still, however, maintain a two-way responsibility that avoids the retention of power in the hands of one sole group. As a whole, it raises the larger question for the people of faith of how they relate to one another as an organization or as an organism.

A focus on the Levites renders evaluations of organizational (church) structure more fluid because the Levites' role changes considerably throughout the period and texts of the Old Testament. According to Deuteronomy (cf. Deut. 18:1–8) they function as priests. They are demoted in the vision of Ezekiel (Ezek. 44:10–14) and serve as temple assistants (also 1 Chr. 23). They serve as guards and porters in Numbers (Num. 4) and as teachers and prophets (1 Chr. 25:1–5; 2 Chr. 17:7–9; 20:14; 35:3). Finally, the dedication of Levite *men* highlights a further issue confronting churches: this ancient model emerges from a strongly patriarchal society: how might this be different today?

x. Instruction for the celebration of the Passover with accommodation for a second date (9:1–14)

Context

Numbers 9 contains two separate topics: the deferred or second Passover (vv. 1–14), and the description of the cloud/fire covering the tabernacle that determined when the Israelites set up and broke camp on their journey (vv. 15–23). Both, in their own way, begin transitioning the narrative of the book from its time of preparation to leaving Sinai, which takes place in 10:11. These two sections are both remarkable, but for different reasons.

The former (vv. 1–14) presents an important and often overlooked discussion on the central celebration for the Israelites that solidified their identity as part of God's people and provides insight for how the Bible interprets its own texts for later application. It is one of a series of laws issued in response to a specific event (cf. Lev. 24:10–23; Num. 15:32–36; 27:1–11 and 36:1–12). In this case, a group of Israelites approach Moses asking that a special exception be made so they can celebrate the Passover, for not celebrating the Passover would mean that they would be cut off from the Israelite community. Furthermore, mentions of Passover often mark significant developments in the Israelite story, coming at the exodus (Exod. 12), here marking God's indwelling of the tabernacle and leaving Sinai, in Joshua 5 when the Israelites cross into the Promised Land, at the completion of the second temple of Jerusalem in Ezra 6, and in the New Testament, of Jesus' inauguration of a new era in Matthew 26; Luke 22.

The latter section (vv. 15–23) has been popular throughout Christian history as an image of God's leading and presence with God's people through difficult times and places. God's presence in this form guides the Israelites through the wilderness as a cloud by day and *the appearance* of fire by night, situated over the tabernacle. When the cloud lifted, the Israelites broke camp. When it stopped, the Israelites set up camp – for as long as the cloud remained. This section is important in terms of the book's structure in that it begins the transition (completed in 10:11) from Israel's preparation to its setting out on the journey.

Comment

The background of Passover is quite complex within the Pentateuch especially and the Old Testament more broadly. According to Exodus 12, describing the first Passover in Egypt the night before the Israelites leave, it was to take place in individual homes. Deuteronomy 16:1–8 instead mandates celebrating the future Passover in the land of Israel at the central sanctuary. Other Passover regulations appear in Leviticus 23:5–8 and Numbers 28:16–25. As in much of the book of Numbers, comparing Numbers 9 with these other treatments highlights the important concerns of this text. In particular, Numbers 9 addresses two circumstances that do not appear elsewhere regarding the Passover that could disqualify a person from being able to participate in the celebration: (1) accidental impurity resulting from contact with a dead body (v. 6) and (2) being distant from home (v. 10).

The regulations for the 'second' or 'deferred Passover' assume that one is familiar with the narrative of the first Passover in parts of Exodus 12 (vv. 2–11, 21–27 and 43–49) and likely also Leviticus 23:5–8 (see also the discussion of Num. 28:16–25). In fact, Numbers 9:1–14 adopts several specific phrases and ideas from Exodus 12:

- celebrating in the late afternoon on the fourteenth day of the first month (v. 3; Exod. 12:6);
- eating it with unleavened bread and bitter herbs (v. 11; Exod. 12:8);
- leaving no leftovers (v. 12; Exod. 12:10);
- breaking no bones (v. 12; Exod. 12:46);
- one regulation for Israelites and resident foreigners (v. 14; Exod. 12:49).

However, none of these topics forms the focus for this section, which instead responds to a problem that arises in this later (second) Passover celebration.

As a whole the section splits into three parts: verses 1–5, 6–8 and 9–14.

1–5. Reading chronologically, verse 1 surprises by providing a date that agrees with Numbers 7 for these events. The date reaches back *before* the events of Numbers 1 – 6, which 1:1 places on the first day of the *second* month of the second year after leaving Egypt, while here the events take place in the *first* month of the second year. This date alerts the reader to the importance of the dates in this section, and specifically of an event to take place *after* the first day of the second month. It is also understandable that the date of the *first* month appears here, because that is when Passover should take place (see Exod. 12:2). These verses, especially verses 2, 4–5, highlight a common cadence in the Priestly material: God commands something to Moses, Moses relays it to the Israelites, and then the Israelites carry it out: *Just as the LORD had commanded Moses, so the Israelites did* (see, e.g., Kellermann 1970: 130).

It should be noted that this passage does not mention the *location* of the Passover celebration: should households eat it in their tents, keeping with the rules set out in Exodus 12:7, or rather at the tabernacle, following Leviticus 17:2–7; 23:7–8 (and in keeping with Deut. 16:1–8)? The issue is perhaps of minor relevance for the immediate setting of Numbers 9 in the wilderness because the

Israelite dwellings remain quite close to the tabernacle. However, this text has a horizon beyond its narrative setting, as the concerns of being 'on a distant way' (v. 10, AT) and comparison with Passover regulations elsewhere in the Bible indicate.

6–8. These verses narrate an exception from verse 5, 'everything that Yahweh commanded Moses, so the Israelites did'. In fact, some Israelites had been unable to carry out the celebration due to factors beyond their control – impurity from handling a corpse (cf. Lev. 22:5; Num. 5:2; 6; 19:13). Nothing has appeared prior to this point on impurity disqualifying someone from Passover celebration, so this regulation must be deduced from similar regulations (cf. Lev. 7:19–21). Yet it makes sense to place this issue here because Moses and the Israelites have set up the tabernacle (Exod. 40:2, 17–33; Num. 7:1) and consecrated its personnel – the priests and Levites (Lev. 8 – 9; Num. 8), which included their purification. Therefore, whether the Passover was celebrated at the tents of each Israelite household or at the central sanctuary, the purity requirement indicates a high level of the divine presence in that space. Furthermore, the language in verses 6–8 uses offering terminology: the verb *q-r-b* ('draw, bring near') and the related noun form *qorbān* ('offering'). The Passover is not viewed as an offering in Exodus 12; however, it has become one through its intertwining with the Festival of Unleavened Bread in Deuteronomy 16:1–8 (without this terminology) and in Leviticus 23:4–8.

The choice of this issue is important because it treats a case in which the individuals do not commit wilful sin or impurity. It is simply something that happened to them, but nonetheless celebration of Passover requires that the Israelites take special precautions in order to avoid exclusion from the Israelite community (vv. 7, 13, or worse, cf. Lev. 10). Though no fault of their own, delaying one of the most important celebrations in Israel's liturgical year was not a small issue. Similarly, an earlier Hittite directive to temple personnel (Chavel 2014: 105; cf. 'Instructions for Temple Officials', §9 in *COS* 1.219) rejects delaying celebration of a ritual celebration for any reason. The fact that Yahweh concedes to the needs of a small group of Israelites shows extraordinary leniency. This is especially true considering that the celebration of Passover determines when Israel will leave Sinai. Yahweh and consequently all Israel must adjust their departure for the Promised Land to not leave behind those who cannot participate in the Passover on the prescribed date.

On a comparative note, the celebration of Passover a month late also appears in 2 Chronicles 30, when King Hezekiah of Judah invites the residents of the former Northern Kingdom of Israel to celebrate a unified Passover, even though the Northern Kingdom had previously been conquered by the Assyrians, largely being resettled by non-Israelites. Issues of impurity pose a problem in that text also, but the reason and the solution are quite different. In 2 Chronicles 30, many of the priests were unclean due to their laxity. And the people do not take measures to ensure their purity, yet Hezekiah's prayer on their behalf brings about God's acceptance of their celebration (vv. 17–20). This action is more in line with Greek changes to the calendar for political or military reasons for events that leaders found too important to omit (Chavel 2014: 152).

In Numbers 9:6–8, the *people affected* take the initiative (*they came before Moses and Aaron*). Furthermore, though he does not play a role elsewhere in the section, Aaron's presence as the representative of the continuing priestly authority (Moses does not have a successor in the same way) indicates that the priests would continue to be available for such issues when they arose in the future.

9–12. Yahweh's reply to Moses concerns not only the specific issue at hand of corpse uncleanliness, but also, going beyond the immediate problem, if someone is far away during the first month when Passover should be celebrated. For both cases verses 11–12 set out *when* and *how* those inhibited from keeping the regulations during the first month should celebrate it. Most important for this passage is that they do it during the *second* month on the fourteenth day, exactly one month later. As in Exodus 12:8–10, 46, no bone shall be broken, which ensures that the meat will not be boiled in a pot, which would require breaking the bones in order to fit the cuts of meat into the vessel. It similarly should be consumed along with bitter herbs and unleavened bread, and there should be no leftovers. Therefore, the celebration significantly mirrors that of Exodus 12, but without indicating specifically *where* it takes place.

While the men's impurity makes sense in the narrative setting, more difficult to explain in the present literary context is the exception made for those far away. At this point in time, the Israelites all camp together around the tabernacle – and no-one asks about this exemption. It has a later time in mind. As such, this points to its writing at a later time when members of God's people either *travelled* to distant locations or *lived* at a distance from the sanctuary. While Sakenfeld (1995: 55–56) notes that the text still leaves some concerns unaddressed, such as a woman's uncleanness due to menstruation or childbirth, the specific cases addressed here, impurity by corpse and travel, function as guidance on how to deal with other cases. The purpose is to teach wisdom in how to fulfil the divine instruction in situations not envisioned by the commandments.

13–14. The final verses highlight two ground rules for Passover that address how one joins and becomes excluded from Israel. The celebration of the feast is not optional for 'Israelites'. Passover represents the most foundational celebration in the Israelite calendar. It marks the beginning of the nation in Egypt, which designates the beginning of the calendar as well. It took place in the *first month*. That is, the Israelites set their calendar by Passover. To belong to God's people meant annual celebration of Passover – if not in the first, then in the second month. This explains why postponing the celebration demonstrates God's leniency in not excluding from his people those who cannot participate in the Passover for no fault of their own. On the other hand, intentional refusal to participate led to one being cut off from the community, which probably meant excommunication. The individual's excluding of themselves by not celebrating leads to the community's action of confirming that status, amounting to poetic justice (Pressler 2017: 73). Verse 13 uses the same term, *nepeš*, that appears earlier in verse 7 for the corpse to describe the person who wilfully refrains from the celebration. It views such a person as quasi 'dead to the community'.

Second, verse 14 picks up on a similar trajectory in Exodus 12:48–49, namely that a resident foreigner (*gēr*) may eat of the Passover, which leads, in Exodus 12, to their being regarded as a native: for there is one regulation for both resident foreigner and native (cf. Num. 15:13–16, 29). This is a common theme in the

Pentateuch: aliens living in the midst of the Israelites receive the same treatment, whether it be for celebrations or economic laws. The same did not hold for the foreign visitor (*nokrî*), presumably someone travelling through for a brief stay, probably a wealthy merchant (for the difference in economic treatment, specifically loaning at interest, cf. Deut. 23:20). A path is staked out for outsiders to become Israelites; Israelite status could be acquired. Thus, as concluded by Glanville (2018: 269; though his comment is directed to Deuteronomy, it applies here as well), 'The *gēr*'s joining the family of Yahweh does not require a "religious conversion" or a "confession of faith". Rather, the *gēr* is caught up in the joy, the community, and the abundance of the family of Yahweh.' The openness to foreigners and the postponing of the Passover are adjustments following an inclusive and welcoming criterion based on God's leniency that Israel should imitate.

Finally, one further significant insight from this text is the way that Moses goes about receiving guidance from God. Unlike the laws given on Sinai, here a situation arises that has yet to be regulated (for similar circumstances, see Lev. 24:10–23 and below, Num. 15:32–36; 27:1–11; 36). In other words, it provides insight on how to respond to new and unforeseen situations: the Bible accounts here for the unaccounted. In verse 8 Moses takes the case before Yahweh and Yahweh provides an answer. God's revelation is continuing, showing that the 'law' was not to be viewed as something rigid, but rather accommodating to the unpredictable and complex circumstances of human reality.

xi. Divine guidance for the marching and settling of the camp through the divine theophany of cloud and fire (9:15–23)

15–23. A new topic begins in verse 15, which refers back to the day of the events of Exodus 40:16, 34–38 (Year 2, Month 1, Day 1). That text reports how the tabernacle, the place where God's presence dwelled with the Israelites, was set up. The significance of this section lies in the transfer of God's presence in the cloud and fire from Mount Sinai (Exod. 24:15–18) to the moveable sanctuary. The tabernacle also receives the rare designation *tent of the covenant* [or *testimony*], which seldom appears (17:7–8; 18:2; 2 Chr. 24:6).

In verse 17 the term *the place* (*māqôm*) hints at the holy nature of the location where the cloud would dwell, regardless of the geographical location, for this term is broadly used for the location of the sanctuary (e.g. Deut. 12:5, 11, 14, 21).

These verses provide a certain rhythm that recalls the 'evening/ morning' of Genesis 1, with their reference to *evening* and *day*. Just as God put the 'lights' (Gen. 1:14) in place and they follow God's will, so the Israelites also follow God's leading.

Israel should move at God's pace, according to God's timing. Following the previous section on the postponing of the Passover, this pace and timing accommodate the needs of a small group of Israelites who would otherwise be left behind and excluded from God's people. With the term *always*, or perhaps 'regularly' (*tamîd*), verse 16 gives the sense that the Israelites remain constant in their obedience to this command, and the repetition *many days* (vv. 19, 20), 'whether by day or by night' (v. 21, AT) and 'days, or month, or many days' (v. 22, AT) concretely demonstrate examples suggesting that *however short or long*, this was the way it was supposed to be (Pressler 2017: 77–78). The Israelites did not decide how long to camp or march. The image is one of dependence and reliance.

Meaning

The Passover story and legal judgment has special relevance for life in several ways: (1) It highlights the importance of the Passover as a special celebration that identifies its partici- pants with the Israelites, God's people. It exudes a deliberate inclusivity towards foreigners and vulnerable people. However, were someone not to take part in the event, either in the first or in the second month, then they would exclude themselves from the Israelite community, which the community would confirm. Within the conception of the text, it was impossible for someone to belong to God's people and forgo celebration of Passover: one was no longer an Israelite unless one partici- pated in the ritual group meal. Passover has not continued its importance in Christian practice, but celebration of the Lord's Supper (communion/Eucharist) now takes its place (cf. 1 Cor. 11:17–34) as a community celebration around food that intends to commemorate the core salvific story. Thus, Numbers 9:1–14 suggests that part of the way for God's people to solidify their connection to God comes through such group feasts. (2) This text reveals the flexibility of God's laws in response to legitimate obstacles to keeping them. As circumstances change – and would change in the future according to this text, which has in mind Israelites being far away from the sanctuary at the time of the celebration of Passover – God provides graciously in answer to prayerful petition for alternative ways to affirm one's identity as part of God's community. Accommodation to the needs of those more vulnerable to changing situations belongs to the purpose of fulfilling the divine instructions in their inclusive and welcoming character. (3) While incidental in this chapter, it should be noted that the Israelites were commanded (Exod. 12:2) to organize their annual calendar to begin by marking the exodus. This way of telling time invites contemporary communities of faith to structure their year, their time, in view of God's history-making action (as done in many denominations that follow the Christian liturgical year). Regardless of whether one can dictate the calendar, the calendar too can function as a means to celebrate and remember God's work *as communities*. (4) Several New Testament authors reimagine Passover for Christians such that *Jesus* functions as the Passover lamb (John 1:29; 1 Cor. 5:7), whose bones must not be broken (John 19:36).

The image of God's presence remaining with the Israelites on their way in the wilderness in verses 15–23 expresses the desire of every person of faith on their journey through life: divine accompaniment. However, the passage highlights their close watch of the cloud lifting or resting and following its lead. The comforting vision (literally in this case) requires close observation and obedience.

xii. Divine royal sign for marching: the silver trumpets (10:1–10)

Context

Numbers 10 completes the transition from the first to the second major section of the book – that is, from preparation for the journey to the actual journey towards the land promised by

Yahweh. This transition began in the previous text, in 9:15–23, and continues in this chapter that splits into four parts. First is verses 1–10 ('Divine royal sign for marching: the silver trumpets'), which concern the fashioning and use of the silver trumpets, necessary in part for announcing that the Israelites should break camp. They then depart in verses 11–28, thus marking the new section. However, the transition to life on the way to Canaan reaches its completion only at the end of Numbers 10.

Comment

1–4. The chapter opens with Yahweh's final command to make something necessary for the journey: two silver trumpets, which God does not instruct to be fashioned along with the other holy furniture in Exodus 25 – 31. Nonetheless, these trumpets played a significant role in Jewish worship in Jerusalem during the Second Temple Period (530 BC – AD 70) – so much so that the Romans displayed them as war spoils on the Arch of Titus in Rome, which they constructed in AD 81 to commemorate the destruction of the Jerusalem Temple in AD 70 as part of the suppression of the Judean revolt.

The priests were to blow these trumpets in order to facilitate an orderly departure from the camps spread out around the tabernacle. This directive contrasts with the movement of the cloud, which in 9:17 signals that departure should commence. These trumpets are also different from the ram's horn (*shofar*) blown on other occasions, such as the beginning of the Jubilee debt forgiveness (Lev. 25:9; they are found together in a worship context in Ps. 98:6). As noted in verses 2–4, different types of trumpet blasts serve different purposes: (1) the primary purpose for this chapter, which is signalling the breaking of camp, but also (2) the gathering of the entire Israelite congregation or only its leaders. A third and fourth set of purposes are added in verse 9 and in verse 10.

5–7. Details of instructions for the first two purposes appear. Exemplary instructions for the trumpet blasts for departure from the camps are given for the camps to the east and south, recalling the layout of the Israelite tribes in Numbers 2. In contrast, verse 7 highlights the nature of the trumpet blast to gather the assembly. Though they utilize different Hebrew verbs in verses 6–7, it remains unclear to modern interpreters just how the trumpet blasts were differentiated from one another (speculation has existed since the rabbinic comments in the Talmud from the second to sixth centuries AD). Even if the text assumes that the audience knows how to tell them apart, most important is the association of a certain blast (*tĕrûʿâ*) with the presence of the divine king in the midst of the camp, which is explicitly related to Yahweh in 23:21.

8. The remark that only the priests, Aaron's descendants, may blow the trumpets as an enduring institution suggests that God, through human representatives, would continually initiate activities that would necessitate their usage. It both recalls the gathering of the people or leaders from verses 3, 7, and points to the further uses coming in verses 9–10.

9–10. The third use for the trumpet blasts (v. 9) points to something that was to take place in the future, when Israel is *in your land*. Then, rather than calling upon the Israelites to do something, the trumpets primarily serve to call *God* to act on Israel's behalf and deliver them from their enemies in battle. In this case, the trumpet blast also implicitly serves to direct the Israelite fighters to engage in battle (a frequent use of trumpets in antiquity), but the onus for victory is placed on God. This use of the trumpets appears in 31:6. The fourth purpose, presumably also intended for life in the land, is the use of trumpets as part of sanctuary-focused celebrations. Verse 10 calls them *days of rejoicing*, which recalls the descriptions of the feasts in Deuteronomy 16:9–15. The verse elaborates that they include appointed (pilgrimage feast) days and the first day of the month, for which special offerings are commanded (Num. 28:11–15). This sounding of the trumpets likely signals the Israelites to gather and celebrate (*t-q-ʿ*, the verb used here, is the same one used for the blast to gather in v. 3). This blowing of trumpets also appears in the narrative of Solomon's dedication of the Jerusalem temple in 2 Chronicles 7:6 as something separate from the general musical worship (cf. Ezra 3:10). The concept of remembering/memorial appears in verses 9–10, but perhaps in a reciprocal fashion: in verse 9, the Israelites are remembered before God so that God secures their military victory. In verse 10, however, the trumpets direct the Israelites' attention towards God in their acts of worship, whose presence then culminates in the divine declaration 'I [am] Yahweh your God!' The military and worship aspects of blasting instruments converge in the notion of the establishment of divine order reflected in Leviticus 25.

Meaning

The continuing responsibility for blowing the trumpets – however this might be conceived when Israel has spread throughout the Promised Land or been scattered in the diaspora – conveys the core theological command that, whether in setting out on a journey, gathering together, engaging in battle or participating in worship and celebration, all such actions that break the daily routine should commence at God's direction, for God is the royal authority who establishes the right order of things. Furthermore, the reciprocal memorial function of the trumpets in verses 9–10 highlights that victory, military or otherwise, lies in God's hands (cf. Pss 20:7; 33:16–18), while the appropriate human response to God's direction and protection consists of worship. A final reflection that trumpets serve to call the people of God to assemble in the divine presence is carried throughout Scripture, in Isaiah 27:13 to call the scattered Israelites, and in Matthew 24:31; 1 Corinthians 15:52 to call all God's people to gather at Christ's second coming – in general for major events in the story of God's people.

2. MARCHING TOWARDS AND FAILING TO ENTER THE PROMISED LAND (10:11 – 14:45)

A. Departure from Sinai in marching order (10:11–28)

Context

Numbers 10:11–28 describes the initial departure from the Sinai Wilderness, building on 2:1–34, which also outlines the general manner in which the Israelites would set out. To understand the importance of this section requires imagining a parade or procession celebrating an important event under human and divine guidance.

Comment

11–12. The second, and longest, part of chapter 10 (vv. 11–28) begins in verse 11, which marks a definitive turning point in the narrative. It provides the date of the Israelite departure, Year 2, Month 2, Day 20, which is nineteen days after the date at the beginning of the narrative (1:1). Israel has camped for eleven months (Exod. 19:1), and all of Exodus 19 – Numbers 10:10

(including the whole of Leviticus) has taken place at Sinai! This date is also the first date in the narrative that postdates the one given in Numbers 1:1, so the narrative now takes a first step forward, rather than providing overviews (7:89; 9:16–23), flashbacks (e.g. 7:1; 9:1, 15) and undated material (5:1 – 6:27).

There is, surprisingly, no mention of trumpet blasts as one would expect from verse 5, but rather the lifting of the cloud in verse 11 that triggers the departure, which recalls 9:17. Their next stop is the desert or wilderness of Paran (v. 12). In contrast to this itinerary, 12:16 reports that the Israelites travel from Hazeroth to the wilderness of Paran. Thus, one might understand verse 12 as a summary of the stops that occur in 11:1 – 12:16, which requires Paran to designate a large region. The wilderness of Paran also appears to be coterminous with the *wilderness of Zin* (cf. 33:36 with 13:21) and reaches northwards from the Sinai Peninsula even to Israel's southern region as far as Kadesh according to 13:26.

13–28. The description of the orderly departure largely follows the directives found in Numbers 2, but with several minor deviations. As mentioned above, one could have in mind something of a military parade when encountering this text: the narrator announces each group and its leader as it goes by, calling the audience to take in and celebrate the spectacle. The length of this section indicates the significance of the event. This departure represents a considerable change from the hurried and mixed crowd described leaving Egypt in Exodus 12:31–38. By this point that mass of different individuals appears transformed into an organized people moving in an orderly manner through God's directives.

Unlike the general directive in 2:17 that the Levites should march after the *second* (southern) group of tribes, verse 17 has two clans, the Gershonites and Merarites, march between the Judah-led tribes of the first group and the Reuben-led second group. Then, according to verse 21, the Kohathites, who carry the holy furniture from the tabernacle, still march between the second and third groups. Verse 21 provides a rationale for this order: the tabernacle complex would be set up by the time the Kohathites arrived at the next campsite so that they could simply bring the holy furniture into the tabernacle. While the logic makes sense, it theoretically leaves the covered furniture waiting to leave at the departure point for a period of time, which is a similar problem to the one that this order attempts to solve. More striking is that the report here does not meticulously follow the divine directive from 2:1, which is otherwise so important and so frequently mentioned in the Priestly material. While this seems less important for the ancient text than for many modern audiences, it is possible to see 2:17 as a general overview that is subject to further detailed application as it is the case here. The text of 10:17, 21 highlights the special theological attention paid to the holy furniture, which is emphasized by receiving explicit mention. It is unclear if this holy furniture includes the ark – which one might presume, according to 3:31; 4:5. In this case, it emphasizes God's location at the centre of the people. However, this contrasts with the ark setting out first in verse 33. Thus, the chapter is concerned more with highlighting the theological significance of various holy items – travelling in the middle of the Israelites because of their extreme holiness, *and* as part of God's provision of guidance for the journey.

B. Human and divine guidance (10:29–36)

A short but striking interaction between Moses and his Midianite relative Hobab comes in verses 29–32 in which Moses pleads with Hobab to come with the Israelites as a human guide. Finally, verses 33–36 return to a narration of the first departure and detail the routines of their journey, focusing on the ark and cloud as divine guides and protectors for Israel. The chapter as a whole provides a complex view of the ways God guides and directs Israel in the wilderness: trumpets, the cloud, the ark and a foreigner.

i. Moses invites his Midianite father-in-law to guide Israel (10:29–32)

29–32. Given the internal focus on Yahweh as the head of the people who determines where and when the camp will be moved, the presence of and request for guidance from Hobab, a Midianite, comes as a surprise. Just as at the beginning of the Israelites' stay at Sinai in Exodus 18, so here at its conclusion Moses' foreign relatives provide guidance. It remains unclear from the grammatical construction in the Hebrew text whether Hobab or Reuel is Moses' father-in-law: the former is presented as such in Judges 4:11, while the latter is in Exodus 2:18. How these identifications accord with the Jethro designated as Moses' father-in-law in Exodus 3:1; 18:1 also goes without answer. Furthermore, while Hobab here is called a Midianite, Judges 4:11 calls him a Kenite. However this is dealt with, his identification as a Midianite is striking in Numbers, given the Midian resistance to and deception of the Israelites in Numbers 22 – 25; 31! This last observation indicates the ambivalence with regard to the inclusion of Moses' relations and their kin's reception of God's favour throughout Numbers, whether Midianite or Cushite (see 12:1).

However, while Numbers 10 omits Hobab's ultimate response to Moses, descendants of Hobab do go on to live in Israel, according to Judges 1:16; 4:11. While not without self-interest (which does not present a problem according to the text so long as Moses' interest is not limited to his own and Israel's success), Moses in effect broadens the offer of God's hospitality to those on the margins of Israel, even inviting them to participate in important and leading functions.

A key message of this short interaction is that God's guidance does not preclude seeking knowledge and insight from other humans, even from those who are apparently outsiders, a message also underscored by the wisdom tradition, which offers the insights of Job, Agur (Prov. 30) and Lemuel (Prov. 31), none of whom count as Israelites in the texts. In return, Moses promises the same treatment for Hobab that God has shown towards the Israelites: to do good to him (v. 32). The Israelites' actions imitate the goodness of God that they themselves have received, following the reciprocal logic of hospitality in traditional cultures (Hobbs 2001; Bailey 2018: 64–68).

ii. Divine theophany and the presence of the ark to guide Israel (10:33–36)

33–34. The tradition that the ark went out *before them* contrasts with verse 21, as mentioned above, but agrees with the role of the ark in Joshua 3:3, 6, when crossing the Jordan River. Reading the traditions of verses 21 and 33 together *theologically* allows for a richer understanding of God's presence both *in the midst of* and *at the head of* the Israelites. In effect, Numbers 10 brings together several important memories of the ark's significance for God's people.

35–36. Perhaps the most important observation on Numbers 10 is that it ends with a climactic song, which pronounces a triumphant tone. Verse 35 is very close to Psalm 68:1, and there are similarities between verse 36 and Psalm 68:17. The psalm depicts a military context, which is also the context here. As with much poetry, the exact interpretation remains hard to pin down, especially for verse 36. The Hebrew texts contains the words 'Return – Yahweh – ten thousands/myriads – thousands/clans of – Israel'. If understood as one poetic line, then, following most translations, it means either 'Return, O LORD *of* the ten thousand thousands of Israel' (NRSV) or 'Return, O LORD *to* the ten thousand thousands of Israel' (ESV). Here Israel is closely identified with Yahweh's army. However, if viewed as two parallel lines like the poetry in verse 35, it reads,

> 'Return, O Lord,
> the ten thousand thousands of Israel.'

In this case, Yahweh is likened to a massive army of ten million that fights on Israel's behalf, which underscores Yahweh as the one scattering the enemies in verse 35. A similar image appears in the presentation of Egyptian pharaohs fighting in battle, both in texts and especially in iconography, where the pharaoh is depicted much larger than anyone else in the picture (see, e.g., the wall relief at Medinet Habu depicting Rameses III defeating the Sea Peoples in the Battle of the [Nile] Delta). An inscription found in major Egyptian temples recounting Rameses II's great battle with the Hittite Empire in 1275 BC praises the help of the Egyptian deity Amun: 'Amun I found more help to me than millions of troops, than hundred-thousands of chariotry, than ten-thousands of men' (*COS* 2.5A, 35).

What takes place in verses 11–36 is an idyllic portrayal of the Israelites' journey: God protects and guides them in the cloud and ark, while they have magnanimous relations with a foreigner who serves as their *eyes*. This chapter – and the entire book up to this point – ends in verses 33–36 on a positive note with no indication of the Israelites' rebellion against Yahweh that begins in the very next verses.

Meaning
The completed transformation from harried slaves to a systematically ordered people on parade on view in verses 11–28 provides one image of God's ability to take a diverse lot of people and fashion them into an organized set of worshippers following divine guidance to establish God's good order. This can certainly be overlaid with the images of the church and the kingdom of God found elsewhere in the New Testament and Scripture as a whole.

The lack of the mention of trumpets but rather the movement of the cloud in verse 11 to signal that the Israelites should set out, as well as the double guidance of Hobab and the ark in verses 29, 33, all juxtapose or overlay various sets of divine and human ways in which God leads and guides his people and even history, including reliance on people outside of or on the margins of God's own people.

C. Rebellion and failure (11:1 – 14:45)

Context
Chapter 11 makes a radical departure from the first ten chapters. In those reports, Yahweh commands and then Moses and the Israelites respond with obedience. Or, as in 9:1–14 (second Passover), a genuine need on the part of the Israelites leads to God's provision of an answer through Moses' mediation.

The first section of chapter 11, verses 1–3, provides a type of prologue with the paradigm of the cycle that repeats often with some variation throughout the following chapters (chs. 11–20). Rather than beginning with divine direction or Israelite intention to live in obedience to God's will, this story begins with an Israelite complaint and ends with the memory of Yahweh's punishment.

The second, much longer section in chapter 11 consists of verses 4–35. It weaves together two themes and concerns: (1) the people's desire for meat, and (2) Moses' desire to share leadership. Both themes appear elsewhere in the Pentateuch, which suggests several questions. First, how does the desire for meat in Numbers 11 relate to the similar narrative in Exodus 16:4–36 but have a drastically different outcome? Second, how does the sharing of leadership responsibilities in Numbers 11 compare with and relate to the similar reports in Exodus 18:13–27 and Deuteronomy 1:9–15, as well as leadership conflicts in Numbers 12; 16 – 17? And finally, what results from the combination of these two topics in Numbers 11?

i. The pattern of rebellion (11:1–3)
Comment

1–3. These opening verses set the tone for most of the material in the next eleven chapters: the Israelites' attitude and actions are marked by complaint, which Yahweh finds evil. This is followed by divine punishment; then the Israelites cry out, Moses intercedes, and Yahweh ameliorates the situation. This pattern also appears in Judges 3:7–11, introducing the cycle that happens throughout that book, though there the evil is in the *eyes* rather than *ears* of Yahweh. In the case of verses 1–3, no definitive reason for their murmuring appears, unlike in other places (Exod. 16:2–3; Num. 11:4–34; 21:4–9). Furthermore, the date of this incident in relation to any others is not given, suggesting that most important is its *thematic* or *paradigmatic* placement at the beginning of the wilderness journey, foreshadowing the nature of the journey.

These verses emphasize the connection between the *burning* of God's anger and a fire breaking out in punishment. These elements lead to naming the location Taberah, 'Burning Place', from the root *b-ʿ-r*, 'to burn'. The breaking out of divine fire indicates something destructive for the humans consumed by it (Lev. 10:2), and yet also something purifying (Num. 31:23–24). The divine fire's danger also recalls the simultaneous threat and promise of God travelling in the Israelites' midst: the fire provides protection and guidance by night (Exod. 13:20–21; 14:24; 40:48; Num. 9:15–16; also Exod. 3:2; 19:18; Deut. 5:22–26).

The danger is alleviated through the people crying out and Moses interceding (coming between) with God. This particular

language otherwise only appears in Numbers 21:7; Deuteronomy
9:20, and it depicts Moses as a mediator between God and people,
a position sometimes occupied by priests and prophets. The
prophetic role will be picked up later in the chapter. In any case,
the supernatural destruction shows God's overall disapproval of
the Israelites' complaining and the risk they run. In this section
God first *hears* the people's complaining (v. 1) and – while it goes
unmentioned – Yahweh also hears Moses' prayer in verse 2, which
leads to the dampening of the fire. To use a pun, the experience
was burned into the people's memory through the naming of the
location 'Burning Place' in verse 3.

ii. Manna and Moses are not enough (11:4–33)

The body of this section is quite complex.

It starts with a first cycle:

- the *people's* complaint (vv. 4–6);
- an aside with details about manna (vv. 7–9);
- and Moses' and God's reaction (v. 10).

Then there is a second cycle:

- *Moses'* complaint (vv. 11–15);
- God's answer (vv. 16–17, 18–20);
- Moses' rebuttal (vv. 21–22);
- and God's repudiation of this rebuttal (v. 23).

The third section contains:

- the implementation of *God's* solution to Moses' (vv. 24–30) . . .
- and to the people's complaints (vv. 31–33).

The final verse (v. 34) provides a transition to the next narrative.

As already noted, this section recalls the provision of manna
and quail in Exodus 16, on which it builds. The challenge is to
understand why and how this topic is woven together with the
shared leadership issue that the narrative also includes.

a. The people's complaint about the manna (11:4–6)

4. The action begins with a group, *the rabble among them*, which is typically how Yahweh's location in their midst is described (see 5:3). This entity, distinct from Israel itself (cf. Exod. 12:37–38), has a *strong craving* or desire. Their presence is somewhat surprising: the structuring of the camp in Numbers 1 – 4 seems to disallow a distinct group, even while Hobab (10:29–32) points to its possibility. The intention is to highlight the association between this group and the Egyptian context behind their craving. This problem originates from *outside* the Israelites, though it quickly catches on with them as well. There are, therefore, positive (Hobab) and negative depictions of outsiders juxtaposed with each other. The most important factor about this *rabble* is that it does not adhere to the structure outlined in Numbers 1 – 4. It is a chaotic element opposed to the divinely commanded order.

An ambivalent element here is desire: neither desire nor craving is, by definition, evil (as one might conclude from the use of the same term in the tenth commandment: 'Neither shall you desire your neighbour's house, or field', Deut. 5:21), nor is there something specifically problematic with the desire for meat. According to Deuteronomy 14:26, when Israelites living at a distance went to worship Yahweh at the sanctuary, they should purchase for their celebratory worship 'whatever you wish [desire] – oxen, sheep, wine, strong drink'. Meat constitutes a central item for ancient Israelite feasts, and feasting was a core activity in worship. Meat also regularly appears on the royal table (1 Kgs 4:22–23). However, in the larger cultural context of ancient Israel and surrounding regions, meat was regularly consumed only in connection with worship, or by elites (see MacDonald 2008b: 64).

As often noted, the Israelites left Egypt with a large number of animals (Exod. 12:38; 17:3), which makes their desire for *some* meat less comprehensible in the light of the overall narrative, though this information does not appear here.

5–6. The problem with this desire lies in the context of Numbers 11, and comparison with the similar text in Exodus 16 proves illuminating in this regard. First, there are two similarities that appear in the two texts: (1) they concern manna and quail; and (2) the pining for life in Egypt includes meat in both cases. Here in verse 5 the people specifically remember fish and various types of produce. Especially the aromatics (leeks and garlic) suggest a certain way in which fish was prepared in ancient Egypt (that fish could be viewed as a type of meat appears clear both from v. 22 below and from Lev. 11:11). As attested in food studies, the specific tastes and smells of particular dishes, or even the naming of such dishes, contain powerful triggers to significant memories (Sutton 2001; Montanari 2006; Altmann 2011: 44–54). In this case, the desire for meat brings up the memory of fish consumption in Egypt and with it a whole way of life.

However, this memory of Egypt is positive, which, while not unique in the Bible (Egypt served as a place of refuge for Abraham, and Joseph rose to power there), does not coincide with the larger motif of Israel as slaves liberated from Egyptian oppression and the contrast between service of Egypt and service of Yahweh. The Israelites here reject Yahweh's provision in favour of Egypt's. There is at least one detail that points to the *modified* nature of this memory: verse 5's *for nothing*. The problem with the rabble's desire is that it is a desire for Egypt's distorted and disordered ideals. The implication that life in Egypt was without bondage points to the way the people idealize a past that did not exist (the helpful term 'countermemory' is suggested by Leveen 2008: 85).

This false memory leads to some important differences between the narratives of Exodus 16 and Numbers 11. Most important is that they have different outcomes: God does not reprimand or punish them in Exodus 16, while here Yahweh becomes angry and strikes them with a plague, as he did against Egypt. To explain this divergence, first, the narrative of Exodus 16 takes place *prior* to the establishment of the covenant and the tabernacle in Exodus 19 – 24; 25 – 40 (cf. Olson 2012: 61–63). These developments mean, as noted in Numbers 5:3, that Yahweh is in their midst, which calls for a different type of interaction and level of trust in God.

Second, manna only begins to be provided in Exodus 16, while its regular provision is assumed here. Unlike in Exodus 16:3, where the Israelites complain about hunger, here the focus is clearly on the desire for meat (vv. 4, 13, 18–23, 34). Thus, the people in Numbers 11 do not suffer from hunger, but recoil from the lack of variation in their diet. Furthermore, this desire includes but also points beyond the physical enjoyment to the elite priestly or royal status that would accompany such regular consumption. They reject the more egalitarian economy of the manna in opposition to the oppressively unequal economy of Egypt (see E. F. Davis 2019: 67–70). The likelihood that it was not the hope for a one-off meal of fish prepared with onions, leeks and melons is reinforced by the way that Yahweh and Moses understand the request in verses 18–23. God speaks of feeding them meat for a whole month, and Moses asks, *Are there enough fish in the sea . . . ?* Therefore, the people rebel against God's provision: they want regular meat in accord with elite ideals that can be realized only through oppression of others. The relationship between elite diet and leadership provides the connection with that thematic thread in verses 15–17, 24–30.

b. Description of the manna (11:7–9)

7–9. The description of manna (explained in Exod. 16:15 as *mān* [Aramaic] 'what' + *hû'* 'it' = 'What [is] it?') is an aside. It builds on the description in Exodus 16:14–15, 31, which states that it is 'like coriander seed, white, and the taste of it was like wafers made with honey'. Here its appearance is compared to bdellium (NRSV has the more general *gum resin*) and its taste to a cake of oil, rather than a honey wafer. Bdellium refers to a type of yellow sap. Manna is often explained as insect secretions on the tamarisk trees found in the Sinai, which can be harvested and eaten in the early morning. However, the biblical texts present it as divine provision.

c. Moses' complaint to God about his leadership role (11:10–15)

11–15. A different theme begins here, where Moses compares the burden of leading the Israelites to that of pregnancy, birth and caring for an infant. This metaphor characterizes Israel as a child and its cry in verse 13 as like the cry of a small child. In rejecting this role of motherhood for himself, however, Moses implicitly attributes it, and thus maternal imagery, to God in verse 12. God is the true mother, provider and sustainer of the people (Moses also uses the *feminine* form of 'you' when speaking of God in v. 15). God as mother also appears in Deuteronomy 32:18; Isaiah 42:14. While Yahweh is predominantly depicted as male, the use of female imagery underscores that the divine image comprises female and male (reflected in Gen. 1:27).

d. God's answer to Moses and to the people (11:16–20)

16–17. Just as the manna and quail themes appear earlier, so, too, does the issue of Moses' sole leadership (vv. 14–17): in Exodus 18, his father-in-law (Jethro in that text) advises Moses to appoint judges to lighten his role as judicial leader (esp. Exod. 18:22, which speaks of a 'burden', as in v. 14 here). Furthermore, the leaders of the tribes that were appointed in Numbers 1:4–16 play no explicit part in this narrative, which suggests that Numbers 11 comes from a different tradition.

18–20. God's answer to Israel comes: they should prepare for a month-long gorging on meat. This length of the feast (cf. Esth. 1:1–4) demonstrates Yahweh's superiority over Egypt, which picks up on the underlying critique in the people's complaint in verses 5–6. God's command (v. 18) to *Consecrate yourselves* in preparation for meat consumption indicates that such an action should take place as *celebratory worship*.

e. Moses and God discuss (11:21–23)

21–23. It is surprising that no punishment comes upon Moses for his lack of trust that God can feed the large mass of people with meat. God only tells Moses to see that God can follow through on the prediction of providing a huge amount of meat. However, unlike the people, and more like the psalms of lament, Moses expresses his doubt *directly to* God. Perhaps, this gap of trust also contributes to understanding the nature of *carrying the people* with which Moses requires assistance: Moses can no longer imagine God's provision being adequate for them, nor does Moses advocate for the people with God, so further leadership is required.

f. God resolves the people's and Moses' complaint (11:24–33)

24–30. Thus, in Numbers 11, the leadership role concerns prophecy rather than judging. Yet how is prophecy conceived in this chapter? Here Moses takes the initiative to gather seventy of the elders: he, not God, chooses them from among the established leadership. Moses' primary position is confirmed in verse 25 by Yahweh speaking *to him*. Then, as a result of God making the spirit rest upon them, the seventy prophesy as a confirmation of their leadership role. However, their prophetic action was such that it was recognized externally, because Eldad and Medad's prophesying causes Moses to be notified (vv. 26–27), thus suggesting it was ecstatic (cf. Saul in 1 Sam. 10:6–13). On the other hand, the only prophetic action on display in the chapter concerns Moses viewing the people's action as evil (v. 10) and failing to serve as an intercessor for the people with God. Thus, the elders are needed to fill this gap of active mediation between the people and God.

Moses' response to Joshua's request to stop Eldad and Medad's prophesying (vv. 28–29) provides a bridge to the narrative in Numbers 12. Moses desires that all God's people might be prophets, but Aaron and Miriam put themselves on Moses' level (12:2–3). However, according to 12:6–8, God's regular communication with Moses places him above other prophets. This topic also arises in Joel 2:28 (quoted in Acts 2) and Ezekiel 39:29. As a whole, Moses welcomes input from outside leaders, whether it be Hobab, or Eldad and Medad.

31–33. The narrative returns to the provision of meat, which builds on a phenomenon known in the region: large numbers of birds migrate through the Levant between Africa and Europe. Migratory birds were so plentiful in ancient Egypt that they were seen as a reliable source of food. Surprising, however, is that the Israelites are far from the Mediterranean coast and yet gather large numbers of birds (ten homers equals ten donkey loads! cf. Kletter 2006). These details move the event into the realm of the fantastic, thereby indicating its miraculous nature. The quail are so plentiful that the people collect them for two days without stopping. However, in the middle of this great harvest, and apparently great feast – though no celebration is reported – Yahweh's anger cuts everything short, striking the people with a great plague, as he did with Egypt. God's declaration of the provision of quail meat for a month does not come to pass. Perhaps the abrupt punishment comes because of the people's method of gathering and consuming at the same time: this was not the sacred consumption in worship of Yahweh commanded in verse 18 but rather a fixation on consumption itself. And, if interpreted in the light of verse 20, the punishment provides poetic justice: they long to gorge themselves on meat, and the overindulgence leads to heavy vomiting, where the meat even comes out the nose. The same goes for their desire for the Egyptian way of life, which was punished by God striking it with plagues. They wanted to be like the Egyptian elite and so got the divine treatment for the Egyptian elite. In the depiction of this tradition in Psalm 78, those who fall by God's strike are qualified as (lit.) 'sturdy' (78:31), from the root *š-m-n* that has the basic meaning of 'growing fat'.

iii. Geographic location (11:34–35)

34–35. The name given to the location, *Kibroth-hattaavah*, 'Graves of Craving', also appears in 33:16–17; Deuteronomy 9:22–23, and recalls the initial problem from verse 4, that the rabble *had a strong craving*.

Meaning

Here complaining leads to dire consequences. Does this mean that all complaint and desire for something absent is therefore wrong? While much of historical Christian tradition has sought to diminish human desire, the biblical witness does not share this impulse: many psalms, especially so-called lament psalms, include passionate longing for a better life and world, including a feast (e.g. Ps. 22, esp. v. 26). Instead, it is the separation of desire's fulfilment from worship of God that comes under judgment.

Numbers 11 provides two locations named in memory of the painful events that took place there. One can draw from these actions the importance of connecting negative events of the past with spatial locations in order to help the people of God remember them. As such, it invites faithful followers to imbue space with meaning so that one's physical surroundings may be marked with the story/stories of faith.

In general, a basic theme from this chapter is that the juxtaposition of good things from known oppressive situations in the past (fish in Egypt) with God's *current* provision (manna) can lead to the desire for the fullness of God's abundance (here *meat*). While such a desire is not evil in itself, the manner in which one receives or takes God's further gift of abundance (here *quail*) comes with the danger of judgment (here *plague*). Taken with some irony, this narrative illustrates, as Deuteronomy 8:3 (Luke 4:4) states, that humans do not live on bread alone. The desire for bread (material goodness) is justified, but they should allow their desire to be fulfilled by God according to God's 'table manners', especially related to worshipful gratitude and economic generosity, rather than the desire for elite luxury for oneself to the detriment of others.

A final direction comes in the interweaving of the desire for an elite lifestyle (regular meat consumption) and Moses' humble desire for shared leadership, especially with regard to the task of intercession. A reversal of values with regard to leadership takes place in Moses' reply to Joshua. The call in this text is for the people of God to desire to *do the work* of leadership rather than to *focus on the benefits* that can accompany leadership. In God's household (economy), everyone is friends with the King, and those who wish a special place at the royal table will end up excluded from it (cf. Luke 14:7–14). And Moses' response to Joshua indicates the importance of valuing input, whether or not the source has been institutionally validated or not (cf. Luke 9:49–50), especially if the person has received divine confirmation through the Spirit.

iv. Miriam and Aaron rebel against Moses' leadership (12:1–16)

Context

While Moses assuaged Joshua's concern about Eldad and Medad prophesying (11:28–29), as if it would somehow lessen Moses' leadership, Joshua's fear that others might seek to usurp Moses' special prophetic role comes to fruition in this chapter. However, the culprits do not emerge from the elders, nor does the problem originate with a foreign riffraff (11:4), but rather with the inner circle of leadership, Aaron and Miriam. Given the similar theme of prophetic leadership, it makes sense to read Numbers 11 and 12 as two aspects of an answer to the same question regarding leading the community of God's people. Moses' humility and integrity allow space for God to take up his defence against his siblings, doing so through the theme of prophecy, thereby picking up on a topic from the previous chapter.

The initial object of Miriam and Aaron's attack consists of Moses marrying a foreign woman. However, the bulk of the chapter concerns their claim to equal status to Moses as receivers of God's word. Also problematic is the punishment falling solely on Miriam. It is unclear how these difficulties resolve, and they may point to a merging of two traditions, as could also have been the case in 11:4–35.

The form of the chapter aligns closely with the paradigm established in the first verses of chapter 11: complaint in verses 1–2, God's response and punishment in verses 4–10, Moses' intercession in verses 11–13, and the end of the punishment in verses 14–15 (Schart 1990: 216–217). This typical structure allows the audience to consider how the narrative in Numbers 12 *differs* or sets particular emphases in relation to the typical form, and how those variations are meaningful: in this case, the complaint is complex, and the bulk of the report consists of God's response.

Comment

1. While included in 11:35 in the Hebrew Bible, and followed by the NASB 1995, NIV, ESV and others, the final statement *While they were at Hazeroth* makes more sense as an opening to this chapter (as in NRSV, NLT), providing it with a location. The geographical term, which means 'farmsteads, unwalled settlements', has not been adequately connected with any known location, though it also appears in 33:17–18; Deuteronomy 1:1.

This narrative does not mention the sibling relationships between Moses, Aaron and Miriam: these remain in the background. However, other familial relationships do play a role in the narrative: father–daughter (for Yahweh–Miriam, v. 14), mother–foetus (also Yahweh–Miriam, v. 12), as well as Moses' marriage. As such, it may also be that Miriam instead represents prophetic and Aaron priestly types of interaction with God. Aaron's priestly role has been on display already (esp. Num. 3 – 4; 5:11–31). Miriam is known from several texts: Exodus 15:20–21 designates her as a prophetess who leads the women in celebration of Yahweh's victory over Pharaoh. She also appears along with Moses and Aaron as a leader of Israel in Micah 6:4. As an aside, it is unclear whether she is the same sister credited with saving

Moses by connecting him with Pharaoh's daughter in Exodus 2:4–8, though this connection is often assumed.

The narrative begins with controversy on the basis of Moses' foreign wife. The Hebrew syntax of the verb (a third-person feminine singular) marks Miriam as the primary instigator, which might provide some justification for the punishment falling on her alone and not on Aaron (though this is hardly satisfying as a solution to the lack of Aaron's punishment: see below). There are two main theories as to the location of Cush and the identity of this wife. One direction is to identify her with Zipporah, known from Exodus 2:15–22; 18:2. In order to draw this conclusion, Cush is equated with the 'Cushan' found in Habakkuk 3:7, which in that verse is parallel to Midian, Zipporah's home in the Exodus texts. The second possibility takes Cush as the region south of Egypt, its usual meaning in the Old Testament (Isa. 11:11; Jer. 13:23: encompassing Sudan, Ethiopia and Eritrea). In this case, the woman represents another wife. Given that Moses' first forty years were spent in Egypt, a wife from Cush becomes plausible. Many interpreters (incl. Calvin) see polygamy as beneath Moses' stature, and rule out this alternative. A focus on a darker skin tone would fit well with the punishment in verse 10 with Miriam's skin becoming 'like snow', if the comparison is one of colour (the word *white* is an interpretive addition that is not present in the Hebrew text) – white versus dark. Because race and ethnic boundaries were not defined *in the same way* in antiquity, such a comparison would not indicate an 'interracial' marriage with the same connotations as in the USA or South Africa where laws existed against such unions. Rather, as argued by Bailey (1991: 179), Miriam may accuse Moses of actually seeking to raise his status by associating himself through marriage with the higher-status Cushites, who were viewed with respect (see Isa. 45:14).

Regardless of the difficulty in identifying the location of Cush, the woman's name or her identity, the issue of mixed marriages (marrying a non-Israelite) is at the forefront here, as it is repeatedly throughout the Bible. Abraham (Gen. 24) and Rebekah (Gen. 27:46) do not want their sons to marry Canaanite women. Such marriages are forbidden in Exodus 34:16 and Deuteronomy 7:2–6. They form a stumbling block for the Israelites in Numbers 25 and for Solomon in 1 Kings 11, and both Nehemiah (13:23–29) and Ezra (9:1–4; 10) condemn them. However, there are also some positive narratives about such unions: Joseph marries the Egyptian Asenath (Gen. 41:45), and Ruth the Moabitess is an exemplary ancestress of David through her marriage to the Israelite Boaz (Ruth 4:13–22). This concern surprisingly receives no further treatment in the chapter.

2. The nature of the complaint changes from concerns about Moses' spouse to the implied notion that he claimed exclusive access to God's speaking. This accusation appears hyperbolic in the light of Moses' desire to share the burden of leadership in 11:16–30 and its fulfilment through the bestowing of prophecy on the elders there. God's confirmation of Moses' special position suggests that the distribution of leadership by God's spirit in the previous chapter does not abolish hierarchy: Moses remains God's chosen leader.

It may be that this change in focus of the charges from verse 1 to verse 2 represents two different traditional accusations brought against leaders and for this reason they are juxtaposed: (1) their family situation disqualifies them, or (2) others do not accept their hierarchical position.

3. The lack of any reaction from Moses (contra 11:10–11) is grounded in Moses' character as the humblest man upon the earth. The inclusion of this statement indicates that Moses was not its writer. The Hebrew term *ānā(y)w*, which appears only here in this singular form, is typically understood as 'humble' or 'meek'. The plural usually refers to the poor or others who have no stature by which to advocate for themselves with judicial authorities and are therefore dependent on divine deliverance (Amos 2:7; 8:4). This understanding provides a transition to the rest of the narrative. However, a counter-proposal is that the term means 'integrity' (Coats 1993: 94), which fits with Moses advocating on behalf of Miriam and Aaron (v. 13) and God's compliment that Moses is a trustworthy steward (v. 7).

4–5. The tension in the story grows when first all three and then only Aaron and Miriam are called to go out to meet God. At this point it is unclear how Yahweh will respond: the invitation to hear from God, including the descending of the pillar of cloud which takes place here, *usually* indicates divine favour, as it did in the previous chapter (11:25; cf. Exod. 16:10; 19:9; 24:15–18; 33:9–10). God instead delivers a message of rebuke to Aaron and Miriam.

6–8. Unrecognizable in English translations are the lines of Hebrew poetry, which are formulated with a chiastic structure as laid out below. This ancient literary form places the most important element in the middle, in this case shining the spotlight on the two lines of verse 7. Moses receives the title of God's *servant*, attributed elsewhere most often to David (2 Sam. 3:18) and other prophets (Jer. 7:25). Furthermore, like Joseph in Potiphar's house (Gen. 39:1–6), God entrusts Moses with *God's* house.

Frame: ⁶ *Hear my words:*
A   *When there are prophets among you,*
 B   *I the L*ORD *make myself known to them in visions;*
  C   *I speak to them in dreams.*
   D   ⁷ Not so with my servant Moses;
   D'   he is entrusted with all my house.
  C'   ⁸ *With him I speak face to face*
 B'   *– clearly, not in riddles;*
A'   *and he beholds the form of the L*ORD*.*
Frame: *Why then were you not afraid to speak against my servant Moses?*
(12:6–8)

God does impart revelation to prophets, including Miriam. However, the superiority of Moses' interaction with God lies in its directness: he does not need to struggle to discern its meaning as with a riddle or dream. Furthermore, with Deuteronomy 13 or 1 Kings 22 in mind, the content delivered through dreams and prophecy must be evaluated and confirmed by others. Moses' pre-eminence is similarly underscored in Deuteronomy 34:10–12. Nonetheless, while God speaks with Moses 'mouth-to-mouth' (this is the Hebrew underlying the idiomatic English translation *face to face* in v. 8), Moses 'sees the form of Yahweh'. This need not imply that Moses sees God completely (cf. Exod. 33:20). Rather, the intimate relationship between Moses and Yahweh resembles other human–divine relationships in Ancient Near Eastern religion according to which Moses 'sees' the divine form and, as a result, also manifests God's form in his person (Exod. 34:29–35; cf. Balogh 2018: 120–124).

9–10. God's speech ends with a statement of God's anger and exit. Its dramatic nature is underscored by the repetition of the mention of Miriam's skin condition.

Why is Miriam punished but not Aaron? Several explanations have arisen: (1) she was the main culprit (she is mentioned first in v. 1), and Aaron was just a later addition to the story; (2) Aaron's position as high priest meant that punishing him would have damaging repercussions for the entire people; (3) it was especially problematic for a woman to question male leadership. None of the three is persuasive. The first falters in that both are named as attacking Moses. The second simply pushes the problem back a step: why was it that only men were allowed to be priests, such that Miriam alone suffers? If Nadab and Abihu could undergo punishment – even death – then surely God and the Israelites could overcome the punishment or impurity of the high priest (cf. Zech. 3:1–5). Finally, one might point to the wise woman of Tekoa rebuking David (2 Sam. 14) as one counter-example showing a woman criticizing a male leader. In the end, it remains unclear, and perhaps stands as a critique of the ancient patriarchy that led to Miriam's suffering for herself and for Aaron (see below). A mediating step takes place through the narration of both Miriam's and Aaron's deaths in 20:1 and 20:22–29.

Miriam's punishment of a skin defilement (on possible medical identifications, see commentary on 5:2) in verse 10 being compared to snow could refer either to the colour, as discussed above at verse 1, or perhaps to snow*flakes*, which could gain support from Psalm 147:16. In this case, her skin was flaking off.

11–13. A better grasp of Miriam's skin condition comes from verse 12 through the comparison of her skin to the appearance of a stillborn infant.

It is ironic in verses 11–12 that Aaron and Miriam require the intercession of the very person whose special role as intermediary they had called into question (E. W. Davies 1995b: 114). For Aaron, as high priest and therefore one who functions *as* mediator between the Israelites and God, to turn to another for intercession demonstrates a certain subordination in contrast to the assertions of equality in verse 2. Aaron articulates Moses' superiority by addressing Moses as *my lord* in verse 11. Aaron also provides a clear example of contrition, acknowledging his foolish sin along with Miriam's.

14. The comparison of Miriam's situation with that of a woman shamed by her father through his spitting in her face can be explained in part through comparison with Deuteronomy 25:9; Isaiah 50:6, which indicate public shaming. Therefore, while it is unstated, God healed Miriam of her skin condition, so now she had to serve a seven-day period of either ritual purification (Lev. 13 – 14) or recovery from shame.

15–16. While Miriam receives little attention in comparison with Moses and Aaron in the Pentateuch, the people's waiting for her indicates that she was highly valued by the Israelites. Just as in 9:6–14, God's pace, and, consequently, Israel's, is determined by compassion towards those in vulnerable conditions. In both cases the condition is impurity. In some ways, one might argue that the people's confirmation of her importance serves as a critique of her separation out from Aaron for individualized punishment in the story. She suffers for both of them. The attack on Moses on account of his foreign wife leads to the suffering of a powerful Israelite woman on account of her and Aaron's unjustified attack.

While verse 3 focuses on Moses' silence in the face of opposition, the truly silent character in the story is the Cushite wife: as a foreigner and a woman, she became the target of those in power. The problem is not with the foreign woman who becomes intimate with Moses, but rather with those persons intimate with Moses by nature of their high leadership positions. Miriam's shaming places her in a similar unprotected situation to that of the foreign wife, a measure-for-measure punishment (Jeon 2022: 212), and in this case the Israelites recognize her plight and her vulnerability, and they restore her. This model should also be envisioned for the foreign women among the Israelites, such as Moses' Cushite wife.

Meaning
Numbers 11 – 12 raises a number of obstacles for leaders. In Numbers 11, Moses attempts to take on a burden that he cannot bear alone, which leads him to despair, lack of vision and

ultimately becoming unable to advocate with God on behalf of the people. In Numbers 12, accusations come from the inner circle, much as the psalmist laments in Psalm 41:9–12. However, in this case Moses steps into the role of intercession for Miriam and Aaron: he stands between humans and God, and God listens to this steward in charge of the divine household.

As with Moses as a leader under siege, the narrative in Numbers 12, especially verse 3, provides the hope for those who are falsely accused that God advocates for them. This model is taken up in the Sermon on the Mount in Matthew 5:5: 'Blessed are the meek, for they will inherit the earth.'

Further, God's unwillingness to entertain the criticism of Moses' foreign wife undercuts any basis for xenophobia and racism and offers some poetic justice: Miriam experiences the ostracism she proposes for Moses' unnamed wife. Furthermore, God and Israel are patient and gracious in waiting for her until she can be restored back to the camp. Neither status, sibling connection nor leadership position can guarantee the respect appropriate for God's choice of leaders and hierarchies. Bringing the weeping of the outsider 'riffraff' of 11:4 together with the silence of Moses' Cushite wife underscores this point further: outsiders, just like insiders, must be judged on a case-by-case basis. Some can lead away from God while others do not.

The New Testament argues that Christ supersedes Moses in two ways in relation to this chapter. First, Hebrews 3:1–6 builds on the notion of Moses being the steward entrusted with God's house in juxtaposition with Jesus, who is God's Son. However, Jesus, as the Son, is the exact reflection of who God is (Heb. 1:3), surpassing Moses in his reflection of the divine image. Second, as the Son, Jesus' knowledge of the Father surpasses the revelation given to Moses (see John 6:46) and accords to Jesus the position to succeed Moses as the mediator between God and humans.

v. The great rebellion and failure to enter the Promised Land (13:1 – 14:45)

Context

While the momentum of the book of Numbers began to shift in Numbers 11 and 12 from the optimistic preparation for the journey to grumbling and punishment during the first stages of the journey to the Promised Land, chapters 13–14 narrate the key turning point of disobedience in the book. The Israelites arrive at the boundary of the land promised to them since Exodus 3:8 and to their ancestors as far back as Abraham (Gen. 12:7; 15:7; 17:8). Instead of entering victoriously, the Israelites' unwillingness to possess the land in response to the spies' reports results in God's punishment of forty years of wandering in wilderness. Rather than a liminal place filled with divine provision – such as of manna, water and divine wisdom in the form of legal precepts – as the wilderness journey had largely been thus far, the wilderness becomes the quintessential place of death.

It is best to begin the narrative with 12:16 ('After the people broke camp from Hazeroth they camped in the wilderness of Paran', AT), which provides a geographic link to 13:3, and also to 20:1. As a result, the whole section from Numbers 13 to 20:1, with its tragic disobedience (chs. 13–14), ritual prescriptions (chs. 15, 18, 19) and leadership challenges (chs. 16–17), can be connected with this location (as argued by Wenham 1981: 16–17). However, location does not play any role in Numbers 15 – 19.

What became the debacle of the Israelites' disobedience to God's command to possess the land of Canaan in Numbers 13 – 14 does not begin ominously. Rather, it begins with a divine command (13:1–2), and, in response, the setting aside of twelve tribal leaders to survey the land (13:3–16). Moses then provides them with detailed instructions on what to observe and bring back (13:17–20), which is followed by the narrative of their exploration (13:21–25). The final section of chapter 13 presents the differing reports of the spies (13:26–33), thus ending the chapter with the open question of which way the people will decide.

The people reject Moses and Aaron's leadership (14:1–10) and thereby God's; they express the desire to return to Egypt in line with the theme already found in chapters 11–12. In dialogue with Moses, God lays out a plan comprising both forgiveness and punishment: this generation will die in the wilderness, but their children will then occupy the Promised Land in their stead (14:11–38). The episode ends with an attempt by the Israelites to go back on their previous decision: they try to occupy the land, but, without God's presence and help, they experience defeat (14:39–45).

Greater depth is brought to the interpretation of this chapter through comparison with Deuteronomy 1:20–25 (cf. Deut. 9:23, and the poetic summary in Ps. 106:24–27), which presents the tradition of the spies and people's unwillingness to enter the land from its own viewpoint. As usual, reading the two presentations in concert brings the theological themes of each text better into focus (see Introduction, 'Reading in concert', for more explanation of this approach).

Comment

a. Divine instruction to survey the land and the choice of leaders (13:1–24)

1–2. The opening verses depict Yahweh as the source of the idea for sending spies, which contrasts with Deuteronomy 1:22–23, where the people take the initiative and ask Moses to send spies. It may be possible to harmonize these two accounts, but such an interpretation misses the question this contrast raises in terms of the *purpose* of sending out spies within the context of each narrative. The goal in this commentary is, rather, to engage with the correlations and disjunctions that appear in and between the texts. In the case of Numbers 13, the overarching goal is to elicit the Israelites' trust in the divine promise (cf. the similar intentions of sending spies in Josh. 2:24; Judg. 18:10), or even the divine land grant that comes in verse 2. God, as the divine and sovereign king, grants the land to the Israelites and wants them to perceive it as a good gift and claim it as their possession by going through it (see Ska 2014: 113–114; cf. Num. 33). The rest of the narrative unfolds under the umbrella of this divine declaration. This point becomes especially pertinent in relation to the differing reports and advice offered by the spies in verses 30–33 and forms the basis for God's severe judgment in 14:11–45. On a smaller note, the narrative's opening with articulating God's giving of the land provides the foundation for the individual instructions appearing in verses 17–20.

3. The location of this narrative – the wilderness of Paran (cf. 12:16; also 13:26: Kadesh in the wilderness of Paran; Deut. 1:19, 46) – does not appear in the same order in the itinerary of camps in Numbers 33, where a plethora of locations come between Hazeroth (33:18; cf. 12:16) and Kadesh (33:36–37). Some texts (20:1; 27:14; 34:4; Josh. 15:3) link Kadesh to the wilderness of Zin (not the same region as wilderness of Sin found in Exod. 16:1) rather than Paran. The two regions were, or came to be seen as, overlapping through the combination of two traditions about the spying (Levine 1993: 54). In mind here for Kadesh is a spring on the southern border of the land promised to Israel.

4–15. The naming of the leaders chosen as spies recalls the choosing of leaders in 1:4–16. However, the individuals mentioned here do not appear outside this narrative, except for Joshua (*Hoshea*) and Caleb. No persuasive explanation has been put forward as to why the order of the tribes differs here from that in other lists such as in Numbers 1 – 4, though it may simply indicate their youth compared to the leaders in Numbers 1 (Morales 2024a: 326). Here, Zebulun and Issachar are separated from each other, as are Ephraim and Manasseh.

The choice of one leader from each of the twelve non-Levite tribes indicates that they performatively occupy the divinely given land as they journey through it, which is meant to be the preliminary act that the people as a whole should bring to fulfilment after their report (i.e. at the end of the chapter).

Their naming initially points in a hopeful direction in the light of the parallel with Numbers 1: the task of taking the census for which the leaders were set apart in Numbers 1 ended successfully. However, the lack of any further mention of the other ten spies again is bound up with their failure to trust God's promise of successful occupation of the land.

16. If read in the light of name changes elsewhere (e.g. Abram > Abraham, Sarai > Sarah in Gen. 17), then the change of Hoshea's name ('he saves') to Joshua ('Yahweh saves') indicates that he will be an important figure in the history of God's people. The alteration from an unnamed saviour ('he') to a Yahwistic name coincides with the revelation to Moses of God's personal name as Yahweh in Exodus 6: according to the narrative chronology, Joshua's parents would not have been familiar with Yahweh as the name of Israel's God at the time of Joshua's birth in Egypt.

17. The verse begins by repeating the language from verse 3 (before the list of names) and now offers specific directions. The extent of the land Moses orders the spies to reconnoitre in this verse and elaborated in verses 21–22 seems jumbled. It is *the land of Canaan* at the start of verse 17, which the latter part of the verse explains as *the Negeb, and . . . the hill country*, which encompasses a smaller region than the land of Canaan as a whole.

18–20. Moses' specific command for the spies' investigation includes information that is important both for taking the land (the nature of the people and their dwellings) and for enjoying its fruits once they dwell there (*good or bad, rich or poor, trees*). The emphasis falls on the latter, evidenced by the directive to bring some of its produce, so that the spies' report should motivate the Israelites to occupy the land. The final statement, *the season of the first ripe grapes*, places the events in the late summer, thus four to five months after leaving Sinai.

21–22. The spies go all the way to *Rehob, near Lebo-hamath*. While interpreters debate the exact location, it might be identified with Beth-Rehob, near Dan in Israel's north, or even farther north-east in the vicinity of Lebweh (i.e. Lebo-hamath) in the Beqa' Valley in Lebanon. If the latter, it correlates with the furthest boundary of the territory ever claimed by the Israelites (cf. Josh. 13:5; 1 Kgs 8:65; 2 Kgs 14:25, 28). The expanse from the southern wilderness to Rehob represents an ideal picture of the land of Canaan (cf. Num. 34:8) that corresponds to the boundaries of the Egyptian province of Canaan before 1200 BC.

However, the narrative in verses 22–23 emphasizes the city of *Hebron*, which is in the southern hills (south of Jerusalem), and the *Wadi Eshcol*, apparently nearby, both of which are much closer to the current Israelite camp. Some interpreters take this as a sign that multiple traditions about the spies have been integrated with one another, though it may also be that verse 21 provides an overview and verse 22 a detailed description of one part of the journey.

Ancient Hebron (Tell er-Rumeide/Tell Hebron) lies 19 miles (32 km) south of Jerusalem and was an important location at various points in Israel's history. A number of the ancestors from Genesis were buried there (Gen. 23:19; 35:29; 50:13), and David ruled from Hebron for seven years before conquering Jerusalem (2 Sam. 2 – 5). The earliest remains of a fortified city there come from the Early Bronze Age III (*c.*2500 BC) and then a new wall was built in the Middle Bronze Age II (*c.*1700 BC), around the time of Abraham in the biblical chronology, which was 15 feet (4.5 m) high in some places (Ben-Shlomo 2018).

The comparison of Hebron with *Zoan* (Tanis) of Egypt highlights the antiquity of the town and therefore its importance. Once thought to be the capital city for the Hyksos Dynasties in the mid second millennium, archaeologists now associate Zoan with the time period around 1000 BC, that is, the biblical period of David. Thus, Hebron is more than seven centuries older than Zoan, and this remark may relate to a building effort of Hebron in David's time.

But, more importantly for this narrative, verse 22 underscores the *Anakites* dwelling there. The term 'Anak' itself in Hebrew means 'neck', or by extension 'necklace', or rather 'long-necked = tall'. The three named Anakites appear again in Joshua 15:14 for the clans that Caleb displaces from Hebron at that time. At least the names Sheshai and Talmai likely come from the Hurrian language, largely known from ancient Anatolia (modern Türkiye) and closely related to the Hittite Empire that exercised influence in the southern Levant (the region of Israel), in conflict with Egypt, until around 1200 BC.

23–24. The short mention of carrying a single cluster of grapes on a pole (or perhaps a platform) emphasizes its great size: both the people and the produce are gigantic. *Eshcol* means '(grape) cluster'; the location is unidentified.

b. Return and report of the scouts with positive and negative features (13:25–33)

25. Adult men, keeping a good pace, would be able to make this journey on foot in forty days. But this is a generalized period and a symbolic number that resurfaces in 14:34, where God condemns the Israelites to wander for forty years, one year for each day of the spies' survey.

26–29. The spies' initial report carries out Moses' imperatives of verses 18–20: two verses highlight the land's bounty, and two highlight the powerful opposition residing there. However, they invert the order from Moses' instructions and end with the note about the land's fortified towns and powerful inhabitants (vv. 28–29). They physically present the fruit (cf. v. 23) and then use the classic portrayal for the land as 'flowing with milk and honey' (cf. e.g. Exod. 3:8, 17; 13:5; 33:3; Lev. 20:24; Deut. 6:3; 11:9; 26:9). This expression is a merism for all food products, from the most basic nourishment for human life (milk) to the superfluous extra that sweetens human life (honey). The expression here communicates 'both sufficiency for everyday life, with the added prestige of Yahweh-given nourishment' (Welton 2022: 19).

The peoples mentioned in verse 29 are largely those viewed as the traditional inhabitants of the land before the Israelites, though their locations can vary (cf. Exod. 34:11; Deut. 7:1; Josh. 11:3).

30–31. There is no notice that the people had become boisterous and were in need of quieting, so mentioning that Caleb 'hushes' them reveals the tension of the moment. These two verses propose opposite conclusions from the same data: Caleb and the others had seen the same land and people, but Caleb focuses on the *land*, while the other spies fix their remarks on the *people* (Schart 1990: 66). They represent different perceptions of the land based on their hearts and eyes (see 15:39).

The fact that it is Caleb who displays trust in God's promise is striking. While it only becomes apparent later in the narrative, he comes from Edomite stock (32:12; Josh. 14:6, 14; cf. Gen. 36:10–11). This description of Caleb is even more surprising in the light of Israel's struggle with Edom in 20:14–21 and Balaam's oracle against Edom in 24:18. In other words, this man with non-Israelite ancestry (and his family) becomes integrated into the Judahite tribe, so much so that he becomes one of its leaders and an outspoken worshipper of Yahweh.

32–33. The spies' negativity increases: their report is 'slandering about the land' (AT) with strong imaginative language: the land eats its inhabitants. The expression may be a generalization denoting the region as a warlike place, with a connotation of divine judgment for rebelling against Yahweh (see Lev. 26:38; Ezek. 36:13–14) that will appear clearly in Numbers 16:31–33. In any case, they argue that the land is unfit to sustain Israel's life, a conclusion that rejects Yahweh's promise of the land as a good gift.

The *Nephilim* appear otherwise only in Genesis 6:4, as a pre-flood mixture of divine fathers and human mothers. They become the main source of the spread of violence that leads to the destruction of creation. By this imaginative association of Canaan with the Nephilim, the spies deepen their perception of the land as a means of death and not of life. Likewise, the inward projection of how these spies *saw themselves* as grasshoppers does not actually inform the audience about how those dwelling in the land actually viewed the spies. The comparison with grasshoppers can be taken in several ways (which can be combined with one another as a layered reading): (1) Leviticus 11:21–22 presents them as the smallest creatures approved for Israelite consumption. However, consumption of clean animals neither bears importance in this narrative, nor would it concern non-Israelites. (2) Grasshoppers or locusts could advance upon a region like an unstoppable and voracious army (cf. 2 Chr. 7:13; Joel 1:4–7). (3) God is described as viewing all earthly inhabitants as little grasshoppers from upon the heavenly throne (Isa. 40:22).

c. The rebellious decision of the people to choose leaders to return to Egypt (14:1–4)

1. Verses 1 and 2 pile up a number of expressions for distress and murmuring, akin to the narratives in Exodus 15 – 17; Numbers 16 – 17. A *rabble* rebelled in Numbers 11; Miriam and Aaron grumble against Moses in Numbers 12; and Levites and other leaders reject Aaron's priestly leadership in Numbers 16 – 17. However, verses 1–2, 5 emphasize that it is the *entire* people (adult men) of Israel who rebel. The intertwining of multiple terms indicates the gravity and confusion of the situation.

2–4. Now, the Israelites wax nostalgic not only about Egypt, but also about the wilderness journey to this juncture, wishing that they had perished in one of these two locations. In pronouncing their punishment in verses 29, 32, God will grant their stated desire to die in the wilderness.

The Israelites' discussion about appointing a new leader to take them back to Egypt seeks to replace Moses and Aaron, who led them out of Egypt. This movement goes beyond the simple expression of nostalgia about Egypt, which appears in 11:18, 20: now they take a step towards returning – an anti-exodus. The enormity of this act is that it seeks to undo God's election of Israel and deliverance of them, rejecting their special relationship (Knierim and Coats 2005: 193).

d. Joshua and Caleb give a positive report and encourage the people (14:5–10)

5. Falling upon one's face is typically a sign of honour or worship, so it is striking that Moses and Aaron take this action *before all the assembly* rather than before God. The closest parallel appears in 16:4, where Moses has the same response when confronted by Korah and associates. That narrative bears similarity to the intention to appoint a new leader on display here in verse 4. However, in Numbers 16, Moses then proposes a test to see whom God has chosen. Here, it is Joshua and Caleb who mount a defence, which might indicate that Moses and Aaron have given up doing anything to stop the people's plan.

6–9. Joshua and Caleb perform a gesture typical of mourning by tearing their clothes. Their speech heightens the rhetoric, proclaiming the land they explored to be (lit.) 'very, very good', which even outstrips God's declaration that creation is 'very good' in Genesis 1:31. Their emphasis lies on the land as a good gift from God that is able to sustain life abundantly, so that when the inhabitants of the land are mentioned it is only to pronounce their doom. They highlight a picture of the future in which God takes centre stage, which contrasts with the lack of a divine presence in the argument of the other spies in 13:27–29, 31–33 (one might call it a practical atheism). The conditional statement *If the LORD is pleased with us, he will bring us into this land* in verse 8 proves foreboding; God is *dis*pleased, so their later attempt at entry in verses 44–45 fails.

The expression 'for they are bread for us' (ESV) used by Joshua and Caleb partially counters the argument used by the other spies in 13:32: the inhabitants of the land, not the Israelites, are the food (however, closer linguistic connection can be found in Deut. 7:16; Ps. 14:4).

The notion of *protection* accorded to the people of the land is literally their 'shade, shadow' (*ṣēl*), which is a common description of the protection provided by various deities both in the Bible (e.g. Pss 91:1; 121:5–6) and in surrounding cultures.

10. Stoning is always carried out by an assembly in biblical texts, often as the punishment after a trial (e.g. Lev. 24:14; Num. 15:35–36; Josh. 7:25), though it could also be the result of mob violence (1 Kgs 12:18). In either case, the punishment intends to serve as a spectacle to make an example of the victims and arouse the rage of the executioners.

The appearance of Yahweh's glory to all Israelites marks this event as extraordinary and pivotal in the relationship between Yahweh and Israel, just as in Leviticus 9:23. There it marks a positive event but here a negative. The text does not state *how* Yahweh's glory keeps them safe; it is likely that all four – Moses, Aaron, Joshua and Caleb – were at risk. In antiquity, the splendour of a deity was understood to be overwhelming for humans, much like the experience of Isaiah in Isaiah 6:1–5 or the Israelites at Sinai in Exodus 24:17; Deuteronomy 5:24, which filled humans with dread. The rejection of God's leaders (Moses and Aaron) brought about a direct response from God, first in the appearance of the divine glory, and then in dialogue with Moses in the subsequent verses. God's glory appears at the tent of meeting, which one must assume was close enough to the gathering to make an impact.

e. God's condemnation and Moses' intercession (14:11–19)

11. With the divine appearance, the whole nature of the narrative changes. The people, Aaron, Joshua and Caleb no longer play active roles while Yahweh and Moses discuss the fate of the Israelites. God's question *How long . . . ?* is an expression of exasperation often occurring as part of a lament. For example, the psalmist in Psalm 13:1–2 asks God how long suffering will continue as a form of critique of God. When God asks this question here, it critiques the persistence of Israel's disobedience (e.g. Exod. 16:28).

The key concept of this entire narrative can be summed up in the opposition of two verbs in this verse: 'this people *despise* me

. . . they [do] not *believe* in me' (ESV; emphasis added). Rather than trusting that God will see them through to the land as a good gift, they reject God and God's plan for them by characterizing the land as a means of death.

12. In response to the people's discussion of replacing Moses and rejecting God's deliverance from Egypt, God proposes destroying the Israelites and making a great nation out of Moses. God suggested this once before, in Exodus 32:10 (cf. Deut. 9:14), when Israel turned to idolatry in making the golden calf. The same proposition here shows the enormity of Israel's rebellion, viewing their unwillingness to possess the land on the same level as idolatry. (As will become evident below, there are more indications that Exod. 32 – 34 provides important context for Num. 13 – 14.)

13–19. Moses takes on the leadership role of intercessor here and pleads with God to maintain the relationship with the Israelites, using several arguments:

(1) He proposes that killing the Israelites will result in the diminishment of God's honour in the view of the peoples living in the land. Verses 13–16 imagine a fairly complicated development: Egypt would receive the report of God's wholesale destruction of the Israelites. They would then tell the occupants of Canaan about it. Those people would thereby conclude that Yahweh was unable to lead the Israelites into the land and fulfil the promise made to their ancestors. The emphasis in these verses is on God's presence in the midst of this people, highlighting God's intimate connection with them that was underscored by the appearance of Yahweh's glory to deal with this situation. Moses' appeal to God's reputation can come across as self-centred to a modern audience. However, if God is the powerful creator and sustainer of the world, viewing God as such means humans enter into a relationship with God starting from the human experience and become able to see reality as it is.

(2) Moses then (vv. 17–19) invokes and summarizes God's earlier self-description (Exod. 34:6–7; see also Neh. 9:17, 31; Ps. 103:8; Jon. 4:2) as loving and forgiving, which God proclaimed after the rebellion and idolatry of the golden calf. Those same qualities are recalled to provide the vision for how Yahweh

should act in this situation. God has thus provided Moses with the elements required to intercede for the people throughout Israel's journey and even its whole history. These elements further underline the connection between the two narratives. Both narratives include manifestations of Yahweh's glory (v. 10; Exod. 33:18). Exodus 33:19 indicates that Yahweh's glory, even the divine identity as a revelation of the divine name, can be basically summarized by the divine 'goodness' (Exod. 33:18). In the end, Caleb's perception of the land as *exceedingly good* (v. 7) and the spies' report as a form of 'slandering about the land' (13:32, AT) reveal what each party thinks of God. The complex description of God's character includes a number of features that cannot be reduced to any one term: *slow to anger*, loving (the term *ḥesed* is difficult to translate, but can just as easily be rendered 'covenant faithfulness' or 'lovingkindness'), *forgiving*, and yet carrying out punishment against the guilty across several generations. The punishment for iniquity taking place for up to four generations has in view a communitarian sense of identity: people do not exist as individuals, but rather as part of extended, multi-generational family units. In contrast to Exodus 34:6–7, verse 19 emphasizes God's forgiveness, and Moses recalls the previous forgiveness from Egypt to this moment.

f. God's forgiveness of Israel, but judgment against the exodus generation (14:20–35)

20–24. God changes from the earlier proposal to destroy Israel as a people to follow Moses' urging. However, God defines forgiveness as compatible with punishment of the generation involved in this rebellion. Divine forgiveness gives Israel another chance to be God's people in the life of another generation (v. 31). God swears an oath – which underscores the gravity of the statement – that all the men who have seen the divine *glory* (implied here is the divine goodness) and *signs* (plagues) done against Egypt and in the wilderness will not enter the Promised Land. Their viewing of those miracles coupled with their inability to perceive the goodness of the land, and therefore the goodness of God, led them to disobedience that results in punishment. The earlier experiences of God's greatness and care for Israel should have provoked trust, as they did in the counter-example of Caleb that appears in verse 24. Caleb is often described as one who, to translate literally, 'is full after me' (32:11–12; Deut. 1:36; Josh. 14:8–9, 14), though here the contrast is heightened even more by stating that he also has *a different spirit*.

In verse 22, the *ten times* that the Israelites have tested God need not be taken literally, instead meaning a great number of times.

25. This verse functions as a narrative break, allowing for a transition to the next section. The names of the Amalekites and Canaanites function as general monikers for 'enemies' here (similar to the use of Amalek and Edom in Balaam's last oracle in 24:15–24); they do not accord seamlessly with 13:29. One might take 'Canaanite' as a general term for residents in the land, similar to the use of Amorites, and 'Amalekite' as the identifier of those nomadic peoples more directly in the vicinity of Israel's present, southern location. The direction of the Red Sea (this identification comes from the LXX, while the Hebrew has 'Sea of Reeds') here likely means towards the Gulf of Aqaba, indicating a different body of water from the one crossed by the Israelites in Exodus 13 – 15. The mention of this body of water functions theologically, however, to indicate that the Israelites are headed back to the *beginning* of their wilderness journey rather than nearing its end (Pressler 2017: 124).

26–27. Verses 26 to 35 return from what apparently was a side conversation carried on by Yahweh and Moses to include Aaron as well. *How long . . . ?* in verse 27 repeats the idea of the Israelites' rejection of Yahweh from verse 11 (with a different term). This section as a whole goes on to declare God's judgment. Some interpreters (e.g. Noth 1968: 97–112; Jeon 2022: 240–257) see the interweaving of two forms of this traditional story at play here – one generally in verses 11–25, and the other in verses 26–38.

28. In accord with the people's expressed desire to die in the wilderness, God condemns them to this fate in an act of poetic justice.

29–30. The identification of those *twenty years old and upwards* who will die in the wilderness recalls the men counted in the census in Numbers 1. It reminds the audience that God (through Moses and the tribal leaders) organized the Israelites into a sacred force on a pilgrimage to occupy the land. Its appearance here marks their failure to live up to that calling.

31–32. The irony continues in that the children, whom the Israelites thought would become captives, will experience God's guidance first-hand bringing *them* into the land, though they, too, will first suffer the consequences of their fathers' rejection of that same divine leadership. No mention of the wives from verse 3 is made. The morbid fate of the fathers is on display in that the 'carcasses' (NKJV) fall in both verses 29 and 32, and 'lie' (better: 'are finished off', from the Hebrew root *t-m-m* meaning 'complete, finish', in v. 33).

33–35. The forty years of wandering equating to the forty days of exploring the land has in mind the length of a generation (though the actual average lifespan was much shorter), specifically the exodus generation condemned above. The children living as *shepherds* likely has in mind the nomadic lifestyle associated with shepherding. These children must bear the 'unfaithfulness' (*zĕnût*; v. 33) of their fathers. This multi-generational consequence describes the interconnectedness of identity and responsibility, as well as the realistic perspective of how the tragedy of previous generations affects future ones. The Hebrew term *zĕnût* otherwise appears only in the prophets (Jer. 3:2, 9; Ezek. 23:27; 43:7, 9; Hos. 4:11; 6:10), who use it with connotations of infidelity to describe Israel and Judah's idolatrous rejection of Yahweh as their God.

g. Death of the ten spies who slandered the Promised Land (14:36–38)

36–38. These verses narrate the immediate demise of the ten spies responsible for slandering the land, one may even say a kind of 'God-less' report: Yahweh strikes them with a plague, so they become the first to die as a consequence of the rejection of God's leadership as a harbinger for the rest of their generation.

h. Attempt and failure to enter the land without the divine presence (14:39–45)

39–40. This final section of the story narrates the attempt by the people to undo their earlier unwillingness to possess the land in quick fashion. However, God has proclaimed that this generation's chance has passed. Therefore, their attempt merely amounts to another act of disobedience.

The section begins with Moses' public announcement of God's judgment against them that was decided in the private discussions of verses 11–25 and verses 26–38. Initially the Israelites respond with mourning. This mourning then transforms (v. 40) into the people's seemingly newfound willingness to obey. Several terms mimic the obedient action of Abraham in Genesis 22:1–4: rising early in the morning, stating *Here we are* (Gen. 22:1: 'Here I am'), going to the place God/Yahweh has commanded (Gen. 22:4), and going up to one of (Gen. 22:2) / the top of (Num. 14:40) the mountains. Similarly, Moses in Exodus 34:2–4 goes up to the top of Mount Sinai early in the morning. They prepare themselves to receive a favourable manifestation of God, but according to their own disposition and not God's. This characterizes a form of religious manipulation of God that encounters strong criticism in Numbers 22 – 24.

41–44. Despite the Israelites' intentions, Moses points out that their venture is doomed before it starts because, regardless of what the people do, Yahweh is not with them. They are in fact trans-gressing God's command (v. 41). Ironically, just as the ten spies did not consider God's role in assisting the Israelites in occupying the land, so the Israelites omit the need for divine help here as well. This omission is underscored in the statement in verse 44 *even though the ark . . . had not left the camp*, as well as in Moses' declaration (v. 42) that Yahweh is not in their midst. This group of people is not the Israelite camp, God's people, as they were organized and ordered in Numbers 1 – 4. Furthermore, it was only when God directed them through the lifting of the cloud and with the ark that the Israelites were to set out, according to 9:17–23; 10:33–35. In the light of these earlier directives, the supposed obedience of the Israelites in verse 40 is unmasked as presumption in verse 43. It is not *follow[ing] [Yahweh] wholeheartedly* as Caleb did (v. 24), but rather *turn[ing] back from following* Yahweh (v. 43). Therefore, their defeat comes as no surprise.

45. The location of *Hormah* remains uncertain, though it reappears in 21:3, where the Israelites will then be victorious. In Joshua 15:30 it belongs to the region of Beersheba, in the southern region of the Negev of Israel. Interpreters commonly associate it with Tell el-Meshash, east of Beersheba.

Meaning
The entire book of Numbers so far has led to the narrative climax in these two chapters: the Israelites prepared for and are now on the cusp of entering the land. At the end of Numbers 13, the Israelites are left with a clear choice: do they embrace Caleb's report in verse 30 that they are able to occupy the land, or do they instead follow the view of the other spies and see themselves as grasshoppers? In the life of faith, one is often confronted with different ways to see or evaluate a situation. Multiple viewpoints can be grounded in perceived, or partial, reality and yet point in different directions: through the eyes of Numbers 13:2, *the land. . . which [Yahweh is] giving*, or 13:28, *the people who live in the land are strong*. This section narrows the choice down to rejection or trust in God (14:11). The journey of the spies was not supposed to be a military strategy for how to defeat enemy armies, but a faithful claiming of the land as God's good gift, similar to God's own claim over many places in Numbers 33. Sometimes, however, fear of opposition from a mentality of dispute and struggle even leads one astray into imaginative speculation, such as in 13:32–33: *a land that devours its inhabitants*, and giants like the Nephilim.

The contrast between Caleb's perception of the land as 'very good' and the way the spies 'slander about the land' indicates a contrast between trusting God's goodness as revealed extraordinarily to Moses and to the whole people, and rejection of that goodness. In the end, it is a question about perceiving the world as a good gift from God that nurtures and sustains life, or seeing it as a kind of death trap that God places to annihilate us. The challenge is for people of faith to embrace God's goodness and long-term promises, like occupying the land for the Israelites in this section, even in those times when fulfilment seems out of reach because real danger might threaten us, though such a conclusion may foreclose on an even bigger picture in which it might not be the case.

God's punishment of the people in Numbers 14 focuses on those who had previously seen (experienced) divine miracles on their behalf. This proclamation of punishment carries with it a warning: God expects people of faith to recall God's work in their past in order to evoke trust in the midst of present challenges as well as hope for the future.

The dialogue between Moses and Yahweh in 14:17–24 offers an intricate reflection on God's character, given the human propensity to sin. Because God offers this self-description in Exodus 34:6–7 (cf. Exod. 33:19), it provides an optimal entry point. However, such narrative presentations that describe God's character contain a number of facets that cannot be reduced to one another: kindness/faithfulness, forgiving, and punishing of iniquity remain both irreducible and interwoven. Therefore, while God does forgive Israel, not giving up on it as the covenanted people by extending the promise to a new generation, this does not exclude the consequences of their lack of trust in God's promised provision. It is on this theme that the author of Hebrews reflects in Hebrews 3:7 – 4:13 when recalling Numbers 13 – 14 as a means to encourage that letter's audience to embrace God's promise of rest in their present moment (Heb. 3:13, 'as long as it is called "today"'). Paul, too, references this story in 1 Corinthians 10:5 to exhort readers and hearers to continue to trust God in the face of trials in the present (1 Cor. 10:13). Even when previous generations of God's people fail, new ones can have hope in God's goodness.

Moses' intercession is remarkable in several ways: (1) It provides a roadmap for how a leader can pray passionately on behalf of those in their care by appealing to God's revealed 'special interests', such as mercy and care for victims of oppression and violence. (2) In contrast to many ancient and modern leaders (despite their rhetoric!), Moses rejects *personal* gain in favour of the well-being of the Israelites.

The interaction between Moses and God also raises the issue of whether God's mind can be changed, which would represent a straightforward reading of this passage and some others. However, this does raise a philosophical difficulty with the traditional understanding of God's perfection and simplicity, atemporality and foreknowledge, according to which God's mind does not change.

The concluding scene (14:39–45) offers a different insight: what should one do after realizing that a grave error has been made? The Israelites do acknowledge their sin, but they are unwilling to embrace the painful consequences that come with it. Instead, they want God to act on their terms. They try a quick remedy, but the damage often cannot be undone so easily. Maintaining faith *after* the acknowledgment of sin requires accepting God's leadership *through* the consequences and the long process of restoration and relearning, rather than assuming that all negative repercussions will disappear.

3. RETURN TO AND PUNISHMENT IN THE WILDERNESS (15:1 – 20:29)

A. Revising instructions of consecration of the people in the Promised Land (15:1–41)

Context

Immediately after the failure to take the land – first out of unwillingness to trust God's superiority over the inhabitants, and then because God had abandoned their efforts – despair presents itself as an easy option. In response, Numbers 15 offers . . . *law*. Why? How can laws function as an antidote to despair? This chapter represents the attempt to press on. Even more, 15:2 quickly offers hope for a future: *When you come into the land* . . . God remains committed to Israel.

The chapter includes several diverse topics, though there are some terminological links back to Numbers 13 – 14 that anchor chapter 15 to this location. Verses 3–16 explain the proportions of grain, oil and drink the people should bring for offerings once settled, thereby reaffirming the land's goodness as a divine gift and providing a vision of a future time when the wandering of the present will have drifted decisively into the past. In verses 17–21 God commands Moses to tell them to bring a tithe of their dough – another manufactured product requiring farming. The chapter even explains how the Israelites can overcome sin against Yahweh once settled in the land (vv. 22–31).

Then, as one of several such narratives in the book (cf. 9:1–14 and 27:1–11), verses 32–36 record an example perhaps related to the stipulations just given. The chapter concludes (vv. 37–41) with a practice intended to help the people keep their focus on Yahweh.

A number of passages from elsewhere in the Pentateuch help with understanding the significance of the various sections in this chapter. The amounts of accompanying flour, oil and drink are best understood when compared with Leviticus 1; 3; 23:10–14; Ezekiel 46:5–7, 11, 14. The purification offering (15:22–29) appears in detail in Leviticus 4. For the value of the physical reminders comparable to those of 15:37–41, see Deuteronomy 6:8–9 and especially Deuteronomy 22:12.

Comment

i. Instructions for offerings with emphasis on proportions of offerings and accompaniments (15:1–16)

1–3. The chapter begins like so many sections in the book with direct speech from God to Moses. There is no indication within the chapter that it must have taken place immediately after the events of Numbers 13 – 14. However, the editorial placement of it here demonstrates God's continued commitment to Israel. The temporal dimension (v. 2) is important for two reasons. First, it reaffirms that the Israelites will take the land and bears similarity to the perspective of Deuteronomy. Second, it provides the reason for the additional requirements for offerings that will follow.

The traditional translation in verse 3 of *'iššê* as *offering by fire* (NRSV, KJV, NASB 1995) should probably be rendered 'food offering' (following NIV, ESV; understood as 'gift' as suggested by Milgrom 1990: 124; 1991: 161–162; see Num. 28:1–2 below for more information; cf. Lev. 24:7, 9).

4–16. The main bulk of this section reiterates and expands on the practice of bringing offerings from Leviticus 1 and 3. The amounts specified here are taken up in the offering calendar in Numbers 28 – 29. Numbers 15 focuses on the added grain (flour), oil, and drink accompaniments, similar to what appears in Exodus 29:38–40; Ezekiel 46:5–7, 11, 14; and Leviticus 23:12–14. Now, coming after Numbers 13 – 14, it serves to emphasize the goodness of the land (that it truly is *šĕmēnâ*, 'oil-like', 13:20; Morales 2024a: 372) in response to the spies' 'slandering about the land'. Such offerings would become possible only when the Israelites have their own farms to produce flour, olive oil and grapes. In any case, when in the land, the offerings should take the form of a festive meal: meat, bread and wine or 'strong drink' (see Introduction, 'The different types of offerings'). Israelites share the 'table' with God. Some of the amounts differ from those in the other texts. For example, in Exodus 29 and Ezekiel 46, the details are only for the burnt offering. The closest comparative text is Leviticus 23:12–14, which provides instructions for items to accompany the burnt offering of a lamb at the time when the firstfruits of the season are harvested. In Leviticus 23:13, the amount of semolina flour is two-tenths of an ephah with an unspecified amount of oil, while in Numbers 15:4 it is one-tenth – assumedly of an ephah though this detail does not appear in the text – of semolina flour mixed with a quarter of a hin of oil. They also share terminology of 'your settlements' in Leviticus 23:14 and Numbers 15:2, and the rest of Numbers 15:2–3 appears in Leviticus 23:10, which brings these texts closer together. One might understand Numbers 15 as expanding and adapting the application of an instruction that Leviticus 23 limited to the celebration of firstfruits of the grain harvest for a burnt offering to then apply to both burnt offerings and sacred offering feasts at various occasions throughout the year. Furthermore, Numbers 15 expands the range to include amounts of accompanying offerings not only for lambs (the young of sheep) and kids (the young of goats), but also for oxen and rams. Also of importance here is that the instructions are given to *whoever presents such an offering* (v. 4), not just to the priests or a leader.

In particular, the section mentions two basic types of offerings: the burnt offering (*ʿōlâ*), for which the whole animal generally goes upon the altar (cf. Lev. 1), and the sacred offering feast (*zebaḥ*), which could be for a prescribed feast or an individual vow.

There was some variation in the animals one could bring, and the size of the animal determined the amount of accompanying flour and drink, as Table 3.1 shows (measurements according to Kletter 2006; Winkler 2016; see Introduction, 'Excursus: weights and measures used in the offering descriptions').

In other words, the larger the animal, the more grain, oil and drink that should accompany it. The proportionality makes sense when viewed in terms of a banquet: in the case of the burnt offering, Yahweh is the only participant, while the sacred offering feast (*zebah*) – translated *sacrifice* in most versions – involves the participation of those bringing it (this appears clearly in Lev. 7:11–16). The greater the amount of meat from a particular animal, the more bread/grain product required as a side dish and wine or 'strong drink' as accompanying beverage.

By making the two parallel, it picks up on the widespread Ancient Near Eastern view that the offerings brought to the sanctuaries of gods functioned as food and drink for those deities (the most common comparison appears in the Mesopotamian flood story *Atrahasis*, when the gods smell the smoke rising from the offerings and descend upon the offerings like flies [3.5.34–35]; for translation see Foster 2005: 227–280). However, Numbers does not suggest that Yahweh actually 'ate' the food. Instead, as verse 3 notes, the part for God was burned, turning it into a *pleasing odour*, which commonly appears in contexts that address offerings for God (also 15:7, 10, 13, 14, 24; 18:17; 28:2, 6, 8, 13, 24, 27; 29:2, 6, 8, 13, 36; often as well in Leviticus, Ezekiel and Exod. 29; cf. Eph.

Table 3.1: Accompaniments for each sacrificial animal in Numbers 15

Verses	Animal	Flour	Oil	Drink
4–5	Lamb/ kid	¹⁄₁₀ (of an ephah) = 1.9 qt; 1.8 l	¼ hin = 0.8 qt; 750 ml	¼ hin = 0.8 qt; 750 ml
6–7	Ram	²⁄₁₀ = 3.8 qt; 3.6 l	⅓ hin = 1.1 qt; 1 l	⅓ hin = 1.1 qt; 1 l
8–10	Bull	³⁄₁₀ = 5.7 qt; 5.4 l	½ hin = 1.6 qt; 1.5 l	½ hin = 1.6 qt; 1.5 l

5:2; Phil. 4:18). This oft-repeated phrase makes Yahweh's sacrificial portion less material, picking up on the ethereal aspect of the divine realm, and yet it shows the importance of the sensuality of worship, in this case, smell.

Overall, 15:3–12 offers an elaboration on Leviticus 7 and a different vision of perfect worship from Ezekiel. As with the later sacred calendar of Numbers 28 – 29, the particular focus of these ordinances lies on the role of the people, those who bring the goods (see v. 4), rather than on the way the priest would burn them on the altar, pour them out, or take some for his and his family's own consumption. Placed after the spy debacle, the purpose of these instructions is to train the people's perception of reality.

The single set of ordinances for native-born and resident foreigner (vv. 14–16) appeared earlier in 9:14 in relation to Passover (see discussion there on the different kinds of foreigners who could be present among Israel). Now these verses expand that participation to a range of worship settings, marking the path to assimilation for outsiders into God's people. Verses 15 and 16 are somewhat repetitive: verse 15 focuses more on the offering prescriptions in verses 2–14, while verse 16 seems to take a broader view, perhaps having in mind the larger Pentateuchal law as a more unified whole (though this position encounters limits in, e.g., Deut. 14:21).

ii. The innovative offering of the first dough (15:17–21)

17–19. This small section addresses a new type of offering, most likely of the bread made from the first dough from the firstfruits of the grain harvest (thus of barley, given that barley was the first crop to ripen in the spring). The Hebrew term *ʿărîsâ* appears only here and in Nehemiah 10:37; Ezekiel 44:30 and probably means 'dough'. As in verse 2 above, this offering is specified for life *in* the land, which makes sense, given that it requires the product of a farm. However, an important development takes place: this type of offering brings worship into Israel's households, into their ordinary and daily life, thus training the people's perception of the goodness of the land in that this offering comes from the *bread of the land* (v. 19). This expression has a parallel in Joshua 5:10–12, when Israel enters the land and the manna ceases after the people eat from the 'produce of the land'. The new offering is a ritual to remember God's providence and care for Israel's life, once with the manna, and now from the produce of the land, God's good gift to Israel.

20–21. The elevation offering for the dough as a cake should take place in the same manner that one presents the elevation offering (of grain) when one finishes threshing (cf. Ruth 3:2). However, Numbers nowhere makes clear how one presented the elevation offering of grain. Perhaps in view is a presentation like that in Deuteronomy 26:2–10.

iii. Instructions for the purification offering (15:22–31)

22–31. These verses provide some updates to the prescriptions for the purification offering for unintentional sin in Leviticus 4:13–21, 27–35 (for the general purpose of the purification offering, see Introduction, 'The different types of offerings'): that chapter included details on the priestly duties for this ritual, as well as the animal offering specifications if the person at fault was a priest or leader in addition to those of the community as a whole or any individual member. Several important additions and changes appear in Numbers 15: (1) the addition of the accompanying grain and drink offering in verse 24, in line with the instructions earlier in Numbers 15; (2) the change from a bull for the purification offering in Leviticus 4:14 to a bull for the burnt offering and a *goat* for the purification offering for the congregation in Numbers 15:24. This change for the purification offering for the congregation aligns with the offering calendar found in Numbers 28 – 29, where a bull is often the burnt offering, and the purification offering is always a goat. (3) There is also the explicit inclusion of the resident foreigner in the community atoned for in verse 26 and this resident foreigner's inclusion in the prescriptions for the individual purification offer in verse 29. (4) Verses 30–31 declare that no amelioration can be made for wilful ('high-handed') sin, which should result in the person being *cut off* from the community.

Overall, the reiteration and discussion of these provisions here provide a contrast to the failure of Numbers 13 – 14 and that of 15:32–36. These regulations in their context prove suggestive in determining what differentiates unintentional (*bišgĕgâ*) sin and defiant sin. However, it is best to begin from within the section itself, which describes as 'high-handed' several acts in verses 30–31: blasphemy, despising the word of Yahweh, and breaking/declaring invalid (God's) commandment. The terminology of high-handedness is also clarified through its usage in relation to rebellion against a human king. In 1 Kings 11:26, Jeroboam 'rebelled', literally 'raised a hand', against King Solomon, and the Israelites exited Egypt with 'raised hand' (against Pharaoh; also Num. 33:3). The image suggests a hand ready to strike (Kellermann 1973: 112). On the basis of these comparative texts, such defiant sin concerns the *motivation* of the perpetrator, something notoriously difficult for humans to discern. It likely requires *knowledge* that the act was an affront to the ruler – in this case, God.[1] Given the use of the root *r-w-m* ('high') in this chapter, there is a contrast between loyalty to God by lifting up a contribution and rebelling by lifting up a hand against God (see Morales 2024a: 381–382).

In specifics, the unintentional sins include not doing 'all *these* commandments . . . spoken to Moses . . . from the day that the LORD gave commandment' (vv. 22–23, ESV). The emphasis provided by verse 23 suggests that 'these commandments' extend beyond those in 15:3–21, having something like the entire Pentateuch in view. This broad focus returns below in verses 37–41.

The distinction between the two types of offences also receives some insight from the prescribed punishment in verse 31, for the person (1) to be cut off and (2) to bear their guilt. The purification offering on one's behalf requires participation in the community of Yahweh's people, and it seems likely that being *cut off* means exclusion from the community as the source of subsistence, safety, identity and meaning for an individual or a group, implying the extinction of progeny (cf. D. P. Wright 1991; Levine 2000: 203–204; Sommer 2009: 77–78). Death may be included in this 'cutting off' (if one reads Exod. 31:14 and 35:2 together, then 'cutting off' can include death for work done on the Sabbath; the same is the

---

1   One might discern a *third* category: sins that are intentional but not necessarily defiant. This category does not appear in Num. 15, but rather in Lev. 5:1; 6:1–7 (Gane 2005: 201–213; Sklar 2013: 43).

case with blasphemy if Lev. 24:16 is brought together with Num. 15:31). The primary purpose of the purification offering consists in purifying the place of God's presence in the community, so that the divine presence can be encountered by those who have sinned as the result of purification and forgiveness, both aspects of atonement (see Introduction, 'Atonement and ritual').

Therefore, verses 22–31 imply that Israel's sin at Kadesh was 'high-handed', explaining the need for the exodus generation to die out or be 'cut-off', and giving the settling generation the remedy or counter-action to avoid the same (see Noonan 2020).

iv. A test case of intentional sin with no possibility of ritual remedy (15:32–36)

32–36. This narrative fits loosely into the literary context with its geographical setting *in the wilderness* (v. 32). However, it does fit well thematically as an illustration of a 'high-handed' sin and the community's necessary response. It presents an offence against the Sabbath rest that flummoxes both the Israelites and their leaders, Moses and Aaron. The particular dereliction, gathering wood, does not necessarily fall under any of the Sabbath regulations strewn throughout the Pentateuch (Exod. 20:8–11//Deut. 5:12–15; Exod. 31:15–17; 35:1–3; cf. Gen. 2:1–3),[2] for it is unclear whether this act constitutes work. However, a foreshadowing allusion to the experience of oppression appears in the use of the verb *q-š-š* ('gather, pick up'), which appears in Exodus 5:7, 12 for the Israelites needing to gather their own straw to make bricks in Egypt. This gathering of straw constituted an added burden to the oppressive labour from which God's salvation – immortalized in the Sabbath practice according to Deuteronomy 5:15 – released them. The action of the man, therefore, reflects a return to Egypt's way of life under Pharaoh's mastery, in rebellion to God similar to that of Numbers 13 – 14. Both episodes do not perceive

---

2 Nehemiah (Neh. 13:15–20) does not apply. The requirement of the death penalty in Exod. 31:14–15; 35:2 for work on the Sabbath does not specify what constitutes work; therefore these texts are not explicitly related to the current text.

God's goodness and care in the gift of the land. The man was living as if still in Egypt even after having been liberated from it (see Novick 2008: 4–5). This framing of an Egyptian form of work and production gives a nod to a narrative with a similar literary role in Leviticus 24:10–23, which deals with blasphemy against God's name by the son of an Egyptian man. In both cases, this highlights the singular instruction (Torah) for both Israelites and foreigners (Num. 15:16, 29; Lev. 24:22).

It is in keeping with Exodus 18:19, 22; Deuteronomy 1:17 and the related events in Leviticus 24:10–23; Numbers 9:1–14; 27:1–11 that difficult cases be brought to Moses (and, according to Deut. 17:8–13, to the priest, who here in Num. 15:33 is Aaron). In fact, the verb for 'be difficult' in Deuteronomy 1:17, *q-š-h*, sounds much like the term for 'gather' and suggests a wordplay on the proceedings here. God hands down the sentence of death by stoning to take place outside the camp, thus separating the death spatially from God's residence.

It has been argued that the lack of clarity concerned whether gathering wood constituted 'work' (cf. Exod. 31:14–15; 35:2), which would result in the death penalty. This uncertainty gives rise to what verse 34 most likely indicates: 'it had not been *decided*' (*p-r-š*; following NASB; Johnson 2020: 210). Thus, the decision from Yahweh represents an interpretive extension of the Exodus regulations. The passage presents an appropriate stoning (v. 36: *just as the LORD had commanded*; also Leviticus 24:23, which provides the basis of a biblical rescript that forms the legal foundation for this decision), which contrasts with the rebellious attempt to stone God's representatives in Numbers 14:10. The section remains vague on its relationship to the 'high-handed' offence in verses 30–31, though their juxtaposition suggests it functions as a reflection of the people's rebellion in Numbers 13 – 14 as a desire to return to Egypt in their approach to life.

v. Tassels of remembrance of the people's identity and consecration (15:37–41)

37–41. Nothing in this section indicates its temporal or geographic setting; therefore, its literary placement at the end of this chapter can be seen as an attempt by the editor to respond to the previous sections, which encompass the material from Numbers 13 to 15:36, and invoke obedience by the repetition of rituals that are able to train and model humans' perception. It makes explicit the reason for the tassels on one's garment found in Deuteronomy 22:12, setting them in conversation with the reason for other concrete reminders of God's teaching such as those in the previous section concerning offerings and worship and in Deuteronomy 6:6–9, which addresses the same topic. One should keep *them* in one's heart (Deut. 6:6), rather than things that can lead astray (Num. 15:39). The reason for such reminders is summed up in verses 40–41, which reaffirm the covenantal bond between Israel and Yahweh: that Yahweh's people be set apart (holy) to the one who delivered them from Egypt.

Surprising connections to Numbers 13 – 14 appear in verse 39. The Israelites should avoid 'chasing' (NIV; *t-w-r*) what comes from their hearts and their eyes – this is the same verb used of the spies' investigation of the land in 13:2, 16, 17, 21 and so on. That 'chasing' or 'investigating' led to the Israelites' unfaithfulness (14:33), and verse 39 here prohibits it because it will again result in unfaithfulness (*z-n-h*, NIV: 'prostitute yourselves'). This way of interpreting the spies' unfaithfulness in chapters 13–14 reveals that the problem was not with the land itself, but with their hearts and eyes that led them to a deceitful perception of the land and, therefore, God. In order to avoid the debacle of Numbers 13 – 14, as well as events like those in verses 30–31, 32–36, verse 38 proposes a concrete mnemonic device to help the Israelites recall *all . . . commandments* (vv. 39–40). God again recommends an external and material item to deal with an internal disposition, just like the worship rituals of the previous sections in the chapter. The tassels' dye was so expensive that the colour indicated royalty (blue or purple). The dye was obtained from snails on the Phoenician coast (for details, see commentary on 4:4–20) and was quite permanent (see Milgrom 1983: 62). The use of tassels was a general mark of high status in the Ancient Near East (Esth. 1:6; Ezek. 27:16). In the context of the previous section (vv. 32–36), when a man was reliving the slavery system of Egypt, the tassels serve as a reminder of the value, even the nobility, of those liberated by God from slavery. But the use of tassels is attached to priestly status and function in Numbers (see Kosior 2018), which aligns well with its use as a reminder of the requirement for the people to be holy. The tassels (*ṣiṣit*) on the Israelites' clothing are little 'crowns' (*ṣiṣ*) like that which forms part of the high priest's garments (Exod. 28:36–38) when in office and which has inscribed on it 'holy to Yahweh'. They are both attached to garments by a blue cord (v. 38; Exod. 28:37). The association with the priestly identity goes further by the meaning of *ṣiṣ* as 'blossom' or 'flower', which becomes significant in the next narrative, when the Aaronide high priesthood is reaffirmed when his staff (lit.) 'blossoms flower' (*wayyāṣēṣ ṣîṣ*, 17:8; Morales 2024a: 389). The tassels, therefore, work not only to connect the people's holiness with the priest, but also to point to the abundance and the goodness of the land under Yahweh's rule against the scarcity of the Egyptian way of life under Pharaoh's mastery.

Meaning
In its literary context, the main point of chapter 15 is to say 'Imagine the future!' and 'Beware the future!'

The detailed description of the offerings that makes up the first half of the chapter (vv. 1–21) recalls festive celebrations for ancient audiences: the food and drink constitute a banquet – either just for God or for God and the people – that looked and smelled appealing. The *pleasing odour* might not please the noses of many today, but its distinctiveness would have served to draw an ancient participant into the experience (cf. the incense in 4:16 as well). The introduction to these sections looks forward to life in the land given by God as a gift, encouraging readers to keep hope in God's provision of a glorious future.

The recurring note in verses 13–16 on the requirements being the same for the long-term resident foreigner – clearly a non-Israelite in this context – and the native Israelite with regard to bringing offerings can be related to Christian inclusion of those from other denominations or perhaps even outsiders in Christian practices such as communion (Sakenfeld 1995: 94). While some differences remain, these verses seek to lower the bar instead of raising suspicion with regard to outsiders seeking to worship God (one might call to mind Acts 15; Gal. 1 in this regard).

Participating in such practices provides an opportunity for both insiders and outsiders to experience and have their perception attune to God's goodness and gifts.

The second half of the chapter, verses 22–41, serves as a reminder for the people of God against disobedience towards the divine and holy deliverer: high-handed rebellion carries dire consequences, while even offences that are unintentional require attention. That is, verses 24–31 present ways in which sin can be both *communal* (or perhaps structural) and *individual*. The distinction made here between unintentional and defiant sin also points to the need for divine assistance to discern human motivations – whether or not they are rebellious in their core. The prescription for a means to deal with sin also suggests God's willingness to forgive and remain present with God's people. Sin does not have to be definitive.

The short episode of the wood-gatherer demonstrates how one can still rely on old approaches and habits, even when the circumstances that led to them are no longer present. It is also an example of the Israelites seeking the continuing guidance of God. Important here is the notion that even the legal stipulations given in Exodus to Numbers to this point did not prove exhaustive, but they allow for, and call for, continued invocation of God's wisdom for difficult cases.

Finally, the command to wear tassels shows the importance of having external reminders of the standing of the people of God in God's eyes, so that appropriate behaviour and treatment of others follows. It impresses further the importance of remembering Yahweh's character as saviour and as holy so that they shape the motivations of both individuals and communities towards the rest and bounty that God provides.

B. Rebellion against Moses and Aaron (16:1 – 17:13)

Context

The next two chapters continue to address the issues of leadership among God's people that appeared especially in Numbers 11 – 12 and challenge the hierarchy established in Numbers 3 – 4. They use several interwoven narratives whose chronology and location remain undefined, especially coming after the various divine prescriptions found in chapter 15. The narrative placement and linguistic connections with the spy story indicate only that they take place sometime after the return to the wilderness in chapter 14, after the defeat at the border of the land. No further details or their order are concerns for the text. The chapters instead address a series of issues that arise after the failure to take the land through exemplary stories: (1) Is Moses' authority still valid? (2) Is the holiness necessary to approach God limited to Aaron and his descendants? (3) Do all Levites have the privilege of the priesthood? And (4) do the Levites have a leadership position over the other tribes (see, similarly, Achenbach 2003: 39–40)?

Overall, these narratives assume Yahweh's separation of the Levites as the sanctuary personnel and Aaron and his descendants as the priests in Numbers 3. However, on the flip side, 15:40 declares the *whole* people of Israel holy, even hinting at a priestly identity, such that they should carry reminders of this fact attached to their very clothing. This proclamation relates to the question of how this shared status plays out in terms of leadership over a number of chapters (chs. 11–18). Chapter 18 summarizes the narrative conclusion of chapters 16–17 in legal formulations. In short, these chapters demonstrate that the shared status does not mean that the whole people have equal authority and leadership responsibility.

A significant challenge in the chapters arises in the attempt to understand the literary connections between the challenge brought by Korah the Levite, by the 250 leaders, and by Dathan and Abiram. After an introduction combining the challengers in 16:1–2, the narrative bounces back and forth between Korah and company (16:3–11, 16–22, 35–40) and Dathan and Abiram (16:12–15, 23–34), though some intertwining takes place. Then Yahweh takes the initiative to confirm Aaron and the priests' authority in 16:41 – 17:11 through the sprouting staff. This final section leads into a conclusion to the contests of ritual ordinances concerning access to the sanctuary and the payments for this service in chapter 18. The climax of Numbers 16 – 17 comes in the final verses (17:12–13), where the Israelites fear that they all will die for having come too close to God at the sanctuary. This recalls the people's similar response in Deuteronomy 5:24–27.

On the whole, the chapters collect a group of narratives *themati-cally*, making this section of text a focal point for discussions of hierarchy and leadership in God's people. Related to the issues concerning leadership in religious communities, the chapters also raise questions about individual and communal punishment for rebellion against God and God's approved leadership. Intertwined are insights on the notion of intercession.

Comment

i. Korah and others challenge Moses and Aaron's leadership based on priesthood prerogatives (16:1–35)

1–2. The chapter opens with introductions to the opponents of Moses and Aaron. Significantly, one is a Levite (Korah) and two others are Reubenite brothers (Abiram and Dathan; the fourth, On, is likely the result of a copyist error given that he does not appear in the rest of the text; see Ashley 2022: 258). Within this constellation, Korah the Levite challenges Aaron's priesthood. According to Exodus 6:18–21, Korah was Moses' cousin – Moses and Aaron's father was the eldest son of Kohath, and Korah's father was the middle son. And according to Numbers 3:27–31; 4:1–20, his clan was responsible for taking care of the most holy sanctuary furniture such as the ark and altars. On the other hand, the brothers Abiram and Dathan pose a different challenge. As brothers from the tribe of the eldest son of Jacob, they contest the leadership of Moses (presumably with his brother), related to a more prophetic theme.

Finally, verse 2 adds that 250 important men in the community join the fray: this was a broader uprising of well-connected, influential leaders. The text emphasizes their significance by describing them with multiple adjectives denoting their elite status in the community, which becomes significant in the final section (17:13; see below).

3. Their challenge to the authority of Moses and Aaron, 'Enough! For the whole congregation, all of them, are holy, and God is in their midst!' (AT), is founded on the statement in 15:40 and aligns with the notion that the Israelites are holy for their God (also Exod. 19:6; Lev. 19:2; Deut. 7:6; 14:2, 21). Yet does this broad holiness for the whole community carry over into (1) their proximity to God's dwelling place (the tent of meeting) similar to the priesthood and (2) the privileges and responsibilities of leadership? The contenders' view of leadership and authority seems distorted. They envision it as self-aggrandizing, lifting oneself over others.

4–7. Moses' answer to the challenge is to let God choose who should take up a priestly, that is, mediating, role between God and the people. Outside this story, rarely does anyone bring a censer of incense into God's sanctuary: we find it in Leviticus 10:1 and 16:12. In Leviticus 16:12 this describes an action that only the high priest carries out, and that only once a year, on the Day of Atonement. The gravity of this moment is heightened through comparison with Leviticus 10:1–2, when fire from God's presence kills Aaron's two eldest sons, Nadab and Abihu, for bringing unsolicited censers with incense. That incident bears much in common with this one in Numbers, with that same fate meeting the 250 challengers here in 16:35.

8–10. Here the story narrows the challenge to Korah and his group of Levites on one side and Yahweh (and Aaron) on the other. Other than Korah, no other Levite receives explicit mention, so his presence becomes representative for a larger group. Moses emphasizes Korah and the Levites' privileged position within the Israelites as a result of God's action in contrast to what Moses terms their 'murmuring against him' (v. 11, AT). *Him* in this context could refer either to Aaron or to Yahweh, and the formulation likely intends the vagueness in order to conflate the two. Korah's expressed desire for the priesthood finds support in Deuteronomy 18:1–8, which grants *every* Levite the privilege of offering sacrifices and eating the portions of these sacrifices given as payment to the priest performing the offering (MacDonald 2012b: 160–161).

11. The accusation of 'murmuring' (*l-w-n*; Exod. 15:24; 16:2, 7, 8; Num. 14:2, 27, 29, 36; 16:11, 41; 17:5; Josh. 9:18; Ps. 59:15) is foreboding in Numbers, always leading to disaster, thereby foreshadowing how the contest will end. Moses' rhetoric also works in such a way that it points out how Korah rejects the very one who has provided him with privilege, thereby painting his striving for the priesthood as a power grab.

12–14. A new section begins here with Moses sending for Abiram and Dathan. The lack of background to this summons and the sudden appearance of the tribute offering (*minḥâ*) in verse 15 indicate that the narrative does not aim for a well-rounded and self-contained story (cf. Blum 1990: 132). The *minḥâ* can also designate a more general offering, as many commentators indicate (cf. Gen. 4:4). It often serves as the basic form of tribute to a superior – also an imperial overlord – which is probably the best way to understand it here.

This section highlights specific features of the leadership contest, especially their refusal – 'and they would not go up' (AT) – in verse 12. Here the text formulates Abiram and Dathan's refusal to go to Moses in the same terms found in 13:31; 14:42 and Moses' 'bringing' (a different form of the same verb) the Israelites up out of fertile Egypt in verse 13. The use of this terminology seems confusing because there was no 'going up' within the camp, but it could indicate (1) going to a place of authority as in Deuteronomy 25:7 (Ashley 2022: 264) as well as (2) an allusion to the exodus as 'going up from Egypt' (e.g. Exod. 1:10; 3:8; 12:38; 17:3; 32:1, 4, 7, 8, 23; Lev. 11:45) and the division between those who are allowed and not allowed to go up the mountain in Exodus 19. Thus, unlike the challenge to Aaron's priesthood in verses 3–11, these leaders reject Moses' political authority after the debacle of Numbers 13 – 14. Furthermore, in verses 13–14 they accuse Moses of leading the people *out of* rather than *into* a *land flowing with milk and honey*. In other words, they call Egypt the fruitful land, offering a very different memory of it from that in Exodus 1 – 14 but in line with Numbers 11:5. By attaching this description to *Egypt*, Dathan and Abiram attempt to fulfil the call in 14:4 to become leaders to take the Israelites back there. In essence, they will not *go up* to Moses because they want to go down to Egypt.

The accusation *Would you put out the eyes of these men?* (v. 14) means deceiving them in some way. In the light of the spies slandering about the land in Numbers 13 – 14, later associated with their unfaithful chasing after their own hearts and *eyes* (15:39), this accusation again becomes a dispute about whose perception of God and the land is correct. The struggle for leadership is revealed to be a question of choosing the kind of leadership that will either form God's people to receive the land as God's good gift, or form an enslaved people back to the ways of Egypt.

15. While Moses does at times become angry with the Israelites (Exod. 16:20; 32:19; Lev. 10:16; Num. 16:15; 31:14), he more often serves as a mediator placating Yahweh on their behalf. In this case, however, Moses communicates his anger *to God*, protecting his own record, arguing that he has not abused his power, following the Egyptian model, by using it to countermand anything – even a donkey – from his opponents (see the similar expression used by the prophet Samuel in 1 Sam. 12:3, which is also found in ancient extra-biblical writings by rulers). His defence does not directly answer their articulated charge, which was leading them into less fruitful circumstances. It instead addresses a universal temptation for leaders: to take advantage of the power at their disposal for their own gain. The proposed ordeal (vv. 29–30) makes Moses' acquittal a supernatural event (see below for discussion).

Moses' prayer that their offering not be accepted (cf. Judg. 13:23; Mal. 2:13; and also several extra-biblical texts; for the opposite, see Ps. 20:3) is a way to ask God to refrain from blessing them.

16–19. The narrative returns to the proposition by Moses in verses 4–7 of an ordeal (or challenge) between Aaron on one hand and the group led by Korah the Levite on the other. In verse 18, Moses joins Aaron in opposition to the 250 challengers at the opening to the tent of meeting. In verse 19, Korah assembles *the whole congregation against them* [Aaron and Moses], indicating how far the community's trust in Moses and Aaron has fallen and how far they were from God's purposes once they had assembled the whole congregation 'before the LORD' (Lev. 9:5) to witness the divine glory (Exod. 40:34; Lev. 9:23–24; Num. 7:89). Thus, now it takes the 'glory of Yahweh' revealed to the whole congregation as the physical presence of God to underscore their authority, similar to 14:10. Yet God's physical presence poses a threat to those in rebellion against God or God's representatives (Moses and Aaron). A similar danger appears in Leviticus 10, and measures are described in Exodus 19:12–15 for steps the congregation must take before encountering God's presence.

20–22. God responds by communicating to Moses and Aaron (in their roles as mediators) the desire to wipe out the whole people except Moses and Aaron (and presumably their families), a suggestion made by God earlier, but that time only for Moses (14:12). They respond by imploring God to focus on the sin of the individual rather than of the whole congregation: presumably Korah is that individual, though the intertwining of the narrative threads renders the statement somewhat metaphorical. As with Abraham's bargaining with God about the fate of Sodom in Genesis 18:23–25, there is some hyperbole here: the whole congregation did come to the tent of meeting for the spectacle *against* Moses and Aaron. Still, a plea is made on behalf of those less actively involved (though the reaction of the people in verse 41 shows how the dissatisfaction had spread; for discussion, see below). This question of the limits of communal responsibility also appears in Ezekiel 18, revealing a continuing conversation between biblical texts (also John 9:1–3).

The title *God of the spirits of all flesh* appears only here and in 27:16 in the Old Testament, but also in the Hellenistic (Intertestamental) Period texts of Enoch, Jubilees 10:3 and the Deuterocanonical 2 Maccabees 3:24; 14:46. It recalls the unity of creation found in the flood story (Gen. 6 – 9), where the term 'flesh' (*bāśār*) frequently appears in reference to human and animal life. As such, it opens the way for the use of creation language below in verse 30.

23–27. Verses 23–34 narrate the confrontation and then downfall of the Korah, Dathan and Abiram households. Speaking through Moses (vv. 23–26), God offers the congregation a chance to reconsider and reidentify with Moses and Aaron instead of with their opponents, which they do (in v. 27). This offer of repentance comes with God telling the people, 'Get away from the *dwelling* of Korah, Dathan, and Abiram' (v. 24, ESV; emphasis added). The text uses the term *miškān*, 'dwelling, tabernacle', in the singular, which is reserved for Yahweh's dwelling elsewhere (except for 16:27) and thus subtly hints at the misplaced worship of these leaders.

The text of verse 25 then returns and weaves in the separate narrative thread concerning Abiram and Dathan, again pointing out that the main goal of the current narrative is to address the question of leadership in the community. Also intriguing in this verse is how the *elders of Israel* have now thrown their support behind Moses and follow him to confront the two Reubenite leaders, which differs from 16:2.

The term *swept away* (*s-p-ḥ*) in verse 26 is also used by Abraham in his bargaining with God about the destruction of Sodom in Genesis 18:23, pointing the reader to consider the issue as a divine judgment. The tragic image of entire families standing at their tent entrances appears in verse 27: the enumeration of the families' generations heightens the tension of the judgment to come.

28–30. Much like stories of the prophets (e.g. Elijah in 1 Kgs 18:36), Moses here provides a sign in order to confirm his status as *leader* in the community. Thus, the challenge between *Moses* on one hand and *Dathan* and *Abiram* on the other concerns Moses' prophetic leadership, rather than Aaron's priestly status, which will be the concern in Numbers 17. This text contrasts with the one at the sanctuary earlier in that it concerns a different context of leadership, given that the question here is whether Yahweh has *sent* Moses (cf. Exod. 7:16; Isa. 6:8; Jer. 1:7).

Moses proposes a sign that would be highly unusual and go against the normal course of human life (v. 29). In other words, if these men should die a normal death, then the people should conclude that Moses is a false prophet. The choice of language in verse 30 is a singular combination: if God *creates something [totally] new* (lit. 'creates a creation'). The Hebrew root *b-r-ʾ* is generally related to original creation (e.g. Gen. 1), so every other use of it draws on the unusual and incredible action. As a result, here Moses starkly contrasts 'the normal ways of the world' with something unexpectedly unique – in this case, the ground opening up and swallowing them alive. As often noted, there is an irony that they 'go down' (v. 33) because they refused to 'go up' (in v. 12) to meet Moses.

31–34. Korah and those associated are swallowed up by the earth, finding the fate that the spies imagined for the whole of Israel when they entered the Promised Land. Korah and the spies share the same faulty perception of God and the land, and now the logical result of that perception comes to fruition. These verses describe the miraculous events using language common to the ancient Ugaritic myth called 'The Baal Cycle', where the god Death (*môt*) opens his mouth and swallows his opponent. *Sheol*, also parallel with *earth* and *ground*, carries out that function here. A similar description appears in Exodus 15:12 of the events at the Red (or Reed) Sea regarding the fate of Pharaoh and his army. Psalm 55:15 expresses the same fate for someone who has betrayed the psalmist.

A point of tension arises in verse 32. While this verse directly states that *everyone who belonged to Korah and all their goods* were swallowed up by the earth, 26:11 declares, *The sons of Korah did not die*. This discrepancy may highlight hyperbole – in this case, the use of the term 'every' was often a part of ancient narratives, a point on display in, for example, the battle reports of the Assyrians, Egyptians and Joshua (Younger 1990). Furthermore, 26:11 also provides another perspective on the question of individual versus collective responsibility. A difference can also be made out between the families of Dathan and Abiram in front of their tents in verse 27, and Korah.

35. The narrative makes a distinction about the fate of the 250 men burning incense at the tent of meeting, picking up the story that was left off in verse 19. These men's punishment fits their offence: on account of the fire burning in their censers, they are burned up by fire.

ii. Redeeming the rebellious censers as a memorial to Aaron's priesthood (16:36–40)

36–40. This next short episode deals with the aftermath of the 250 men's offering. Yahweh commands Eleazar to collect the censers of the dead men and then form them into a sheet of bronze for an altar. Eleazar, son of Aaron, may act as a sign showing that he is moving into the role of the high priest, to which he will fully ascend in 20:28. It may also be an attempt to keep Aaron, as the current high priest, separate from corpses, though Aaron's location between the living and the dead in 16:48 complicates this interpretation.

Eleazar literally must pick up the pieces from the midst of the fire. It remains unclear *which* altar receives the metal plating, so the point of the story lies more in these censers staying within the holy space, regardless of the intention with which they were brought (the text does not explain the motives of the 250

men). Thus, *whatever* is offered in the sanctuary becomes holy.
Nonetheless, this plating was intended to function as a sign of
this disastrous incident. If the altar onto which this plating was
attached was the altar for burnt offerings, given that it was plated
with bronze according to Exodus 38:2, then its place was in the
courtyard. This location was accessible to all (clean) Israelites
bringing an offering. The notion of a material reminder of God's
holiness here and with Aaron's staff (Num. 17:10) serves as one of
the themes combining Numbers 15 (the fringes on garments in
15:38–40) with Numbers 16 – 17.

iii. Aaron's incense offering and atonement for the people (16:41–50)

41–50. The most surprising episode in this chain of events
comes in the response of the broader congregation of the Israelites
to the deaths of these rebellious leaders. They turn *against* rather
than *to* Moses and Aaron, accusing them of responsibility for
these deaths. The use of *rebelled* or 'grumbled' (NIV; from the root
l-w-n) in verse 41 forges a connection with the similar provo-
cations from chapters 11–14. As they gather against the two
leaders, again Yahweh's glory appears in the cloud, apparently as
protection for them and to announce the divine decision between
the two parties. As expected, God takes Moses and Aaron's side,
once again expressing the desire to destroy the congregation
(v. 45). Moses and Aaron again intercede on behalf of the people,
demonstrating this core act of leadership: to act for the good of
those under one's care, even when they accuse the very same
leaders of harm.

Aaron's intercession takes the concrete form of the *appropriate*
use of a censer filled with incense according to the narrative: he
must plunge into the plague-stricken people to make atonement
for them. This action requires a high sense of responsibility for the
people, given that they had just attacked his leadership. However,
in verses 46–47, it is the failure of the Levites to protect the holy
sphere (1:53; 8:19) that contributes to death among the Israelites,
and Aaron must restore the appropriate boundaries between
priest and people, which, quite dramatically, is a mediation that is
the difference between life and death (v. 48). Uncharacteristically,

atonement here takes place *without* a blood sacrifice (also in Lev. 5:11–13, but with flour; see Peres 2021).

The count of the dead as 14,700 people (v. 49) represents a significant step towards the fulfilment of God's promise that this entire generation would die in the wilderness (14:35), though it tragically also includes some from the *next* generation as well.

iv. Aaron's staff buds as divine confirmation of his priesthood (17:1–13)

1–13. This final leadership challenge instead begins with divine initiative and develops out of a Hebrew wordplay in which the term *maṭṭê* means both 'staff' and 'tribe', thus each *maṭṭê* stands for a *maṭṭê* (though the English text instead uses the phrase *ancestral house* in order to differentiate the two in this story; e.g. vv. 2, 3). By putting *Aaron*'s name on the staff for the tribe of Levi, God presumes that Aaron is the leader of the Levites, which has been up for debate in these chapters. The issue of leadership and the use of a 'staff' will play an important role in chapters 20–21. However, the main focus of this challenge is between the Levites and the other tribes, though it does not explicitly say for what responsibility until the very end of the section, in verse 13. Here the exclamation *Everyone who approaches the tabernacle . . . will die* is a reminder that the challenge is about cultic proximity to the divine presence and reflects especially on the deaths of the 250 leaders, who served as representatives for the people as a whole. If they could not bring offerings to the sanctuary, then certainly the rest of the people could not do so. This verse expresses the need for mediation between God and the people. As such it underscores Aaron's role in the previous section and leads into the ritual prescriptions in Numbers 18. For this reason, Yahweh requires the twelve staffs to be placed at the tent of meeting, *before the [ark of the] testimony, where I meet with you* (v. 4, NRSV margin).

Yahweh indicates the choice of Aaron through a miraculous sign (v. 8) in which Aaron's staff not only blossoms, but even bares ripe almonds after a single night in the sanctuary. Aaron's staff is not returned to him, unlike those of the other leaders. It instead remains in the sanctuary as a reminder of God's choice, in keeping with 15:38–41 and 16:39–40. Similar to the case of the spies and Korah, this challenge is about whose leadership is able to nurture Israel's life and whose leadership is sterile. For this reason, the miraculous sign indicates fertility and life, pointing to divine blessing and the good gift of land, against aridity and the death of those who want to go down to the old ways of Egypt.

The section ends with the affirmation of the hierarchy set out in Numbers 3 – 4 of Aaron's priesthood. However, it does not provide the same confirmation of Moses' political and prophetic leadership. This omission may point to Eleazar's pre-eminence over Joshua that will emerge in the ensuing chapters.

Meaning

The questions put forth by chapters 16 and 17 are incredibly relevant, especially for church communities in cultures shaped by democratic values: followers of God in these contexts may ask with 16:3, 'Why do you elevate yourselves over the community of Yahweh?' What gives someone the right to lead, to exercise authority? Chapter 16 overlays different traditions of power struggles as something of a diptych. The narrative structure itself intimates the similarities of rebellions by different community leaders, despite the divergence in the chief actors (Korah, the 250 leaders, or Abiram and Dathan). Yet the people's response (16:41–50) shows that all Israel blamed Moses and Aaron for the failure and punishment, rather than the rebels. Only the challenge initiated by God resulting in Aaron's budding staff, a confirmation of God's promise of life in a good and fertile land, brought about a *peaceful* conclusion (as insightfully noted by Pressler 2017: 157).

In a world that lays emphasis on individual value and 'rights', these texts highlight a different organizational structure. While the whole people of God (and all humans) bear equal value and status, this equality is not a justification for power struggles and does not entitle nor burden all with equal responsibilities when it comes to leading God's community. When this passage is read in the light of Numbers 1 – 4, readers are invited to accept the roles in the spiritual community that God accords us. This does not mean one cannot challenge problematic leaders (cf. e.g. 1 Kgs 12; Gal. 2:11–14)! The almost universal misuse of even legitimate authority

leads followers to question leaders' motivations. Moses sets a
high bar for leaders attempting to acquit themselves of charges of
grabbing or abusing power: God approves of leadership that leads
to life. Those who see authority and leadership as concentration of
power diminish access to the resources intended to promote life
and flourishing for the people by concentrating these resources in
the hands of a few. Instead of following the logic of innocent until
proven guilty, the narrative reveals that only a supernatural intervention will prove the leaders' legitimacy. This type of proposal
invites modern-day authorities to tread very carefully in their
appropriation of power.

This section provides narratives to depict an aspect of the
tension between God's desire to dwell *among* the Israelites and
their rejection of divine leadership and divinely appointed leaders.
Various leaders want to draw near to God, but their motives seem
to be to profit personally from the power which that proximity
affords to the detriment of the common good. It points out the
warped motivations that draw people to positions of power,
inviting followers of God to reflect on their motivations for
desiring leadership and the dangers that such positions hold, both
to their holders and for followers.

Also, as with some other stories in Numbers (21:6; 25:9),
these chapters indicate some level of collective responsibility
and punishment: the families of Abiram and Dathan are held
responsible for the actions of these two men and are swallowed
up by the earth with them. There is a conversation within both
chapter 16 (see v. 22) and the larger Old Testament about collective
responsibility (Deut. 24:16; Ezek. 18). Based on those verses,
readers might be inclined to look for something that the *families*
of these two men did wrong in Numbers 16; however, there is
no evidence of this. Rather, it is better to understand this case in
the light of Numbers 13 – 14, where the failure of one generation
has consequences for the next, even when they are not guilty and
are even objects of God's mercy and forgiveness. The chapter
understands humans as interconnected with one another, and,
therefore, bearing some level of responsibility for one another
(like Gen. 4:9; Luke 10:25–37), and more for those close to us than
those distant. On the whole, the Bible invites audiences into this

complex *conversation* rather than providing a definitive *answer* about the issue. Such an approach proves more effective, especially in a globally connected world with historically particular and global challenges such as colonialism, slavery, genocide, wars, climate change, a world economy, and pandemics that also have consequences way beyond their historical and geographical limits.

A further small insight comes from Eleazar's making a metal plating for an altar and the preservation of Aaron's living staff before the presence of God. As a permanent part of the worship setting, this plating becomes an enduring reminder of the danger of approaching God improperly, and Aaron's staff is a reminder that nurturing life and facilitating the people's access to it is the purpose of a divinely legitimate leadership. Though only applicable in Christian communities by analogy, this text highlights the question of what contemporary form and motivation improper worship and leadership might take, and how communities of faith can remember and reappropriate the resources received through fault-filled means in a way that does bring God glory.

C. Reaffirming the responsibilities and limits of priests and Levites (18:1–32)

Context
The prosaic ordinances outlining the various responsibilities of, and payments received by, the priestly family of Aaron and the tribe of Levi in relation to the sanctuary come as a response and supplement to the narrations of chaotic conflicts around access to the sanctuary in chapters 16–17. Chapter 18 most immediately answers – if obliquely and only in part – the Israelites' question of 17:13, *Are we all to perish* [for approaching God's dwelling, the sanctuary]? This chapter reaffirms the protective buffers, first of the priests and then of the Levites, between God and the rest of the Israelites. As such, it recalls the camp order of the early chapters of the book (especially 1:51–53; 3:6–13; 4:15–20; 8:14–22) and constitutes part of the complex answer to the question of how a holy God dwells amid humans of ambivalent character.

However, this chapter also takes great interest in the way that God provides for the Aaronide priests and Levites through

offerings and tithes brought to Yahweh. God establishes what
they can and cannot take from these resources. In the light of the
previous discussion about leadership (chs. 16–17), there are limits
to the benefits priests and Levites receive from their privileged
position. The chapter makes several strong distinctions: between
the most holy parts of offerings only to be consumed by male
priests, dedicated items that whole priestly families may enjoy, and
the tithe of agricultural goods given to the Levites. These lines
impress the sanctuary's hierarchy into the concrete functioning of
the sanctuary. Striking contrasts appear between the distribution
of the various offerings and the justifications for such portions
here and in Leviticus 1 – 7; 22:1–16; 27:26–33; Deuteronomy
14:22–29; 15:19–23; 18:1–8; and Ezekiel 44:10–31.

Comment
i. The division of cultic responsibilities between priests and Levites (18:1–7)

1–7. In this and the following sections, Yahweh speaks directly
to Aaron, which only otherwise happens in Leviticus 10:8 after
a similarly tragic event at the sanctuary that brought about
the deaths of his two sons, Nadab and Abihu. In both cases
strangeness (*zār*) approaches Yahweh's dwelling: in Leviticus 10 it
is strange fire, in Numbers 16; 18:4, 7 it is strangers (*outsider*, NRSV;
'unauthorized person', NLT). This same language appeared earlier
in 1:51, but especially in 18:7 it encompasses both non-Levites
and Levites not belonging to Aaron's family. These instructions,
therefore, function in the context as direct responses to the narratives of chapters 16–17 and the attempt of outsiders to usurp the
priesthood. Coming after the election of Aaron in the previous
narrative, God's direct revelation to Aaron in effect *performs* this
choice of Aaron and his priestly descendants' mediatory role
between God and Israel. A close link is forged to the prior narratives by using the same term for God's wrath, *q-ṣ-p*, in verse 5 as
in 16:22, 46 (also 1:53).

The notion of *bear[ing] responsibility for offences* in verse 1 appears
in a number of other Priestly-affiliated texts in the Pentateuch
(e.g. Exod. 28:38, 43; Lev. 5:1, 17; 7:18; 16:22; 17:16; 19:8; 20:17, 19;
Num. 5:31; 9:13; 30:15); in this context it concerns the wrong people

carrying out tasks at the sanctuary or those duties performed incorrectly. One example (from Lev. 7:18) is the consumption of meat from a shared offering feast on the third day after the feast took place. Now, rather than the perpetrators, such as the 250 leaders offering incense, it is the priests who bear the responsibility unless they restrain those lay leaders from improper action (or point out their mistake). Such an enactment can be seen in the narrative of King Uzziah (2 Chr. 26:16–21), who barges into the Jerusalem temple to offer incense and is struck with a skin defilement (*ṣāraʿat*) when rebuked by the priest.

There is a play on words in verses 2 and 4 for the tribe of Levi: the root *l-w-h* with which the name is associated means 'to join', and the Levites are *joined to you* (i.e. Aaron). However, as one would expect from Numbers 3, there is a clear hierarchy, specified in verses 4–5, in which the Levites perform their service at the tent of meeting *while* the priests attend to the altar and the holy things. In verse 7 it also accords the work *behind the curtain*, that is, in the Holy of Holies, to Aaron. It is used as a general overview term here when compared with Leviticus 16:12, 29–34, which prescribes that only the high priest should enter the Holy of Holies, and that only once a year.

The positive affirmation of the Levites' role as assistants (and *brothers* in vv. 2, 6) to the priests omits any hint of the conflict between Korah's Levites in chapters 16–17.

ii. Resources belonging to the priests (18:8–20)

8–14. After delineating the responsibilities of the priests and Levites, verse 8 begins a new section with a repeated oracle from God to Aaron describing the priests' payment (perquisites) for their work. This section draws quite extensively on Leviticus 6:16–18, 26–29; 7:6–10, 32–36; 22:1–16; 27:26–27.

The section begins (v. 8) with a solemn declaration by Yahweh, 'I *myself* give to you . . .' (see, e.g., NIV). Their livelihood depends not on their status, but on their dependence on God's care. Then it separates into the most holy portions that only priestly men may eat (vv. 9–10) and those that their households may consume (vv. 11–19). The first group draws on the conceptions of the tribute, purification and reparation offerings found in Leviticus 6 – 7, which gives some detail on the portions of these offerings reserved for priestly consumption. Unlike Leviticus 6 – 7, which names those invited to the table and the place of their consumption, the presentation in Numbers 18 focuses solely on the priests, who are guests invited to a regular feast reserved for a special few. The unique expression in verse 9 *reserved from the fire* refers to the portions of the offering not burned on the altar.

More attention is dedicated to the innovative distribution of the processed firstfruits of crops and firstborn ordinances in verses 11–19, which are subsumed under the category of elevation offerings (things dedicated to God) and set aside for the priestly household – though priests' wives are not expressly mentioned. Nestled within these dedicated goods in verse 14 are also *every devoted thing (ḥerem)*, which often refers to killing humans in war and the livestock and other spoils (cf. Deut. 20:17; Josh. 2:10; 6:18; 8:26), though it may also indicate dedication to God without the possibility of redemption for human use (Lev. 27:28; cf. Num. 21:2).

Additional note: the firstfruits and firstborn offerings

The Pentateuch (and Ezek. 44:30) offers several different visions as to who receives the offerings of firstfruits and firstborn. In some cases, the texts simply place different accents; in others they diverge on central points.

As part of the narrative about Israel's last night in Egypt, Exodus 13:1–2, 11–16 reports Yahweh claiming all firstborn human and animal males of the Israelites. It divides them into two categories: humans and donkeys, which one must redeem (e.g. with a sheep), and all firstborn male calves that belong to Yahweh. It then provides a justification, relating the practice to Yahweh's rescue of Israel from Egypt through the killing of Egypt's firstborn human and animal males, rendering this Israelite practice an act of remembrance. The use of the term 'sacrifice, shared offering feast' (the verb *z-b-ḥ*) in Exodus 13:15 hints that the (lay)person offering the animal participated in the enjoyment of its consumption, though no more than a subtle gesture is given.

In Exodus 22:29–30, the focus lies on the requirement for the worshipper (esp. farmer) to bring the firstfruits and firstborn, and that they belong to Yahweh. In contrast, Exodus 34:19–20 underscores that one was to redeem firstborn boys and donkeys, otherwise the donkey was to be strangled.

While brief mentions appear in Deuteronomy 12:6, 17, more details come in Deuteronomy 14:22–27; 15:19–23. All these texts, in contrast to Ezekiel 44:30 *and* Numbers 18, invite the *worshipper* and their family to partake in celebratory feasting of the firstfruits and firstborn. No mention of the priest is found in these texts from Deuteronomy, though in Deuteronomy 18:4 the firstfruits of the crops are accorded to the priests, as well as the first fleece of the sheep. Finally, Deuteronomy 26:1–10 provides detail on how a worshipper should bring the firstfruits of the crops to the sanctuary, whereupon the priest will put the goods before the altar and the worshipper should recite a version of the exodus narrative. However, in Deuteronomy 26:11, the worshipper and household consume the goods (without any mention of priestly participation!).

In contrast, Ezekiel 44:30 says nothing specifically about firstborn animals – though these may be included in the 'every offering of all kinds from all your offerings' reserved for priests. The verse does, however, clearly give the agricultural firstfruits to the priests. Nothing is said about their families, which may simply indicate a difference in emphasis from that in Numbers 18.

In Leviticus 27:26–27 the focus is twofold: first there is a declaration that the animal – specifically the types of animals that could be sacrificed – *belongs* to Yahweh, so no-one can *dedicate* it to Yahweh. Second, if it is an unclean animal, it is either redeemed for the owner's use at its value plus 20% (thus like a vow, cf. Lev. 27:13); or, if it is not redeemed, it may be sold for its value, presumably by the responsible priests, who are the ones present to officiate at the sanctuary rituals in Leviticus 27. No mention is made of *human* firstborn here.

15–18. These verses, which address the firstborn, bring together concerns found in several other texts. First, verse 15 makes it explicit that these offerings, which belong to Yahweh, are given *to the priests* – something implicit in other texts but not stated directly. Second, the mention of *both* humans and animals recalls Exodus 13; 22; 34, though the language *first issue of the womb* is especially close to Exodus 34:19 and 13:2, 12, 15 (which, however, specifies firstborn *males*). The discussion of *redeeming* the human firstborn likewise overlaps closely with Exodus 13:13, 15; 34:20. However, while those texts also speak of redeeming a donkey, which is an unclean animal, the formulation of redeeming an unclean animal coincides with Leviticus 27:27, which also addresses the *price* at which it can be redeemed (its value plus 20%). This same calculation appears in Leviticus 27:6, 13, which addresses things that a person vows to give to Yahweh but later decides they want to keep. Specifically, the value of a one-month-old to five-year-old boy is placed at five shekels (also in Num. 3:47). To redeem it, this amount plus 20% must be paid. The exact calculation in Numbers 18:16 actually replaces a priest's assessment of the value found in Leviticus 27:11–12. The description of the weight of a sanctuary shekel as *twenty gerahs* also appears elsewhere, in Exodus 30:13; Leviticus 27:25, showing even closer links with Leviticus 27.

The description of the ritual procedure with the animals that one can sacrifice comes in verses 17–18. The calf, lamb and kid (of a goat) are sacrificed in the manner of a shared offering feast according to the procedures described in Leviticus 3:2–5 and 7:30–34. Thus, it takes known procedures and applies them to an offering that had not yet received detailed prescriptions, though only the priests' families consume the meat of the firstborn (which contrasts with Deut. 15:20). And this is what takes place overall in verses 15–18: the passage adapts concepts and language from other Pentateuchal texts and applies it to this situation.

19. A rare statement about a *covenant of salt* appears in this verse (see Lev. 2:13). The preservative property of salt is commonly appealed to in interpreting this expression as indicating the perpetuity of the covenant (see 2 Chr. 13:5 and Sklar 2013: 100). However, 'salt' also functions as an idiom for shared meals as an indication of partaking in a covenantal relationship, implying mutual hospitality and loyalty (see Milgrom 1991: 191–192). In Ezra 4:13–14 the idiom of the sharing of resources is contrasted with the retention of revenue from the king, so the use here is relevant to indicate the just revenue, neither less nor more, that the priests receive from the offerings as a gift from Yahweh.

20. While the statements in verse 20 conclude the discussion of the priestly gifts with another address to Aaron, this address also functions as a transition to God's declaration of gifts for the tribe of Levi. However, verse 20 itself looks forward with hope to life in the land – after the wandering – with a special bond between God and Aaron's priestly descendants. *Yahweh*, not a section of the land, will be their portion and inheritance. Similar statements appear in Deuteronomy 18:2; Ezekiel 44:28. By including the provisions for the *Levites* in an address to Aaron, the responsibility for distributing these tithes to the Levites lies with Aaron's priestly descendants, who should not keep these contributions for themselves.

iii. Resources belonging to the Levites (18:21–32)

21–24. These verses likewise envision life in the land and dedicate Israel's *tithes* to the Levites as payment for their work at the sanctuary. The nature of tithes in Old Testament texts contains many complexities. In the broader biblical and Ancient Near Eastern material, a tithe often concerns a tax given to the political authorities (e.g. 1 Sam. 8:15; for discussion, see Altmann 2011: 221–226). Within the Pentateuch, however, it always concerns contributions connected with Yahweh's sanctuary or its personnel, and appears in Leviticus 27:30–33; Deuteronomy 14:22–29; 26:12–14.

In Deuteronomy's conception, those bringing the tithes consume them as households (including outsiders such as widows, immigrants and Levites) *at the central sanctuary*, though every third year they collect them *in their villages* for these outsiders. In Leviticus 27:30–33 an innovation of a tithe of animals emerges, and both the animal and dry goods tithe are designated 'holy'. This designation likely means they are to be given to the sanctuary personnel, though the Levites never appear in a separate group in Leviticus, certainly not as those receiving the tithe, which instead comes to the fore in Numbers 18. One can deduce the contents of the tithe in Numbers 18:30 (from the threshing floor and vat), which excludes animals.

A justification for the gift of the tithes to the Levites for their work in verse 22 answers the question raised in 17:12–13: rather than the Israelites as a whole, or their elders, the *Levites* serve as intermediaries and representatives for the people at the sanctuary. For like the priestly descendants of Aaron, the Levites also remain (relatively – see discussion on Num. 35) landless even after the Israelites take the land (v. 23). Similar discussions appear in Deuteronomy 10:8–9; 18:1–2; and Ezekiel 44:28.

25–32. This final section relates the remuneration given to the Levites to the sacred portions of the priests. Now Yahweh turns to Moses, who should command the Levites to tithe, just as the Israelites at large have tithed. Perhaps the change of address to Moses from Aaron intends to function as a check on the priests' authority in general, and their privileged position of access to resources in particular: it is not *they* who deliver the message that the Levites must tithe to them. In any case, the Levites' tithes go to Aaron and the priests. In verse 30, the instruction goes to considerable lengths to describe how the Levites should pass on the best part of what they have received as their tithe. A purpose of this tithe emerges in verse 31, which is that the Levites' households in effect desacralize their portion of the tithes such that they may consume them *in any place* and not just at the sanctuary. Furthermore, this consumption can still take place in a way that maintains the layers of protection between God's wrath, Aaron's priestly descendants, the Levites and the Israelites at large. Thus, a larger purpose of this section is the determination of the relationship, at least in terms of the distribution of contributions (which one can imagine as taxes and tribute), among God's appointed servants.

Meaning

The main interest of this chapter is the delineation of the gift exchange between the people, Yahweh, and the priests and Levites. It assumes a life of abundance in the land God gives, beginning with the presupposition that God provides generously for Israel. In response, the people bring a wide variety of gifts to the sanctuary for God, which God distributes in an orderly fashion among all the participants, in this chapter in ways that build on and diverge from discussions of the tithe in other parts of the Pentateuch. Here the emphasis lies on the just portions for priests and Levites given their privileged access to resources, which caused the power struggle in chapters 16–17.

However, this passage presents a great pitfall in what remains unsaid: what if spiritual/religious authority, like that of the Aaronide priests mandated here, is used for *personal* gain, rather than in service of the larger people of God? To use the image of Numbers 17, what if Aaron's staff becomes as sterile as the staffs of the other tribes? Broadening one's perspective to include the voices of critique in both the Old Testament (e.g. Lev. 10; 1 Sam. 2; Isa. 1; Jer. 7; Amos 5) and the New (e.g. Jesus' strong words for the religious leaders in Matt. 23) indicates that the Bible itself actively identifies and rebukes this typical human abuse of power through concentration of resources (Olson 2012: 117–119). Nonetheless, as discussed in regard to earlier chapters (e.g. Num. 3 – 4; 16 – 17), neither Numbers 18 nor the Bible as a whole abandons or pushes to end hierarchies with clear power differentials. In 1 Corinthians 9:13–14, Paul also argues that some religious workers are entitled to financial remuneration for these efforts (also 1 Tim. 5:17–18). As in James 3:1, Numbers 18 emphasizes the intrinsic danger bound up with leadership of God's people (vv. 1, 22–23, 32).

D. The purification from corpse impurity (19:1–22)

Context

Chapter 19 is dedicated entirely to the ritual of the red cow that addresses the problem of contact with human death. However, it does so in a manner unlike any other in the Bible with its combination of the burning of a *red* cow, its burning taking place *outside* the Israelite camp, and, finally, the application of the ash–water mix carried out by a non-priest. As an overview, this chapter first details the preparation of the cleansing agent (the ash of the red cow) in verses 1–10. In verses 11–22 there are details on the situations concerning when and how the ash should be used: situations when encountering a human corpse.

The placement of this chapter, like many in Numbers, is surprising: why does a chapter detailing a ritual restoration of those who have had physical contact with a corpse follow the discussion of the tithes to the Levites and priests in Numbers 18? Several answers are possible, though certainty remains elusive:

1 This chapter serves as a *structural* element in the continuing transition from the exodus generation that exited from Egypt to the settling generation that will enter the land (Morales 2024a: 463). The congregation, as a group that is larger than the individual, receives a means to carry forward in the face of widespread death.

2 In fact, many of the older generation have already perished because of the various rebellions in Numbers 16 – 17, and the deaths of two leaders – Miriam and Aaron – follow in Numbers 20, as do initial conquests of Arad (in the south) and the Transjordanian territories of Sihon and Og, all in Numbers 21. Thus, much death surrounds this chapter.

3 If Numbers 18 addresses the roles of the *priests and Levites* as a partial answer to the people's lament in 17:12–13 that they will all perish, Numbers 19 concerns the *people's* role in maintaining the purity of the camp and, consequently, of Yahweh's sanctuary that can allow Israel to remain alive and experience positive encounters with the divine presence (Morales 2024a: 496).

The ritual has similar concerns to Leviticus 5:2–3; 11 15; 21; Numbers 5:1–4; 6:6–10; and 9:6, 10–11 (also Ezek. 14:16; 39:12, 15), so there would have been some justification for including it in one of those contexts as well. None of these texts explains, however, the process of purification from contact with a human corpse for the general population. Some overlap exists with the ritual performed when the victim of an unresolved homicide is found in the open country in Deuteronomy 21:1–9.

Comment

1–10. Similar to several other chapters in Numbers (chs. 2 and 4), Numbers 19 begins with Yahweh speaking to Moses and Aaron. This opening suggests that the material will concern the sanctuary in the middle of the Israelite camp. However, most of the action takes place at a distance from the sanctuary, though with a significant relationship to it (cf. vv. 4, 13, 20). There is a complex set of protagonists here: the *people* (Israelites) select a cow and bring it to Moses (and Aaron), who in verse 3 pass it on to Eleazar.

From verse 3 with the mention of the *son* of the high priest, Eleazar, it is clear that this ritual differs from a typical purification offering. While Eleazar is *chief* over the Levites (3:32) and has performed several important actions (cf. 4:16; 16:37–39), the text provides no explanation for the choice of the priest's son here. Interpreters usually suggest two likely and overlapping reasons. First, Aaron the high priest will die in the next chapter, so Eleazar begins to take on the mantle of high priesthood. Second, the continuing holiness required of the high priest would lead to the performance of this ritual by another priest, given that they become unclean in the process, perhaps similar to what occurs in 16:37–39 (Milgrom 1990: 158).

This ritual involves several actors. There is Eleazar, who serves as the model priest, but there is also a person who slaughters and who burns the cow (this may or may not be the same person), and the one who gathers up the ashes. Nothing suggests that the last two persons need to be priests, so it was presumably unimportant. This inclusion of lay Israelites – and even resident non-Israelites who live among the Israelites long term (the *gēr*, often translated 'alien') – highlights the responsibility of the entire Israelite community to deal appropriately with dead bodies.

The steps of the ritual to prepare the cleansing agent in verses 2–10 are fairly straightforward:

1 The community brings an unworked, unblemished red cow to Eleazar (and presumably later to the high priest; v. 2).
2 Eleazar (or an important priest) takes it outside the camp, and someone slaughters it there (v. 3).
3 Eleazar sprinkles some of its blood towards the sanctuary with his finger seven times (v. 4), though apparently still outside the camp. This action likely purifies the sanctuary, even from a distance (see below), thus making it possible for God to remain present there (cf. 5:3).

4 The cow's body is burned whole – including its blood – along
   with some hyssop (or more likely marjoram, given that hyssop
   does not grow in the region), crimson thread and cedar wood
   (vv. 5–6). The importance of this action is that the priests
   receive no payment for this procedure, unlike with other
   offerings. Furthermore, the blood becomes part of the ash,
   which may signal the reservation of the ash's potency for later
   use by individual Israelites as needed. The hyssop/marjoram,
   crimson thread and cedar wood (and water and blood) appear
   earlier in Leviticus 14:6 as a mixture sprinkled on someone
   who formerly had a skin defilement when pronouncing them
   pure.
5 The priest washes his clothes and bathes, as does the one who
   slaughtered the cow: both remain unclean until evening (vv.
   7–8).
6 A third person gathers the ashes and puts them in a safe place
   outside the camp: this one as well must wash and remains
   unclean until evening. Now the ash is available for whoever
   will need it (vv. 9–10).

Why a *red* cow? The emphasis on the colour red (*'ādōm*: applied
to the cow, the crimson thread and cedar bark) and explicitly on the
sprinkling of the blood (*dām*, phonetically similar to the Hebrew term
for 'red') towards the sanctuary underscore the highly meaningful
nature of blood. In the Bible, blood is associated with both death
and life (cf. Gen. 9:4; Lev. 17:11, 14). Contact with blood can make
the pure person impure, while blood serves as the key ingredient in
processes allowing the impure person to rejoin the congregation of
the pure (cf. Gorman 1990: 202–203). As such, it has incredible power.
Things that come into contact with blood undergo a change in status.
    The choice of a *cow* may result from a parallel with the choice
of a female animal for individual, lay Israelite transgressions in
Leviticus 4:27–28, where the animal is a female *goat*. A cow, which
is much larger, would render considerably more ashes available to
the members of the Israelite community (in 1 Sam. 6:14 and 16:2
cows are also sacrificed under special circumstances). Nonetheless,
the closest parallel comes in the ritual performed for an unresolved
homicide in Deuteronomy 21:1–9, which also calls for a cow.

A key connection is articulated in verse 9, which calls this ritual a purification offering. Other texts that mention a location for the purification offering (e.g. Exod. 29:36; Lev. 4; 8; 16; and Num. 8:7) place it at the sanctuary. In the unique ritual here, the question arises: why does all this take place *outside* the camp, rather than in the sanctuary?

In order to understand the significance of this ritual sacrifice in more depth, comparison with similar processes in Leviticus 5 is helpful, through which an answer emerges for the location of the ritual in Numbers 19. In Leviticus 5:2 the text pronounces unclean anyone who has touched something unclean, specifically the corpse of any animal, which contrasts with touching a *human* corpse in Numbers 19. The remedying procedure for several cases of impurity, including that of an animal carcass, appears in Leviticus 5:5–13:[3]

1 One should confess (v. 5).
2 One should bring a purification offering – a female of the flock (sheep or goat) or cheaper replacement (vv. 7, 11).
3 The priest sprinkles some of the blood upon the side of the altar in the case of the birds (v. 9) and presumably the female sheep/goat, though this is not mentioned.
4 The priest atones for one's transgression (vv. 6, 13).
5 The transgression will be forgiven (v. 13).

No confession appears in Numbers 19, and the purification offering itself happens outside the camp and *in advance* of the transgression. This juxtaposition in *time* (before rather than after the offence) provides a likely explanation for the *location* of the

---

3 However, the regulations for touching an animal carcass are elaborated upon and changed in Lev. 11:24–40. In addition to the descriptions of different categories of animals and what makes them unclean, this section changes the process by which they become clean: rather than bringing a purification offering as in Lev. 5, now they must simply wash their clothes and wait until evening, and then they will become clean (vv. 24–25, 39–40).

slaughter of the animal outside the camp. Furthermore, the blood remains in the animal, thus becoming part of the ash. When needed, the ash is mixed with water to become the *water for cleansing*. The term for *cleansing* (*niddâ*, vv. 9, 13, 20–21) is not the typical one but instead refers to bleeding, menstruation or defilement in other contexts (e.g. Lev. 12; 15); thus, the water might more literally be rendered 'waters [for removal] of defilement'. In Leviticus 12, the blood of menstruation and of the parturient is called (lit.) 'blood of impurity' (Lev. 12:4, 5), but the same flow of blood postpartum is the source of her purification (Lev. 12:7; see Erbele-Küster 2017). Therefore, *niddâ* fittingly qualifies a ritual in which the preparation causes participants to become impure in a transitional state on the way to complete purity (Maccoby 1999: 94–117).

The actions in the first ten verses result in the preparation of a highly powerful purifying agent: when added to water, the ashes of the mixture of cow, hyssop/marjoram, scarlet thread and cedar set a purification process in motion.

Like 9:14; 15:14–30; 35:15 (also in Exod. 12 and Lev. 16–25), verse 10 explains that the ritual applies to Israelites as well as to resident foreigners, so it concerns maintaining an appropriate community environment for God's sanctuary.

11–15. Only now does the text provide a general description for the situation in which the ash should be used: when one touches a human corpse. However, the first steps towards purification do not specifically mention the ash from the cow, which will be detailed only later in the chapter. Rather, verses 11–12 indicate that the entire purification transition process lasts for seven days; if not completed in this time, then it apparently became impossible. Furthermore, the important actions take place twice, on the third and seventh days (explained in vv. 17–20). The seven-day period for ritual cleansing appears in Leviticus 13 – 15 also.

The central importance of this ritual emerges from verse 13, which notes two consequences that result from failure to carry out the ritual: Yahweh's sanctuary becomes impure, and the responsible person will be *cut off from Israel* (see commentary on 15:22–31). God cannot dwell among the people because God cannot come in contact with impurity. Therefore, that person must be separated from the community of God's people.

Of similar significance is the power accorded to death. The fact that those who have contact with the dead must be separated from God's presence (they are impure), and must consciously undergo purification rites to be able to come near God's presence once again, indicates that the God of Israel should not come in contact with death. One might say that it is an explosive ritual declaration that Yahweh is the God of the living.

As with many ritual instructions, further questions may arise. In this case, they concern the *location* of contact with the dead: verses 14–15 provide extra details on a situation where someone dies in a tent. If indoors, then everyone who has been in the tent while the person was dead and all open containers become unclean. The contamination of open containers represents an innovation: in Leviticus 11 – 15 it is solely touch that passes on impurity, not indoor proximity. The contamination by a corpse in a tent reveals that the person's personality (*nepeš*) emanates from the person's corpse (*nepeš*; see 5:1–4 above) and travels in the air like a form of energy (cf. Frevel 2012: 389–391; Feder 2021: 153–157). That explains why the sprinkling of blood towards the sanctuary is capable of purifying it from a distance in the specific case of the red cow ritual. Just as contamination occurs through the air when a corpse is found in a tent, the same goes for the purification of Yahweh's tent.

16. This verse explains that an outdoor situation is different: then one must actually *touch* the corpse or come into direct contact with the place where the corpse was buried. This distinction generally aligns with the prescriptions concerning skin defilement and bodily fluids in Leviticus 14:46–47; 15:4–27, as well as priests becoming impure through touching a human corpse in Leviticus 22:4. Numbers 6:1–10 extends this impurity to the Nazirite (male or female), so it then includes non-priests, though only those who have set themselves apart. What is peculiar here is the contamination through contact with a grave. Perhaps the contamination through the air in the open, instead of in a tent, occurs exclusively when one steps on a grave because the person's *nepeš* travels upwards (Maccoby 1999: 18).

17–20. These verses discuss the use of the ashes, finally connecting back with verses 2–10: a person mixes ash from the cow with fresh water, dips some hyssop/marjoram into the mixture, and sprinkles it onto the unclean person (and onto the tent and its furnishings as well if the contact with the corpse took place inside). This sprinkling explains the purifying of verse 12 that takes place on days three and seven. Verse 19 adds that the unclean person must also wash their clothes and bathe with water – these are common purification acts throughout Leviticus and Numbers, and also in the Dead Sea Scrolls and John the Baptist (Matt. 3). Verse 21 notes that the one sprinkling becomes unclean through this action and must wash his clothes and bathe, becoming clean in the evening.

Unlike the ritual actions for impurity of skin defilement found in Leviticus 14:1–9 that bear some similarities (seven days, cedar, crimson thread, hyssop/marjoram and sprinkling blood), Numbers 19 makes no mention about the person made unclean through contact with a human corpse needing to live outside the camp. On the backdrop of these other texts, Numbers 19 addresses some of the same issues but in a different manner, and some additional circumstances come to the fore. First, Numbers 19 is the only text that gives a *positive* ritual for all Israelites for what to do when coming into contact with a human corpse. It also gives more information suggesting how a corpse causes impurity. In terms of the type of ritual action, it is the only offering that is burned away from the altar and sanctuary, outside the camp with the blood. It is also different in that much of the ritual action can be done by any clean member of the community – with little priestly involvement. This broadens the responsibility to all Israel. And, if a member of the community fails to take this ritual seriously, it will even affect the sanctuary (vv. 13, 20), that is, God's presence in the community.

21–22. The final statement deals with the person involved in administering the ritual and notes that this person remains impure until evening and can pass on that impurity to whatever they touch. This apparent transfer of impurity – though a lesser degree since it ends in the evening – from the person originally needing purification for contact with a human corpse raises questions about the way that purification might be imagined. Is the water mixture a magnet or sponge that sucks up the impurity or that attracts it away from the original bearer such that it sticks on the person sprinkling the water on them? The text does not provide details on how to conceive of the transferal, but simply indicates that all involved in the preparation and administration of the ritual become impure for a certain amount of time.

Meaning

At a most basic level, this chapter highlights the significant impact that human death has on everyone coming into contact with it, sometimes not even by touch. In the case of this text, no difference arises between one's intentional and one's accidental contact with human remains. As indicated by the growing recognition of post-traumatic stress disorder, coming into contact with a human corpse brings humans into contact with their own human limits. It marks a disjunction and should be treated in such a way that grants a designated period of time to acknowledge its reality. Such contact has powerful effects on a human community, requiring an extensively prepared and twice-administered ritual. It also hinders God's dwelling in the midst of human communities.

Given the broad reach of the ritual – it would extend from those mourning a close relative, implied by the context inside a tent, to those who happened upon an unknown human bone distant from settled land – the importance of the ritual lies in its efficacy to restore human communities connected with God, whose tent is in their midst, despite the deep ruptures that death brings into life.

In its context, coming after chapters 11–17, an abiding lesson from this chapter comes in the challenge to conceive of ways to deal with the failures of our corporate past. How does a community of faith move beyond a community's or a family's sins? It requires rituals to transition from mourning, trauma and guilt to forgiveness, restoration and life.

According to Hebrews 9:13–14, Christ acted as a high priest offering his own blood, which brings about eternal redemption for the conscience, while the ashes of this ritual (among others) purify the physical body. For both texts, the ability to have God dwell in one's midst so that one can encounter the divine presence is the goal, and Hebrews argues for the unique efficacy of Christ's sacrifice in that it requires no repetition.

E. Death reaches the centre of the exodus generation (20:1–29)

Context

As with many other portions of the book, chapters 20–21 are formed by a compilation of varied materials. Within the literary structure of Numbers presented in the Analysis, the end of chapter 20 and beginning of chapter 21 mark a separation in the flow of the narrative, from the pessimistic end of the exodus generation to the more optimistic beginning of the settling generation. Nonetheless, these chapters comprise a literary unit with thematic links of great significance within the structure and overall message of Numbers (see below).

From the perspective of the wilderness journey, that is, geographically, chapters 20–21 form a unit marked by the movement from Kadesh to the plains of Moab, at the eastern border of Canaan. Given that Numbers depicts two main geographical movements, from Sinai to Kadesh (Num. 1 – 20) and from Kadesh to the plains of Moab (Num. 21 – 36), the itinerary details in chapters 20–21, especially in 21:10–20, are significant. There is a much more focused and determined march than in the previous leg of the journey that was marked by constant failures and delays. Using geographical referents, chapters 20–21 describe a thematic movement of the new generation of Israelites turning towards faithfulness and victory (Pressler 2017: 186; Ashley 2022: 328).

In 20:1 we find a geographical and chronological note relevant for fitting chapters 20–21 in the overall structure of the book. The community of Israel settled in Kadesh, in the desert of Zin, in the first month. The last chronological reference in the book was in 10:11, the second month of the second year. The last geographical reference was in 12:16, the desert of Paran, but with the later specification that it was at Kadesh (13:26). To determine the exact time and place of chapters 20–21 in Israel's wilderness journey, Numbers 33 and Deuteronomy 1 – 3 must be considered. Numbers 33:38 establishes the date of Aaron's death, narrated in

20:22–29, as the first day of the fifth month of the fortieth year. This specific date might imply that Israel arrived at Kadesh twice, once in the second year (12:16; 13:26) and then in the fortieth year (20:1). In Deuteronomy 1 – 3, when Moses rehearses Israel's wilderness itinerary, Kadesh is the place where Israel spends a long time (Deut. 1:46), probably most of the thirty-eight year-period they took from Kadesh to entering the plains of Moab (Deut. 2:14). This conundrum is commonly explained by source criticism or by differentiating two places called Kadesh, one in the desert of Zin (cf. Num. 27:14; 33:36; Deut. 32:51) and one in the desert of Paran, which is Kadesh-barnea (cf. Num. 13:3; 32:8; Deut. 1:19; Josh. 14:7). Not to dismiss the geographical and chronological incongruity and possible solutions, they are less helpful for understanding the function of chapters 20–21 in the overall structure of the book.

The location at Kadesh directs the reader to interpret the events of these chapters in the light of the previous events at Kadesh, more specifically, the rebellion of Israel and their failure to enter the Promised Land in chapters 13–14, as well as the leadership struggle in chapters 16–17. These are the two central themes in Numbers 20 – 21. The lack of a specific year suggests that a chronological contrast does not constitute the primary difference between the older exodus generation and the new generation which will enter the Promised Land. The narrative depicts a new beginning of the wilderness journey, focusing more on the new generation, with different dynamics between the people, their leaders and Yahweh. Rather than a fresh start, there is an important transition between the two generations. The new is formed out of the old in a process of learning to trust Yahweh and act accordingly. The geographical association with Kadesh and the impression of closeness in time create proximity between the old and the new generation with the intention to show the transition between their experiences.

Chapters 20 and 21 are linked thematically by the occurrence of parallel episodes of complaint (20:2–13; 21:4–9), petition (20:14–21; 21:21–23) and the motif of water (20:2–13; 21:16–20). The water motif, which is related to issues of leadership marked by the use of the staff, has contrasting purposes. In Numbers 20, the water motif is part of a complaint episode with the tragic result of Moses and Aaron, the people's main leaders, wrongly using the designated staff, being declared guilty by Yahweh and deserving of death outside the Promised Land. In Numbers 21, the water motif is a poem of gratitude sung by the people in celebration of the generosity of their leaders who provided water for them using their staffs. For this reason, chapters 20–21 are considered together in this commentary, with shared *Context* and *Meaning* sections, so that the contrast between the exodus generation and the settling generation is better appreciated, with Numbers 20 pointing to the end of the first and Numbers 21 pointing to the beginning of the latter (for the *Meaning* section, see below, at the end of Num. 21).

Comment
i. Miriam's death (20:1)

1. Three terms designate Israel in this verse: (lit.) 'sons of Israel', *the whole congregation* and *the people*. This combination is uncommon and occurs only here and in 16:41, when the people accuse Moses and Aaron of killing fellow Israelites in the context of conflict between the people and the leaders.

No year is given, only a reference to the first month. Kadesh in the desert of Zin is called Meribath-kadesh in other texts (27:14; Deut. 32:51), differentiating it from Kadesh-barnea, associated with the desert of Paran.

A short note reports that Miriam died and was buried in Kadesh. The conciseness of the report does not minimize its importance. Several deaths have occurred since Numbers 11, but Miriam is the first individual whose burial is reported. Her death occurs together with Aaron's (vv. 22–29). Placing Miriam's death with her older brother's confirms her leadership role (cf. Mic. 6:4). Miriam's death marks the arrival of death for the older generation of Israel's leaders. However, her death is not explained as a direct divine judgment against her, as in the case of Moses and Aaron (v. 12). Maybe this is a form of balancing the events of Numbers 12, when Miriam and Aaron challenged Moses' leadership but only she was punished by God. Lastly, Miriam's death heads chapters 20–21, which prominently connect the water motif to the role of leadership (20:2–13; 21:16–20). Miriam's character is repeatedly associated with water, especially in her song after Israel's liberation through the Red Sea (Exod. 15:20–21), which is immediately followed by a divine provision of water (Exod. 15:22–27). This last episode is marked by the term 'bitter' (*mārîm*), a wordplay on Miriam's name that is picked up in Numbers 20:10 in Moses' accusation of the people as *rebels* (*hammōrîm*).

ii. Moses and Aaron's rebellion results in announcement of their death (20:2–13)

a. People's complaint at lack of water at Meribah (20:2–5)

2–5. The conflict in this episode (20:2–13) is stated twice, first in the narrator's voice (*there was no water*, v. 2), then in the people's voice (*there is no water to drink*, v. 5). Various expressions connect this episode with others in the wilderness journey. *The people quarrelled* [or *disputed*: *wayyāreb*] *with Moses* in verse 3, just as in Exodus 17:2. The Hebrew verb *r-y-b* ('disputed') explains the name of the place as Meribah in both episodes (here in v. 13; Exod. 17:7). The first movement by the assembly, *they gathered together against Moses and against Aaron* (v. 2), connects this episode with the Korah rebellion in chapters 16–17 (16:3), as does the first saying of the people, 'If only we had perished with our brothers in the presence of Yahweh' (v. 3, AT; cf. 16:35). The use of the verb 'to perish' (*g-w-ʿ*) refers back to 17:12–13, when the people expressed their concern that all of them would die like those who had participated in the rebellion of Korah. Here, then, instead of worrying about a shared fate, they ironically express their desire for such a fate. The people justify their complaint about 'this bad place' because of its lack of 'seed, figs, vines and pomegranates' (v. 5, AT). These fruits were brought from Canaan by the spies in 13:23, connecting this episode with the definitive rebellion in chapters 13–14. The term 'seed' (*zeraʿ*) may connect this episode with 11:4–9, when *the rabble among them* desires better food than the manna, which is compared to coriander *seed* (*zeraʿ*, 11:7; cf. Exod. 16:31). These connections to other episodes of murmuring and rebellion could create the expectation for divine judgment on the people, but that is not what happens.

b. Divine instruction for Moses and Aaron to respond to the people's need (20:6–8)

6–8. Moses and Aaron fall on their faces, as they normally do in response to the people's rebellion, especially in anticipation of their intercessory role (14:5; 16:22, 45–46). Yahweh's glory appears as it did in the preceding punishment of the people for their rebellion (14:10; 16:19, 42), but this time it leads to instructions for facilitating divine provision for the actual needs of the people. This episode breaks the pattern of other murmuring and rebellion stories in Numbers: complaint → punishment → intercession → relief (MacDonald 2012a: 132).

Yahweh 'says a word' to Moses (v. 7, AT): Moses and Aaron, in the assembly's sight, must 'say a word' to the rock to make water spring from it in order for Moses to give the assembly and their animals something to drink (v. 8). The instructive aspect of the 'word' is emphasized.

c. Moses and Aaron fail to trust in and sanctify God (20:9–13)

9. It is not explicitly said which staff Moses took. Moses and Aaron's staffs play important roles in the exodus and wilderness narratives as signs of the divine power and their authority (cf. Exod. 4:1–5, 17; 7:17; 14:16; 17:1–7; Num. 17:1–13). However, the qualification of the staff 'from the presence of Yahweh' (AT) can only refer to Aaron's.[4] The struggle for leadership in chapters 16–17 comes to a closure with Aaron's staff divinely chosen and put in the sanctuary 'as a sign for the sons of rebellion' (17:10, AT).

10–13. Instead of speaking to the rock, Moses speaks to the assembly. He accuses them of being rebels (v. 10), as if they are the 'sons of rebellion' to whom Aaron's staff is a sign and associating them with the crucial rebellion in chapters 13–14 (14:9). Later, however, the accusation is turned against Moses and Aaron by Yahweh, here in verse 24 and later in 27:14. By raising his hand and

---

4   In v. 11, the Masoretic Text has 'his staff', so Moses'. However, this might be an editing error, with the original text as 'staff' as in v. 8. This reading is supported by the LXX (Propp 1988: 22).

striking the rock with the staff (v. 11), Moses follows his actions on other occasions when Yahweh instructed him to do so (Exod. 7:17; 14:16; 17:6). Moses and Aaron repeat actions that earlier worked as signs of their authority (Exod. 17:1–7). This episode, however, takes place after the affirmation of their leadership in chapters 16–17, and when the people are in true need. Yahweh's care and providence constitute the main issue of this episode, the first focused on the new generation. Yahweh meets their need despite Moses and Aaron's failure, showing that Israel's life depends on careful obedience to Yahweh's words more than the obedience of its leaders. Yahweh's instruction to use Aaron's staff, preserved in the ark blooming, budding and bearing fruit (17:10), indicates the function of leaders as mediators of the divine presence and blessing by facilitating the people's access to resources to meet their needs, instead of concentrating power and resources. This has been demonstrated at several points in chapters 16–19, and yet Moses and Aaron repeat former actions, even emphatically by striking the rock twice, to affirm their leadership and not to provide for the people. Moses and Aaron's failure is highlighted as profoundly serious. Moses had even *lifted up* [or *raised*] *his hand*, a combination that reflects the 'high-handed' sin of 15:30 (Morales 2024b: 25) and associates Moses and Aaron's failure here with that of Israel in chapters 13–14.

Yahweh's glory had appeared only to Moses and Aaron, while on many other decisive occasions it had appeared to the whole people (Exod. 16:7; Lev. 9:6, 23; Num. 14:10; 16:19, 42). Part of their role as leaders in this episode, then, was to manifest Yahweh's glory to the whole people. By focusing on their authority, instead of on their mediatory function, Moses and Aaron do not sanctify Yahweh. The provision of water, then, is associated with the divine word, presence and blessing represented by Aaron's staff. For this reason, even though Moses and Aaron fail, water is abundantly provided. Yahweh is sanctified 'in them', that is, in the waters of Meribah (v. 13), manifesting the divine glory as a blessing that sustains the life of the new generation of Israel, even apart from their most notorious leaders. This is relevant in the light of Miriam's death at the beginning of the chapter and the prospect of Moses and Aaron's deaths in the near future.

iii. Edom denies passage to Israel and threatens it with military aggression (20:14–21)

14a. Because of its proximity to the territory of Edom, 'on your borders' (v. 16, AT), the location has to be Meribath-kadesh, modern-day Petra. The occupation of Edom in the time portrayed for the Israelite settlement is characterized by tribal organization, as the reference to '*Shasu* tribes of Edom' in Egyptian correspondence in the Late Bronze Age attests (cf. Kitchen 2003: 473–474). The reference to a *king*, then, must be applied to any ruler, most probably one or more chiefs (cf. Gen. 36:19–28, 31–43).

14b–17. In the Late Bronze Age, kings of great kingdoms such as Egypt and Hatti treated one another as brothers in their diplomatic correspondence (Podany 2010). The brotherhood between Israel and Edom is used to appeal to kinship solidarity, based on obligations of protection and generous treatment, especially in situations of vulnerability. That is why the message starts with a rehearsal of Israel's history in Egypt and their deliverance through divine intervention (cf. Deut. 26:5–9). Israel's commitment to a brotherly dialogue with Edom is a mark of their previous encounter as brothers in Genesis 32 – 33. In both episodes, Jacob/Israel sends out messengers to Esau/Edom (cf. Gen. 32:3–4) with the intention of being on good terms when they meet. In the present episode, it might be that it is an invitation for Edom to contribute to Israel's salvation, as when Yahweh heard Israel's voice and 'sent out a messenger' to deliver them (v. 16, AT). Israel's intention is for mutual care and cooperation, a mark of kinship solidarity. Contrasting with Esau's response in Genesis 33, here Edom turns down Israel's appeal, and, therefore, the brotherly relation and responsibility, and insists on *meeting* Israel with military power (vv. 18, 20).

18. Edom's reply is threatening, confident of its military success against Israel (cf. Amos 1:11). A completely different picture is presented in Deuteronomy 2:3–8: Edom is fearful of Israel, who is warned by Yahweh not to fight them, and they pass through Edomite territory with no harassment. This discrepancy highlights the different purposes of Numbers and Deuteronomy in their depictions of Israel's encounters with other peoples. The importance of Israel's commitment to brotherly solidarity by means of dialogue and cooperation, and Edom and other peoples' aggressive responses, will be explored in the Balaam Pericope (chs. 22–24).

19. Israel insists on getting permission to go through Edomite territory by adding the criterion of paying for any resources they might consume on the way (cf. Deut. 2:6–7).

20–21. The threat of verse 18 is now acted upon. Israel's intentional use of kinship terms implies certain ethical demands that Israel must observe, including avoiding conflict. Even when Edom fails to keep these demands by attacking Israel, Israel does not. Deuteronomy 2:5 explains that Israel cannot fight Edom and take any of its land because Yahweh has given it to Esau as his inheritance.

vi. Aaron's death (20:22–29)

22–23. The exact location of *Mount Hor* is unknown, and it is possibly not a specific toponym but just a reference to 'the mountain top'. However, the reference to the borders of Edom suggests a location near Meribath-kadesh.

24. The idiom for death, 'to be united to his people' (AT), is used only in the Pentateuch (Gen. 25:8, 17; 35:29; 49:29, 33; Num. 27:13; 31:2; Deut. 32:50). It is probably derived from the practice of burying a family member with deceased kin in a shared family grave. Yahweh's justification for Aaron's death is his and Moses' rebellion, inverting Moses' accusation against the people in 20:10. Literally, they rebelled against 'my [Yahweh's] mouth'. This expression highlights that in the episode of the waters of Meribah, Yahweh addresses Moses with a 'word' and Moses must address the rock with a 'word' as well (20:7–8).

25–26. Aaron's death as the death of the first high priest is highly significant. There are some hints that this is not only Aaron's death report (contra Knierim and Coats 2005: 235). Although we should not expect Aaron to be dressed with all his high-priestly apparel (see Exod. 28; Lev. 8:7–9) because he is not on duty, the instruction to put Aaron's clothes on Eleazar implies that they were not Aaron's common clothes. The high-priestly apparel attaches him to specific areas of the tabernacle and his responsibilities in them. Furthermore, it points to royal and heavenly features, associating the high priest with the divine council (Milgrom 1991: 1016–1017; Nihan and Rhyder 2018). The verb 'to remove' (*p-š-ṭ*) is better translated as 'to strip' (so NRSV) and carries a humbling, even derogatory, meaning.

27. Because Aaron's death will be an occasion for the transfer of the high priesthood to his son Eleazar, everything is done *in the sight of the whole congregation.* The high priesthood is of public interest as it relates to the life of the assembly before Yahweh, so the whole people are included as witnesses.

28–29. Aaron's death is part of the divine punishment for the rebellion of the exodus generation in chapters 13–14, and his and Moses' rebellion in 20:2–13. Aaron and later Moses are mourned by the people for thirty days (cf. Deut. 34:8). Describing Aaron's death with the verb 'to perish' recalls the conclusion of the rebellion of Korah in 17:12–13, in which the people fear that all of Israel will *perish.*

Later, in chapter 35, the death of the high priest has ritual and social consequences. It marks the end of the blood-guilt for those who have caused someone's death inadvertently (see 35:25). The high priest effects atonement for the community in his cultic function and in his death. The placement of Aaron's death here and its resulting atonement might explain the transition from the failure of the exodus generation to a more successful journey for the settling generation. The death of the first high priest, even as a divine punishment for his rebellion, atones for Israel and opens the way for the new generation.

4. FLASHES OF HOPE FOR THE NEW GENERATION (21:1 – 25:18)

A. The pattern of success (21:1–3)

Comment

1. This episode interrupts Israel's stay at Mount Hor (20:22; 21:4) and follows a thematic rather than a geographical logic, as does all of Numbers 21. The two geographical references are important mainly to establish a connection between this episode and Israel's failure to possess the Promised Land in chapters 13–14. *Arad* is specifically said to be in the *Negeb*, the dry southern region of Canaan (cf. 13:17, 22). *The way of Atharim* (*hāʾătārîm*) is most probably a reference to the way taken by the twelve representatives to explore (*wĕyātûrû*) the land (13:2).[1] As Arad takes some Israelites captive, it seems as if Israel is again defeated by the Canaanites (cf. 14:45).

---

1 This is how ancient versions, such as the Targum (Aramaic) and Aquila (Greek), understood the Hebrew.

2–3. The rebellion in chapters 13–14 is marked by opposition to their leaders and by complete disregard for Yahweh's presence in the midst of the people. They rejected divine help to possess the Promised Land (14:11) and then tried to possess it on their own without the divine presence (14:41–44). Now, as they are being attacked, the people's reaction is quite different. They appeal to Yahweh for help by making a vow that imposes obedience on them. If Yahweh gives the Canaanites to Israel, they will completely devote (*ḥerem*) the Canaanite cities to Yahweh. Although related to a military context, so the spoils of war are not claimed for individual or public use, *ḥerem* in the Israel–Canaan relationship sets off-limits boundaries in order to bring about the formation of a specific identity defined by covenantal loyalty to Yahweh (Glanville 2021; cf. 18:14). In this vow, the verbs are in the singular, pointing to collective decisions and actions. There is a real sense of the determination and unity of the whole people, without any mention of Moses or any other leader. However, this is not rebellious behaviour, as in chapters 13–14. In the light of Miriam and Aaron's deaths, as well as Moses' failure as a leader, this episode shows the possibility of Israel's success as a people, the new generation, without their main leaders.

Yahweh responds to the vow and gives the Canaanites into Israel's hand. For its part, Israel completely devotes them and their cities. Arad and its king are not mentioned, so the reference to (lit.) 'the Canaanite' and the generalized *them* and *their towns* gain a more representative meaning. Israel's victory here, then, anticipates Israel's success in possessing the Promised Land and completely devoting Canaan to Yahweh. The conclusion of the episode is an aetiology for *Hormah*, which is derived from the root *ḥ-r-m*. In 14:45, the exodus generation was defeated by the Canaanites as far as Hormah – they were destroyed. This time, the new generation's trust in and dedication to Yahweh invert the outcome and Israel completely devotes (*ḥerem*) Canaan to Yahweh at Hormah.

B. Remedy for failure through the copper snake (21:4–9)

4a. Another part of the itinerary is given. Israel must go south, by the road of the Red (or Reed) Sea, to go around the land of

Edom. In Deuteronomy 2:1 this route is taken before Israel sends messengers to Edom and can go through its territory (Deut. 2:8). This difference might be explained by fluctuating Edomite boundaries. Deuteronomy 2 uses 'Mount Seir' as a reference to Edom, but Mount Seir is to the west of the Arabah. However, in Numbers 20 – 21 the boundary of Edom is established to the east of the Arabah. The move to the south, then, is explained as necessary to go around the territory of Edom known by the authors of Numbers, because of Edom's refusal to let Israel pass through it (20:20–21).

The southern location of the copper snake episode is quite relevant archaeologically. The Timna Valley, in the south part of the Arabah, near the Red (or Reed) Sea, is well known for its copper mines with intense activity under the Canaanites during the eleventh and tenth centuries BC (Yahalom-Mack and Segal 2018).

4b–5. The people's impatience is literally described as 'shortness of throat', because they lack food and water and their throats are disgusted with their food. Despite the use of the complaint formula *Why have you brought us up out of Egypt to die in the wilderness?* (cf. Exod. 14:11–12; 17:3; Num. 14:2–4; 16:13; 20:5), this is not an episode of murmuring without cause. When compared with Numbers 11, the current episode is not about displaced or unregulated desire (cf. 11:4). Food is scarce and unsatisfying.

6–9. Venomous vipers (*Echiscarinatus*) are common in the Sinai Peninsula and the southern region of the Negev. The expression 'fiery snakes' (see NRSV margin) is already indicative of the metallurgical crafting of the copper serpent, but also points to the religious aspect of these creatures. The words for 'copper' (*nehošet*) and 'snake' (*nahaš*) sound alike and serve as a pun, as recognized by the medieval Jewish commentator Rashi (1999: 254). The repetitive Hebrew root *s-r-p* ('fiery') is always related to fire, implying the metallurgical process, so that Yahweh's instruction for Moses to craft a *śārāp* (v. 8) is fulfilled by his crafting of a copper snake (*nehaš nehošet*, v. 9). The use of the term *śārāp* intentionally associates these snakes with heavenly creatures, the seraphim (e.g. Isa. 6:2, 6), also related to the cherubim (e.g. Gen. 3:24), both of which protect the divine realm from human access (Hartenstein 2007; see 23:21–24 below).

The immediate active response from God breaks with the pattern of murmuring episodes. Here the people's complaint serves a more positive purpose. The people truly repent and appeal to Moses to intercede on their behalf. Again breaking with the murmuring pattern, Yahweh does not answer Moses' intercession by merely doing away with the snakes, but provides a means for those injured to show active trust in divine providence for their healing. More importantly, Yahweh's provision is not limited to this occasion, but seems to serve the people in any future accident.

Archaeological and biblical evidence suggests that we are dealing with a cultic object. Hezekiah's cultic reform described in 2 Kings 18 refers to the copper snake ('Nehushtan') made by Moses that had become a cult object to which people burned incense. Dated in the early Iron Age, a small copper snake was found in Timna, inside the inmost part of a tent sanctuary (Amzallag 2016). The healing efficacy of the copper snake depends on its cultic function as an image of the divine presence. This is similar to the use of Aaron's staff in the previous episode that addressed the lack of water (20:10−13). Furthermore, Aaron's staff turned into a snake (*tannín* in Exod. 7:9, but *naḥaš* in Exod. 7:15) and was preserved in the inmost part of the tabernacle like the copper snake in Timna, 'in the presence of Yahweh' (Num. 20:9, AT), 'before the [ark of] the testimony' (17:10, AT), whose covering was formed by two cherubim (see above, 7:89; cf. Exod. 25:20, 22).

This episode of the 'fiery snakes', then, points to Israel's proximity to the divine presence and the dangers for Israel when a sacred space is approached inadequately. It might even reflect an early tradition of a healing ritual by incantation with repetitive sounds using the consonants *n-ḥ-š*, which reproduce the hissing sound of snakes. This is ritually parallel to other Ancient Near Eastern incantations that, like this episode, conclude with the prognosis 'he will live' (AT; Hurowitz 2004). This incantation aspect will be criticized in Numbers 22 − 24 with the association of *naḥaš* with cursing (see 23:23; 24:1). However, the positive aspect of this episode will be picked up in Numbers 22 − 24 as well, with Israel's access to the environment where it can enjoy an intimate, trusting and obedient relationship with God, the source of its blessing, that can be associated with the garden of Eden and the Promised Land (see 23:23; 24:5–6). The triumphant note that concludes this episode provides the new generation with access to the divine presence and healing by means of a cultic object and a ritual that can be used to give life even in the future, independently from the leadership of Moses and Aaron.

C. Successfully arriving at the plains of Moab (21:10–20)

10–13. This itinerary omits the point from which Israel sets out and lists a selection of campsites. It does not correspond well with the same itinerary in 33:41–49. The purpose is to locate Israel in Amorite country, at the eastern edge of Moab, and to delineate Moab's boundaries: the Zered River on the south and the Arnon River on the north. It attests that Israel travelled up to the east of Moab.

14–15. The whole system of streams of the Arnon is mentioned, as well as their position in relation to the border of Moab, with 'the settlement of Ar' (AT) a possible reference to *Ar* [*'ar*] *of Moab* (21:28) or 'city [*'îr*] of Moab' (22:36).

Quoting from *the Book of the Wars of the LORD*, mentioned only here in the Bible, anticipates a successful enterprise as Israel moves close to the Promised Land. The poetic text gains an epic character with slight textual emendations, making Yahweh the subject of the verbs:

> Yahweh came in a whirlwind;
> he came to the streams of Arnon.
> He marched through the streams,
> turning aside to the settlement of Ar,
> leaning toward the border of Moab.
> (Christensen 1974: 359–360)

Emendations are typically hypothetical, but this change fits well with the character of other epic texts in the Old Testament with theophanic features (Deut. 33; Judg. 5; Ps. 68; Hab. 3:3). The subsequent verses then quote a song that shares features with Deborah's song (!) in Judges 5 in relation to the leaders of

Israel and their staff. The emended text fits the theme of the divine presence accompanying Israel in chapters 20–21, which is especially demonstrated by means of signs related to Israel's leaders' staffs (see above, 20:10–13; 21:7–9).

16. Exactly like 20:7–8, Yahweh speaks to Moses to gather the assembly to give them something to drink.

17. Moses gets out of the picture and Israel acts. Similar to what Moses was instructed to do (20:8), Israel's Well Song is a word directed towards an object, the well, to give its water ('Come up, well!' [AT]), and an encouragement to do so (*Sing to it!*). The poetic text in verses 14–15, the Well Song and the Heshbon Song (21:27–30) are probably all from *the Book of the Wars of the LORD* (Greenstein 2017).

18–19. Resembling known Bedouin well songs, the second part of Israel's Well Song clarifies who was responsible for the enterprise. Three leadership titles are used, all of them present in Deborah's song in Judges 5: *śārîm* ('chieftains') indicates tribal hierarchy (Judg. 5:15); *nĕdîbê* (*nobles*) concerns those with the economic status and disposition to commit their resources to the common good (Judg. 5:2, 9); and *mĕḥōqēq* is a lawmaker (Judg. 5:14), a designation used for Moses in Deuteronomy 33:21, hence its use in the singular here. So we could expect a reference to Moses' staff, but instead we have a reference to (lit.) 'their staffs'. The term for *staff* here (*mišʿenet*), related to an ordinary work object like a shepherd's staff (Ps. 23:4), is different from other occurrences in the exodus and wilderness narratives (*maṭṭê*, Exod. 4:2; 7:9; 17:5; Num. 20:8) and from Judges 5:14 (*šebeṭ*). The difference probably results from the use of a quotation from an earlier source (*the Book of the Wars of the LORD*) preserving a traditional song. This is not necessarily the instrument used to dig the well, although Bedouin well songs attest to this, but an indication that they demonstrated their leadership (cf. Judg. 5:14) by providing water for the people. Where Moses and Aaron failed as leaders by centralizing their authority when they should have facilitated the people's access to resources and power, these leaders from the people succeed. Therefore, their staffs, like that of Aaron, function as objects that indicate the divine presence in the people's midst and divine providence for them. Their success is precisely in the plurality of leaders (cf. 11:16–17; Frevel 2018: 102), an important lesson for the new generation moving forward, as it has been for the whole of Numbers 20 – 21. There is, then, a reversal of chapters 17–18, when the staff of Israel's leaders was a sign of their rebellion against Yahweh, Moses and Aaron. For this reason, the last part of verse 18 belongs to the Well Song: (lit.) 'from the wilderness a gift'.

Even though apparently an itinerary, all the terms in verse 19 are unknown toponyms, but with significant meanings. *Nahaliel* means 'estate of God' or 'God is my estate', and *Bamoth* means 'heights', often used in compound names for Moabite territories (e.g. *Bamoth-baal*, 22:41). Digging wells successfully asserts land rights (e.g. Gen. 20; 26), so it is possible that this last part of the Well Song attests Israel's rights to disputed Moabite territory, the theme of the final narrative in verses 21–35.

20. Other references to the territory of Moab are given to determine Israel's final position at this point. The use of the definite article in 'the Jeshimon' (*the waste-land*) implies a specific place, probably north of the Dead Sea on both sides of the Jordan (33:49; 1 Sam. 23:19).

D. Victory over King Sihon and King Og (21:21–35)

This is the first battle that results in Israel's possession of land, later given to the tribes of Reuben, Gad and half of Manasseh (32:33). It becomes the successful paradigm for taking possession of Canaan as a whole (Deut. 31:3–4), although the land's status as part of the Promised Land is liminal (cf. Josh. 22:9–34). For this reason, this narrative is well preserved in Israel's collective memory, as attested by its frequent mention in biblical literature (Deut. 1:4; 2:24 – 3:22; 4:46; 29:7–8; 31:4; Josh. 2:10; 9:10; 12:1–5; 13:10, 21, 27; Judg. 11:18–26; 1 Kgs 4:19; Neh. 9:22; Pss 135:10–12; 136:17–22).

21–22. Sihon is approached in a similar way to Edom in 20:14–17, though Israel sends messengers, not Moses. Following the theme of Israel's leadership transition in chapters 20–21, Israel's victory over Sihon, like the battle at Hormah (21:1–3), does not depend on Moses' leadership. Sihon is not treated in terms of brotherhood, like Edom, but there is still an appeal to an amicable encounter in which Israel does not initiate any aggression of military action.

23–25. Sihon, like Edom, denies Israel's request and gathers an army to battle Israel (cf. 20:18, 20–21). Instead of turning away, as in the case of Edom's attack, Israel defends itself. Similar to Yahweh's action against Egypt, Israel strikes Sihon (cf. Exod. 7:20, 25; 8:12; 9:25; 12:12). By defeating Sihon, Israel takes possession of his land, from the Arnon in the south to the Jabbok in the north (v. 24), with the specification of Jazer, according to the LXX, as a location on the border of Ammon. This is a summary statement about a process of conquering and rebuilding its towns (v. 25; cf. 32:33–42), culminating in Israel settling in them.

26. Amorite presence in the Transjordan is described here as a conquest of previous Moabite territory. Historically, there is no evidence of significant occupation in this region before the stronger Moabite polity built by King Mesha in the ninth century BC (Jeon 2022: 31). Heshbon in the early Iron Age was just a small village. This corresponds well with the identity of the Amorites as semi-nomadic herdsmen, originally from northern Syria, who occupied the highlands east and west of the Jordan River (Fleming 2016: 1–30). The region became politically disputed between Israel and Moab in the ninth century BC. According to the important Mesha Stele, an extra-biblical inscription from the ninth century, Israel's king, Omri, had defeated Moab and annexed the territory to Israel.

27–28. The Heshbon Song in verses 27–30 has two functions in this context: it corroborates the information given in verse 26, that Israel's possession of this region did not infringe on Moabite territory; and it serves as an ironic taunt song, because it turns Sihon's victory over Moab into Israel's victory over Sihon. The irony is indicated by the term *ballad-singers* (*hammōšĕlîm*), from the root *m-š-l*, repeatedly used in Balaam's oracles, which reverse the intended curses into blessings (23:7, 18; 24:3, 15, 20, 21, 23).

Parallel descriptions of Heshbon in verse 27 as 'fortified' (*built*) and [*well*] *established* are ironically inverted by parallel images of destruction in verse 28. Also parallel is the *devour*[*ing*] of Ar of Moab with the *swallow*[*ing*] *up* of the heights of the Arnon. The second part of this parallel requires explanation. 'Bamoth' is often used in compound names for Moabite territories, but here it is used topographically (translated *heights*).

29. *Chemosh* is the Moabite national deity. In many ways, these verses reflect a retributive theology typical of biblical explanations for Israel's and Judah's destruction and exile. Moabites are called *people of Chemosh*; the deity, presumably as an act of judgment, hands over his people to an enemy, which is the explanation given in the Mesha Stele (lines 5–6) for Moab's subjugation to Israel in the ninth century BC; and there is a lament over the nation's fortunes: *Woe to you . . . !* A modified version of Moab and Heshbon's destruction is found in Jeremiah 48:45–46 as part of a prophecy against Moab.

30. There are several textual difficulties in verse 30, leading to various proposals of changes and interpretations. The geographical movement from Heshbon to Dibon parallels verse 28, with Dibon substituting for the *heights of the Arnon*, both to the south. If 'Nophah' (see, e.g., ESV, NET) is read as 'Nobah', which might be close to Jogbehah (cf. Judg. 8:11), this is a reference to a region north of Heshbon, already on the way to the Jabbok River, near Ammon's border. That would be a parallel to verse 24, *from the Arnon to the Jabbok*. The reference to *Medeba*, near Heshbon, is interesting as it is mentioned in the Mesha Stele (line 8) as a town where Israel's King Omri dwelt. If the connection with verse 24 is held, verse 30 concludes the Heshbon Song by moving from Sihon's military victory over Moab to Israel's military victory over Sihon, confirming its ironic purpose. So verse 30 could be rendered as follows:

> We [Israel] have overpowered them;
> Heshbon has perished as far as Dibon.
> We have shattered them as far as Nophah [Nobah],
> which reaches to Medeba.
> (NET)

31–32. A modified form of the assertion of verse 25 about Israel settling in Amorite towns is replicated in verse 31. *Jazer* refers to the northern region of the Amorite territory, near Ammon's border (cf. v. 24), reaffirming Israel's complete possession, from south to north, of Sihon's land. This detail comes after the conclusive summary of verse 31 to make a transition to Israel's encounter with Og, king of Bashan, a fertile area to the north, east of the Sea of Galilee.

33–35. According to 34:7–12, the region of Og's kingdom is part of the Canaanite territory given to Israel by Yahweh. This explains some important differences from Israel's encounter with Sihon. There is no diplomatic encounter between Israel and Og, who comes straight to battle. But Israel does not attack Og's army right away. There is a divine message to Moses confirming Israel's victory as the result of Yahweh's promise to give Og, his people and his land into Israel's hand. Finally, Israel's victory is described as resulting in the destruction of Og, his descendants and his people, reflecting the practice of complete devotion (*ḥerem*; cf. Deut. 3:6).

In Deuteronomy 3:1–11, we find two details about the identity of Og and his kingdom that enable a better understanding of the importance of this short narrative in Numbers. Deuteronomy 3:5 characterizes some of the towns as fortified, and 3:11 calls Og one of the remaining Rephaim. These two details connect the success of the new generation against Og with the failure of the older generation to take possession of Canaan in Numbers 13 – 14. There the Canaanite towns are also described as *fortified* and their inhabitants are called the offspring of Anak (Num. 13:28). The so-called Anakites are related to the Rephaim in Deuteronomy 2:11, and Numbers 13:33 associates them with the Nephilim of Genesis 6:4, which might imply a mythical identity for an extraordinarily tall, strong and violent people (see Num. 13:33 above). Hence, although the account is short, Israel's victory over Og is crucially important. This is the inversion of the older generation's failure and the beginning of Israel's conquest of Canaan, starting with a great victory over its most feared population. Numbers 21, then, is framed by two very successful military victories by Israel (cf. 21:1–3).

Meaning
Miriam and Aaron's deaths framing Numbers 20, and the two successful military victories framing Numbers 21, suggest that

these are not unrelated. Israel's move into the Promised Land is pictured as a transition that requires a process of formation of the new generation from the old. In Moses and Aaron's rebellion, we learn that in this transition, the assertion of authority goes against the purpose of leadership as laid down in chapters 16–19. And if leaders are more avid to dispute or affirm their authority than to serve, they will become unnecessary. God's intentions and promises will be fulfilled without them.

Although it is a consequence of his failure, Moses himself gives Israel a partial substitute for his leadership. In the episode of the bronze serpent (21:4–9), Moses manufactures a cultic object related to Aaron's staff, which is one element that represents the divine presence in the midst of the people, to serve as a means of divine healing for them so as to preserve their lives as they learn to trust God and to approach God's presence carefully.

The immediate and future absence of Miriam, Aaron and Moses as leaders provides Israel with the possibility of putting into practice their own diversified leadership. In the Well Song, a plural leadership make use of their status and resources to provide for the basic needs of the whole people, digging a well with their staffs and giving them water. The use of staffs and the provision of water affirm that Israel's leadership is mediating God's care and presence in the midst of the people. They have learned to sanctify God in the eyes of Israel.

The cultic and practical means of making God's presence and blessing available to the people show how they are entangled. Our worship experience as a community of faith in certain times and places, and how we live our ordinary lives in community, should inform and reinforce each other as means to create environments where God can be encountered and the needs of people can be met.

Israel's success in this new phase without Moses' leadership is then affirmed in their military victories in 21:1–3 and 21:21–35 that overcome the failure of the older generation in chapters 13–14.

Water provision and the use of a staff as means to depict God's presence and care for God's people are well illustrated by Psalm 23. But in these episodes in Numbers 20 – 21 we learn, together with the new generation, that there is a responsibility for the people to realize and experience this presence and care themselves. This is the result of an interdependent and cooperative dynamic between leaders and people in the effort to provide resources and healing for their lives, especially by those in privileged positions for the benefit of the more vulnerable. This process of formation must be seen as a paradigm for every generation of the people of God. For God's intention and purpose for God's people is to be among them, as a good shepherd, providing for them and making them safe.

E. Balaam's oracles/divinations (22:1 – 24:25)

Context

In the previous chapters, other peoples opted for aggression even when Israel offered dialogue and negotiation (20:14–21; 21:21–35). Battle seems unavoidable, and Israel's hope lies solely in divinely ordained military success. Other peoples' aggression and Israel's success are relevant as Israel arrives at the *plains of Moab* (22:1), and they are carefully addressed in the Balaam Pericope (chs. 22–24).

Israel's encounters with other peoples on the last leg of its journey also suggest an interest in defining Israel's identity in relation to them (see Introduction, 'Israel's identity and its neighbours'). This important theme dominates chapters 22–24, especially in the artistically and theologically fantastic Tale of the Jenny (22:21–35). With some textual and thematic links to chapters 22–24, this theme will be explicitly addressed in chapter 25, also appearing in subsequent chapters (chs. 26, 27, 31–33, 36). Israel's geographical and cultural proximity to other peoples in the Transjordan makes it a liminal space where different identities are negotiated, with boundaries constantly formed and blurred (Pardes 2000: 129–130; see also Diamant 2009: 61; Stone 2014: 88). Therefore, the Balaam Pericope is central to the development of this part of Numbers.

In Balaam's fourth oracle (24:15–24), which bears the greatest resemblance to the oracles of Israel's prophets, Israel's relations to Moab, Edom, Midian and Amalek gain more theological importance by being viewed in the light of their origins back in Genesis. One main aspect is the textual and theological link between

Numbers 22 – 24 and Genesis 12:1–3 in the expression *whomsoever you bless is blessed, and whomsoever you curse is cursed* (22:6; 24:9; cf. Gen. 12:3). The divine election of Abraham's family determines Israel's identity and future, as well as that of the other peoples it encounters.

Blessing and cursing also connect Numbers 22 – 24 to Genesis 3 (see Savran 1994). These are the only two biblical texts in which a talking animal appears. The serpent and the jenny have knowledge of God unknown to their human interlocutors, and their interactions determine the paths of the narratives and the human characters. While the serpent's interaction with humans leads to enmity, cursing and death, Balaam's interaction with the jenny leads to reconciliation, blessing and the preservation of life. The contrasting results of the human interactions with the serpent and the jenny – curse and blessing – designate the latter as a reversal of the former.

Animal imagery and reversals are also a characteristic of another Balaam tradition outside the Bible. Reconstructed fragments of a wall text inscribed in plaster at Tell Dēr ʿAllā, in the upper Jordan Valley, just 2 km (1.25 miles) north of the Jabbok River, contain a reference to Balaam son of Beor, the seer of the gods, who received a divine night vision (see Dijkstra 1995). Besides a clear reference to the same name and patronym, several other features are shared between these Balaam traditions. Reconstruction of the text of the inscription remains challenging, as does the definition of its language,[2] but the following can be attested clearly: Balaam receives a troubling divine vision at night that causes him to weep. He then communicates to his people that the gods have decided to afflict the land with doom consisting of the overturning of the natural and the social world in a description of reversals based on animal imagery, and death will reign (Milgrom 1990: 475). It can be affirmed with some certainty that Balaam pronounces doom on his own people, which is not well received by them, causing Balaam to confront them more stringently with a form of

---

2   The best option is an Aramaic dialect with Canaanite influences. See
    Robker 2019: 277–278, 300–301; cf. Wolters 1988: 108, 112.

social critique against oppressors and tyrants in association with curses, sorcery and incantation (lines 34, 35 and 39; see Dijkstra 1995: 55–59). This is the first extra-biblical example of a religious specialist similar to Elijah and Elisha, who came from the same region in Gilead, just 30 km (19 miles) north of Tell Dēr ʿAllā (see Diamant 2009: 104).

A comparison of the two traditions makes it reasonable to investigate Balaam as a possible historical figure. Balaam is a diviner and not a sorcerer (e.g. Num. 22:8; see Robker 2019: 342; Wiggershaus 2021: 205). In the Deir ʿAlla Inscription, Balaam receives his visions from El, the chief deity who leads the divine assembly, of which the most relevant participants are the Shadday – lower gods. El and Shadday also appear in the Balaam Pericope, as well as Elohim and Elyon. However, the only explicit reference to Balaam's religious devotion and obedience in the biblical text is to Yahweh. It is possible that the Balaam tradition was adapted to Yahwistic religion. Nonetheless, the biblical text maintains Balaam's polytheistic environment and paints a complex picture. Israel is blessed by the whole divine assembly and not only by Yahweh. Yet their blessing is subordinated to Yahweh's authority over Israel and other nations within the divine assembly.

The Transjordan region of Gilead is the best candidate for the origins of Balaam traditions. This is the location where the Deir ʿAlla Inscription was found and where the biblical narrative positions Israel's camp. However, the Balaam Pericope also associates Ammon (see on 22:5) and Aram (23:7) with him. Ammon and Gilead overlapped in the region of the Jabbok River, especially during the second half of the ninth century BC, when Hazael of Damascus exercised influence in the entire Transjordan (see 2 Kgs 10:32–33). Therefore, the historical figure of Balaam likely lived in the Ammonite territory near the Jabbok River and had Aramean roots. This would explain the Aramaic linguistic character of the Deir ʿAlla Inscription, and it fits well with the most recent and acceptable date for the inscription around 800 BC (see Robker 2019: 274, 278). The similarity on several levels between the Balaam Pericope and the Deir ʿAlla Inscription may even suggest that the latter originated or at least was preserved in Israelite circles in Gilead (Levine 2000: 230).

The importance of the Balaam Pericope and its intricate textual
and thematic connections to its literary context raise the question
of composition. Typical source-critical models have proven inadequate (Robker 2019: 37). Furthermore, the following structure
suggests an intricate cohesiveness:

A Balak's perspective on Israel (22:1–4)
B First set of three divinations to decide whether Balaam
   should go with Balak's messengers (22:5–35)
   B1 First divination: denial (22:5–13)
   B2 Second divination: approval (22:14–20)
   B3 Third divination: qualified approval (22:21–35)
      B3a The messenger of Yahweh blocks the way, the
         jenny sees him and swerves, Balaam strikes the
         jenny (22:21–23)
      B3b The messenger of Yahweh blocks the way, the
         jenny sees him and swerves, Balaam strikes the
         jenny (22:24–25)
      B3c The messenger of Yahweh blocks the way, the
         jenny sees him and crouches down, Balaam
         strikes the jenny; two dialogues that qualify
         Balaam's actions follow (22:26–35)
C Balak requires Balaam to see Israel as he does and curse it
   (22:36–41)
D Second set of three divinations to decide if Israel is cursed
   or blessed (23:1 – 24:24)
   D1 First divination/oracle: Israel is blessed (23:1–12)
   D2 Second divination/oracle: Israel is blessed (23:13–24)
   D3 Third divination/oracle: Israel is blessed (23:25 – 24:14)
      D3 + 1 Fourth divination/oracle: Israel is blessed
         and other peoples are cursed (24:15–24)
      D3 + 1a First oracle/poem: Israel, Edom and Moab
         (24:15–19)
      D3 + 1b Second oracle/poem: Amalek (24:20)
      D3 + 1c Third oracle/poem: Kenites/Midianites
         (24:21–22)
      D3 + 1d Fourth oracle/poem: Ashur (24:23–24)
E Balak and Balaam part ways (24:25)

In the *Comment* below, other tripartite elements connecting the structure and theme of the whole Balaam Pericope, and the 3 + 1 structure of the second set of divinations (D), will be presented.

Lastly, the Balaam tradition appears in other parts of the Bible. It is significant that Numbers 31 rejects the more positive view of Balaam in chapters 22–24. Numbers 31 holds Balaam responsible for Israel's profanation in the Baal-peor incident of chapter 25 (31:16; cf. Rev. 2:14), and Balaam is killed by the sword with other Midianite chieftains (31:8; cf. Josh. 13:21–22). The development of this tradition is puzzling (see Frevel 2020: 155–189). A negative view of Balaam is also found in Deuteronomy 23:4–6, where he is associated with Mesopotamia and curses Israel (cf. Josh. 24:9–10; Neh. 13:1–3). The negative view of Balaam in 2 Peter 2:15–16 and Jude 11 is based on his greed, assuming that he did accept Balak's honours. The *star* mentioned in Balaam's fourth oracle (Num. 24:17) is alluded to in Matthew 2 in its association with Jesus as a messianic figure. Some texts from Qumran (4Q175, 4Q266, 4Q269, 1QM XI, 6) also associate Balaam's star with an unnamed messianic figure. Neither Matthew nor the Qumran texts mention Balaam as the source of the oracle. However, the presentation of the magi as foreign religious specialists in Matthew 2 may stand in parallel to Balaam (see Robker 2019: 257).

Comment
i. Balak's perspective on Israel (22:1–4)

1. Israel arrives at *the plains of Moab across the Jordan from Jericho*, the place where they will stay for the rest of Numbers and all of Deuteronomy (see 26:3, 63; 31:12; 33:48, 50; 35:1; 36:13; Deut. 34:1, 8). Despite this designation, Israel is encamped in a region to the north of Moab's borders (21:10–12; see Frevel 2020: 127).

2–4. The context for Balak's initiatives against Israel is their victory over the Amorites (21:21–32). One of the main motifs in the Balaam Pericope is sight as a form of interpretation of reality and the divine will. Here, Balak 'sees' what Israel has done to the Amorites and interprets it as a threat. Balak's reasons for this conclusion become clearer in verse 4. He fears that Israel's camp will exhaust the natural resources around Moab and Midian, an issue that emerged already with Edom (20:17, 19) and the Amorites

(21:22). The association of the *surroundings* with grazing (35:2–4) explains Balak's analogy of Israel with an ox chewing or licking (*l-ḥ-k*) the vegetation. This rare verb is used to depict a humiliated enemy 'eating dust' (Ps. 72:9; Isa. 49:23; Mic. 7:17). Balak views Israel as a domestic ox subservient to its master, like a subjugated enemy, but also threatening to exhaust natural resources because of its great size (cf. Exod. 1:9, 12).

ii. First set of three divinations to decide whether Balaam should go with Balak's messengers (22:5–35)

a. First divination: denial (22:5–13)

5–6. For the origins of Balaam, see the *Context* above. Like Balak, the name Balaam might mean 'destroyer'. The Hebrew term *pethor* has a meaning relevant to the narrative: 'visionary land'. The text qualifies Balaam's location with reference to 'the river' (AT), taken here as the Jabbok, and 'the land of Ammonites'. Whatever Balaam's origins, the text characterizes him neither as Moabite nor Israelite. He is an outsider.

When Israel approached Edomite and Amorite territory, they sent out messengers (*mal'ākîm*) to negotiate a peaceful encounter (20:14; 21:21). Balak also dispatches messengers (*mal'ākîm*), but his intentions are to curse Israel, so that he can 'strike [*n-k-h*] and expel them from the land' (v. 6, AT; cf. 21:24, 35). This context associates cursing with military violence and expulsion from the land, implying subservience caused by exclusion from relationships and environments of well-being and blessing. Balak attributes to Balaam the power of cursing and blessing with his concluding expression: *whomsoever you bless is blessed, and whomsoever you curse is cursed* (v. 6).

7–13. The messengers are identified as *elders of Moab and . . . elders of Midian* (v. 7), and then as chieftains of Moab (v. 8) or chieftains of Balak (v. 13). Both terms can refer to tribal leaders. For the connection between Moab and Midian, see on 25:6–18. They bring Balak's words to Balaam, and also 'sorceries' (*qĕsāmîm*, v. 7). These likely refer to the results of previous divinations conducted by specialists at Balak's court (Wiggershaus 2021: 91–92). Divination was commonly employed for discerning divine decisions in cases of war. Balak thus requests from Balaam a curse in response to the divination reports he has already received.

Balaam's response (v. 8), asking the messengers to wait for the night, reveals that he will enquire of Yahweh about the issue. That he *rose in the morning* (v. 13) might imply that his divinations occurred as visions in dreams, which corresponds with how Balaam is depicted in the Deir ʿAlla Inscription.

In the exchange between Balaam and God, Balak's message (vv. 5–6) is repeated (v. 11), but not exactly. It omits that Israel sits 'in front' of Balak,[3] that Israel 'is more powerful' than Balak, and that Balak attributes to Balaam the final word on cursing and blessing. More importantly, Balaam changes 'curse' (ʾ-r-r) to 'condemn' (q-b-b), and 'strike' (n-k-h) to 'battle' (l-ḥ-m). The differences between the messages intentionally soften Balak's language. Perhaps Balaam's purpose is to make it easier to receive God's permission to work for Balak (Guimarães 2022: 25–26).

In God's reply, Balaam is commanded not to go with Balak's messengers, and, more significantly, Balak's attribution of curse and blessing is completely denied in the divine affirmation that Israel is blessed (v. 12).

b. Second divination: approval (22:14–20)

14–20. The messengers inform Balak that Balaam will not come, but instead of attributing the refusal to Yahweh, they attribute it to Balaam himself (v. 14). Possibly considering the matter to be a typical political negotiation, Balak sends a second delegation of greater honour (v. 15), later qualified as his servants or retainers (v. 18). This qualification connects this group more closely to Balak's court, probably being his direct representatives.

Payment for Balaam's services, never mentioned explicitly by the first group, is the focus of the second delegation. Balaam is informed that he will receive 'exceedingly great honour' (v. 17, AT), which he interprets as valuable material compensation, 'the

---

3   The LXX and 4QNum include this part, and Robker considers this reading of v. 11 older than the MT, arguing that the omission is based on literary style to avoid redundancy (Robker 2019: 76). However, this does not explain the other omissions and the changes of vocabulary.

fullness of silver and gold' of Balak's house (v. 18, AT). Material compensation and submission to Balak's rule go hand in hand.

The requirement is recalled in the expression 'condemn [*q-b-b*] for me this people' (v. 17, AT). Balak wants to be 'capable' (*'ûkal*) of striking Israel and expelling them (v. 6). Balaam denies that he is 'capable' (*'ûkal*) of doing anything against the word of Yahweh, his God (v. 18).

A common divinatory practice in the Ancient Near East was to repeat the same enquiry to a deity to confirm or deny a previous interpretation. However, deities were not fond of multiple enquiries on the same issue. Three was apparently the perfect number of times for diviners to compare divinations without overly pestering the deity (see Koch 2010: 45, 48). Here, however, Balaam makes a decision after only two contradictory results. Given the contradiction, he should have tested his results a third time. As with his softening of Balak's request when reporting it to God, his hastiness suggests he was willing to accept Balak's proposal.

c. Third divination: qualified approval (22:21–35)
The change in Balaam's interpretation about the possibility of meeting Balak poses some questions: are Balaam's divinations reliable? Is his willingness to meet Balak going to lead him to acquiesce to Balak's request to curse Israel? The built-in suspense is definitive for understanding the Tale of the Jenny.

The divine permission for Balaam to accompany the second group of messengers to meet Balak (22:20) and the divine anger when Balaam does so (22:21–22) are typically used as evidence to argue that the Tale of the Jenny is an independent piece of folk literature that disrupts the Balaam Pericope (see Milgrom 1990: 468–469). However, this scene must be interpreted in the light of the practice of divination in the Ancient Near East. As noted above, given the contradiction between Balaam's interpretations of the first and the second divine responses, he should have tested the results a third time. The divine anger clarifies that Balaam misinterpreted the divine will (see Wiggershaus 2021: 207–208, 211–213). The Tale of the Jenny functions as the third divination (see Moyer 2012: 170). This narrative invites the audience to witness the process of divination and to interpret the divine decision.

There are several textual links between the Tale of the Jenny and Israel's encounter with Edom in 20:14–21 (Gelblum 2023). For example, the Israelites are committed to sticking to the 'path' through Edom's territory, not 'swerving to the right or the left' or passing 'in the field and the vineyard' (20:17), but Edom blocks them, 'going out with a sword' (20:18) and a 'strong hand' (20:20). Therefore, Israel 'swerved' (20:21). In the same way, the jenny 'swerved' from the 'path', going 'in the field', because the messenger of Yahweh blocked it 'with a sword . . . in his hand' (22:23). Another time the messenger stands in a 'vineyard' until the path is too narrow to go 'to the right or the left' (22:24).

These links between the narratives are foundational for understanding the role of the Tale of the Jenny in the overall message of the Balaam Pericope. This comparison renders Israel and the jenny analogous. The terms governing the actions of the jenny in 22:21–35 describe the actions of Israel in 20:14–21. Edom is then mainly associated with Balaam (cf. Frisch 2015: 106), reflecting a tradition found in Genesis 36:32 about the first king of Edom, who is called 'Bela son of Beor'. Edom's aggressiveness against Israel, his brother, serves as an archetype for all peoples who treat Israel as an enemy in Balaam's fourth oracle (cf. Isa. 34; Ezek. 35 – 36; Obad.; Amos 9:11–12).

21. *Got up in the morning* is also attested in the Deir 'Alla Inscription (line 3) in a context of divination, suggesting the possibility that the Tale of the Jenny is the third divination that communicates the divine will to Balaam about Balak's proposal. Donkeys were commonly used in ancient Israel and Mesopotamia for agricultural draught labour and threshing, as well as for carrying loads and riding (Borowski 1998: 93, 97). Donkey riding was related to people of high status, even royalty. The high material value and status was especially associated with jennies (*ʾātôn*; see Judg. 5:10; 1 Chr. 27:30; Job 42:12; Zech. 9:9). Although the detail of Balaam saddling his jenny seems mundane, it becomes significant as we understand the meaning of the Tale. The verb *ḥ-b-š*, literally 'binding', is also applicable to 'ruling' (Job 34:17; Isa. 3:6–7). This accords Balaam high status, and it also points to the gendered aspect of Israel's identity and its relationship with other peoples, which will be explored in Balaam's second oracle (23:24) and in chapter 25 (cf. Stone 2014: 97).

22–23. The reason for God's anger is explained above. Different from other occurrences, here the 'messenger of Yahweh' (*mal'ak yhwh*) is not identified as Yahweh (cf. Gen. 16:7–13; Exod. 3:2–6; Judg. 13:3–23), but a representative in parallel and opposition to Balak's messengers. He stood in the way as 'an opponent' (*śāṭān*) with his sword in hand. This first occurrence of the term *śāṭān* in the Bible does not carry the more specialized meaning it has in 1 Chronicles 21:1. Besides the correspondence with Numbers 20:14–21, where Edom blocks Israel's path, threatening it with the sword (20:18), the imagery here also points back to Genesis 3. There, God also positions a representative, a cherub, with a sword to bar the way back to the garden of Eden (see on 23:23 below).

Balaam does not see the messenger of Yahweh while his jenny does. This is definitely ironic given Balaam's profession and international fame as the 'seer of the gods' and the common characterization of the donkey as stupid, stubborn and lazy (Way 2011: 87). Because the jenny sees the danger, she 'swerved from the path' (AT; cf. 20:21), and Balaam *struck* (*n-k-h*) her. Balaam does to the jenny exactly what Balak wants to do to Israel: to strike it (22:6).

24–27. The messenger of Yahweh blocks the way for a second time (v. 25), but the path is fenced in on both sides (v. 24). In an attempt to avoid the danger, the jenny swerves and 'presses' (*l-ḥ-ṣ*) Balaam's foot against the wall (v. 25). For a second time, Balaam 'strikes' (*n-k-h*) her. The messenger of Yahweh blocks the way a third time (v. 26). The spot is described as a *māqôm ṣār* (v. 26), commonly rendered a *narrow place*. The verb 'pressing' (*l-ḥ-ṣ*) in verse 25 and the adjective *narrow* (*ṣār*) are relevant here. The former is characteristic of Israel's experience of 'oppression' in Egypt (e.g. Exod. 3:9; Deut. 26:7; Judg. 2:18; 1 Sam. 10:18; Pss 42:9; 106:42; Isa. 19:20), modelling the exhortation for Israel not to 'oppress' the stranger (Exod. 22:21; 23:9). The latter shares the root for the verb *ṣ-r-r*, which Numbers uses almost as a technical term for the aggressiveness that results from the tense relationship between Israel and other peoples and nations (10:9; 25:17, 18; 33:55). Both terms point to oppressive dealings that restrict the means of life for the other (see 25:16–18).

The use of the term *ṣār* in this scene connects with Israel's relationship to other peoples in chapters 25 and 33 from the perspective of animal imagery. In Numbers 25, Israel submits itself to a subservient relationship with the Moabites comparable to a domestic animal ploughing the field under a yoke (25:2–3). Something similar appears in 33:55 with the description of Canaanites as *barbs in your eyes and thorns in your sides*. As with Israel in these cases, the messenger of Yahweh and the jenny only 'oppress' Balaam because of his willingness to curse Israel, so that Balak can 'strike' Israel as he had 'struck' the jenny. Balaam's violence against the jenny is the outcome of him being 'enraged', which is exactly how God feels about Balaam and the reason for the messenger's opposition to him with sword in hand (22:22).

28–30. Even if the jenny sees the divine representative clearly and communicates this to Balaam through her unusual movements, Balaam remains unable to discern what is going on. Therefore, the divine endowment of human speech to the jenny overcomes *Balaam's* inability and not the jenny's. Rather than mentioning the divine messenger, the jenny questions Balaam's violence, given her long and faithful service to him. Clarifying the appropriate relationship between them precedes his overcoming the inability to discern the divine presence and intention (see Stone 2014: 91–92).

The jenny uses a curious idiom in her question: 'three feet [*times*]' (v. 28). The use of 'feet' for 'times' is seen again with the messenger of Yahweh (vv. 32, 33) and with Balak (24:10). The tripartite structure of the Balaam Pericope is highlighted in this idiom. It also highlights the identification of the jenny with Israel in the reversal of Balaam's three 'strikes' against the jenny and his three 'blessings' towards Israel in his three forthcoming oracles (see 24:10). Furthermore, the idiom is also associated with Israel's three annual festivals in which, according to the Hebrew of Exodus 23:17, they would 'see . . . the face . . . of Yahweh' (see Exod. 23:14–19).

Balaam's answer is full of rage. He wishes he had a sword to kill the jenny (v. 29), but he cannot see the actual sword endangering his life, not the jenny's. He accuses the jenny of mocking him (v.

29), a serious accusation. This verb (*hit'allēl*) is used for violent acts intended to shame the victim (Judg. 19:25; 1 Sam. 31:4; Ps. 141:4) or as a description of the divine judgment on Egypt's dealings with Israel (Exod. 10:2; 1 Sam. 6:6). The jenny's reply (v. 30) rejects Balaam's accusation by qualifying it with a difficult expression: *hahaskēn hiskantî*. The common rendering, *Have I been in the habit of . . . ?* (NRSV, NIV), is too general. Levine offers a more precise rendering: 'Have I ever . . . sought to gain an advantage?' He recognizes that this is 'an educated guess' (Levine 2000: 158), but it fits very well with a main theme in the Balaam Pericope that will be suggested in the *Meaning* section. The expression is constructed with the repetition of the same verb from the root *s-k-n*, which is associated with advantage or profit (Job 15:3; 22:2; 34:9; 35:3) and with a position of privileged service (1 Kgs 1:2; Isa. 22:15). The jenny states that she has never abused her position to act violently and gain advantage over him. Her reply reminds Balaam of her long and close companionship (v. 30). This appeal for recognition of her faithfulness to their relationship and her purpose, even in a position of servitude (remember Balaam is the one who 'saddles' or 'rules' the jenny, v. 21), rhetorically demands that Balaam owes her trust and care, not violence and rageful killing (see Howard 2008: 27). Companionship, even kinship, is also Israel's appeal to Edom (20:14) and will be implicitly underlined in Israel's relationship to the other nations in the fourth poem of Balaam's last oracle (24:15–24). Israel is not to take advantage of its position as a people elected by Yahweh. That is not the purpose of Israel's election in Genesis 12:1–3, as will be argued below. The violent tension between Israel and other peoples is only a result of their aggressiveness towards Israel to curse it. Balaam's short reply, *No* (v. 30), is an embarrassing acknowledgment of the validity of the jenny's appeal.

31–35. When Yahweh 'unveils' (*g-l-h*) Balaam's eyes, Balaam sees what the jenny saw (v. 31; cf. v. 23). The unveiling of Balaam's eyes by Yahweh here is not punctual, as he later will be characterized as the one with 'unveiled eyes' (24:4, 16, AT). The divine messenger replicates the jenny's behaviour, repeating her question about being struck three times (v. 32). Again, clarifying the appropriate relationship between different but linked entities is required before affirming any religious expertise to discern the divine presence and intention. Only then does the messenger of Yahweh inform Balaam of what the audience already knows: the messenger is positioned as *an adversary* or 'opponent' (*śāṭān*). The last part of verse 32 is difficult, but the best textual option and rendering is, 'your path is shaky before me' (Robker 2019: 78). This concrete image of the scene is also a metaphor for Balaam's adventure so far: his 'shaky' divination, his 'shaky' business with Balak, and his 'shaky' treatment of his jenny.

These three related matters displease the messenger of Yahweh (*before me*). He was sent to stop Balaam's ill intentions and would have struck him were it not for the jenny's swerving (v. 33). The messenger of Yahweh would do to Balaam what he, representing Balak and the nations, intended to do to Israel and did to the jenny, who did nothing but serve him faithfully and save his life. The sword that Balaam wished he had to kill the jenny intended to kill him. This same logic will be applied later in 31:8 for Balaam's death, which is specifically and intentionally qualified as occurring *with* [or 'by'] *the sword*. This expression intensifies the connection between Balaam and Edom, for Esau is said to live 'by [the] sword' in relation to his brother Jacob (Gen. 27:40). However, it completely ignores the transition of Balaam's character hereafter (see Pardes 2000: 133).

In this third divinatory experience, Balaam recognizes that his inability to see reflects his inability to know or discern (*y-d-* '), leading him to sin. So he repents and is willing to return home (v. 34). Only after his experience with the jenny does Balaam gain insight and share her discernment of the issues at hand. The jenny's perception of the appropriate relationship between her and her master, which is a discernment of the divine presence and intention, defines Balaam's new insight into Israel in its relationship with other peoples, making him ready to speak the word of Yahweh in the matter (see 24:4 below). Therefore, the messenger of Yahweh allows him to go (v. 35).

iii. Balak requires Balaam to see Israel as he does and curse it (22:36–41)

36–41. The Arnon River marks the outer border of Moabite territory (v. 36; 21:13). 'The city of Moab' (*'îr mô'āb*) is a reference to the Ar of Moab (*'ār mô'āb*, 21:15, 28), which is placed at the border of Moab as well (21:15). By meeting Balaam at the border of Moabite territory, Balak demonstrates proper royal protocol. The same could be said about his offering of a banquet for Balaam and the more prestigious chieftains (v. 40). Although Balaam accepts Balak's invitation, he notes that divine intention rather than Balak's treasures guides his actions (v. 38).

Kiriath-huzoth is an unidentified site (v. 39). However, its location can be derived from two possibilities related to *Bamoth-baal* (v. 41). Numbers 21:28 makes reference to 'bamoth' and to 'baal', not as a toponym but still in relation to Ar of Moab in the region of the Arnon River. In this case, Balak did not take Balaam far from where they had met. However, in verse 41, from Bamoth-baal it is possible for Balaam to see Israel's camp. In this case, Bamoth-baal would be north of the Arnon, near Nebo and Heshbon. Kiriath-huzoth might then be a variant for Kiriathaim (32:37; Jer. 48:1). Both possibilities depend on understanding Bamoth-baal not as a toponym, but as a religious and topographical term, 'the heights of Baal', high places dedicated to religious activities.

iv. Second set of three divinations to decide if Israel is cursed or blessed (23:1 – 24:24)

Divination is typically binary. The first set of divinations (22:8–12, 19–20, 21–35) were enquiries concerning the divine will as to whether Balaam should go with Balak's messengers or not. Balaam's second set of divinations also concerns two options: blessing or cursing. Balaam states the results clearly in 23:20: 'I was taken to bless' (AT). As is typical of divination in the Ancient Near East, these are subject to revision and appeal (Wiggershaus 2021: 175), which explains Balak's insistence that Balaam should keep trying from different places and angles. As noted above, there was a three-time limit for such divine enquiries.

a. First divination/oracle: Israel is blessed (23:1–12)

1–2. No special cultic preparation appeared for the previous set of divinations. Here, Balaam instructs Balak to build seven new altars where seven burnt offerings can be sacrificed. The use of sacrifices in divinatory and enchanting rituals shows that they are not forms of manipulating the deities, but of invoking their presence so that their will can be discerned. The requirement for new altars is curious if Bamoth-baal is a cultic site. It may be that Balaam recognized the incompatibility of using cultic objects dedicated to Baal in his enquiry of Yahweh (cf. Noth 1968: 182).

3–4. While Balak stands, Balaam says he will walk. The verb *h-l-k* is very prominent in the whole Balaam Pericope and might have an enhanced meaning here concerning a ritual movement of perambulating in an attempt to meet with the divine presence (see Levine 2000: 166). Even with all this preparation, Balaam makes it clear that Yahweh has the initiative: 'Perhaps Yahweh will allow himself to be encountered by me' (v. 3, AT).

5–6. Here, as with the case of the jenny, Yahweh makes it possible only for Balaam to go and speak to Balak, without providing the exact words.

7–10. Throughout the Balaam Pericope, the narrator qualifies Balaam's speeches as *māšāl* (v. 7; 23:18; 24:3, 15, 20, 21, 23), a term for songs or proverbs (e.g. Prov. 1:1), but never used in the Bible for prophetic speeches. The first part of the oracle (vv. 7–8) introduces the situation from the previous narrative, but it provides new information and insight. It says that Balak brought Balaam from Aram, from the mountains of *qedem* (v. 7). Egyptian texts use *qedem* as a toponym for the Syrian desert, but that cannot be the reference here, given that it is a mountainous region. Maybe it is better to understand *qedem* literally as 'east' without any specific reference ('east' in relation to where?).

Balaam's description employs two different verbs, 'to curse' (*'-r-r*) and 'to doom' (*z-'-m*). In Balaam's own words (v. 8), there is the same verb 'to doom' and one he used before, 'to condemn' (*q-b-b*, 22:11). Their appearance in close proximity here illuminates their peculiar meaning. Cursing, as explained above, implies exclusion from nurturing relationships and environments (see 22:5–6). Here, to be condemned and doomed implies an agent that causes such exclusion. An Akkadian cognate to the root *q-b-b* is especially connected to royal and divine decrees (Levine 2000: 170–172). So its association with 'curse' implies that Balak is looking for a divine decree of condemnation and doom against Israel through Balaam. From the beginning of Balaam's first oracle, he discerns that God does not condemn and has no indignation that will doom

Israel (v. 8). Balaam's divination makes it clear that despite the ups and downs on the wilderness journey, Israel is not cut off from its relationship with Yahweh, the source of its blessing.

Balaam sees and observes Israel (v. 9; cf. 22:41; 24:17), and what he sees is a peculiar people. Israel is separate from and not reckoned among the peoples. In other words, Israel is elect. The expression 'dwell alone' associates Israel with Yahweh, who 'dwells' (*š-k-n*) among them (5:3; 35:34). Israel's relationship with Yahweh renders its relationship with other peoples secondary with regard to identity, safety and prosperity. Therefore, the last lines of Balaam's first oracle (v. 10) recall Yahweh's special promises to the patriarchs of progeny as numerous as 'the dust' (Gen. 13:16; 28:14) and define Israel's standing with God as *upright* (see 23:21 below). Balaam desires to *die the death of the upright*, meaning that he wants to be in the appropriate relationship with Israel, therefore with God, as part of their life and destiny, a desire which he does not receive according to 31:8.

11–12. Balak makes it clear that Balaam 'truly blessed' Israel (v. 11, AT). Yahweh's relationship with Israel is not breached.

b. Second divination/oracle: Israel is blessed (23:13–24)

13–14. Balak does not give up. He wants a decree of condemnation (*q-b-b*, v. 13). Maybe a breach in the relationship between Yahweh and Israel can be perceived if only the 'outskirts' (*q-ṣ-h*) of the Israelite camp are in view. There is an intertextual and theological link here to 11:1, where Israel's complaints enrage Yahweh, whose fiery anger consumes 'the outskirts [*q-ṣ-h*] of the camp' (AT).

15–17. These verses are almost identical to 23:3–5. The differences are the following: Balaam does not mention any ritual walking; he changes the subject of the verb that designates the encounter (*q-r-h*) from God to himself ('I will let myself be found', v. 15, AT) and the divine initiative changes from God (Elohim, v. 4) to Yahweh (v. 16).

18–20. The second oracle starts like the first (see v. 7), but it gains a kind of exhortative character by calling Balak to *rise, hear* and *listen* (v. 18). Balaam declares that the divine will established in the first divination is firm and will not change (v. 19). While Balak 'took' Balaam to curse (22:41), God has 'taken' him to bless.

The inconsistency of Balaam's divinatory skills in Numbers 22, influenced by his desire to accept Balak's proposal, gives way to his consistent discernment of and obedience to the divine decision in Numbers 23, after his experience with his jenny.

21–24. Some implications of the first oracle are made explicit in the second. Israel's upright standing before God is now expressed as a verdict. God does not 'observe iniquity . . . see sin' in Israel (v. 21, AT). Considering Balaam's dialogue with the jenny and the messenger, this is an affirmation that so far Israel has not taken advantage of its election to harm other peoples (cf. 22:29, 34 above). The presence of Yahweh with Israel is qualified as 'the blast [*tĕrû'â*] of the king in it' (AT), perhaps a reference to the blast of the silver trumpets (10:5–6) for Israel's military action (10:9).

Images of three animals appear in verses 22–24. The first one is the analogy between God (El) and *the horns of the wild ox* (v. 22). Balak spoke of Israel as a domestic ox (*šôr*) in a subservient position that threatened to consume the resources of Moab's surroundings (22:4–5). But now, from God's perspective, Israel is a wild ox (*rĕ'ēm*), with God as its powerful and dangerous horns. Taking advantage of the shared identities of both terms (see Deut. 33:17), the animal imagery ironically reverses Israel's identity in relation to Moab, from subservient to aggressive.

The second image is the 'serpent' (*naḥaš*) in verse 23 that appears in a play on the term for 'divination' (also *naḥaš*). Ironically, the affirmation that 'there is no *naḥaš* in/against Jacob' follows closely after an episode in which many in Israel die from the bites of serpents (*nĕḥāšîm*) sent to them by God as punishment for their complaint (21:4–9). But its combination with the parallel term 'sorcery' (*qesem*; cf. 22:7) reveals a more complex concept. The choice of the term *naḥaš* reinforces an intertextual connection between chapters 22–24 and Genesis 3. The serpent in the garden of Eden represents a form of human knowledge of the divine will apart from their intimate, trusting and obedient relationship, so that this knowledge becomes human power to control and defy the divine for personal gain (Savran 1994: 51–52). This form of religion is repudiated in Numbers 22 – 24 by the frustration of Balak's plan. The affirmation that 'there is no *naḥaš* in/against Jacob' also reverses the consequences of humanity's giving in to the *naḥaš*'s proposal in Genesis 3. As the messenger of Yahweh gives way to Balaam and his jenny, the reader is informed about Israel's access to the environment where it can enjoy an intimate, trusting and obedient relationship with God, the source of its blessing (see 24:5–6 below).[4] Ironically, while this is possible in 21:4–9 by the manufacturing of a *naḥaš*, the cultic copper serpent, here it is by the removal of *naḥaš* as a form of sorcery against Israel.

The third image appears in verse 24 comparing Israel to a lion eating its prey. This image reverses the two previous depictions of Israel. Balak's view of Israel as a subjugated ox consuming all resources from Moab's surroundings is turned into a lion that consumes its prey, drinking the blood of 'the pierced' (*ḥ-l-l*). The last term has a military meaning important for Israel's relation to other peoples (31:8). In addition, its religious connotation of 'profanation' points ahead to the Baal-peor episode. There, submission is gendered, so Israel is 'profaned/pierced' (25:1) as a woman, which is reversed by Phinehas's action of piercing (25:7–8). A gender reversal is also envisioned here by turning Israel as the female jenny crouching down (*r-b-ṣ*) under Balaam (22:27) into a male lion (for the gender of the term *lābî'*, see Strawn 2005: 311–319) that 'gets up' and will not *lie down* (*š-k-b*).[5]

---

4   For discussion on the cherubim, see 7:89. The association between the *naḥaš* and the cherubim (*kĕrūbîm*) of Gen. 3 is complex, but warranted. In Num. 21:6 we have the expression *hannĕḥāš îm haśśĕrāpîm*, so that a connection between *naḥaš* and *śĕrāpîm* is well established in the tradition of Numbers, probably by how seraphs were viewed as a form of winged serpent. But it is also true that cherubs and seraphs are closely related in their identity and function as part of the divine throne room in the sanctuary (Exod. 25:17–22; 1 Kgs 6:23–29), so that Israel's access back to the garden of Eden is represented by its experience in the cult. For a thorough comparison of cherubs and seraphs in biblical tradition and the Ancient Near East, see Hartenstein 2007.

5   Maybe the association between *naḥaš*, *kĕrūbîm* and *śĕrāpîm* gave rise to the use of the analogy between Israel and a lion, as *kĕrūbîm* are typically compared to a sphinx, a mythical creature that could be depicted with the body of a lion, with wings and a human head.

c. Third divination/oracle: Israel is blessed (23:25 – 24:24)

Even with two oracles confirming God's intention to bless Israel, a set of divinations comprises three attempts, so Balak will not give up on his plan before he exhausts all his chances. Balaam's third oracle confirms the first two and goes a step further. A second part is added to the third oracle, following the 3 + 1 emphatic structure as found in Proverbs 30:18–31 and Amos 1:3 – 2:6 (Milgrom 1990: 206). The second part of the third oracle itself then carries the same structure of 3 + 1, as it is composed of four poems. Balaam's oracles are defined by the Hebrew word *māšāl* (23:7, 18; 24:3), and his final oracle repeats this word four times (24:15, 20, 21, 23). The emphatic confirmation that Israel's blessing is the divine decision also comes from an important change in the character and function of Balaam and his oracles. The last two oracles are also called an 'utterance' (*nĕʾūm*, 24:3, 4, 15, 16). Prophetic discourse is typically characterized as direct divine speech using the expression 'Yahweh's utterance' (*nĕʾūm-yhwh*; e.g. Isa. 1:24; Jer. 1:8; Ezek. 5:11; Hos. 2:13; Amos 2:16; Obad. 8; Mic. 4:6; Nah. 3:5; Zeph. 1:2). Balaam's role changes from a diviner to a prophet, now speaking the direct words of Yahweh through the divine spirit (Num. 24:2; see Savran 1994: 35–36; Levine 2000: 191, 235; cf. Wiggershaus 2021: 108, 205–206). What defines Balaam's relationship with God here is his being under the *spirit of God (rûaḥ ʾĕlōhîm)*, which Moses wanted for all Israel (11:29).

25–30. Balak wants to try for the third time to reverse the divine verdict concerning Israel (v. 21). The place where Balak takes Balaam now reflects this intention. The summit of *Peor* (v. 28) is ominous given the events to come in chapter 25.

24:1–2. In the light of his discernment that the divine will is to bless Israel, Balaam abandons his common divining techniques, marking this final oracle as a prophecy. He neither perambulates nor invokes any *nĕḥāšîm* (cf. 23:23). Balaam faces the wilderness and sees all of Israel's tents, *tribe by tribe*. God's approval of this change in attitude is expressed by putting the divine spirit upon Balaam.

3–4. The introduction to Balaam's final oracle is exactly like those for the other two (23:7, 18). But for the first time, his oracle has a superscription with Balaam's name and credentials, which is typical of biblical and Ancient Near Eastern prophetic speeches (cf. Deir 'Alla Inscription, line 1; Isa. 1:1; Jer. 1:1; Ezek. 1:3; Hos. 1:1; Amos 1:1; Mic. 1:1). Several points of the Balaam Pericope suggest that his sight is significant for his divination. Now it becomes his title: he is a man whose eyes are opened, who sees the vision of *the Almighty* (Shadday) with eyes 'unveiled' (*g-l-h*; cf. 22:31).

5–9. A general positive assessment of Israel's camp with its tents and tabernacles – pointing back to chapters 1–4 – is presented in verse 5: they are good (*tôb*, echoing the refrain of divine approval of God's creation in Gen. 1). The meaning of such goodness is spelled out with botanical imagery resembling the garden of Eden, for example *like gardens beside a river* (v. 6). This confirms that God's blessing towards Israel is compared to the accessibility of an environment where they can enjoy an intimate relationship with an abundance of resources. Here, this environment is not a specific geographical place, but Israel's camp wherever it goes. Israel's camp is like the valley of a wadi swerving through a territory, just like the swerving of the jenny (22:23, 26, 33) and the commitment that Israel would not swerve within Edom's and Sihon's territory (20:17; 21:22). Israel's swerving, like the jenny's, serves the lives of others, so that responding to it aggressively, as Balaam did to the jenny, and Edom, Sihon and Balak intended to do to Israel, is completely unjust and results in cutting them off from the benefits of a relationship to Israel.

The text and language in verse 7 are obscure. The images of buckets flowing with water and Israel's seed in plentiful water build on previous experiences of Israel's wanderings. The former reinforces Israel's new confidence in God's providence in the Well Song (21:17–19). The latter image of Israel's *seed* (*zera'*) in plentiful water responds to Israel's complaints in 20:5 about God bringing them out of Egypt to a place of no seed and God's provision of 'many waters' from the rock in 20:11 (Morales 2024b: 182). In this sense, this divine blessing answers two major concerns that led Israel to rebel against God: lack of sustenance and fear for their descendants (14:3, 31). The second line (in the Hebrew) of verse 7 refers to an Israelite king *higher than Agag*, the name of an Amalekite king defeated by Saul (1 Sam. 15:1–9; see Num. 24:20 below). Amalek is the first threat to Israel in its exodus journey

(Exod. 17:8–16), the first obstacle in Israel's way to the Promised Land (Num. 13:29). Amalekites are perceived as particularly violent towards vulnerable people (Deut. 25:18; 1 Sam. 30:1–3). This reference to Amalek, then, confirms the association of Balaam and Balak with aggression towards the vulnerable, the jenny and Israel. Amalek's appearance here makes sense thematically, as Amalek comes from Esau/Edom (Gen. 36:12). The affirmation about Israel's king being higher than Agag need not carry messianic connotations. Yahweh is described as Israel's king in Numbers 23:21, so this is an affirmation about the superiority of Yahweh's rule over Israel and its opposition to any human political power that might threaten it as a vulnerable people.

Animal images return in verses 8–9, but this time the reason for their use to depict Israel is clearer. The *horns of a wild ox* are explained above (23:22). Playing with Balak's fear that Israel would consume resources like an ox (22:4), Balaam speaks of Israel consuming the peoples (*gôyim*). These peoples are said to be Israel's enemies, using the term *ṣār* that is associated with the important root *ṣ-r-r* (see on 22:24–27 above). Because these peoples treat Israel oppressively while it is vulnerable, God gives Israel the upper hand against them. The second part of verse 8 is textually problematic, but in the light of the animal imagery it can be rendered 'their bones he breaks; his loins he smashes' (see Levine 2000: 197–198). The reference to loins as the sides of the body and the change to the singular ('his') might point to it being a description of Israel smashing the sides, that is, borders, of Moab in 24:17. The last line of verse 9 expands on the reason for imagining Israel as a violent animal: Balak's intention to curse Israel, viewed as a domestic and subjugated ox, leads to the divine reversal that turns Israel into a violent animal against Balak and every other people who treat Israel in this way. Another important reversal takes place here. While Balak attributes the power to bless or curse to Balaam (22:6), Balaam recognizes that this is a divine matter mediated by Israel. Cursing or blessing others depends on how they treat Israel: they are blessed if they bless it, and cursed if they curse it (cf. Gen. 12:2–3; see *Meaning* below).

10–13. There is an important movement of anger among the three main characters of the Balaam Pericope. God is the first to be angry, showing dissatisfaction with Balaam's decision (22:22). Then Balaam is angry with his jenny for acting unexpectedly (22:27). In both cases, the character's anger comes within the third instance of the three-part structure. The same pattern occurs here. Balak is enraged by the third of Balaam's oracles, which confirms the divine blessing of Israel. Balak is enraged because Balaam sided with God in his decision to bless Israel, whom he calls his enemy (*'ōyēb*), a term with no connotations of oppressive behaviour like *ṣār* in verse 8. The use of the expression 'three feet/ times' again reinforces the paradigmatic function of the Tale of the Jenny for the Balaam Pericope. As Balaam struck his jenny 'three times', which Balak wanted him to do to Israel, now he blesses Israel *three times*, reversing and frustrating Balak's plan. Because Yahweh 'kept' (*m-n-'*) Balaam from going with Balak's first messengers and Balak recommended Balaam not to 'keep' (*m-n-'*) from meeting him, Balak blames Yahweh for 'keeping' (*m-n-'*) Balaam from the glory he offered him.

14. Before returning to his place, Balaam gives final confirmation of his siding with God in blessing Israel. He calls it a 'counsel' (*yā'aṣ*), like the one given by another foreigner, Moses' father-in-law (Exod. 18:19), about what will happen between the two peoples, Israel and Moab, in the latter days (*bĕ'aḥărît hayyāmîm*). This last expression stresses a definitive outcome, like Balaam's end (*'aḥărîtî*, 23:10).

15–19. This final part of Balaam's oracle extends the tripartite structure to emphasize Balaam's siding with God in his decision to bless Israel and to frustrate Balak's intended aggression. For this reason, this part is not considered a fourth oracle, but an amplification of the third. They both are described as an 'utterance' (*nĕ'um*) and share the same superscription (vv. 15–16; cf. vv. 3–4), with one slight addition here, 'knower of the knowledge of the Most High [Elyon]' (AT), which emphasizes Balaam's attunement to the divine knowledge and intention.

Balaam's religious skill is again associated with his sight (v. 17). He sees and observes, just as he literally saw and observed Israel in 23:9. However, now it concerns something about Israel that is not temporally (*now*) and spatially (*near*) immediate. The imagery used in the second part of verse 17 points to a royal figure originating from Jacob and Israel. The divine character of kingship in the Ancient Near East, including in biblical traditions, is commonly conceptualized by celestial bodies (Gen. 37:9–10; Judg. 5:19–20; Isa. 14:12; see Levine 2000: 201).

Directly related to Balak's intended aggression towards Israel, Balaam sees this Israelite royal figure smashing Moab's 'sides' (*pa'ătê*, v. 17). There is possibly a double meaning here. 'Sides' might imply borders of a territory (NRSV *borderlands*; cf. 34:3; 35:5), connecting it to the 'loins' of verse 8, and also the head's temples (cf. Lev. 13:41). The second option, then, would recommend emending the Hebrew from the verb *qarqar* ('tear down') to the substantive *qodqōd* ('scalps of the head'), following the text of the Samaritan Pentateuch and Jeremiah 48:45. In this case, we would have a divine action against Moab's territory and its leaders, that is, 'heads', called 'sons of Seth' (see Ashley 2022: 422). The reference to Adam and Eve's son after Cain killed Abel (Gen. 4:25–26) points to a general identification of peoples who share a common kinship (see Milgrom 1990: 208). The appeal to identification and symbiosis is also the basis for Balaam's jenny to question his aggressiveness towards her. It might be, then, that when those close to Israel, such as his brother Esau, act violently in an attempt to dominate it, God will act against them and elevate Israel over them.

Such an interpretation makes the transition to Balaam's view of Edom and Israel in verses 18–19 smoother and more logical. Edom represents the people closest to Israel, struggling for dominance within a context of family and divine blessing (cf. Gen. 27). Edom's aggressive response to Israel when it was vulnerable (20:14–21) leads to the divine decision to make its territory, given by God (see Deut. 2:5, 9, 12, 19), the property of its enemies (see Num. 24:8, 10 above). In contrast, Israel is envisioned as one who is strong and wealthy (*ḥāyil*; e.g. 31:14; Judg. 3:29; Ruth 2:1) holding a ruling position in relation to those who attempt to destroy it. Then the last part of verse 19 returns to the relationship between Israel and Moab by making reference to Ar of Moab (see 22:36 above), from which Israel will deport the remnant survivors. Although violent, this is a prophetic reversal in which Israel, the weaker party, is elevated against the strong ones who threaten it.

20. The notion of reversal in which the strong is subdued by the weak reinforces Balaam's second poem (*māšāl*), now against Amalek. In a contrasting parallel, Amalek is called the '*beginning of nations*' (AT), an archetype of all nations in their violent power against vulnerable people, but Balaam sees its *end*.

21–22. The third poem (*māšāl*) concerns the Kenites. Like Edom, Moab and Amalek, the Kenites were geographically and culturally close to Israel. Biblical tradition presents them as a subgroup of Midianites (see Judg. 1:16; 4:11). However, as a nomadic group of metal-workers, they were associated with various peoples. The Kenites also gain a more archetypical character by being referred to as Cain/Kain. Balaam again sees a reversal. The Hebrew word for Kenites (*qênî*) sounds like the word for 'nest' (*qēn*), so the poem depicts their strong dwellings as nests on the rock. The image of a high nest is reversed to a land down on the ground and trampled by cattle, which is the sense of the Hebrew term *bāʿēr* (cf. Exod. 22:4). This is typical for lands that had their populations exiled, and that is the explanation given in the last part of the poem.

23–24. This is the last of Balaam's four poems. The Hebrew of the Masoretic Text for verse 23 is corrupted, and scholars have advanced several textual and interpretive solutions. The reconstructed Hebrew and translation preferred here is: 'He saw Og[6] and took up his poem [*māšāl*], saying: "Woe! Who can live from the Northland?"'[7] This reconstruction maintains the structure and pattern of Balaam's last four poems. Balaam sees a character directly related to the narrative world of Numbers and connects it to the narrative of origins from Genesis to create an archetype. Here, the connection is between Og, the king of Bashan (21:33–35), and Eber, who is part of the lineage that generates Abraham (Gen. 11:16–25) and whose immediate forefather is Shem (Gen. 10:21).

---

6   Addition found in the LXX and Vulgate.

7   Following Levine 2000: 206. Instead of considering it as a reference to a divine imposition, 'when God [El] puts this in place' (*miśśûmô ʾēl*), Levine revocalizes the text and creates one expression to form a geographical reference, 'from the Northland' (*miśśemō ʾl*).

This pattern of Balaam's fourth oracle also recommends the textual reconstruction for 'Northland'. The parallelism between Asshur and Eber makes sense in the light of Genesis 10:21–22, where Asshur and Aram appear together as Shem's descendants. From Israel's perspective, Aram (Syria) is to the north, and the relationship between Eber and Syria is attested in Neo-Assyrian and Neo-Babylonian texts (Levine 2000: 206). The threat to Asshur and Eber comes from the ships of Kittim. Once again, we are in the realm of origins. Kittim appears in Genesis 10:1–4 as a people descended from Noah through Japheth who lived on the coast and are typically identified as Greeks. These Kittim will 'oppress' ('-*n-h*) Asshur and Eber. In a political context, this means subjugation with payment of tribute. More importantly, it is the term used for Egypt's subjugation of Israel (Exod. 1:12). Subjugation was a form of extinguishing a people, therefore Balaam's fourth poem concludes with an expression used earlier (v. 20): their end will be complete demise as well.

v. Balak and Balaam part ways (24:25)

25. The end scene communicates without any dialogue. There are three instances in which the verbs *q-w-m* ('get up') and *h-l-k* ('walk') occur together in chapters 22–24. The first is in 22:13, where Balaam gets up and tells Balak's messengers to walk back to their land because Yahweh did not let him walk with them. In the second, 22:21, Balaam gets up and walks with Balak's messengers. Now, after all his oracles of blessing on Israel frustrate Balak's plan, Balaam gets up and walks to his place. Following the three-part pattern of the Balaam Pericope, the final and decisive indication that Balaam sided with God and parted ways with Balak appears in the third repetition of these terms.

Meaning

Numbers 22 – 24 provides a theological perspective on what happened in chapters 20–21. Even when other nations aggressively threaten Israel in its vulnerable condition, God ensures their safety just as they were provided with healing from serpent bites (21:4–9). But the artistically rich and theologically profound construction of chapters 22–24 provides a vision for how God intends to open access to the divine presence, blessing and life to all, through the elected people, even when they do not understand the divine intentions and fight against them.

The blessed state of Israel in chapters 22–24 appears to reverse humanity's fate after Genesis 3. The access to an environment of intimate and trusting relationship with God, leading to abundant life, once shut, is now reopened (cf. Savran 1994: 41–43; Akil 2008: 75). In the foundational narrative of Israel, this perspective connects the garden of Eden with Canaan (Pardes 2000: 137). However, there is also an expansion of the concept of 'promised land' beyond a specific geographic location. Balaam's oracles are affirmations about the similarity of Israel's camp to a lush garden as a source of life, confirming its theological characterization in Numbers 1 – 4 as an environment that shelters and maintains the divine presence in its midst.

God's intention to bless all other peoples through Israel is defined by this view of Israel's camp. As a result, the interaction between Israel and the other nations defines the way in which divine blessing and cursing occur. Not only is the identity of Israel as God's people important here, but also Israel's vulnerable condition and the close relationship, even kinship, among all humanity. Following the logic of Genesis 12:1–3, God will bless those who bless Israel and curse those who curse it (cf. 24:9). But God's election of Israel is intended to bless all the families of the earth (Gen. 12:2–3; cf. Frevel 2020: 25).

There is an intriguing reflection here on the role of Israel's leaders in relation to the people of Israel, and the people of Israel in relation to other peoples. God responds to the dispute over leadership and authority in chapters 16–17 with instructions in chapter 18 concerning the limits of the just portions that Levites and priests could gain from the offering. They should not take advantage of their privileged access to the divine presence or their religious expertise to concentrate power and resources for themselves and thereby impede the people's access to God and to divine blessing. This constitutes Moses' and Aaron's failure in chapter 20. An expansion of this theme occurs in chapters 28–29, after the integration of some foreign groups into Israel in chapters 26–27, with instructions concerning Israel's worship that include the annual festivals. What is expected from Israel's leaders in relation to the people – facilitating access to the divine presence and blessing in the form of distributing resources instead of concentrating them – is expected from Israel as a whole in relation to other peoples. Comparing Israel's wilderness journey to the Promised Land to Israel's festival pilgrimage in the light of the peculiar use of the expression 'three feet/times' in the Balaam Pericope, Israel should not take advantage of its privileged position as God's elect in its encounters with other peoples. Instead, it should be a mediatory facilitator of other peoples' access to life and blessing that Israel's relationship with God provides.

God's intention is universal in scope. If there are elected, privileged and expert groups in relationship with God, they must serve the benefit of others, and not their own personal gain. This is especially true in contexts in which some are in vulnerable positions in relation to others. There is no real religious expertise and true knowledge of God without recognition of the appropriate relationships that truly advance God's intention to encounter all humanity, even all of creation, as a life-giving force experienced in truly embodied reality in which material resources and relationships promote the flourishing of all.

For this reason, the Tale of the Jenny is so relevant. It critiques forms of knowledge of God that intend to control and manipulate the divine power in order to castigate vulnerable people and elevate those in power. Similar to the serpent's approach in Genesis 3, the direct interest in divine knowledge in distrust of God's intention and disregard for relationships moves humanity away from God and blocks the way to life and blessing, leading instead to death. The jenny, representing the true knowledge of God, questions Balaam about his violence against her in the light of the appropriate relationship between them as those who share life together and depend on each other (cf. Pressler 2017: 210–211).

There is a serious challenge here for religious experts such as pastors, missionaries, professional theologians or biblical scholars. Knowledge of God and God's ways in the world only goes as far as the recognition of common humanity, even common creatureliness, and discernment of the appropriate relationships that this implies. Specifically, religious leaders should act to promote easier access to God's life for others. This raises the question of how God responds to other people's hostility and aggression towards God's people with violent images of them. Again, the character of the jenny provides significant insight.

Balaam initially represents false religion associated with violence against, and cursing of, Israel. After his dialogue with the jenny, Balaam receives corrected knowledge of God and his character transitions to identifying with Israel. He then becomes a medium of blessing to Israel. The jenny shows how Israel must be a source of blessing for others, including those who act violently against it (see Gelblum 2023: 338).

Viewing others as animals commonly serves to create boundaries between insiders and outsiders and define outsiders as less than human to justify aggression against them. Even if the text is critical of Edom, Moab, Midian, Amalek and Asshur as typically aggressive towards the vulnerable, they never lose their shared humanity or even kinship with Israel in the oracles of Balaam. In the Balaam Pericope, these identity boundaries, created through animal images, are themselves subverted by an animal. The jenny crosses the human–animal divide in her dialogue with Balaam, and also the animal–divine divide in her knowledge of God (see Stone 2014: 90–91). The crossing of boundaries by the jenny shows that the way forward to reconciliation is to assume the value of being a vulnerable outsider, not being part of the centres of power and violence. This is a model for the development of Balaam's character. Just as divine revelation comes unexpectedly from the jenny, crossing the animal–divine divide, it also comes unexpectedly from Balaam, a pagan and foreign diviner, crossing the Israel–nations divide. God's most elevated words of blessing on Israel do not come from an insider, not even from Moses, but from Balaam, an outsider. The rigid divide between insiders and outsiders blurs in the figures of the jenny and Balaam, and a more dynamic and ambivalent identity of God's people is created (see Pardes 2000: 133; Diamant 2009: 109). When God's people are a blessing to others, even those who wish and act to destroy them, the resulting cycle of reciprocal blessing entails amicability and cooperation that are mutually beneficial and can even blur their different identities.

Finally, then, the role of the jenny undercuts the reading of Balaam's oracles from a triumphal perspective. Violent animal images depicting Israel's overcoming of other peoples' aggression towards it (23:22, 24; 24:8, 9) are used to communicate a reversal from the perspective of those in weak and vulnerable positions struggling to survive violence at the hands of the powerful. Israel, however, never loses the identity of the jenny. God's people are still called to be a blessing to others and not a curse. Balaam's oracles use violent animal imagery to depict Israel opposed to those who want to curse and destroy it. As with the question posed to Balaam by the jenny and the messenger of Yahweh, these oracles reflect divine concern and anger at the abuse of a vulnerable creature. Considering the logic of cursing and blessing of Genesis 12:1–3, the reversal is not a final judgment on Edom, Moab, Midian, Amalek or Asshur. They instead represent those abusing their positions to destroy God's plan to bless all humanity and creation through God's people. The critique is that in their abuse of power they actually cut themselves off from access to the divine life and blessing, so that they will eventually die out, as in the divine warning for humanity in Genesis 2:16–17. The use of biblical texts such as Balaam's oracles against peoples to dehumanize them reveals blindness and ignorance of the knowledge of God, a false religion that does not recognize the appropriate relationships that promote divine life and blessing. The Balaam Pericope is a message of hope for subjugated people. It cannot be used by those holding power against others (see Pressler 2017: 220). God's election and blessing of Israel never becomes a reason to attack others. As a textual construction, the Balaam Pericope represents an attempt to dialogue with those in power across rigid divides, even when this is considered asinine, for there is no guarantee of avoiding violence against ourselves (see Stone 2014: 99).

F. Faithfulness amid unfaithfulness (25:1–18)

Context
Coming immediately after the extraordinary divine blessings of Balaam's oracles in chapters 22–24 and the military victories over

the Amorites in chapter 21, Numbers 25 returns the audience to the ambivalent actions of the Israelites on the final stage of their journey to Canaan. The story had left them in the plains of Moab across the Jordan from Jericho in 22:1 – in other words, on the cusp of entrance into Canaan. Israel's stay in Shittim reflects Israel's experience in the Transjordan as it negotiates its identity as the people of Yahweh among other inhabitants. The Transjordanian context puts Israel in contact with groups close to Israel's identity but not really part of it (cf. 24:15–24), specifically Moabites (Gen. 19:30–38; Ruth) and Midianites (Gen. 25:1–2; see Levy 2008: 255). It also contributes to the biblical discussion about the legitimate status of Transjordan as part of the Promised Land (Num. 32; Josh. 22:9–34).

Chapter 25 concludes the focus on the first generation exiting Egypt. It recounts one final tragic story on Israel's wilderness journey, offering a closing pendant for this generation to their breaking of the covenant back in Exodus 32 – 34. In both cases, the covenantal blessing and Israel's apostasy are related to cultic feasting involving consumption of food with sexual connotations (cf. Exod. 32:6).

There are some confusing details in the chapter: why does it speak first of the *Moabites* and then the *Midianites* (cf. 22:4, 7)? Why does Yahweh conclude a covenant of *peace* with Phinehas for his *violent* action? Where did the plague come from? Theologically and ethically, the chapter also presents serious problems that must be addressed if we are willing to engage faithfully with it.

Comment

i. The daughters of Moab and submission to Baal (25:1–5)

1. Conquering and settling in Moabite territory (21:24–26) gave occasion for Israel to live alongside its inhabitants. The opening line names the location, *Shittim* = 'The Acacia Trees', which reappears in Joshua 2:1; 3:1 as the place from which the Israelites cross through the Jordan to begin taking possession of the Promised Land. It is a place bursting with anticipation, yet Israel will not leave it for the rest of Numbers or Deuteronomy. The fact that the location remains the same but the *generation* changes provides a warning: entering and possessing the land cannot be

taken for granted; it depends on continual loyalty to Yahweh. This first experience of coexistence with other peoples is a negative representation showing what Israel must avoid, pointing back to Exodus 34:10–16. The verbs used in 25:1–5, 'fornicate' (*z-n-h*), 'invite' (*q-r-ʾ*), 'feast' (*ś-m-ḥ*) and 'worship' (*ḥ-w-h*), replicate the prohibition in Exodus 34:14–16. In fact, Exodus 34:14 also includes the character of Yahweh as zealous, thereby invoking a term (*q-n-ʾ*) that shows up in Numbers 25:11, tying together the two disparate parts of this chapter.

While in Shittim, Israel began to profane themselves, polluting that which was sacred (cf. Exod. 20:25; 31:14; Lev. 18:21; Num. 18:32). The narrative opens with fornication (*z-n-h*), an expression commonly used for Israel's unfaithfulness to Yahweh by engaging in idolatrous worship (e.g. Isa. 57:3; Jer. 2:20; Hos. 2:7) and entering into alliances with other nations (Ezek. 16:26, 28). The ambiguity between sexuality, idolatry and political alliance appears intentional. The expression 'daughters of Moab' (lit.) should be interpreted in the light of this ambiguity. Villages around prominent cities are called 'daughters' (32:41–42; Judg. 1:27), especially in Moabite territory (21:25, 32; Judg. 11:26; Isa. 16:1–2). This will explain the association between Moab and Midian in the second part of the chapter (see vv. 6–18 below).

2–3a. Israel's mistrust of Yahweh in the wilderness is reflected in its ways with food and drink. This last appeared when Israel complained about the quality and quantity of food available (21:5). It is no small matter, then, that Israel is offered the chance to enjoy abundant and desirable food in this foreign religious feast. The term for invitation (*q-r-ʾ*) is used for participants of royal banquets (1 Kgs 1:10, 19, 26) and cultic feasts (1 Sam. 9:13, 22; Zeph. 1:7) where the formality of table communion marks social bonding with mutual loyalty, even shared identities. In this event, Israel worshipped (*ḥ-w-h*) foreign deities. Religious, political and sexual submission is implied in the ambiguous use of the expression 'bonded [*ṣ-m-d*] to Baal-peor' (AT). Baal-peor might be a local manifestation of the deity Baal, or a typical Moabite toponym (cf. 23:28; 32:38; 33:7).

The verb used for this event (also in Ps. 106:28) derives from the noun 'yoke' (cf. 1 Sam. 11:7; Jer. 51:23). It implies that Israel works on the fields, ploughing, as a form of religious service to Baal, the 'owner' of the land. Israel's bondage to Baal also has a sexual connotation, given the basic meaning of Baal as husband and master. In serving Baal as a domestic animal working his fields, Israel appears like a submissive wife to this foreign deity. Politically, Israel is a submissive wife to this deity's people. Ironically, Israel is envisaged as a submissive wife to the 'daughters of Moab'. Overall, Israel changes its allegiance, trusting others to provide for its life by submitting to these people's ways of living, that is, breaking Yahweh's covenant and purposes in forming Israel as a people.

3b–4. Yahweh's reaction compares to the anger of a cuckolded husband. Later, in verse 11, the use of the affective term *jealousy* (*qinʾah*) confirms the comparison by linking it to the ritual prescription in Numbers 5 concerning the 'jealous husband'. Yahweh's instruction to Moses for dealing with Israel's apostasy concerns only 'the heads of the people' (AT; cf. 1:4; 32:28). Apparently, they must be considered responsible. What Moses must do to them is unclear, but it is certainly a public act, indicated by the expression 'facing the sun' (AT), something like 'in broad daylight'. The meaning of the verb *h-q-ʿ* remains difficult. Based on its use in 2 Samuel 21:6, 9, 13, a form of execution by impalement is suggestive. However, the basic meaning of the verb points to bodily dislocation or dismemberment (Gen. 32:25), and it is used metaphorically for relational alienation between Israel and Yahweh (see Ezek. 23:17–18). Therefore, Yahweh commands the public recognition of these family leaders' dismembering themselves from the divine covenant and people.

5. Moses summons the judges of Israel, recalling Exodus 18:25 and pointing to more prominent leaders than the general heads of the people of verse 4. This also connects this episode with the positive participation of Moses' Midianite father-in-law in Israel's formation. This both serves the transition in focus to the Midianites in the next section (vv. 6–18), and reinforces an important pattern concerning the relationship of Israel towards foreigners. Inclusive episodes are juxtaposed with others establishing limits to this inclusiveness (Pressler 2017: 224–225). Moses uses an explicit violent verb ('to kill', *hārag*) that was not used in the previous verse.

ii. Phinehas's demonstration of faithfulness to Yahweh (25:6–18)

This episode likely comes from a different tradition from the previous one, given that it introduces a plague and public mourning at the tent of meeting. The two episodes illuminate each other in the final form of the chapter. Several textual details reinforce the ambiguity between politics, cultic rituals and sexuality in characterizing Israel's apostasy. The focus on Midianites might be explained by an association between tent villages around Moabite cities, 'daughters of Moab', and Midianite nomadic caravanners and raiders (see 31:10; cf. Judg. 6:2–6; also see Monroe 2012: 230). The combination of Moabites and Midianites recalls the political threat in Balaam's narrative (22:4, 7; cf. Josh. 13:21–22) and points forward to Israel's war with the Midianites (31:1–12).

6. A clear marker of a new section occurs here: *wĕhinnē* ('Now look!'), which calls for the reader's attention. The first action described concerns the consummation of a marriage but resembles a sacrificial offering: an Israelite man 'comes in and brings' (the verbs *b-w-ʾ* + *q-r-b*) to his brothers at the door of the tent of meeting. These terms often pertain to sacrificial language (see Lev. 1:3; 2:2, 8; 4:3–4, 14), anticipating a cultic experience (see below, v. 13). Instead of a sacrificial animal, however, the Israelite man brings a Midianite woman. The mourning, in the combined context of the idolatry of Baal-peor and the divine punishment, also sets a contrast to a cultic feast, including that of verse 2, which makes this action untimely (cf. Joel 2:15–16).

7–8. We first hear about Phinehas in Exodus 6:25. His name is of Egyptian origin and means 'the southerner', referring to someone of darker skin colour from the Nubian region (Spencer 1992). Phinehas is always associated with violent protection of the cult and preservation of Israelite identity (31:6; Josh. 22:13, 30–34; Judg. 20:28; see Organ 2001). 'From the assembly' (NRSV *left the congregation*) locates Phinehas with those weeping at the door of the tent of meeting. His violent action points to the priests and Levites' protection of the boundary between God's holiness and impurity (cf. 3:10; 18:1–7), although the use of a spear is surprising given that no military instrument is ever mentioned as part of the tabernacle paraphernalia.

The political, religious and sexual ambiguity of the whole narrative will find its peak in the wordplay presented here: Phinehas goes to the tent (*haqqŭbbâ*) and penetrates the couple into her belly (*qŏbātāh*). The best comparison for this structure is the pre-Islamic Arabic Bedouin *kubbe*, a small tent used for divination in a context of war, typically attended by the tribal chieftain or a female priest of a noble tribal family (Morgenstern 1942/1943: 207–223). *The plague* may insinuate Israel's conflictual relationship with the Midianites, who are likened to a plague of locusts despoiling the land in Judges 6:5 and 7:12, pointing to the battle in Numbers 31.

Politically, the relationship between the Israelite man and the Midianite woman signifies a peace agreement between the two people. Religiously, the *qŭbbâ* stands as a rival sanctuary to the tabernacle, its cult and its priesthood, where a foreign woman and a non-Levite male attempt to ritually obtain divine favour and blessing. This is especially relevant after the strong critique of religiously manipulating God in chapters 22–24, and the fact that Zipporah, Moses' Midianite wife, was a ritual specialist who was able to avert divine punishment (Exod. 4:24–26; Dozeman 2008). However, Israel would be submitting to a different deity and be integrated into a different people, giving in to a different identity from the one intended by Yahweh. It is that which prompts Phinehas to act so severely and violently. Stabbing her *qŏbātāh* reinforces the cultic and sexual ambiguity of Israel's relationship with the Midianites. The term occurs elsewhere in the Bible only in Deuteronomy 18:3 as a reference to the belly (*qēbâ*) of a sacrificial animal as part of the portion of the sacrifice that belongs to the priest. (Another option is that *qŏbātāh* is related to *nĕqēbâ*, female genitals.) As noted above, the language used in verse 6 for the Israelite man's action resembles that for a sacrifice; ironically, they bring about divine rescue by actually becoming a sacrifice at the hands of Phinehas.

Israel is presented as a wife to Baal and his people, submitting to them and their ways. Phinehas's violent penetration of his victims with his spear is an affirmation of Israelite identity against this submissive role and spurious forms of religion. The only relationship in which Israel must be submissive is that with

Yahweh. Once Phinehas's actions have got these relationships straight, the plague over Israel is contained.

9. The highest number of deaths in the whole of the wilderness journey is recorded here. This final strike against the older generation marks its demise and the establishment of the new generation by the new census in the next chapter. The use of a *plague* to do so corresponds with Yahweh's intention in 14:12.

10–13. In the first episode of the chapter, Israel's apostasy was described in the light of Exodus 34:15–16. Now, Phinehas reflects the role of the Levites at Sinai. They too act violently against guilty Israelites (Exod. 32:25–29) as a means to effecting *k-p-r* ('atonement', Exod. 32:30) because of Yahweh's jealousy (*q-n-'*, Exod. 34:14). Like the Levites set apart to Yahweh then (Exod. 32:29), Phinehas is also rewarded.

The effect of Phinehas's actions is summarized in the expression [*he*] *made atonement for the Israelites* (v. 13), which expands on previous descriptions of Yahweh's anger turning back (vv. 4, 11) and containing the plague (v. 8). Divine anger, human sacrifice and a plague lead interpreters to conceptualize *k-p-r* here as ransom or a form of scapegoating (see Milgrom 1990: 277–278; Monroe 2012; Ashley 2022: 439). However, as shown above, Phinehas's action re-establishes the right relationships between Yahweh and Israel, and between them and other peoples and deities. Ordering relationships and bringing them into alignment is an act of atonement (see Introduction, 'Atonement and ritual'), which is declared to be the priests and the Levites' function according to 8:18–19. It protects those near Yahweh to guarantee safe encounters in a context of disruption of relationships (cf. 1:50–53). By engaging in cultic companionship in submission to foreign deities and their ways in this chapter, Israel betrays Yahweh and their companionship turns into hostility. According to the logic of hospitality in ancient cultures, hospitality turns into hostility when expected behaviours are not followed (Matthews 1991). By re-establishing appropriate boundaries for the relationship between Israel and foreign peoples with Israel's primary dependency on Yahweh, Phinehas guarantees the means for Israel and Yahweh to meet again in amicable encounters of worshipful commensality.

For this reason, Yahweh rewards Phinehas and his descendants with the priesthood permanently (cf. Exod. 29:9; 40:15) and a *covenant of peace* (v. 12), which is ironic in the light of Phinehas's violent action. The language of *shalom* connects Israel's renewed companionship with Yahweh to the hospitality experienced between Moses and his Midianite father-in-law, Jethro. Their encounters are marked by mutual utterances of *shalom* (Exod. 4:18; 18:7, 23) in the context of mutual hospitality where Moses experiences safety in Jethro's tent and Jethro experiences safety in Moses' tent. This peaceful relationship is possible because, even though Jethro is a Midianite priest (Exod. 2:16), he never threatens Israel's relationship with Yahweh. As a foreigner who recognizes Yahweh's sovereignty (Exod. 18:9–10), he facilitates and cooperates with Israel's submission to and participation in Yahweh's covenant.

That is not the case for the 'daughters of Moab' and the Midianite woman. They are instead set as rivals to Yahweh's covenant and sanctuary. They go against Yahweh's intentions in forming Israel as a people, because they establish Israel as submissive to them. From this comparison, we see that Israel and other peoples can benefit from relationships of mutual hospitality. However, when the relationship is unequal and Israel becomes submissive, that is a call for hostility. This explains why Yahweh commands Moses, who previously benefited from Midianite hospitality, to grant Phinehas a covenant of peace, precisely because he responded with hostility towards the Midianites.

14–15. The identity of the Israelite man and the Midianite woman are revealed at the conclusion of the story. This form of emphasis unveils relevant information for understanding the meaning of the whole episode. Their high sociopolitical status is confirmed in Zimri's title as *nāśî'* of the ancestral house of Simeon, a designation of leadership in the overall structure of Israel's camp (1:16). Cozbi is identified as the daughter of Zur, the head of a league of Midianite tribes, a political unit compared to a nation (Ps. 117:1). Verse 18 also calls Zur a Midianite *nāśî'* (see Josh. 13:21), and 31:8 even calls him a king.

Even more significant for interpreting the story is the meaning of their specific names. Cozbi comes from the Semitic root *k-z-b*, with two main meanings: 'deceitful' and 'voluptuous' (Lutzky 1997). 'Voluptuousness' or 'abundance' was applied to women's attractiveness, even to their genitals, and was a characteristic of Mesopotamian deities such as Ishtar and Asherah, implying that Israel was seeking safety and provision from a source other than Yahweh. Therefore, this meaning evokes notions of idolatry with sexual connotations similar to the root *z-n-h* in verse 1. The 'deception' meaning appropriately describes Israel's participation in religious feasts with lavish food in expectation of living in abundance by submitting to a foreign power and way of life, whereas the outcome is death and weeping. Zimri shares the name of another biblical character who leads a coup to kill Israel's King Elah and his whole family (1 Kgs 16:7–20). This name thus designates political betrayal, as when Jezebel calls Jehu, who has just killed her son Joram, king of Israel, a 'Zimri' (2 Kgs 9:31). The Simeonite chief's name highlights political betrayal of Yahweh's kingship over Israel. These names indicate a metaphorical level of meaning of the whole scene for Israel's relations with foreign people in Transjordan.

16–18. As in verse 12, Yahweh's instruction to Moses carries the weight of Moses' personal relationship with the Midianites. Instead of demonstrating peace and hospitality, Moses must treat the Midianites with hostility and strike them. In other words, Moses must replicate Phinehas's actions because Midian treated Israel with hostility first. The verb *ṣ-r-r* is related to the substantive *ṣ-r*, 'narrow', so here it basically means to restrict the means of life of the Midianites, that is, to oppress them (cf. 22:25–26, where *ṣ-r* is combined with *l-ḥ-ṣ*, a very common verb for oppression in Hebrew, e.g. Exod. 3:9; Deut. 26:7; Judg. 2:18; Ps. 42:10; Isa. 19:20). The mark of this hostility is deception, with the root *n-k-l* used twice and combined with the name Cozbi, which also means 'deceit'. The hospitality offered to Israel by the 'daughters of Moab' and Cozbi in her *qûbbâ*, as shown above, tricked Israel into a submissive, even oppressive, relationship, risking Israel's identity and life. From the perspective of the biblical author(s), the Midianites' deceptive hospitality is revealed as an attempt to oppress Israel by 'narrowing' their means of life. By calling these episodes *the affair of Peor* and *the affair of Cozbi*, the conclusion connects the two parts of the chapter.

Meaning

The promise and experience of abundance may deceive and lead to oppression and death. The formation of Israel as a people in relationship to Yahweh starts with a new understanding of abundance through distribution and limits that eliminate oppression and nurture human flourishing (E. F. Davis 2009: 66–79). In its first experience of settled life in relationship with other peoples, Israel is deceived by abundance to the point of becoming submissive and potentially oppressed again.

Hospitality and hostility are set alongside to determine Israel's identity in relation to other peoples. This framework is useful for revealing that personal and communal identities are fluid (see Leveen 2010: 400–403). Exploring Israel's identity negotiation with the Midianites is historically and theologically complex. Their proximity and differences amount to a thin line between hospitality and hostility. Comparing the mutual hostility described in Numbers 25 with the overall mutual hospitality between Moses and Jethro serves a crucial purpose in biblical narrative: teaching discernment (see Introduction, 'Israel's identity and its neighbours'). When should Israel engage in mutual hospitality and cooperation with other peoples, and when must it protect its identity to the point of hostility? Discerning the difference is the difficult task that biblical authors model for later generations, including us. Hospitality and cooperation demand identity negotiation that does not evade each particular identity but is able to promote shared benefits.

We cannot consider the meaning of chapter 25 without struggling with its violent language and images. Theirs is a world of war (ch. 31) and of foreign raiders looting and destroying fields and houses (Judg. 6:2–6), which differs starkly from the experience of many of us, although large numbers today are still caught up in the horrors of violence and wars. However, part of the process of discernment promoted in this chapter requires of us what Julia O'Brien calls ideological critique and faithful engagement (O'Brien 2008). This is especially true of the characterization of foreign women in this chapter. For the biblical writer, otherness and deceitfulness are portrayed as hyper-sexualized foreign women. This theological language depicts relationships, including that between humanity and God, from a perspective of domination and conquest with gendered sexual connotations. Such language sidelines women's experience of violence and abuse, something that feminist approaches to the Bible have shown. A faithful engagement with the text demands recognition of how this theological language, commonly misunderstood, can lead to violent consequences in real people's lives.

It also demands that we compare and contrast it with other depictions of foreign women in the Bible, in this case especially Canaanite Tamar (Gen. 38), Midianite Zipporah (Exod. 4:24–26) and Moabitess Ruth. In Numbers itself, Zelophehad's daughters, likely comprising a group of foreign women, become a model of integration and faithfulness for Israel (see chapters 26, 27, 36). These foreign women, sometimes even in sexual contexts, played a central role in Israel's formation as a people. They became part of Israel's identity in cooperating with Yahweh's purpose for Israel, other peoples and the whole creation. Ours is the responsibility to discern well the biblical text and our own world for the purpose of safe encounters of mutual benefit between ourselves and others.

5. A NEW GENERATION PREPARES TO ENTER THE LAND (26:1 – 36:13)

A. Organizing the camp of the settling generation (26:1–65)

Context

Following the name given to the book in Greek and many modern languages, Numbers 26 is full of numbers in yet another census. As discussed in the Introduction, the two censuses of Numbers serve an important structural and theological role. In spite of important similarities, differences abound. Some differences highlight each census's unique purpose in the theological message of Numbers.

Each census takes into account a different generation of Israelites. The transition from the exodus generation to the settling generation, as part of a divine judgment, heightens the gravity of the question concerning who really belongs to Israel. While the last blow against the exodus generation in chapter 25 established some boundaries between Israel and other peoples in Transjordan, the second census follows up with an internal accounting of who is part of Israel.

The first census centred on the organization of the people around the tabernacle with the divine presence among them as the definitive feature of their identity. As is clear in 26:52–56, the second census focuses on the division of the Promised Land, sharing out the divine blessing of the land among the Israelites as the defining feature of their identity. These two features are complementary and not exclusive. The focus on land division explains why the second census is structured by tribal clans. They reflect most of the names in Jacob's genealogy in Genesis 46:8–27. Therefore, the seventy individual Israelites who entered Egypt (Exod. 1:5) are now approximately seventy clans, though without a one-to-one correspondence between the individuals of Genesis 46 and the tribal clans in Numbers 26. Still, the order of the census in the LXX follows Genesis 46, while the MT follows the same order as the one presented in Numbers 1. The structure based on tribal clans is expressed by a standard formula, with some variations, giving the clan names, indicating that the second census is actually a mix of census and genealogy (Gane 2004: 734).

A tribal clan (*mišpāḥâ*) is a social unit defined by kinship relations, biological or adoptive. Therefore, the second census establishes the kinship ties that form Israel as a people. To be part of God's people depends on being in a family integrated into an Israelite tribal clan. The association between tribal clans and another social unit, the house of the father (*bêt 'āb*, v. 2), means that participation in a tribal clan depends on, and gives one the right to, land ownership within that clan (cf. Levine 2000: 333–334).

This genealogical feature of the census sets it apart from military and economic censuses in the Bible (Josh. 8:10; 1 Sam. 11:8; 2 Sam. 18:1; 24; 1 Kgs 20:15; 2 Kgs 3:6). It depicts a condensed and cohesive picture of Israel, its tribes, clans and families, taking into account its diversity and the possibility of adoptive kinship ties through different means of shared identity. This theological and ideological purpose of the second census of unity in diversity in a representative group appears in other Ancient Near Eastern literature (cf. Jeon 2022: 182).

Comment
i. Second census (26:1–51)

1–2. The instructions for the second census are similar to those for the first (1:2–3). Eleazar replaces Aaron as the priest, indicating the change of generations. The fact that the census takes place under divine orders differentiates it from royal affirmations of power leading to divine punishment (2 Sam. 24). This point is made by the chronological reference of the census being taken *after the plague*, inverting the sequence of divine punishment: census → plague.

3–4. Moses and Eleazar communicate with Israel about the census and link it back to the first census, referring to the 'sons of Israel going out of the land of Egypt' (AT). The specific expression 'sons of Israel' almost always means merely 'Israelites'. In the context of genealogies, however, it is better understood as 'descendants'. This addresses the problem of referring to this group as 'going out of Egypt'. This is not about the exodus generation, but their descendants.

5–7. Reuben is called the *firstborn* and is positioned first in the list for this reason, as in the first census (1:20). Reuben gave rise to four clans: Hanochites, Palluites, Hezronites and Carmites (cf. Gen. 46:9; Exod. 6:14; 1 Chr. 5:3). Their total is 43,730, a small decrease from the 46,500 of the first census.

8–11. The Palluites are set apart to account for an important event involving some of their families. Dathan and Abiram, Pallu's descendants, were part of a 'banner/faction' (*nēs*, v. 10; cf. Exod. 17:15) against Moses and Yahweh together with other men (Num. 16). While their families are presumably cut off from Israel, verse 11 states that the descendants of one of the faction's protagonists, Korah, survived (see v. 58 below).

12–14. Simeon gives rise to five clans: Nemuelites, Jaminites, Jachinites, Zerahites and Shaulites (cf. 1 Chr. 4:24). Genesis 46:10 and Exodus 6:15 include one more of Simeon's sons, Ohad, adding that Shaul was the son of a Canaanite woman. These divergences show that the tribal clans and the individuals in the genealogies are not necessarily identical, suggesting the possibility of being integrated into a tribal clan as a foreigner, even a Canaanite. Simeon's total number is 22,200, an enormous decline from the

59,300 of the first census. Zimri, one of the protagonists of the Baal-peor episode, is described as the leader of a Simeonite family and a descendant of Shaul in 25:14, which might explain this drastic decrease in number as a form of divine punishment.

15–18. Gad gives rise to seven clans: Zephonites, Haggites, Shunites, Oznites, Erites, Arodites and Arelites (cf. Gen. 46:16). Their total is 40,500, a non-negligible decrease from the previous 45,650 men in the first census.

19–22. A short notice concerning the eldest sons of Judah and their deaths (cf. Gen. 38) introduces Judah's account. No reason for their deaths is given, but the Canaanite location seems important enough to appear here, as it does in Genesis 46:12. Some parallel with the deaths of Aaron's two sons might be in play (see vv. 63–65 below), leading to the conclusion that lineage is not a warranty for authority, as Judah's authority is slightly emphasized in the first census by his highest number of descendants and position in the camp. Judah fathers three other sons, but the sons of Perez are elevated to Judahite clans (cf. Gen. 46:12), so Judah gives rise to five clans: Shelanites, Perezites, Zerahites, Hezronites and Hamulites. Their total is 76,500, a small increase compared with the 74,600 total in the first census. Even with the deaths of two sons, Judahites increase, highlighting God's promise to Jacob's descendants in general (Gen. 46:3). Singling out Perez, the son of Tamar, a foreigner, probably Canaanite, and accounting his sons as Judahite clans underlines their kinship ties as part of Israel.

23–25. Issachar gives rise to four clans: Tolaites, Punites, Jashubites and Shimronites (cf. Gen. 46:13; 1 Chr. 7:1). Their total is 64,300, a significant increase from the 54,400 total in the first census.

26–27. Zebulun gives rise to three clans: Seredites, Elonites and Jahleelites (cf. Gen. 46:14). Their total is 60,500, a small increase from the 57,400 from the first census.

28. The structure of the text in verses 28–34 reveals that each of Joseph's sons form their own tribe and are not counted as clans. As such, summaries appear for the total for Manasseh and for Ephraim, and not for Joseph. Manasseh, Joseph's firstborn, comes first this time (cf. Gen. 46:20; unlike Num. 1:32–35). For a census marking the transition between generations, one would expect the second-born to be prioritized, as was the case in the first census, and in accord with the narrative of Ephraim's priority over Manasseh in Genesis 48. However, the inversion makes Manasseh the seventh tribe, a significant position (Ashley 2022: 448), and leads us to pay closer attention to Manasseh's account in the following verses.

29–34. One direct clan is associated with Manasseh here, the Machirites (contrast Josh. 17:1–3). Four further generations of Machirites are listed as part of clans associated with Manasseh: Gileadites, and through Gilead, Iezerites, Helekites, Asrielites, Shechemites, Shemidaites and Hepherites (cf. 32:39–40; 1 Chr. 2:21–24; 7:14–19). Through the line of Hepher comes Zelophehad, who is not counted as a clan. He is singled out because of his daughters Mahlah, Noah, Hoglah, Milcah and Tirzah. The account of Manasseh is quite extraordinary, running through several generations and including the names of five women. Furthermore, its final number increases to 52,700 from the 32,200 total in the first census.

The need to account for so many generations relates to the division of Manasseh's clans between Transjordan and Cisjordan, and the inheritance by the five daughters of Zelophehad, which will be the theme of 27:1–11. This expansion of generations provides important details about how this census establishes kinship ties. All Gilead's clans (Iezerites, Helekites, Asrielites, Shechemites, Shemidaites, Hepherites) and three of Zelophehad's five daughters (Hoglah, Noah, Tirzah) are toponyms of Canaanite city-states. All but Hepher (see Josh. 12:17) and Tirzah (see Josh. 12:24) are attested in the Samaria Ostraca (Niemann 2008). Gilead itself is a Transjordan region south of Bashan (see 32:34–42). Manasseh's genealogy may indicate a movement of integration of foreigners into Israel by establishing their kinship ties with Manassite clans (cf. J. Davis 2022: 230–257). Strong support for this comes from Zelophehad's daughters. In this patrilineal structure, they claim their right to inherit their father's portion of the Promised Land, which is divinely confirmed (27:1–11). Interestingly, Caleb's right to land inheritance is divinely decreed as well (14:24), and both have to remind Joshua of this divinely given right (Josh. 14:6–14; 17:4). For Milgrom, the need for divine sanction in both cases is explained by their shared foreignness (see 32:12; Milgrom 1990: 224). The same dynamic of Numbers 25 might be in play here. Canaanites may be integrated into Israel as long as the right relationship between them, analogically compared to that of husband and wife, is observed. Again, the use of 'daughters' here is a political idiom referring to villages/ towns (cf. 25:1; Ashley 2022: 449). For this reason, the meaning of Zelophehad's name is relevant. It is probably a combination of Hebrew *ṣel* (shadow/ protection) and *paḥad* (fear/ awe; see Levine 2000: 322). Considering all of these details and the purpose of the second census, Zelophehad's daughters stand for the possibility of the Canaanite population finding protection within Israel as long as they are integrated into Israel's identity as the people of Yahweh (see Introduction, 'Israel's identity and its neighbours').

35–37. Ephraim gives rise to four clans: Shuthelahites, Becherites, Tahanites and Eranites, the last one through Shuthelah (cf. 1 Chr. 7:20–21). Genesis 46:21 and 1 Chronicles 7:6–8 list Becher as part of Benjamin and not Ephraim. Their total is 32,500, a significant decrease from the 40,500 total in the first census.

38–41. Benjamin gives rise to seven clans: Belaites, Ashbelites, Ahiramites, Shuphamites, Huphamites, Ardites and Naamites, the last two through Bela. Genesis 46:21 and 1 Chronicles 7:6–12 present very different lists. Most important, however, is that both lists change the progeny connections. For example, Genesis 46:21 considers Ard and Naaman as direct descendants of Benjamin, not of Bela, while 1 Chronicles 7:12 lists Shephupham and Hupham as great-grandsons of Benjamin through the progeny of Bela. The fluidity in how the genealogies are constructed shows that the important element is that certain clans are under the patrilineage of a specific tribe. Their total is 45,600, a significant increase from the 35,400 of the first census.

42–43. Genesis 46:23 agrees that Dan gives rise to only one clan, here called the Shuhamites, and Hashum there. Their total is 64,400, a slight increase from the 62,700 total of the first census.

44–47. Asher gives rise to five clans: Imnites, Ishvites, Beriites, Heberites and Malchielites, the last two through Beriah (cf. Gen. 46:17; 1 Chr. 7:30–31). Their total is 53,400, a significant increase

from the 41,500 total of the first census. Asher's daughter Serah is
mentioned but is not accounted for by a clan. It is certain that the
twelve patriarchs also had daughters and not only sons, but their
male descendants are listed because clan formation is patrilineal.
So why mention Serah? Given the focus on clan kinship in the
census, perhaps Serah is a relevant Asherite village/town.

48–50. Naphtali gives rise to four clans: Jahzeelites, Gunites,
Jezerites and Shillemites (cf. Gen. 46:24; 1 Chr. 7:13). Their total is
45,400, a significant decrease from the 53,400 total of the first census.

51. A conclusion is presented with a total number of 601,730,
a small decrease from the 603,550 of the first census. This is
not the totality of Israelites, but only of those who will inherit
land; therefore, the next section is about how to go about the
allocation. The almost equal, but still lower, number of Israelites
is meaningful. In spite of the exodus generation's failure leading
to divine punishment, Israel remained fruitful (see Table 5.1).

Table 5.1: Comparison of census figures in Numbers

	Census 1	Census 2	Difference
Reuben	46,500	43,730	−2,770
Simeon	59,300	22,200	−37,100
Gad	45,650	40,500	−5,150
Judah	74,600	76,500	+1,900
Issachar	54,400	64,300	+9,900
Zebulun	57,400	60,500	+3,100
Ephraim	40,500	32,500	−8,000
Manasseh	32,200	52,700	+20,500
Benjamin	35,400	45,600	+10,200
Dan	62,700	64,400	+1,700
Asher	41,500	53,400	+11,900
Naphtali	53,400	45,400	−8,000
TOTAL	603,550	601,730	−1,820

ii. Logic of land distribution among the tribes (26:52–56)

52–56. The conclusion emphasizes the purpose of the second
census. The constant repetition (6 times) of the root *n-ḥ-l*,

'inheritance' and 'inherit', works as the leading motif that unifies
the concluding chapters of Numbers (e.g. 27:7, 8; 32:9, 11; 33:54;
34:2, 5, 13, 17; 35:8; 36:2, 3). However, the verb driving this section
is *ḥ-l-q*, 'apportion', as a divine command ('the land will be
divided'), repeated three times. And this allotment must follow
two methods: by lot and by size of tribe. The territory is determined by the size of the tribe and no favouritism is allowed. The
phraseology of the divine instruction accounts not only for the
'clans' but for every name mentioned (v. 53: *according to the number
of names*), which would include all the women listed in this census.

iii. Census of the Levites (26:57–62)

57–62. While in the first census the Levites were set apart
because of their special tabernacle duties, here they are set apart
because they will not inherit any portion of land (v. 62), although
they will receive places in which to settle (cf. 35:1–8). A first set
of clans follows the three main levitical branches: Gershonites,
Kohathites and Merarites (cf. 3:17; Gen. 46:11; Exod. 6:16). A
second set of clans is presented explaining their connection with
the first three branches: Libnites, Hebronites, Mahlites, Mushites
and Korahites. Their total is 23,000, a slight increase from the
22,000 total of the first census (3:39). Some clans disappear from
the first census: Shimeites, Amramites, Izharites and Uzzielites.
The Korahites are descendants of Izhar (16:1) and Amram is
mentioned in verse 58 as Kohath's descendant, but the Shimeites
and Uzzielites are completely lost in the second census. This
comparison again shows that clan formation focuses on kinship
more than on direct progeny. It also shows that the second census
has more to it than just a listing of clans and numbers. The
second census could list Izharites as a clan and eliminate Korah
from view because of his rebellion (chs. 16–17), but verse 11 has
already mentioned that the Korahites survived and they come to
be one important levitical clan, even appearing to be responsible
for several biblical psalms (Pss 42; 44–49; 84–85; 87–88), with
historical evidence of their existence in the ostracon from Arad.
Even if Korah, representing the exodus generation and its rebellions, died, there is still hope for his descendants (see Gane 2004:
736).

The mentioning of Amram, without considering him a clan, is also relevant. His mention calls attention to his wife Jochebed and her descendants. In verses 58–60 the verb *y-l-d* (bear/ bring forth) is repeated four times, emphasizing the role of mothers in producing descendants and clans. Priestly marital restrictions might also explain the need to draw attention to Jochebed (cf. Lev. 21:7, 13–14; Ezek. 44:22). There is no restriction for priests to marry only Levites, but the expression *daughter of Levi* emphasizes the quality of the priestly lineage until Eleazar. However, the recollection of Nadab and Abihu's deaths shows that obedience and fidelity supersede lineage in importance for the priestly office to guarantee the divine presence with the new generation.

iv. Reminder of the reason for a second census (26:63–65)

63–65. This concluding remark reminds the reader of the reason why a second census was necessary: the death of the whole exodus generation as the result of divine judgment. This note works as a warning and as a message of hope for the settling generation. Even in the context of a census, Israel's identity as God's people is defined by entering and maintaining the covenant in a trusting relationship with Yahweh. This is underscored by highlighting Caleb and Joshua as those whose lives were preserved through God's promise, even though neither appeared in either census as part of any significant lineage or clan. Caleb is of Kenizzite origins (32:12; cf. Gen. 15:18–21; 36:10–11) and was integrated into the tribe of Judah (13:6) by receiving his land portion in Judah (Josh. 14:6–15).

Meaning

The hope of the future through descendance is a profound and basic human value. Some countries, such as Brazil, have been considered the country of the future. Even if this hope remains deferred, it can determine the lives of generations living to provide their descendants with a better life than their own. In response to such settings Alves, a Brazilian theologian, constructing a hopeful image of a new human community, entitled his work *Tomorrow's Child* (Alves 1972). The notion of bringing about a new and bright future through procreation is both analogical and literal. Alves speaks of the future as conception and birthing, the bringing forth of life into the present as we look to the future (see Alves 1974: 562–563). Even when the present is bleak and seems to abort life, the community of the present generation is called to maintain a 'stubborn commitment to the future of our grandchildren', so that the new generation, the seed of the future, might live (Alves 1974: 569).

The second census is constructed with such hope. Even if the exodus generation was punished and died without the fulfilment of the divine presence in the land, there is still hope for a new generation. But that does not come about without the difficult transition from one generation to another in chapters 15–25. The exodus generation, while knowing they will not receive God's gift of the land, remains responsible and must commit to bringing forth the seed of the future, trusting in how God has acted in the past. 'This weaving of the past into a bleak present while awaiting a better future is a striking dimension of Numbers' (Leveen 2008: 39).

Bringing forth life for the future is not limited to biological lineage. The second census shows that descendance is about more than bloodline. It is about kinship formation by inclusion and integration into the covenant community. Foreigners, even some Canaanites, have their place secured within God's people for posterity, by adopting Israel's covenant and being adopted by family groups in Israel. Characteristic of the second census is the presence of women who bring forth new descendants to God's people biologically and otherwise. Zelophehad's daughters, or foreign towns under divine protection, can bring forth life for those who did not belong. Levi's daughter can bring forth life even if priests and Levites endanger their descendants. These women represent the community that brings forth the future of God's people. The second census is full of hope: it guarantees the inclusion of those who want to be God's family.

B. Land distribution outside tribal patrilineage: Zelophehad's daughters (27:1–11)

Context

The setting for chapter 27 and the remainder of Numbers appears in 26:63–65: the Israelites are camped at the edge of the land, separated from it only by the Jordan River. Beginning with Numbers 27, these final chapters deal largely with issues that concern settlement in the land that they will possess in the future. There is, therefore, an underlying tone of hope that the people will receive the land promised to them. Furthermore, unlike difficult cases that arose earlier (cf. chs. 9; 15), these chapters are addressed to the new generation that was counted in the previous chapter. Specifically, 26:33 mentions Zelophehad, who has five daughters but no sons.

Chapter 27 splits neatly into two sections. Verses 1–11 address the issue of the inheritance of a man who dies with daughters but no sons, first for the initial division of land (vv. 1–7) and then once settled (vv. 8–11). Such a question would arise within a patriarchally organized society for which *land* and *legacy* are closely interwoven. This issue also arises in Genesis 38; Leviticus 20:21; Deuteronomy 25:5–10; and Ruth. The treatment here is the first part of a narrative about Zelophehad's daughters that continues in Numbers 36 and Joshua 17 with a revision of the decision that God hands down here.

In verses 12–23, God reminds Moses of his impending death because of the events narrated in chapter 20 and also Deuteronomy 32:48–52. A different version of these events appears in Deuteronomy 31. As a result, Joshua is appointed successor to Moses, at least in terms of military leadership. The fulfilment of the proclamation of Moses' death and Joshua's assumption of leadership take place in Deuteronomy 34.

Comment

This first section concerns inheritance in the land, which points to the future. Some of the land of the tribe of Manasseh, to which these women belong, had already been taken in chapter 21 and would be allotted in chapter 32. That land was in the Transjordan (east of the Jordan River), while, according to Joshua 17:1–6, these women receive portions in the Cisjordan (the region west of the river). Furthermore, given the connection to both Numbers 26 and Joshua 17, the narrative of these daughters is not just about individual family or clan inheritance, but also about the political relationships between different peoples.

Inheritance in Ancient Near Eastern cultures (and most ancient cultures) generally went to the sons (Westbrook and Wells 2009: 93–101). Key concerns were maintaining the family's coherence and subsistence, so the firstborn often received a larger share, as also dictated by Deuteronomy 21:15–17. As a result, daughters typically received dowries (a wedding gift) rather than a share of the inheritance. However, numerous exceptions of women receiving inheritance appear throughout the Ancient Near East, from the pre-Babylonian writings of the Sumerians to the Judean community at Elephantine in southern Egypt in the fifth century BC. Furthermore, biblical texts also make use of the alternate strategy of levirate marriage, where a brother of the dead man marries his widow in order to produce children in the dead man's name (cf. Gen. 38; Deut. 25:5–10; Ruth 1; 4; though see Lev. 20:21, which seems to outlaw the practice!). Given that this option does not appear in this chapter, it may offer a different solution, though the women's mother had also died according to the logic of Numbers 26 (assuming that Zelophehad belonged to the generation that came up out of Egypt, contra J. Davis 2022: 226).

1. The initial division of land taking place upon the Israelite conquest is addressed in verses 1–7. In this setting it is significant that these five daughters are named here (v. 1), in 26:33; 36:11, and in Joshua 17:3, given that many women appearing in the Bible are not. Furthermore, they are almost the *only* women mentioned in the census (other than Serah, daughter of Asher, in 26:46 and Moses' mother, Jochebed, in 26:59). Their appearance therefore marks their initiative (confirmed by God's answer in v. 7) as exemplary. Their entrance into a public (male) space before the tent of meeting also demonstrates courage (like that of Tamar in Gen. 38:25–26). Their initiative prevents them from being pushed to the margins of society, providing themselves with economic security.

As noted earlier, the names of three of the women, Tirzah, Noah and Hoglah, correspond to place names in Northern Israel. Tirzah served as capital of the Northern Kingdom of Israel under Baasha (1 Kgs 14 – 16), while Noah and Hoglah appear in eighth-century records, likely for wine deliveries (the Samaria Ostraca; see, e.g., Dobbs-Allsopp et al. 2004: 423). It may be that this narrative marks the memory of the incorporation of non-Israelites from this region into the Israelite people (J. Davis 2022: 246–248).

The detailed genealogy for Zelophehad's daughters (v. 1) is convoluted: especially *a member of the Manassite clans* is redundant, and Judges 5:13–17 (cf. the opacity in Num. 26:29–30; Josh. 17.2) views Gilead and Machir as separate clans, not as father and son (J. Davis 2022: 243). This evidence shows that genealogies functioned to indicate the changing relationships between groups of people in terms of familial bonds.

2. The extended list of the people before whom the women present their argument indicates the daunting nature of their case.

3–4. The daughters base their case on their father's status *relative* to those participating in Korah's rebellion in chapters 16–17. While it has been argued (Milgrom 1990: 231) that the participation of a father in Korah's rebellion would automatically disqualify offspring from inheriting land in Israel, the mention of Korah's own sons in 26:11 calls this conclusion into question.

The issue at hand in their petition concerns the one-time division of the land (cf. Josh. 17). The connection of the issue of land inheritance with continuation of their father's *name* suggests that memory is seen as tied to a territory and to the thriving of one's descendants in that place.

5. The difficult nature of this case comes to light in that Moses does not himself issue a ruling, but instead brings it before God.

6–7. There are two parts in God's response to Moses. The first concerns the specific complaint of Zelophehad's daughters and affirms the women's claim as just. The implementation of the judgment appears in Joshua 17:3–6 as part of the allotment for Manasseh. That allotment demonstrates the exceptional nature of the daughters' action: each daughter receives a portion of land equal to Zelophehad's brothers' portions. However, unlike the term used for 'giving' an inheritance to the male figures, the verb used for transferring the land to the daughters (ʿ-*b*-*r*) appears only for the women (vv. 7, 8) and not with the inheritance of men, thereby connecting the two sections. The use of this verb indicates the special nature of this action, with the women functioning more as intermediary holders of the land between grandfather and grandson (cf. 1 Chr. 2:34–35 and Milgrom 1990: 232–233).

8–11. The generalizing statute applies the ruling of Zelophehad's daughters to a related but slightly different topic: the passing on of the inheritance of an Israelite man dying without sons rather than the first division of the land among clans and households.

There is no resolution in this section for how the ordinance of inheritance by a daughter in verses 8–11 relates to the practice of levirate marriage to a widow. The lack of reference to levirate marriage here is a gap in the text: it could indicate the tacit *acceptance* or *rejection* of that practice. These verses insert the daughter into the expected chain of inheritance rights of male relations to the head of the household.

C. Transfer of leadership from Moses to Joshua (27:12–23)

This constitutes a separate section that is still linked to the earlier verses in the chapter in dealing with an extraordinary transfer of leadership; both sections address extraordinary transitions from the present to the future. This case concerns the administrative and especially military leadership of the Israelites as a whole. The section bears similarities to the narrative of Aaron's death in 20:22–29. A gradual transfer of leadership responsibilities began then, with Moses playing smaller roles in chapters 21–26.

12. The section begins with a command for Moses to ascend a mountain to view the land that Yahweh has given to the Israelites. Different versions of this command appear in Deuteronomy 3:21–28 and 32:48–52 (cf. Deut. 31:23). That version specifies the mountain as Mount Nebo and the land Moses views as that on the other (west) side of the Jordan, where Moses will not enter. The two of them function in some ways as a frame around all the legislation and speeches that appear from Numbers 28 to Deuteronomy 32. According to the narrative, Moses carries out this command only in Deuteronomy 34:1. Joshua's installation is presented differently in Deuteronomy 31:7–8, 14–15, 23, where it is broken up by a command to recite the Torah every seventh year and by a lament by Yahweh that the Israelites will become disobedient.

The Israelites have camped across from Jericho since Numbers 22:1, and 33:48 identifies the mountains of Abarim as the location where the Israelites camped *before* reaching the plains of Moab. Therefore, either Moses (and Joshua) travels back to that location, or this section narrates an event that took place at an earlier point in time but was placed here for other, perhaps thematic, reasons.

13–14. The nature and purpose of Moses' death are brought into comparison with Aaron's. The reason God gives for both of their deaths refers to the events in 20:1–13, and both die on a mountain after transferring (some of) their authority to their successors (cf. 20:22–29).

15–17. Moses' response concerns the well-being of the Israelites, thereby displaying an important quality of good leadership: he requests a successor so that they will be cared for. Both here and in the parallel report of Deuteronomy 31:7, *Moses* takes the initiative to ask Yahweh for a successor to lead the Israelites. A different account of the interaction appears in Deuteronomy 3:23–28, where Moses pleads with God to let him enter the land.

The phrase *the God of the spirits of all flesh* appears elsewhere only in 16:22. In that context it concerned God's role as the ultimate and just judge, able to mediate in overwhelming situations. Here the focus instead lies on divine provision, requiring significant foresight to provide the best leader. If comparable to the similar phrase in Genesis 6:17 ('all flesh in which is the breath of life'), then it emphasizes the universality of God's rule over humans and animals, and how Israel's leadership, within its limits, must reflect God's cosmic rule.

The type of leadership emphasized is military, underscored in the language of *go out/come in* and *lead . . . out/bring . . . in* in verse 17. The meaning of these terms comes to light through comparison with 1 Samuel 18:13–16; 2 Samuel 5:2, where it is used of humans, and Judges 4:14, where it is God who goes out before Israel's army. The comparison of the Israelites to *sheep without a shepherd* reappears in 1 Kings 22:17; Ezekiel 34:5, in both places concerning political leadership, much in line with the common descriptor of kings in the Ancient Near East as shepherds of their people.

18–23. Joshua has impeccable qualifications: he served as Moses' aide (Exod. 24:13; Num. 11:28), as a leader in battle (Exod.

17:9–13) and as one of the two spies who remained faithful to God
(Num. 14). However, unlike Eleazar taking over from Aaron,
Joshua does not belong to Moses' clan or tribe. The consecration
of Joshua to military leadership further marks the changing of an
epoch. Joshua has the spirit '*in* him', which differs from the spirit
coming upon the elders in 11:25 but replicates the language used by
Pharaoh about Joseph (Gen. 41:38). The parallel in Deuteronomy
34:9 calls Joshua 'full of the spirit of wisdom'. The expression here
may indicate permanence in contrast to the fleeting prophecy in
Numbers 11 (Budd 1984: 307).

Moses ritually lays his hands upon Joshua (v. 18) to appoint him
to a specific function or status (see 8:10 above), so that he endows
Joshua with *some of your authority* (v. 20, NRSV, NIV; *hôd*: literally
'majesty, honour') rather than all of it. This Hebrew term appears
only here in the Pentateuch and usually applies to God or kings.
This difference, along with the need for Joshua to consult Eleazar
the priest for God's direction, rather than having direct access
as Moses does, indicates that Moses possessed pre-eminence
over all subsequent leaders of Israel. It also indicates a different
relationship between Moses and Aaron from what would now be
the case between Joshua and Eleazar (cf. ch. 12). The epoch of
Mosaic leadership differed qualitatively from succeeding times.
Rather than Joshua hearing directly from Yahweh, this text
emphasizes that he must consult the priest for divine guidance
through the *Urim*. This Urim, often found together with the
Thummim (Exod. 28:30; Lev. 8:8; Deut. 33:8; Ezra 2:63; Neh. 7:65),
appears to be a form of divination to discern God's intention
between two options through something like a casting of lots,
according to 1 Samuel 14:41. In contrast, Joshua 1:7–8 lays weight
on meditation on the Instruction (Torah/law) given by Yahweh
to Moses for Joshua's success. This 'book of the law' concerns
especially Deuteronomy in the context of Joshua 1.

There are several parties involved in the transfer of leadership:
Moses the current leader, Eleazar the priest and the whole congregation. The whole assembly must witness the transfer of Israel's
main leader because they, too, have some responsibility for their
leaders. While Joshua's installation in Deuteronomy 31:7 does
occur 'in the sight of all Israel', the locus of action is the tent,

with the pillar of cloud appearing to show God's approval of the events (Deut. 31:14–15). In Numbers 27, however, the focus is placed on the Israelites, often identified as *the whole congregation*. Its importance may foreshadow the distinctions between the tribes that will dwell east of the Jordan and those whose allotments are in the Cisjordan (cf. ch. 32).

Meaning

Anxiety around male heirs features prominently in the narrative text of Genesis (e.g. Gen. 15 – 21), and Zelophehad's daughters take up this concern. Their initiative to guard the name (memory) of their father leads in fact to the maintenance of their own memory in both this narrative and Joshua 17. However, it confirms the basic patriarchal outlook of the text (Sakenfeld 1988), which also demonstrates the value of communal embeddedness more than one's individual advancement. There is some malleability on display here with regard to the traditional patriarchal system. Likewise, in Job 42:15, Job's daughters receive gifts from their father 'along with their brothers', indicating that the biblical texts do know of a scenario that provides resources for daughters beyond the special situation of a man having no sons. However, Job is not an Israelite, and his situation reflects an extraordinary divine blessing. The requirement for inheritance by Zelophehad's daughters might also indicate their complete trust in God's abundant goodness to give them a good land. In any case, it is clear that these texts do not set out to make fundamental changes in the traditional cultural ways of passing on land, but instead seek to deepen connections between communities and the land on which they live, which may instead prove countercultural to capitalist notions of immovable property as a commodity to be bought and sold.

The second section of chapter 27 delves further into another of the key themes of the book: the transfer of leadership responsibilities from the foundational period of Moses and Aaron connected with Sinai and the wilderness to the regular time of life in the land. Moses recognizes the Israelites' need for leadership, though God ordains that it be different from Moses' time, with a rebalancing of the relationship between military (political) leadership and the priest. The transfer of leadership is not a private matter between those in leading positions, but it involves the whole community which the leadership is intended to benefit. The entire section takes place under the spectre of verses 12–13, which recall Moses' failure. Thus, even with Moses' authority or splendour, audiences are invited to remember the problematic nature of human leadership. One could argue that this indicates that the emergence of God's kingdom on earth is not tied to personalities, one particular political system, or a specific ordering of the relationship between faith leaders and political leaders. A significant fact for Joshua's instalment in 27:18 is that he is *a man in whom is the spirit*.

Stretching forward to the New Testament, Moses' desire for a shepherd is adopted and fulfilled in Matthew 9:36 (cf. Mark 6:34; 14:27; John 10:11–16; Heb. 13:20; 1 Pet. 2:25) in Jesus, who is concerned for the Israelites, whom he compares to 'sheep without a shepherd'. The New Testament authors argue for the superiority of Jesus' leadership over that of both Moses and Joshua, inviting audiences to deeper trust in God's guidance through Jesus.

D. Festival calendar (28:1 – 29:40)

Context
These chapters follow the second census in Numbers 26, which numbers the new generation of Israelites, now given their opportunity to take possession of the land God had promised them. Numbers 27 then surprisingly addresses land inheritance by daughters (27:1–11) and the transition of leadership from Moses to Joshua (27:12–23), both of which emphasize the imminent possession of the land. Following these pointers towards life in the land, chapters 28–29 now detail the most important action that the Israelites should carry out: the worship of God. Given that especially the annual festivals appear quite seldom in the rest of Numbers (only Passover in ch. 9), in this context oriented towards occupation of the land these chapters function as a promise about life in the land (Pressler 2017: 255).

Chapters 28–29 are one of numerous treatments in the Pentateuch of the festival calendar, alongside Exodus 23:14–18;

34:22–23; Leviticus 23; and Deuteronomy 16:1–17 (additionally Ezek. 45:18–25). In addition, Exodus 29:38–41 contains prescriptions for the twice-daily offering with amounts of accompanying grain, oil and drink coming from Numbers 15:4–10, and Sabbath and monthly offering regulations also appear in Ezekiel 46:1–7. Outside the Bible, several Ancient Near Eastern civilizations have also left offering calendars behind, indicating that such calendrical records were a common scribal practice (Thames Jr 2021).

What was the reason for this repetition of and variation on the same theme? The repetition shows the central importance of the topic of worship of Yahweh, that is, the expression of honour, devotion and gratitude. Its significance lies in the necessity of honouring and celebrating Yahweh with concrete gifts as a gathered community. And, while such celebrations often include communal feasting, an aspect highlighted in Deuteronomy 16, the specific offerings mentioned in Numbers 28 – 29 consist almost entirely of details about the precious things set aside for Yahweh alone, items that the gathered congregation *does not eat or drink* – burnt offerings and purification offerings (apart from the mention of vows and free-will offerings and shared offering feasts in 29:39).

As so often, one can also enquire why this discussion appears here. In addition to the contextual emphasis on preparation for life in the land in chapters 27–36 already suggested, an answer may emerge from the way this presentation of offerings goes beyond all the others through its systematic delineation of regular offerings, also of the daily offerings, and then working its way towards less frequent events from there. The presentation builds from the daily offerings (28:2–8) to those additionally required weekly on the Sabbath (28:9–10), monthly (New Moon: 28:11–15) and finally to the annual festivals (28:16 – 29:38).

As such, it incorporates the regulations of amounts for the accompanying grain and drink offerings found in 15:1–10 into the regular cycle of offerings, which contrasts with the amounts found in Ezekiel 46:13–15.

Rather than the celebration aspect and emphasis on the location that are especially prominent in Deuteronomy 16, Numbers 28

– 29 places its emphasis elsewhere, intending to make a different point. These chapters largely follow the outline of the calendar in Leviticus 23 for the annual festivals, adding a detailed and systematic account of the offerings provided for each occasion. This account goes beyond all the others in its attempt to *sanctify time* (Pressler 2017: 256). It provides a regular morning and evening rhythm to a life in God's kingdom in addition to the weekly (in Lev. 23:3), monthly and yearly one (Lev. 23; Deut. 16; etc.). Finally, the offerings here detail the *public communal* offerings: these form the baseline of offerings from the community at large to which individuals could add their private gifts of thanksgiving or purification offerings. Its relation to the other calendars appears more as collation than alteration (Budd 1984: 314), which is different from some of the others.

Comment
i. Introduction (28:1–2)
1–2. The chapter opens with the customary divine communication to Moses, who acts as the intermediary between God and the Israelites. Verse 2 piles up general terms for the various kinds of offerings as a way of including all of them, which ESV appropriately renders, 'My offering, my food for my food offerings, my pleasing aroma'. There is some question as to whether to render the Hebrew term *'iššê* as 'offerings by fire' or 'food offerings'. While linguistically related texts from Ugarit (fifteenth century BC in modern Lebanon) indicate the meaning 'food offering', even the LXX in the third century BC already understood the term as 'fire offering'. In terms of the logic of the offerings, it is best to follow Milgrom (1990: 124), who excludes the possibility of 'fire offering' because this designation does not include the purification offering, which is also burned.

Perhaps the most important phrase in verse 2 concerns each offering being brought *at its appointed time* (*bĕmô 'ădô*): the way that *time* is sanctified in each action constitutes the central element in these chapters, and one that now combines the festivals – which is often the use of this term – with the daily and Sabbath offerings.

Additional note: the amounts of offerings

Table 5.2 provides an overview of the public offerings for each
occasion, based on the repeated amounts of ³⁄₁₀ ephah of grain
for a bull, ²⁄₁₀ for a ram and ¹⁄₁₀ for each lamb, as well as ½ hin of
drink offering for each bull, ⅓ for each ram, and ¼ for each lamb.

ii. Daily morning and evening offerings (28:3–8)

3–8. The daily offerings focus around one male lamb in the
morning and one in the evening – always accompanied by grain,
oil and drink offerings – constituting a repetition of Exodus
29:38–41. These constitute the baseline communication of a
continual (or *regular*, in Hebrew the term *tāmîd* in v. 3) response to
God's provision of a land and wealth that yield the valuable goods
from which the Israelites can make offerings back to God. Several
other texts also provide comparison: Numbers 15:4–5 provides
the amounts of accompanying grain, oil and liquid. Twice-daily
offerings appear in 2 Kings 16:15, but this royal adaptation tells
of morning burnt offerings and evening tribute offerings. Ezekiel
46:13–15's vision outlines a once-daily morning offering with
different amounts of accompanying grain and so on, all brought
by the leader.

A comparison of these verses with those in Exodus 29 reveals
several differences: the passage in Numbers 28 repeats Exodus
29 almost word-for-word except for changing the drink offering
from 'wine' in Exodus 29:40 (and Num. 15:5) to *šēkār* in verse 7
here. The meaning of this term is contested: either a strong grape-
based alcohol such as grape schnapps/grappa, or beer made of
wheat or barley. On the one hand, its appearance here may favour
a grape-based beverage focused on the increased alcoholic content
because the fruit of the vine remains a constant throughout
biblical sacrifice, and wine is specified in verse 14 (cf. comment
on 6:3). On the other hand, this unique specification might imply
that beer is envisioned in the other references to drink offering in
Numbers 28 – 29 (see Welton 2020: 113; cf. Deut. 14:26). Another
change is 'you [sing.] shall do upon the altar' in Exodus 29:38 to
'you [pl.] shall bring to Yahweh' here in verse 3 (AT). This latter
difference results from the difference in addressees: Exodus 29

Table 5.2: The amounts of offerings in Numbers 28 – 29

Celebration	Text	Burnt offering: lambs	Burnt offering: bulls	Burnt offering: rams	Purification offering: goat	Tribute offering w/ oil (ephah)	Drink offering (hin)
Daily offering	28:3–8	2	0	0	0	0.2*	0.5
Sabbath offering	28:9–10	2	0	0	0	0.2	0.5
New Moon	28:11–15	7	2	1	1	1.5	3.1
Passover	28:16	0	0	0	0		
Feast of Unleavened Bread	28:17–25						
Day 1		7	2	1	1	1.5	3.1
Day 2		7	2	1	1	1.5	3.1
Day 3		7	2	1	1	1.5	3.1
Day 4		7	2	1	1	1.5	3.1
Day 5		7	2	1	1	1.5	3.1
Day 6		7	2	1	1	1.5	3.1
Day 7		7	2	1	1	1.5	3.1
Firstfruits / Weeks	28:26–31	7	2	1	1	1.5	3.1
First of seventh month	29:1–6	7	1	1	1	1.2	2.6
Tenth of seventh month	29:7–11	7	1	1	2	1.2	2.6
Festival of Booths	29:12–38						
Day 1		14	13	2	1	5.7	10.7
Day 2		14	12	2	1	5.4	10.2
Day 3		14	11	2	1	5.1	9.7
Day 4		14	10	2	1	4.8	9.2
Day 5		14	9	2	1	4.5	8.7
Day 6		14	8	2	1	4.2	8.2
Day 7		14	7	2	1	3.9	7.7
Day 8		7	1	1	1	1.2	2.6

* Amounts for the tribute and drink offerings in each line are total amounts. For example, each of the two lambs for the daily offering is accompanied by 0.1 ephah of grain with oil and 0.25 hin of liquid. Therefore, the total amount of accompanying tribute offering (for both lambs) is 0.2 ephah and of accompanying drink offering is 0.5 hin.

solely concerns the actions of the *priests*, while here in verse 2 the
intended audience is the *Israelites*. The subject changes in verse 4
back to the singular, indicating that these actions now concern the
priest (supported by the addition of 'pour out in the sanctuary' in
v. 7).

However, Numbers 28 provides several additions; some are
small clarifications, but verse 6 is added in its entirety: 'The
regular burnt offering ordained [lit. 'done'] on Mount Sinai as
a sweet aroma, a food offering for Yahweh' (AT). This addition
makes a conscious reference back to Exodus 29, suggesting the
normative nature of the stipulations given on the mountain of
revelation, even though no record exists of this offering taking
place at that time (but see Lev. 9:17).

iii. Sabbath offerings (28:9–10)

9–10. On the Sabbath, two additional lambs augment the
daily fare – a regulation found nowhere else in the Pentateuch.
As a result, a cycle emerges that is punctuated by the doubling of
offerings every seventh day. That said, there is a striking omission
here: while 28:18, 26; 29:1, 7, 12, 35 forbid occupational work, no
such stipulation appears for the Sabbath. Perhaps this was understood as self-explanatory because of the Ten Commandments
(Exod. 20:8–11 / Deut. 5:12–15), especially given the judgment
in Numbers 15:32–36 (and Exod. 35:1–3) on the man gathering
firewood on the Sabbath. Its omission likely points to the expectation that the audience is familiar especially with Leviticus 23
(Nihan 2008; here at v. 3), though the reliance on Leviticus 23
remains unclear until verses 16–25 on the Passover (see below).

iv. Monthly New Moon offerings (28:11–15)

11–15. Also mentioned in Numbers 10:10 and Ezekiel 46:6–7
(but with different amounts!), a big jump in the number of animals
takes place on the first day of the lunar month, calling for two
bulls, one ram and seven male lambs, in addition to the regular
offerings. However, in addition a purification offering of a goat
is required, a first in this list (cf. 6:11, 16). While purification
offerings on behalf of a priest were burnt in full (cf. Lev. 4:11–12),
for the same offering brought on behalf of individual Israelites in

Leviticus 6:26, 29 the presiding priest and male members of the priest's family could consume parts of it.

This stipulation implies a regular cleansing of God's dwelling from human imperfection, in order that God might continue to live among Israel. One can note that the comparative *rarity* of the purification offering shows that the purpose of the offering did not consist in keeping God's anger at bay (contra Wenham 1981: 200); the burnt offerings – which were the type offered on a twice-daily, weekly and New Moon (monthly) rhythm – instead focus on the regular reminder that God is superior to humanity: Yahweh rules, not humans.

Also striking here, verse 15 mentions for the first time in the chapter the bringing of a male goat as purification offering (also v. 30; 29:16, 19, etc.). Elsewhere in these chapters this same offering appears simply as *one male goat . . . to make atonement for you* (v. 22). Atonement appears primarily in Exodus, Leviticus and Numbers (also Ezekiel), and is discussed above in the Introduction ('Atonement and ritual'). The two descriptions are combined here in verses 22; 29:5, 11.

v. Passover and the Festival of Unleavened Bread (28:16–25)

16–25. A shift takes place between verses 15 and 16: up to this point, the text has treated regular offerings that one can mark off as twice-daily, weekly and monthly (every four weeks). From verse 16 onwards the text treats several annual occasions that are, however, clustered around the first and even more the seventh month of the year.

This treatment of Passover and Unleavened Bread carefully separates the two just as its source does (Lev. 23:5–8), making clear that one should celebrate Passover on the fourteenth day of the first month (in v. 16), and Unleavened Bread, though not explicitly named, as part of the same festival block during the seven subsequent days (vv. 17–25). These two chapters are more similar here than with regard to any other feast. The description of verse 16 assumes knowledge of how one should celebrate the day (thus Exod. 12:1–13). While the location does not appear in verse 16, the fact that verse 17 calls the fifteenth day (that is, the first day of Unleavened Bread) a pilgrimage feast (*ḥag*) leaves open the possibility that Numbers allows the Passover to be celebrated at home, like Exodus 12 (unlike Deut. 16:1–8). Then the people gather at the sanctuary for the explicit offerings that take place for the next seven days. Comparison with Leviticus 23 reveals very few differences: verse 16 here omits the time of the Passover observance, a central element in Exodus 12:1–13; Leviticus 23:5; and Deuteronomy 16:4, 6 and the central offerings of the daily provisions of bulls, rams and lambs for each day during Unleavened Bread. This omission results from the overlap with the time of the evening offering in verses 4, 8, making repetition of the time unnecessary.

There are several differences between the celebrations in Exodus 12; Leviticus 23; and Numbers 28 on one hand, and Deuteronomy 16:1–8; perhaps also 2 Kings 23:23; 2 Chronicles 30; and 2 Chronicles 35 on the other, which concern the *location* of the celebration of Passover (at home in the former and at the central sanctuary such as Jerusalem in the latter) and the number of days of the Passover–Unleavened Bread celebration. It spans eight days in Leviticus 23:5–8 and Numbers 28:16–25 versus seven in Deuteronomy 16:1–8. One way of understanding these differences is that the practice of rituals regularly changes throughout time and in different locations, but the ritual itself remains intact. A further example comes in the future-oriented Passover described in Ezekiel 45:21–24, which envisions a prince figure leading the celebration and describes different amounts of accompanying tribute offerings, no lambs, and different numbers of other animal offerings. This is an exciting example of how God's laws are not static but rather incarnational: they allow for human particularity, and are able to minister to different people and groups in different historical situations.

vi. Festival of Firstfruits and Weeks (28:26–31)

26–31. The chapter folds in the Day of Firstfruits into (the festival called) Weeks (v. 26): unlike the other annual celebrations, the text does not name a particular date for this pilgrimage, nor does Numbers designate it a pilgrimage *feast*, contrary to how it appears in Deuteronomy 16:9–12. However, in this way it follows Deuteronomy in not prescribing an extra trip to the sanctuary (tabernacle or temple) for Firstfruits, though Deuteronomy (and Exod. 23:16–17; 34:22–23) does envision a trip to the sanctuary for its *Festival of Weeks*. This celebration relates directly to the agricultural harvest, coming seven weeks after the ripening of the barley if one can assume Leviticus 23, so geographic location determined when regions would celebrate. In order to understand when this would take place, these verses are best read in conjunction with Leviticus 23:9–21. However, two significant challenges arise in that the Numbers text differs in terms of the offerings it prescribes. First, Numbers omits the so-called wave offering (Lev. 23:9–14) that takes place after Unleavened Bread and the accompanying offering that Leviticus 23 foresees celebrating the firstfruits of the grain harvest, when one waves a sheaf and brings a lamb for burnt offering with the accompanying tribute offering and drink offering. Second, Leviticus 23:14 comments that this offering must be fulfilled before one can eat of the new grain harvest. However, Numbers 28 does not mention this celebration, jumping instead to fifty days later and Firstfruits/Weeks, which appears in Leviticus 23:15–21.

According to this formulation of the festival, one might suggest the Israelites were therefore not required to be present at the sanctuary for the Day of Firstfruits/Weeks (cf. Milgrom 1990: 245). Given the specificity of making an offering of the new year's grain, however, it may instead indicate that the celebration lasted only for a *day* (and different days depending on when one's grain ripened!), rather than a week, like the spring Festival of Passover/ Unleavened Bread or the autumn Festival of Booths.

Furthermore, what is prescribed initially is different. It states, 'when you bring a tribute offering of new grain' (v. 26, AT; *minḥâ ḥădāšâ*). This phrase otherwise occurs only in Leviticus 23:16. In Leviticus 23 this offering is specified as two loaves of bread, which seems to be assumed here. In both cases it probably indicates bread made from grain from the new, rather than the previous year's, harvest (Lozinskyy 2022: 67–68). *Then* one brings a number of the regular burnt offerings and a purification offering. Also, the numbers of rams and bulls in Leviticus 23:18 are reversed in Numbers 28:27 (two rams in Lev. 23, two bulls in Num. 28). This discrepancy indicates the flexibility, once again, of celebrations: in

different settings, the Israelites perform their worship in ways that
bear resemblance to one another, but are not entirely the same.

vii. First day of the seventh month (29:1–6)

1–6. While Numbers 28 and 29 belong together as a presentation
of the daily, weekly, monthly and yearly festivals, the fact that all of
Numbers 29 focuses on the events of the seventh month shows the
centrality of these events for Israel's life under God's rule.

The NRSV in verse 1 reads *a day for you to blow the trumpets*, though
the Hebrew merely offers 'a day of shouting' (*yôm terû'â*; or 'day
of acclamation', following Lozinskyy 2022: 99–100). The term
appears several times in connection with a variety of celebrations
(in addition to shouts of alarm or war cries in 10:5–7, which are
less relevant here), in relation to worship settings (Ezra 3:12; Ps.
27:6) and in everyday life (Job 8:21).

The opening day of the seventh month at a later time (in the
Jewish Mishnah, dated *c.* AD 200) served as the beginning of the
new year complete with a feast, but there is little support for a *new
year's feast* in the biblical texts themselves (except that Ezek. 40:1
places the beginning of the year in the seventh month; note also
Neh. 7:73). Rather, in Exodus 12:2, the spring month of Abib,
when one celebrated Passover, is designated the first month of the
year (also Ezek. 45:18, 21). The occasion here in verses 1–6 instead
marks the beginning of the most sacred month, with both the
tenth and fifteenth to twenty-second as holy days.

The text here relies on some parts of Leviticus 23:23–25,
though the Leviticus description indicates that the sound is one
of remembrance. This celebration does not otherwise appear in
the Pentateuch. In fact, Numbers 10:10 instead designates the
beginning of every month with this, or a similar, sound. These
verses expand on the acclamation, laborious work prohibition,
and undefined 'present a food offering to Yahweh' of Leviticus
23, furnishing the day with a large number of offerings, almost
equivalent to those for the Feast of Unleavened Bread and the
New Moon. Thus, with the inclusion of the daily and New Moon
offerings (v. 6, minus the monthly purification offering), only the
outlays for Tabernacles/Booths later in the same month are larger
for individual days.

viii. The Day of Atonement (29:7–11)

7–11. The tenth day of the seventh month, as verse 7 calls it here, appears as the 'Day of Atonement' in Leviticus 23:26–32 and at length in Leviticus 16 (there is very close similarity between Lev. 16:29 and Num. 29:7). The practices on this day extend beyond particular offerings to doing no work at all and practising self-humiliation. It is striking that almost the sole omission from Leviticus 23:27 in Numbers 29:7 is the name of the day in Leviticus. This points to the reliance of Numbers on the audience's familiarity with the name of the celebration. Second, the Numbers treatment of the celebration provides new ways to honour the day in relation to the other festivals: the community of Israelites should humble themselves and refrain from *all work* (not just 'laborious', 'regular' or 'occupational' work, which is required during other annual celebrations). No detailed description of this 'self-humiliation' appears in the Pentateuch (cf. Lev. 16:29, 31; 23:27, 32; Num. 30:13). It is literally a form of castigating ('-*n-h*, 'to oppress, humiliate, do violence to', according to *HALOT* 853) one's self, vitality, body or throat (*nepeš*). For this reason, it can easily be considered a form of rigid fasting, although other forms of self-denial or contrition, such as sexual abstinence, might also be practised (see Stökl 2003: 34–37; Gane 2005: 312–315; cf. Ezra 8:21; Ps. 35:13; Isa. 58:3; Dan. 10:12). By leaving it unstated, the audience must fill in the gap in the text in the way they see best.

And, in addition, a number of public communal offerings should be brought – one bull, one ram, seven lambs, and one goat for the purification offering. This description leaves out the detailed ritual from Leviticus 16, though it does mention a second purification offering here in verse 11, which one might understand in terms of the two goats or the two purification offerings (one goat and one bull) in Leviticus 16. The expression *the sin-offering of atonement* (*hakkippurîm*, v. 11) appears only otherwise in Exodus 30:10, perhaps also being a reference to the events on the tenth day of the seventh month as here in verse 11, but in a somewhat undefined manner. In any case, when viewed only in the context of Numbers 28 – 29, this sacred day appears quite similar to other sacred days.

The theological significance of this passage lies, again, in its differences from Leviticus 23 (and Lev. 16). Leviticus 23:28–32 emphasizes that breaking the prohibitions on work or self-humiliation on this day will bring about exclusion from God's people – a punishment found in Numbers 9:1–14 (esp. v. 13) for Passover, a celebration mentioned only in the single verse of Numbers 28:16 in this passage (though also central in identifying with God's people in Exod. 12:43–49). Leviticus 16, on the other hand, provides further details for the particular actions of the high priest in this ritual. In contrast to both of those discussions, Numbers 29 adds the regular public offerings to be carried out at the sanctuary – one bull, one ram, seven lambs and their accompanying grain offerings and drink offerings. In this case, the three presentations largely dovetail, with each elaborating a different aspect. However, the numbers and types of burnt offerings differ: in Leviticus 16 there is one bull and two rams (in addition to the two goats as purification offerings).

ix. Festival of Tabernacles (29:12–38)

12–38. By far the greatest amount of text and the largest number of offerings appear in conjunction with the 'Festival of Yahweh' from the fifteenth to the twenty-second of the seventh month. Elsewhere this celebration is called 'Booths' (the Hebrew 'Sukkot' also translates as 'Tabernacles'). In Exodus 23:16; 34:22 it is called 'ingathering', which highlights the agricultural connection: the feast takes place after completion of the autumn harvest (also Lev. 23:39). The festival or feast (*ḥag*, v. 12) indicates a pilgrimage celebration. These verses build on Leviticus 23:33–36 (though Lev. 23:39–43 offers further details), with almost every word other than the name of the festival as 'booths' from Leviticus 23:34–36 being repeated here in verses 12, 35–36 (the beginning and end of the discussion). Also omitted from the discussion in Numbers 29 are aspects of this festival that are specific to it, such as the use of fruit and branches of trees or the construction of and dwelling in booths for the seven days as a reminder of the trek from Egypt to the land as found in Leviticus 23:40–42.

The main details in the verses in between consist of the numbers and kinds of animals brought each day for burnt and purification offerings. Unlike any other discussion of Booths or the celebration of Unleavened Bread in the spring, the number of bulls descends from thirteen to seven for days one to seven of the celebration. Then, on day eight, the number agrees with the amounts from the first and tenth days of the seventh month and is more in line with the amounts from Unleavened Bread and Weeks. Like the main feast in the spring, Unleavened Bread, Booths also requires a purification offering for each day of the celebration. Like Leviticus 23:35–36, verses 12 and 35 prohibit regular or laborious work on the first and eighth days.

There is a question of how to relate the command to celebrate for seven days (v. 12) with a festival that includes an *eighth* day (vv. 35–38). The mention of *seven* days may simply serve to mark out the traditional number of completion, which leads to a 7 + 1 understanding of the days of the festival's duration, which also emphasizes the movement from the thirteen bulls on the first day (v. 13) to the *seven* on the seventh day (v. 32).

What made Booths so significant that Numbers requires such a higher number of regular offerings? The main answer to this question lies in the agricultural cycle of the year. By the time of Booths, the harvests for the year had been brought in, thus making it the most plentiful season in terms of food on hand. Coupled with this is the fact that it was the time when the main field work of the year had come to a close, so it represented the best season to praise Yahweh in gratitude for the year's bounty. The reason for the declining number of bulls each day remains unclear, though the fact that the sum of days one to seven is seventy suggests completion, and it may also represent an earlier cultural tradition of the Levant going back to the second millennium (Ayali-Darshan 2015). In any case, the feast also served as an important time in several narratives and other texts such as 1 Kings 8 (dedication of Solomon's temple, also 2 Chr. 7); Ezra 3:4; Nehemiah 8 (reconstitution of the community after the exile); and Zechariah 14:16–19 (future gathering of nations in Jerusalem to worship Yahweh).

It should be noted that the first and eighth days' prohibition on work does not forbid celebration. Refraining from work could easily indicate a time of enjoyment (the *assembly* in v. 35 need not have been solemn; cf. Amos 5:21). However, the return to a lesser number of offerings on day eight indicates a return to 'normal'.

x. Private offerings (29:39–40)

39–40. According to verse 39 the offerings laid out above are 'in addition to your vow offerings and your free-will offerings, for your burnt offerings, and for your tribute offerings, and for your drink offerings, and for your shared offering feasts' (AT). This verse makes it clear that the offerings detailed in the previous two chapters concern regular, community-wide, public offerings. An individual or family would often bring other offerings. These included those to fulfil vows and those simply as free-will offerings – for which no mandate existed. Both types concern animals that those bringing them would participate in consuming (cf. Lev. 3:1–16 for the part that the officiating priest receives, while Lev. 7:16–18 notes that a consumption of either free-will or vow offering takes place at the sanctuary on the day of sacrifice as well as the following day).

Meaning

Given that Numbers 28 – 29 takes its place among *numerous* other discussions of Israel's festival calendar, several directions take on significance, especially in the light of the strong rejection in the book of Hebrews of Israel's ability to achieve God's favour through such animal offerings.

(1) As seen in other chapters, Numbers seeks to update and provide another point of view on central topics. In doing so, it provides guidance on the interpretation of the Bible from within the Bible itself. These chapters take several interpretive steps that one can learn from:

- Explication/clarification: Numbers 28:16–25 makes it clear how one could combine the celebration of Passover and Unleavened Bread by celebrating them back-to-back. This may be implicit in Deuteronomy 16:1–8, but Numbers 28 states clearly that they occur one after the other, to avoid misunderstanding.
- The most prominent source text for Numbers 28 – 29 is Leviticus 23. For the most part, Numbers 28 – 29 fills in the

'public offerings' into the celebrations mentioned in Leviticus
23, sometimes even omitting the name of the celebration!
This shows that sometimes the biblical texts *assume* that
readers are aware of other, earlier texts. That is, they assume a
certain amount of biblical literacy to understand their point.

(2) The central message of the content of Numbers 28 – 29,
coming after the first chapter concerning the allocation of the
land to specific tribes, clans and families in Numbers 27, is that
the Israelites acknowledge God's reign by allocating valuable
goods as gifts to Yahweh from the land they will receive. In
other words, as a community they provide regular daily, weekly,
monthly and yearly valuable goods to express their response of
gratitude and worship for God's provision of the land – so that
God will continue to dwell in their midst. While Numbers 7
outlines a punctiliar experience of consecration and worship by
the exodus generation, in Numbers 28 – 29 the settling generation
is reminded of the constant cycle of consecration and worship
for life in the land. Modern communities of faith can likewise
consider appropriate rhythms of showing concrete gratitude to
God from generation to generation that can sanctify spaces and,
most importantly for Numbers 28 – 29, time.

(3) The manner in which this giving-back takes place serves
to structure the days, weeks, months and yearly cycle in such
a way that the relationship with God is part of every morning
and evening, and there is an ebb and flow to the sacred times
of the year that corresponds to the yearly cycles of abundance
(harvest). These chapters provide the people of God with a
structure for community worship – some of which took place
with the entire community (presumably) present, such as the
Feast of Unleavened Bread in the first month and the Festival
of Booths in the seventh month. However, much of the worship
took place while most of the people remained at their respective
homes. Therefore, worship took place whether an individual was
present or not.

Daily worship appears in the Psalms (61:8; 88:9; 145:2), but
it is in these chapters of Numbers that the entire overview of
prescribed Israelite worship appears.

Furthermore, the fact that these chapters describe the *public* worship taking place at the sanctuary with and without the presence of the community indicates that, in the Old Testament, there was a distinction and an overlap between public and private worship. The main daily actions by and for the community of burnt offerings and their accompanying grain and drink serve as signs of subservience to Yahweh's authority. One might go so far as to suggest that worship takes place *by* and *for* the people without the necessity of their continual physical presence. They are then drawn into worship twice a year in the sanctuary, while also celebrating from afar during Firstfruits/Weeks and Passover.

The implied danger of this structure is that, as Isaiah 58 shows, there could be daily worship in the sanctuary without the required expression of the people's worship in ordinary life through their ethical and compassionate treatment of their neighbours (especially those enslaved and hungry in Isa. 58:6–7). Two features in the community's worship prescribed in Numbers 28 – 29 are intended to avoid the dichotomy: the practice of self-humiliation and generous free-will offerings.

(4) The repetition of the number seven – the number of feasts, the number of days with sacred convocations without work, the number of days of the Feasts of Unleavened Bread and the 7 + 1 of Booths, and the emphasis on the seventh month (the entirety of Num. 29) – implies a fullness and completeness to this way of worshipping Yahweh through an annual cycle of offerings. That is to say, Numbers 28 – 29 shows how God's people can worship twice daily – every day, compounded by further celebrations throughout the weeks, months and year – every year. Life in God's kingdom (in Numbers: in the Promised Land) consists first and foremost of worship.

Overall, when read together with the New Testament, such as John 4:20–24, faithful worship requires the orientation of one's whole self – in spirit and in truth – towards God. Even in the narrative of John 4, spiritual and truthful worship still involves bread, harvest and a generous host. As in John 4, how one reconciles the details of Numbers 28 – 29 with, for example, Leviticus 23; Deuteronomy 16; Ezekiel 45–46 for one's own place and time has value, but it must be combined with personal action and heart focus. Nonetheless, the rhythms described in Numbers 28 – 29 highlight the way that regular worship practices can shape community and individual life into habits of worship. Worship does not include the same types of offerings in the present time, even if material resources distributed and consumed communally must still be present, requiring people and communities of faith to construct regular – perhaps morning and evening – practices such as study, prayer, sharing the table, hospitality and care for others.

(5) The methodical structuring of time according to worship in these chapters provides a fundamental challenge to other ways of organizing time, such as work and school routines, national holidays and economic cycles. It does not necessarily exclude these: there are work-related and economic concerns in the weekly Sabbath cycle and in the agricultural underpinnings for the celebrations of Firstfruits (which is not given an exact date!) and the seventh month, which generally coincided with the harvest of other crops. However, the *worship calendar* overruled all these other economic and political concerns as a matter of sanctification of time so that God could be present with the people of God wherever they resided.

E. Instructions for vows (30:1–16)

Context
Generous free-will offerings conclude the instructions about public worship at the sanctuary in Numbers 28 – 29. The voluntary participation of the community in joyful consecration to God by extending God's good gifts to their neighbours, modelled by the Nazirite vow in Numbers 6, is necessary to avoid the dangers of fixed public worship devoid of personal commitments to God and others. Numbers 30 then gives a general rule about vows (cf. Lev. 5:4; Num. 15:3, 8; Deut. 23:21–23) followed by subcases. After an introduction (v. 1), the general case is established (v. 2), followed by four subcases addressing specific concerns related to vows made by women: (1) a young woman who makes vows while living in her father's house (vv. 3–5); (2) a woman with a pre-existing vow who gets married (vv. 6–8); (3) vows made by a widow or a divorcee (v. 9); (4) vows of married women (vv. 10–12). The structure of the rest of the chapter remains vague (see

Eichler 2021). The best option is to see verses 13–15 as a reformulation of the main point made in the four subcases and verse 16 as their conclusion.

It is certain that vows implied a high economic cost. This aspect, more than self-imposed personal renunciation (cf. 29:7–11), is the focus of Numbers 30. Some examples of vows can be seen in Leviticus 27, where people, animals, houses and land are consecrated, that is, made available to use for the community by priests at the sanctuary. The relation of Numbers 30 with the surrounding literary context confirms this. In 29:39, vows (*neder*) are connected to costly voluntary offerings (*nĕdābâ*) during the annual festivals in Israel's cultic calendar, appropriate occasions for fulfilling vows (see 1 Sam. 1). The context of war, as in the case of Numbers 31, is also appropriate for vows. The only occasion Israel makes a vow in Numbers is in the context of war (21:1–3) as a petition for success with a commitment to dedicate the spoils to Yahweh in the form of *tribute* (*mekes*, 31:25–47) and *offering* (*qorbān*, 31:48–54). The specific status of women in relation to owning and managing the most valuable asset in ancient Israel as part of its covenant with Yahweh, land inheritance, is the main topic of Numbers 27 and 36. Even whole tribes negotiate their part in Yahweh's covenant and land inheritance by means of an oath (*š-b-ʿ*), as seen in Numbers 32. Therefore, the literary context of chapters 27–36 centres on distribution regulation of ancestral property as a religious, even a cultic, issue (cf. Grossman 2007).

Numbers 30 and the surrounding context assume that women have legal rights to goods and property and some significant freedom to make vows that would affect their whole household (cf. Num. 6). It is for this reason that so much attention is given to their vows. Numbers 30 guarantees women's socio-economic and religious freedom, protecting them from any religious guilt in a patriarchal structure in which their fathers and husbands could interfere in their religious commitments.

Comment
i. General case of vows (30:1–2)

1. Yahweh normally addresses Moses first, who transmits the message to Israel (e.g. 28:1–2). The indirect speech only to the *heads*

of the tribes of the Israelites could reflect a scenario similar to that of
Numbers 36. Tribal leaders address Moses with concerns about
a specific topic, which Yahweh answers through Moses with the
formula 'this is the word that Yahweh commanded' (36:6, AT).
This exact formula is found here in verse 1. Moses then addresses
the Israelite leaders to answer concerns they have brought to his
attention concerning sacrificial offerings and their effect on family
possessions (Achenbach 2003: 612–613). As in Numbers 36, Moses
and the community struggle to adapt earlier divine instructions
to the innovative rule that gives rights of ownership of goods and
property to women.

2. This is a general rule that is not limited to vows made by men
(cf. Deut. 22:21–23; Prov. 20:25; Eccles. 5:4–5). The third-person
masculine singular is commonly used as representative of male
and female in divine instructions (e.g. Exod. 12:3; 28:21; Lev. 7:8;
19:3; Num. 9:6; see Knierim and Coats 2005: 291; Eichler 2021:
323).

Three Hebrew roots form duplications of verb plus noun ('vow
a vow'; 'oath an oath'; 'bind a bond') in typical Hebrew style.
Baruch Levine rigidly differentiates each term to emphasize the
peculiar historical meaning of a 'binding agreement' (*'issār*) as
a contractual document, sometimes associated with a covenant
(Levine 2000: 427–430). The formal aspect of this agreement
makes it appropriate for more important negotiations, such as
property transfer, which is relevant for the discussion below.
However, the text uses the terms as complementary rather than
distinctive, as interpreted in the Damascus Document of the
Qumran community (Schiffman 1991: 201). The oral, rather than
written, character of the vow or oath is emphasized. The current
verse presents the expression *all that proceeds out of his mouth*, and
variations of it appear throughout this chapter (vv. 6, 8, 12), as well
as a constant use of the verbs 'hear' (*š-m-*ʿ) and 'keep silent' (*ḥ-r-š*).

The profound and serious religious feature of vows is affirmed
by taking Yahweh as the one to whom a vow is made, and by
classifying the failure to fulfil it as profanation (*ḥ-l-l*). Profanation
is the use of a sanctified or consecrated (*q-d-š*) item for common
and personal use (Lev. 19:7–8). A vow establishes an obligation to
Yahweh that will be fulfilled at the sanctuary in the form of an

offering, a dedication of a valuable item to the divine realm for religious use by the community (Achenbach 2003: 612–613). What has been vowed is already considered God's property to be offered at the sanctuary for the benefit of the community even before it is actually delivered. Not fulfilling the vow means that the goods are used for personal benefit and become profaned, that is, put to common use. Unlike Leviticus 27, Numbers 30 does not present the option of redeeming a consecrated item (see Lev. 27:15).

ii. Vows made by women (30:3–16)

a. A young woman who vows while living in her father's house (30:3–5)

3–5. The first subcase is of a woman who still lives in her father's house. The combination of the two qualifications *within her father's house* and *in her youth* points to unmarried women under the authority of the social unit called the 'father's house', at the age at which a man takes responsibility for his own acts (see Cocco 2020b: 190). The first subcase offers a simple criterion for the validity of an unmarried woman's vow: it is valid if her father keeps silent about it on the day he hears of it, and it is not valid if her father objects on the day he hears it. The text assumes that the responsibility to fulfil such serious vows ultimately falls not on the daughter but on the father, who holds ownership of the house's goods (Frevel 2020: 369). A protective aspect of the instructions appears in the conclusion. If her father objects to her vow, Yahweh will forgive her. She will not bear any guilt for profanation.

Of special interest is the use of the term that defines the vow as 'standing' (*q-w-m*). It is a priestly term for evaluations of goods in relation to the Year of Jubilee and vows in Leviticus 27. The value established by the priests 'stands' (*q-w-m*, Lev. 27:14, 17), just as the unmarried woman's vow 'stands' if her father does not object. One possible vow is the consecration of ancestral property (Lev. 27:14–24) or, more specifically, the usufruct of the land or its produce, which is exclusively offered to the sanctuary (Milgrom 2001: 2382). After the Year of Jubilee, the land and its produce return to their household owners, or they can become the permanent property of the sanctuary and the priests (Lev. 27:21). Such a connection reinforces the notion that the vows envisaged in Numbers 30 are related to ancestral property, especially land.

b. A woman with a pre-existing vow who gets married (30:6–8)

6–8. The second subcase is a logical sequence of the first one. A woman makes a vow while single and then gets married. This is characterized by the first expression in verse 6, literally, 'if she becomes to a man', which is an idiom for getting married (Lev. 22:12; Deut. 24:2). With the term *thoughtless* [or 'rash'] *utterance* (*mibṭāʾ*), the text recognizes that she did not anticipate marriage and the implications of her vow therein. The same criterion for validity or invalidity of the previous subcase applies here (vv. 7–8). The ambiguous position of the daughter and the husband in relation to the father in this subcase is reflected by the use of two verbs that are otherwise specific for the daughter–father and the husband–wife relationship for the other subcases (see Cocco 2020b: 197–200). Here, the husband not only opposes (*n-w-ʾ*) her vow, as a father does (v. 5), but he annuls it (*p-r-r*) (vv. 12, 13, 15). The case of Zelophehad's daughters in Numbers 36 concerns what would happen to their ancestral inheritance when they married, a similar scenario to this subcase.

c. Vows made by a widow or a divorcee (30:9)

9. The third subcase addresses vows made by women who are not under male authority: widows and divorcees. Their vows are always binding, following the logic of the general rule presented in verse 2.

d. Vows of married women (30:10–12)

10–12. This fourth subcase could be understood as referring only to widows and divorcees living in their deceased or ex-husbands' houses (Schiffman 1991: 211–212). In the Temple Scroll (11Q19 LIV), the subcase of the widows and divorcees is moved to the end of the section dealing with vows to avoid any misunderstanding. The progression of the subcases here leads to the most common of the cases, that of the married woman (Ashley 2022: 478). The same criterion for validity or invalidity of the first subcase of an unmarried woman living in her father's house applies here, with the husband as equivalent to the father, but annulling (*p-r-r*) the vow rather than opposing it (*n-w-ʾ*).

e. Reformulation of the main point of the divine instruction for vows made by women (30:13–15)

13–15. A final summary of the criterion for the four subcases is presented with some variations in terminology. Two variations are noteworthy. The vow is described not merely as binding upon oneself (*nepeš*), but as 'to afflict oneself' (*lĕʿannōt nāpeš*). The significance of the expression is omitted, as is the case in 29:7. Some biblical texts associate similar expressions with fasting (Isa. 58:3, 5; Ezra 8:21) and other forms of contrition (Ps. 35:13). The use of this exact expression, however, associates these vow instructions with the Day of Atonement (Lev. 16:29, 31; 23:27, 32). In later Jewish traditions, the requirement to afflict oneself on the Day of Atonement was mainly about fasting and resting, but other forms of abstention, such as from sexual intimacy, were also considered part of the expression's meaning (see m. Yoma 8:1; m. Taʾanit 1; Stökl 2003: 34–37). Even if these practices were important, the purpose of associating these instructions on vows with the Day of Atonement was to integrate them into the total consecration required for this day, and it qualifies the types of vows envisioned in these instructions. As mentioned in the *Context*, these vows would be fulfilled at a cultic festival, and now a specific association with the Day of Atonement arises. Because the Day of Atonement marks the beginning of the Year of Jubilee (Lev. 25:8–10), the use of this specific expression supports the argument that the kinds of vows envisioned in Numbers 30 are intrinsically related to ancestral inheritance and land property with implications for the Year of Jubilee.

The second variation is the use of the expression 'bear her sin' (*wĕnāśāʾ ʾet-ʿăwōnâ*). This is an important Priestly concept that deals with the guilt of sinful actions (e.g. Exod. 28:43; Lev. 5:1; 7:18; 19:17; 24:15; Num. 5:31; 9:13; 14:33–34; 15:30–31; 18:1, 22, 23, 32). It works as a metaphor in which sin is considered a burden. If the person who commits the sin bears it, then they suffer its consequences. If another person bears it, the expression is equivalent to the former person being forgiven (Schwartz 1995: 8). This accords with the use of the expression as a variation of the conclusion for the other subcases in which the woman is forgiven by Yahweh. In this case, the third-person masculine singular who bears the sin is none other than God (Eichler 2021: 323–324). In the Priestly theology, the expression does not merely connote the forgiveness of the guilty party, but it also indicates the removal of the sinful action from the sanctuary, specifically on the Day of Atonement (Schwartz 1995: 16–17). As part of the complex system of rituals, the living goat 'bears . . . all their sins' (*wĕnāśāʾ . . . et-kol-ʿăwōnōtām*, Lev. 16:22, AT). As with the first expression, this variation not only qualifies what was previously said – that Yahweh will forgive her – but also connects these specific vows with the Day of Atonement.

The connection with the Day of Atonement and the Year of Jubilee is relevant for Zelophehad's daughters. This is made explicit by the leaders of Gilead (36:1–4), who show concern for what might happen to their tribe's land portions in the Year of Jubilee should these women marry outside their tribe.

f. Conclusion for vows made by women (30:16)

16. As a conclusion, this verse omits the general rule and the third subcase on widows and divorcees. It becomes clear that the main concern of these instructions on vows is to promote order and the stability of the household and its goods by regulating the relationship between husbands and wives, and unmarried women with their fathers while in their houses (see Pressler 2017: 265).

Meaning

Not long ago, single women in the USA were still required to have a man's signature to secure their own mortgages (S. Davis 2016: 30). In Brazil, the former Civil Law from 1916, in effect until 2002, prohibited a married woman from accepting or rejecting her own inheritance without her husband's legal approval. Unfortunately, the instructions on women's vows in Numbers 30 bear some resemblance to these problematic modern legal practices. One should not evaluate this from the perspective of a Western ideal of individual autonomy. The ancient Israelite sense of identity, for all, was collective. Identity was understood from the perspective of one's role as a member of the group. Most ancient Israelite women may not have striven for a life independent of male figures because life was harsh for women in such positions (see Ruth and Naomi's case). But their cooperative work and status in ancient Israel are more important than the contemporary view of biblical womanhood and manhood is willing to admit (see Meyers 1983; 2014). Nonetheless, Numbers 30 builds on a patriarchal order to address situations of possible conflict within it. This asymmetry of rights and elevation of male authority should be recognized (see Meyers 2013: 201; Pressler 2017: 272) and placed in conversation with other biblical texts that elevate women's authority over goods (such as the cases of Ruth and Hannah in the OT, or Mary and the poor widow in the NT). Such steps allow one to appreciate more positive aspects in the biblical text.

As shown above, Numbers 30 also assumes women's right to make use of household goods and property in their relationship with God, and it protects women from any religious guilt in cases when a male authority figure in the household might restrict her faith commitment. According to one Qumranic interpretive tradition of Numbers 30, the annulment of a vow by the husband or father was his obligation only in case the fulfilment of the vow would lead to a violation of the covenant and the Torah (Damascus Document XVI, 10–12). From this perspective, the content of the vows in Numbers 30 would not require male intervention because they are extraordinary forms of Torah observation.

The biblical text itself invites, or even demands, innovative inter-pretation that should end up eliminating the gender asymmetry assumed in the text and promoting gender reciprocity. Numbers 30, together with Numbers 27 and 36, works with a dynamic of expanding and constraining female rights in constant revision and innovation of the Torah as Israel prepares to enter the Promised Land. As argued by Leveen, in this final section of Numbers, legal adaptation is crucial to its message for establishing precedents for how Israel will engage with the Torah in the constant formation of its identity in changing circumstances (Leveen 2008: 172–174; cf. Douglas 2001: 160–171). Considering the precedent presented in Numbers 30, some possibilities of following its logic in new situations emerge.

There are at least three parties entangled in the instructions concerning vows made by most women: a woman, a male figure and God. When the male figure restricts the woman's vows, it is God who ultimately abdicates from receiving what is God's rightful possession, the goods and property vowed to the sanctuary for the benefit of the woman, her family and the community. God bears the loss to preserve the family's well-being. This is a similar argument to Jesus' critique of a tradition of property consecration as a vow. A son consecrates to God his ancestral possessions, offering them to the Temple as *qorbān*, which impedes their use for helping his parents when they are in need. In this case, God should take the loss for the well-being of the family. But the *qorbān* tradition gave occasion to the violation of the Torah for the benefit of the temple and its staff to the detriment of the family's well-being (Mark 7:9-13; par. Matt. 15:3-6).

God sets a precedent and a model for how to manage conflict when changing circumstances, here especially related to the expansion of a woman's rights, demand that God's people engage innovatively with their own identity and faith commitments. This model creates more room for reciprocal relationships between genders in families and in society, promoting a more symmetrical marital dynamic in which shared decisions and responsibilities prevail over power negotiation in which only one party, typically the man, has the final word.

F. War against the Midianites (31:1-54)

Context
After a long hiatus into legal regulations, the narrative thread picks up here on the events from 25:17-18, where Yahweh commanded Moses to strike the Midianites because of their deception that led to Israel's oppression. Between chapter 25 and chapter 31, a complete change in Israel's generations has occurred (ch. 26). The new generation does not intermingle with the Midianites as the first generation did in chapter 25. However, it comes as a surprise (addressed even by Calvin and the medieval Jewish commentator

Rashi) that *only* the Midianites and *not* the Moabites – who hired Balaam along with them (22:2–4) – experience God's vengeance. The punishment of the Midianites is also surprising in that Moses found refuge with a Midianite priest and married a Midianite (Exod. 2:11–22), and Moses petitions his Midianite relative to guide and accompany the Israelites to the Promised Land in 10:29–32.

Two other factors determine the context of chapter 31: the mention of Moses' impending death in verse 1 (cf. 27:13), and the location of the Israelite camp on the plains of Moab by the Jordan at Jericho in verse 12.

The chapter begins with the preparation for battle as part of a divinely ordained war, and the battle and destruction of Midian (vv. 1–12). More central in this recounting is the question of what to do with adult female and boy captives and how to purify the plunder (vv. 13–24). This gives way to a detailed accounting and regulation for dividing up the plunder between those who fought in the battle and the rest of the Israelites (vv. 25–47). The final section (vv. 48–54) reports an additional offering to Yahweh by the officers who led the attack.

Comparison with several other scriptures illuminates this chapter: 1 Samuel 30, where David enacts a similar rule for dividing the spoil; Judges 7 – 8, which narrates Gideon leading a small troop to defeat the Midianites; Deuteronomy 20:10–18, which sets out ordinances for taking the spoils of war and destruction of idolatrous cities; and Numbers 19, which describes the ritual through which those who have touched a dead corpse can become clean. Comparison with the disastrous events of Judges 21 may also cast a negative light on Moses' commands (see vv. 17–18 below). Finally, a reference to the same battle also appears in Joshua 13:21–22.

Comment

i. Preparations for war (31:1–6)

1–2. The opening verses indicate that this war was fought in response to Yahweh's command, not the Israelites' will (cf. Exod. 17; Josh. 6:17, 21; often part of the practice of *ḥerem*, 'devote to destruction', as found in 21:2–3).

3–6. Yahweh commands Moses to select a surprisingly small army for this battle: twelve thousand in total, one thousand from each tribe. While no comment appears, the command is like that of Judges 7, where Gideon selects a small force at God's behest to fight against the Midianites so that the Israelites cannot take credit for the victory (Judg. 7:2).

The command for Phinehas, son of the high priest Eleazar, to bring sacred vessels and the signal trumpets (cf. 10:9) indicates the religious character of this battle in the light of Phinehas's violent action in chapter 25, providing further support for Yahweh's initiative in the matter. Commentators disagree about whether these sacred vessels necessarily included the ark in order to provide a contrast to 14:44 (see E. W. Davies 1995b: 323; Ashley 2022: 485), but verse 6 does not make this explicit. In any case, as in Deuteronomy 20:2, a priest accompanies the army, but no speeches like those in Deuteronomy 20 take place.

ii. Victory over the Midianites (31:7–12)

7. The declaration that the army does as Yahweh commanded and kills *every* man draws on a frequent trope for reporting military victory throughout the Ancient Near East (Younger 1990). This literary hyperbole may preclude the need to posit that there were various groups of Midianites, and the Israelites here only attack one of them (contra Wenham 1981: 209).

8–12. According to 24:25, Balaam had returned home. Here in verse 8 he reappears among the Midianites (see also Josh. 13:21–22). The effect of including Balaam here goes against the tradition in chapters 22–24 that provides a positive transformation of his character. This reappearance of Balaam builds on the association of Balaam with Edom (see commentary on 22:21–35), especially how the sword marks Edom's life (Gen. 27:40). While the angel had spared Balaam in 22:34, the sword of God – now placed in the hands of the Israelites – strikes him down this time.

A favoured explanation for the conflation of the Midianites with the Moabites in this chapter and in chapter 25 comes to light in verse 10, with the mention especially of *their encampments* (*ṭîrōtām*), a relatively rare term (only 7 times in the OT), which in Ezekiel 25:4 designates places where nomadic groups dwell.

Thus, given the characterization of the Midianites as nomadic, they could have come to dwell *in* Moab (cf. Ezek. 25:10), around Moabite towns, which also provides an interpretation for the expression 'daughters of Moab' in 25:1 (see commentary on 25:6–18). Because this prophecy against Moab appears in Ezekiel, a prophetic book arising no earlier than the exilic period (sixth century BC), attempts have been made to explain the names of the Midian kings in verse 8 (who also appear in Josh. 13:21–22, but not as kings) as coming from the sixth or later centuries (Achenbach 2003: 617; Frevel 2020: 219–221).

iii. Treatment of Midianite women and purification of soldiers (31:13–24)

This section addresses a second, interwoven set of obstacles in the chapter that have to do with the purification of the fighters and their plunder, and the problem with letting the non-virginal women remain alive. These concerns respond to the ordinances from chapter 19 (purification after contact with human corpses) and, according to verses 14–16, retribution against the Midianite women responsible for corrupting Israelite men in chapter 25, likely through a reconciliation with Deuteronomy 20:10–18.

13. Moses and the other leaders meet the returning army *outside* the camp in order to maintain the purity of God's camp (cf. 5:2), which comes as a surprise after verse 12 stated that they 'brought the captives, spoils and plunder to Moses and Eleazar the priest and the Israelite assembly *at their camp*' (NIV; emphasis added). English translations obscure the Hebrew, which reads 'to the camp' (using the same preposition as 'to Moses'). The reason for meeting outside becomes clear in verses 19–24, namely that the warriors and plunder must first go through various purification processes. In other words, even killing at *God's command* brings about impurity.

14–16. These verses recall the events of chapter 25, though from a different perspective in which the Midianite women seduced Israelite men to join with them in sexual trysts and offer feasts dedicated to foreign deities *on Balaam's advice* (v. 16). Here, as in chapter 22 (but in strong contrast to chs. 23–24), Balaam appears in a more negative light. His death aligns with the prohibition on sorcery (*q-s-m*) in Deuteronomy (cf. Deut. 18:10), although this term is used differently in chapters 22–24.

Upon the army's return, Moses does not praise God for the victory, but rather becomes angry with the army's leaders for allowing the Midianite women to live. According to Deuteronomy 20, the Israelites should treat enemies far away differently from those in the land: they could take as plunder the women, children, livestock and other goods from faraway lands, but they should destroy everything belonging to enemies in the land Yahweh promised so that they would not be led into idolatry. The situation here, with the Midianites, presents a conundrum: the Midianites do not occupy Israel's Promised Land, but they have already caused the Israelites to worship other deities.

17–18. Moses' response, killing all boys and non-virginal women and girls, seeks to maintain the separateness of the Israelites. This command draws closer to the regulations for peoples *in* the land, but leaving virgin women and girls and allowing for the Israelites to take plunder of other goods is a compromise between the two. However, the only other situation in which all men, male children, and non-virginal women and girls are killed appears in Judges 21:10–12. That chapter describes a horrific series of events in Israel's history, thus casting a pall over the events here. In Judges the tragic events do lead to the avoidance of the complete eradication of the Benjaminites; in this case, it should, however, have that result for the Midianites. The *lack* of divine involvement in this command leaves a gap for critique of Moses' order (K. Brown 2015), as does any indication that the Israelites carry out Moses' command. (One can also note the further appearances of the Midianites as a strong foe in Judg. 6 – 7.)

19–24. The command in verses 19 and 24 for the troops returning from battle to camp outside the main camp aligns with the requirements of 5:2–3 and chapter 19 for purification from contact with a human corpse. This is also the same for plunder of cloth, skins and wood (vv. 20, 23), which all together follow 19:11–21. This report comes as a surprise given the *lack* of mention of such a purification process for the Israelites after battles in 21:1–3, 21–35 (battles against the Canaanites and Amorites) or in chapter 25.

It is striking in verse 21 that Eleazar the priest rather than Moses declares Yahweh's ordinance for the purification of metals, though it is attributed to *the statute of the law that [Yahweh] has commanded Moses*. This deviation, coming at the end of Moses' life, provides an insight into the way that the instructions given to Moses should be applied after Moses' ensuing death, referenced in verse 2. Furthermore, the command to purify the metals with fire (v. 23) does not appear anywhere else for such plunder in the biblical tradition, so Eleazar's instruction shows how innovation is intrinsic to biblical law. Such action recalls Moses' directive to Aaron in Leviticus 10:10–11 (cf. Deut. 17:8–13) to discern between clean and unclean and 'to teach the people of Israel all the statutes that the LORD has spoken to them through Moses'.

iv. Treatment of plunder (31:25–47)

25–47. This section describes in detail the allocation of the plunder, given the special compromise situation outlined above. The amount of plunder taken is staggering, and, along with the miraculous lack of *any* Israelite casualties (v. 49; see below for discussion), suggests hyperbole, as noted above is often the case in Ancient Near Eastern reports of military victories (such as in the Mesha Inscription from Israel's ninth-century neighbour Moab). There were only twelve thousand Israelite fighters who, according to verses 32–35, took around 800,000 animals in total. If one can deduce that there were as many Midianite fighters as girls who had not had sexual relations with a man, that would total 32,000 Midianite fighters whom the Israelites killed. Tallies of spoils are found in, for example, the Neo-Assyrian ruler Tiglath-Pileser's Summary Inscription 4 (*COS* 2.117C) for animals and people from Arabia, the Annals of Sargon II (*COS* 2.118A) or reports of Sennacherib's campaigns (*COS* 2.119). These kings date to the ninth to eighth centuries BC. Such lists also appear in Egyptian inscriptions of Thutmose III (e.g. *COS* 2.2A) from the fifteenth century BC.

The spoils are divided in half, with one half going to those who fought, and the other half going to the rest of the (non-Levite) Israelites (v. 27). In this regard the ruling mirrors the one made by David for his troops in 1 Samuel 30:20–25. However, in Numbers

31 special provisions are made for the priests and Levites – in other words, for those set aside to do the work at God's sanctuary. A portion – a tax of 0.2% – was given by the fighting men to the *priests*, while the half given to the Israelites was subject to a 2% tax given to the *Levites*. Thus, those who fought received a far larger portion of the plunder per person than the rest of the community (contrary to David's ruling in 1 Sam. 30).

According to verses 36–40, each combatant received approximately twenty-eight sheep and goats, three head of cattle, two or three donkeys, and one woman or girl.

v. Soldiers' voluntary offering of plundered jewellery for their atonement (31:48–54)

48–54. This section narrates the contribution of gold jewellery by the army officers as an elevation offering that is intended to ransom their lives, though it remains unclear exactly why this is needed. It could come as an acknowledgment that the counting of the men in the army was a tenuous action (cf. Exod. 30:12; 2 Sam. 24), always endangering those who do it because one might begin to trust in one's own strength, rather than in Yahweh's provision.

The mention of no loss of Israelite lives in the battle in verse 49 takes on extra significance in that it contrasts with the deaths of the entire exodus generation in the wilderness, as proclaimed by God in 14:29–31. A declaration of no loss of life to a fearful enemy is a hyperbolic trope also appearing in Neo-Assyrian texts (*COS* 2.115B, Ninurta-Kudirrī-uṣur–Suḫu Annals #2, col. 2) and points to Yahweh's ability to protect the Israelites, even on the battlefield.

The awkward verse 53 may indicate that the individual troops had participated in this offering, perhaps by giving from their plunder to the officers, who then passed on the gold to Moses and Eleazar in verse 51. On the other hand, it may underscore the largesse of the officers, if the others do not give anything.

A similar gift of jewellery after the defeat of the Midianites appears in the Gideon story in Judges 8:24–27, and in that case some kind of worship object, an ephod, is made from the gold. Numbers 31 does not state what becomes of the offered gold, though its purpose, as a memorial of/for the Israelites before God, might indicate some use in the tabernacle as with the censers that were turned into an altar plating in 16:36–40. This contrasts with the offering in Judges, which leads the Israelites away from Yahweh. Leaders often gifted precious metals to temples after military victories in antiquity, so this act fits cultural expectations. The lack of a designated leader for this battle, however, means that the group of commanders are the ones who bring it. The commanders give a considerable amount: 16,750 shekels of *gold* compared with the ½ shekel of *silver* per person for the census in Exodus 30:12–16, which would call for only six thousand shekels in the case of Numbers 31 for the twelve thousand combatants (for the modern equivalent of a shekel, see commentary on 3:44–51).

Meaning

God's call to Israel to avenge the Midianites – along with various other texts in the Old Testament that mandate and narrate divine calls to battle (e.g. Deut. 7:2–5; Josh. 2 – 12), and especially to drive out (*g-r-š*), devote to destruction (*ḥ-r-m*) or destroy (*š-m-d*) another people, while also enslaving those who surrender (Deut. 20:10–11) and taking women and children as booty (Deut. 20:14) – contrasts markedly with other commandments in the Old Testament to love and welcome the stranger, as well as with Jesus' call to be peacemakers (Matt. 5:9). In response, how should people of faith respond to Numbers 31, as one example of such a scriptural text?

One can first recognize the impulses that come to the fore in such commands. According to verse 2, the killing takes place to redress a prior harm against Israel that led to worship of other deities. Both the impulse to redress wrongs and the impulse to avoid foreign worship require little substantiation. Rather, it is the *means* by which humans act towards such ends that raise critique.

Furthermore, the literary language takes up the hyperbolic rhetoric found in narratives of military campaigns from throughout the Ancient Near East, which serve to magnify the superiority of the victor – in this case, Yahweh. Also, Joshua 13 – 23 indicates – despite the praise Joshua receives for the military victories in, for example, Joshua 10 – 11 – that the use of the language of the killing of 'all' (men/people) is not meant literally. To miss the rhetorical function of this language and these biblical texts is to miss their point, which is not about the killing and destruction of others, but the assertion of Yahweh's power to protect the life and identity of Yahweh's ethnically and culturally diverse people, even in its formation here in the Pentateuch, in the face of various threats. (For a further possibility, see the *Meaning* section for Num. 36.) The rescue of Rahab and demise of Achan, for example, underscore the primary importance of acclaiming Yahweh's superiority and trust in Yahweh's provision for making one an 'Israelite', rather than ethnic origin (see Num. 26; note also Moses' *Midianite* father-in-law in Exod. 18:9–12 and his *Midianite* wife in Exod. 4:24–26).

Lastly, these battles are first *God's*, not the Israelites', and they are primarily *God's* to fight by the means that God chooses. All war in the Bible comes in response to sin, especially oppression of the weak. God chooses to become involved in Israel's own predicaments, even when they concern violence, showing God's concern for all spheres of human reality (Chapman 2013). Christ comes as the Prince of Peace – a martyr rather than a warrior in his life on earth, though his depiction in Revelation (19:11–16) includes warlike imagery.

G. Transjordan and the unity of the tribes (32:1–42)

Context

Israel's conquest of Transjordan in chapter 21 functions as a boost of hope for the new generation who have just seen the ultimate failure of the exodus generation in the person of their great leaders, Moses and Aaron (20:1–13). But what was once the reason for hope for Israel's future becomes a serious threat to it in chapter 32. The request by several tribes to settle in Transjordan and not cross the Jordan to Canaan is interpreted by Moses (vv. 7–15) as a rebellion akin to the doubting of Yahweh's promises in chapters 13–14. Is the settling generation repeating their ancestors' failure to enter Canaan?

In the dialogical negotiation between Moses and Israel's leaders and the Gadites and Reubenites, their anxiety concerning Israel's unity emerges, for the Jordan River works as a hard border to the east of the Promised Land (34:11–12; cf. Gen. 15:18–21; Exod. 23:31; Deut. 32:49; Josh. 1:4). A common territory can serve as a defining factor for a common identity (see Gen. 10:5, 20, 31; McEntire and Park 2021: 35). Numbers 32 addresses how to maintain this unity with a divided territory that includes portions not previously promised by Yahweh.

In Deuteronomy 3:12–20, recording the same episode and issue, the question of Israel's unity is solved by the sole initiative of Moses, who is said to give these territories to the Israelite tribes and impose their responsibility to help the other tribes settle in Canaan. Here, the fear of fracture and rupture is solved by a dialogical process to discern the divine will for new circumstances. A proposal viewed initially as a rejection of Yahweh's promises opens into new possibilities of being God's people. Israel's unity is affirmed by appealing to kinship language (v. 6), committing to a shared destiny (vv. 17–18), submitting to Moses and Israel's leaders (v. 25; cf. vv. 27, 31), and following after Yahweh (vv. 11, 12, 15) to be in the divine presence (vv. 20, 21, 22, 27, 29, 32).

Historically, Israelite presence in Transjordan is not so different from what we know about its presence in Canaan. However, political disputes over this area among Israel, Moab and Aram (Syria) in the ninth and eighth centuries are attested and raise the question of a cohesive identity of its population (see J. Davis 2022: 84–114). Relevant information appears on the ninth-century Mesha Stele from a Moabite king, and the biblical narratives of Samuel and Kings (see 1 Sam. 11; 13:7; 1 Kgs 19:15; 2 Kgs 3; 8:7–15; 9:14–15; 10:32–33). This political reality lies behind the theological disputes, of which Joshua 22, together with Numbers 32, represent the most important witness. Although polemical, both texts affirm that Transjordan might be part of Israelite identity (see Introduction, 'Israel's identity and its neighbours'). The theological debate concerns the commitment of people in Transjordan to Yahweh's covenant.

Comment
i. Reuben, Gad and half of Manasseh's request to settle in Transjordan (32:1–5)

1. This verse sets the scene. It refers to Reubenites and Gadites, following their birth order (cf. Deut. 3:12, 16). The rest of the chapter consistently (7 times) puts Gad first (vv. 2, 6, 25, 29,

31, 33, 34/37), attesting to Gad's political activity in the region witnessed by the Mesha Stele (line 10, *COS* 2.137). The specific geographical area defined as *the land of Jazer and the land of Gilead* is not completely clear. However, the construction 'the land of X' must be a reference to the land around cities (v. 33). *Jazer* is known as a city with surrounding villages from 21:32. *Gilead* is used as a reference to a large region in verses 26 and 29, even as a referent for the whole Transjordan (vv. 39–40; Deut. 3:12–13; Josh. 22:9), and also as a Manassite clan eponym (Num. 26:29–30; 27:1; 36:1).

2–5. In a similar depiction to 27:1–2 and 36:1, the Gadites and Reubenites come to Moses, Eleazar and the Israelite leaders to make a request that will require some negotiation and discernment. Even more than in the other cases, this scene is characterized by courtly terms: *your servants* (*ʿăbādêkā*, vv. 4, 5, 25, 27, 31; cf. 31:48–49) and *if we have found favour in your sight* (v. 5; cf. Esth. 7:3).

They request that certain lands in Transjordan be given to them as a possession by Israel's leadership so they will not cross the Jordan (v. 5). Israel already settled in Transjordan in 21:25, 31, but now the Gadites and Reubenites want it as a permanent holding (*ʾăḥuzzâ*). To be given a land from the Israelite leaders as *a possession* is to receive it as an inheritance of the Promised Land from Yahweh (27:4, 7; 33:53; cf. 26:54; 34:13).

The land given by Yahweh so far contrasts with the land 'struck' (*n-k-h*) by Yahweh, a reference to the kingdoms of Sihon and Og in 21:24, 35. The Gadites and Reubenites specify this land by listing nine cities, all in central Transjordan, near Heshbon, between the Jabbok and the Arnon rivers (Levine 2000: 485; see the map in J. Davis 2022: 153). *Heshbon* was said to be Sihon's capital (21:26) and *Jazer* is mentioned among Heshbon and Dibon (21:32). Some of the cities listed here are targeted in prophetic judgments against Moab (see Isa. 15:2, 4; 16:8–13; Jer. 48:1, 22–23, 32–34; Ezek. 25:9). In the Mesha Stele, *Dibon* is King Mesha's city (lines 1–2, *COS* 2.137), *Nebo* is said to be conquered from the Israelites (line 14, *COS* 2.138) and Baal-meon (here, *Beon*, see v. 38) is a city fortified by Mesha (line 9, *COS* 2.137). With this geographical disposition, it is possible to understand the division between Gilead and Jazer in verse 1 to be referring to larger areas. *Jazer* might stand for the region around Heshbon, between the Jabbok and the Arnon, and *Gilead* to the region above the Jabbok (J. Davis 2022: 100). However, the qualification of 'the land of X' in verse 1 remains relevant because it designates the land around the cities where cattle and flock could be tended, which is the reasoning of the Gadites and Reubenites when choosing this land (v. 4).

ii. Moses reprimands the request (32:6–15)

6–15. Moses is right to interpret their request as a rebellion because they conclude with a desire not to cross the Jordan (v. 5). The crossing of the Jordan was a movement required for Israel to settle in Canaan, so it becomes an event marking Yahweh's gift of the Promised Land (v. 7; Deut. 32:47; 34:4; Josh. 1:2, 11, 15; 3 – 4). For this reason, crossing ('*-b-r*) the Jordan, repeated seven times through the chapter (vv. 5, 7, 27, 29, 30, 32), will be definitive to establish the legitimacy of the Gadites and Reubenites as true Israelites living in Transjordan.

Moses accuses the Gadites and Reubenites of following the rebellious pattern of their parents. They stand in their place as a 'sinful breed' (v. 14, AT). This unique expression bears the double meaning of a sinful generation that multiplies (procreates) sinful acts. Moses recalls the events of Numbers 13 – 14 and describes them as a discouragement from entering the land that Yahweh gave them (v. 9) and provoking Yahweh's anger (vv. 10, 13–14). What happened then was evil in Yahweh's eyes, which contrasts with the appeal of the Gadites and Reubenites to find 'favour in the eyes' of Moses (v. 5, AT). Moses fears that the settling generation will repeat the same mistakes of not considering the goodness of the land as Yahweh's gift and will increase the anger of Yahweh (v. 14), who will abandon Israel in the wilderness, which will destroy Israel for ever (v. 15). The Gadites and Reubenites would then be guilty of the destruction of Israel, qualified as corruption (*š-ḥ-t*), implying the breaking of the covenant as in Exodus 32:7, an event that lies behind Numbers 13 – 14.

Moses' speech includes important elements that illuminate the rest of the chapter. Crossing the Jordan will be emphasized as a criterion to mark Israel's identity and faithfulness to Yahweh's covenant. Kinship responsibility is used by Moses as the basis for his argument (v. 6), so the question is whether the Gadites and Reubenites will act as *brothers* to the other tribes. The verb 'to discourage' (*n-w-ʾ*, v. 7) appeared in chapter 30 for the possibility of fathers and husbands opposing a woman's vow (30:5, 8, 11). This fits well with the correspondence between kinship and shared land implied in the negotiation happening in the current chapter. Not surprisingly, then, Moses speaks of an oath made by Yahweh to give Canaan to the patriarchs (v. 11). Only here and in 14:16, 23 does Yahweh make an oath concerning the Promised Land. Also important in verse 11 is the use of the term 'ground' (*ʾădāmâ*) to define the Promised Land, eliminating the territorial limitations that the term 'the land' (*hāʾāreṣ*, v. 9) carries (cf. Gen. 12:3). Lastly, loyalty to or rebellion against Yahweh is defined as 'following after me' or not (vv. 11, 12). This expression was used about Caleb and Joshua's commitment to Yahweh in 14:24, in contrast to the rebellion of the other Israelites, hence their mention in verse 12 (cf. Deut. 1:36). This is a contrast to the accusation in verse 14 that the Gadites and Reubenites are following in the footsteps of their parents, so to speak, when they should follow after Yahweh.

iii. Explaining the intention of the request and their commitment to unity (32:16–19)

16–19. The Gadites and Reubenites already have 'come to' Israel's leaders (v. 2), but after Moses' reply they 'approach' him (AT). The verb *n-g-š* reinforces the courtly context (1 Kgs 20:13), even as a divine court (Isa. 41:1, 21; 50:8; cf. Num. 4:19; 8:19). The scene might be characterized as the establishment of the terms of a binding agreement (see Ashley 2022: 500). Like their parents (14:3), the Gadites and Reubenites show concern for their little children. They want to fortify the towns Israel has conquered in Transjordan to protect their families from the inhabitants of the land. Those towns, therefore, were not completely destroyed and neither were their inhabitants (see Josh. 13:13).

Unlike their parents, however, they make a strong and important commitment to Yahweh, represented by Israel's leaders. They will not only join Israel in battle, they will go 'before Israel' (v. 17, AT). Their reasoning for such commitment is based on Moses' rhetorical question regarding kinship responsibilities (v. 6). They

will make the other Israelites 'enter their place' (v. 17, AT) and
won't go back to their houses until every Israelite receives their
inheritance (v. 18). Their destinies, then, are shared and intertwined, creating the notion of unity (Leveen 2017: 48). By leaving
their little children behind in solidarity with Israel, the Gadites
and Reubenites risk the future of their tribes for the benefit of
Israel's future. This is a clear sign of their identity as God's people.
The willingness to risk their lives for the benefit of the group is
one of the strongest expressions of communal identity, what Jacob
Wright classifies as 'performing peoplehood' (J. L. Wright 2020:
78), which is typical of international politics in the Ancient Near
East (see 1 Kgs 22).

iv. Moses' proposal of a covenant (32:20–24)

20–24. Moses' reply is constructed conditionally with positive
(vv. 20–22) and negative (vv. 23–24) outcomes resulting from the
terms established by the Gadites and Reubenites. This structure
is modelled on covenantal agreements found in biblical traditions with blessings and curses (Lev. 26; Deut. 27 – 28). This is
confirmed by the important expression 'according to what came
out of your mouth' (v. 24, lit.; cf. 'according to this word' in v. 20)
found in the context of oath-making (30:3).

Moses turns the whole binding agreement into part of a
covenant with Yahweh. What was said to be done 'before Israel'
(v. 17) is now repeatedly said to be done 'before Yahweh' (vv.
20, 21, 22). Even more, fulfilling their commitment renders
the Gadites and Reubenites free from any obligations towards
Yahweh and Israel (v. 22), an expression depicting the fulfilment
of the terms of an oath (2 Sam. 3:28). Their failure to fulfil their
commitment, meanwhile, would be considered a sin against
Yahweh (v. 23). The consequence of this sin is depicted as if
their sin is personified (cf. Gen. 4:7) and will 'return' to them
in a kind of boomerang effect. Moses' terms, then, qualify this
negotiation as a covenant, but not only between the Gadites
and Reubenites and the rest of Israel, but between them and
Yahweh. The kinship responsibility and solidarity previously
emphasized by Moses and the Gadites and Reubenites, which
marks Israel's unity and identity, gains a theological aspect as

finding its foundation in the covenantal relationship between Israel and Yahweh.

v. Agreement with the terms of the covenant and confirmation of its future validity (32:25–33)

25–27. Because Moses theologically qualifies this oath-making as a covenant, the Gadites and Reubenites must agree with the terms again. Now they use the expression 'before Yahweh' (v. 27) and not 'before Israel' (v. 17), submitting to Moses' terms, and make explicit for the first time that they will cross the Jordan (v. 27). But a more political feature emerges in the terms *your servants* and *my lord* (vv. 25, 27), which characterize this covenant as one between vassal and suzerain. This is relevant in the light of political disputes over Transjordan between Israel and Moab, especially because Mesha, the Moabite king, had a close relationship with the tribe of Gad (J. Davis 2022: 106, 155). The vassalage of Gadites and Reubenites in relationship with Israel's leaders and Yahweh (see below, vv. 31–32) is not merely a matter of language. Their initiative to spearhead Israel's battle in Canaan fits Ancient Near Eastern expectations that vassal kings would take this position in their suzerain's battles (J. L. Wright 2020: 73).

28–30. Moses gives Eleazar, Joshua and Israel's leaders the responsibility to enforce the covenant in the future. Verse 30 sets out the consequence for the Gadites and Reubenites if they fail to fulfil their part of the agreement. Most commentators understand the consequence to be that the Gadites and Reubenites would be taken with the rest of the Israelites into the land of Canaan, where they would receive their possession (e.g. Ashley 2022: 501). However, this seems out of step as a consequence of their sin against Yahweh, as affirmed in verse 23, and makes little sense in the context of international politics in the Ancient Near East. One could suggest that verses 23 and 30 do not belong in the same literary source (Feldman 2013: 411–412), but the terminology points to a better solution. The key factor is the verb '-*ḥ-z*. The root of the verb forms the noun for *possession* (*'ăḥuzzâ*), which is thematic for the chapter (vv. 5, 22, 29, 32). In verse 30, the verb is in the passive stem (*niphal*), with no explicit subject or other feature, such as an imperative form, that could denote a reflexive mode (cf. Gen. 34:10; 47:27; Josh. 22:9, 19). Two occurrences of the verb in this stem are illuminating. Genesis 22:13 and Ecclesiastes 9:12 depict animals 'caught' (*'-ḥ-z*) in a sort of trap so that they are taken as a possession to serve human needs. Therefore, a syntactical solution that fits well with the overall purpose of the chapter is to translate our verse as follows: 'If they do not cross with you, armed, they will be taken by you as a possession in the land of Canaan.' The Gadites and Reubenites hoped to receive their possession in Transjordan, a good land for their animals, but if they do not fulfil their oath and break the covenant with Yahweh and Israel, they, in a typical biblical ironic reversal, will be taken as a possession, like animals, as war spoils to Canaan to serve Israel. The Gadites' and Reubenites' relationship with Israel would follow the model of submission depicted in 25:2–3.

31–32. Again the Gadites and Reubenites agree. But they make explicit something that was implicit in their previous response in verses 25–27. The words to which they submit and will fulfil are said to be Yahweh's (v. 31) and not Moses', which would make him, implicitly, their master. Here, however, we see that it is Yahweh who should be seen as their ultimate master. To be in covenant with Yahweh means to be in covenant with the representatives and people of Yahweh, submitting to all that makes them God's people.

33. This verse does not fit easily with the previous narrative. The whole negotiation between the Gadites and Reubenites and Moses and Israel's leaders was conditional, future-oriented, and to be enforced by Eleazar, Joshua and other Israelite leaders. Here, as a conclusion to the covenant between them, Moses seems to ignore all of that and give them what they first requested. More problematic, however, is the introduction of the half-tribe of Manasseh as part of Israel who will settle in Transjordan, which is now explicitly associated with the kingdoms of Sihon and Og. It is very probable that verses 33, 39–42 formed a separate tradition, more immediately connected to the narratives in chapter 21. This close connection can be seen in Deuteronomy 2:26 – 3:22 where, right after the conquest of Sihon and Og's kingdoms, Moses gives parts of Transjordan to the Reubenites and Gadites (Deut. 3:12) and to the half-tribe of Manasseh (Deut. 3:13–15; cf. Achenbach

2003: 374–375; J. L. Wright 2020: 69–70; J. Davis 2022: 112, 180). The inclusion of verses 33–42 is important to account for the half-tribe of Manasseh and their possession in the Transjordan, as well as make an explicit connection between the conquest of Sihon and Og's kingdoms and the request made by the Gadites and Reubenites.

vi. The land given to Reubenites, Gadites and Manassites in Transjordan (32:34–42)

34–42. A list of towns built by Gadites and Reubenites, as well as towns conquered by Manassites, is presented. Verses 34–38, with the list of towns rebuilt or fortified by the Gadites and Reubenites where their small children, wives and livestock would stay, would work well as the conclusion of the negotiation between them and Moses and the Israelite leaders in verses 1–32 (see Kislev 2016: 620–621). But now, combined with the list of towns conquered by Manassites, this last part of the chapter represents a more complete picture of Israelite presence in Transjordan.

In comparison with verse 3, some towns are added while others appear with different names. *Atroth-shophan* is probably a village 'daughter' around Ataroth, while *Beth-nimrah* stands for the previously mentioned Nimrah, just as *Sibmah* stands for Sebam and *Baal-meon* for Beon. Maybe verse 3 already presents their modified names, as is recommended in verse 38. The towns that did not appear in verse 3 are *Aroer, Jogbehah, Beth-haran, Kiriathaim* and Kenath/*Nobah*. *Aroer* is near Dibon right above the Arnon River, *Jogbehah* is just north of Jazer, *Beth-haran* is by the side of Shittim in the plains of Moab and *Kiriathaim* is south-west of Nebo and is mentioned in the Mesha Stele (line 10, *COS* 2.137).

When it comes to the half-tribe of Manasseh, its location depends on information from Numbers 21 and Deuteronomy 3. The actions of Jair are associated with Og's kingdom, comprising the whole of Bashan to the border of Geshur, east of the Sea of Galilee (Deut. 3:13–14). *Kenath*, the city conquered by Nobah, appears only here and in 1 Chronicles 2:23, where it is closely associated with Jair and Geshur. Kenath appears in the Amarna Letters from the Late Bronze Age and much later becomes one of the cities in the Decapolis, some 80 km east of the Sea of Galilee (Wenham 1981: 216; Levine 2000: 498).

Israelite presence in Transjordan, according to this list, goes from Aroer and Dibon in the south, just above the Arnon River, to Kenath in the north-east, just above the Yarmuk River. The list also presents divisions between the two-and-a-half tribes. The towns rebuilt by the Reubenites in verses 37–38 are grouped at the centre, while the towns rebuilt by the Gadites in verses 34–36 enclose the Reubenites from the south and north. The half-tribe of Manasseh, then, occupies the region to the north of the Gadites. This division is less logical than the ones found in Deuteronomy 3 and Joshua 13. There the Transjordan is divided into three parts: Bashan to the north, occupied by the half-tribe of Manasseh, Mishor to the south, occupied by the Reubenites, with Gilead in the middle, occupied by the Gadites.

Apart from geographical matters, verses 39–42 present relevant information on kinship relations between Manassites and their land possessions. Machir is said to be a descendant of Manasseh, just like Jair, while Nobah's affiliation is not given, but he must be a Manassite. In 26:29–33, Manasseh has only one direct descendant, Machir, and the rest of the tribe comes from Machir's descendant, Gilead. In 1 Chronicles 2:21–22, Gilead is also a descendant of Machir, and Jair's affiliation to Machir is from his mother's side, while his patrilineal descendance comes from Caleb, now integrated into Judah. There is, as mentioned in Numbers 26:29–34, a blending of genealogy and geography, especially relevant for the tribe of Manasseh and its association with the broader region of Gilead, that can be a general reference for all the Transjordan occupied by Israelites (see Leveen 2017: 66). The Gileadite descendance of Machir, through matrilineage, fits well with the characterization of Jair's and Nobah's territory as 'daughters', farming villages around towns (v. 33) where livestock were kept (cf. v. 1). The more fragile affiliation of Transjordanian populations with Israel explains the need to integrate them through genealogical associations (26:29–33) and covenantal oath-making, as is the case in the current chapter. This also explains the anxieties of Manassite women about losing their possessions or inheritance to other tribes for lack of male heirs (ch. 27), and the same anxiety of Manassite men if their 'daughters' marry outside their tribe (ch. 36).

Meaning

What makes a people? Better, what makes God's people? Numbers 32 provides an answer addressing new circumstances when one foundational factor for that identity goes missing: living in a shared territory in fulfilment of God's promise. An important part of the answer is the sense of kinship through mutual solidarity, responsibility and a shared destiny. This, however, can be applied to any communal identity. Anthropological, psychological and neurological studies have shown that social cohesion is based on this sense of kinship (Whitehouse 2021: 89). The family-like bond is defined by the willingness of individuals to self-give in favour of the group (Whitehouse 2021: 99–101). This level of family-like social bond emerges from shared meaningful experiences, especially overcoming threatening experiences together. But such experiences can be intentionally routinized ritually and narratively to promote a shared identity (Whitehouse 2021: 106–112).

It is possible to see these elements in Numbers 32. The Gadites and Reubenites are willing to risk their lives and future for Israel. Their shared meaningful experiences are then ritually and narratively marked through an oath-making covenant and textual memorials that can be replicated in the future to promote similar meaningful experiences. More relevant to the specifics of Israel's identity is that these factors are framed with the divine presence and submission to Mosaic authority. When Israel finally prepares to cross the Jordan in Joshua 1, these three components of Israel's identity are emphasized: relationship with God, submission to Torah and kinship allegiance (Leveen 2017: 48).

Numbers 32 shows that these three elements do not have a rigid form and can be negotiated to account for new circumstances. The Transjordan context implies the possibility of detaching God's people's identity from a specific territory, as well as integrating outsiders into God's people. Such possibilities were crucial in Israel's history of negotiating its identity among different people, from its early stage when settling in Canaan to much later in the exilic and post-exilic period (Leveen 2017: 189–199; see Introduction, 'Israel's identity and its neighbours'). For Christians who do not share the same territory, language, history and lineage as ancient Israel and Judea, Numbers 32 offers a rich theological foundation for a communal identity as God's people. Through shared meaningful experiences promoted by common rituals and narratives based on biblical festivals and texts converging now around Jesus, it is possible to find a shared identity with all of God's people to the point of becoming God's family. But it also imposes openness when establishing our identity in relation to other cultures, religions or what is commonly called 'the world'. Exclusive antagonism or complete assimilation are not the only options. Dynamic negotiation based on our common humanity, shared experiences and reciprocity is not only possible, but necessary for the common well-being of all, and even to create a mature identity of God's people as family living in God's world to fulfil God's purpose for all people.

H. Mapping Israel's itinerary from Egypt to the plains of Moab (33:1–56)

Context

Notes on Israel's travel itinerary are spread throughout Exodus–Deuteronomy. However, nothing compares with Numbers 33. It lists forty-two places in a sequence based on the formula 'they set out from X and camped in Y', with few, albeit important, interruptions. Israel's starting point is Rameses in Egypt (v. 3) and its final point is Abel-shittim in the plains of Moab (v. 49). Three short notes structure the presentation by placing Israel 'on the border of' a certain place (*the wilderness*, v. 6; *the land of Edom*, v. 37; *Moab*, v. 44) and the last placement of Israel is *in the plains of Moab* [across the Jordan from] *Jericho* (v. 48).

Even without certainty about most of the places, the path from Egypt to Transjordan in this chapter is uncommon. Egyptian military campaigns in the Levant took the international coastal route towards Megiddo and went east to the King's Highway in Transjordan. Israel's southwards trajectory into Sinai (v. 15) and then from Kadesh (v. 37) through a very obscure route to the Transjordan (vv. 45–49) is completely unexpected from a geographical perspective (Jeon 2022: 25–27).

From a literary perspective, chapter 33 can be compared to Ancient Near Eastern itineraries reused in royal annals (see Roskop 2011: 50–81). Neo-Assyrian annals, for example, use equivalent verbs to the formula used throughout Numbers 33. They incorporate itineraries into these records of royal activities, serving as royal propaganda especially in military campaigns (G. I. Davies 1974: 58–60; Roskop 2011: 152–153). None of these features appear in Numbers 33, even where one might expect them, such as in the war with Amalek at Rephidim (v. 14; cf. Exod. 17:8–16).

The introduction of the itinerary, recollecting Israel's liberation from Egypt at Passover (v. 3; cf. Exod. 12) and fulfilling the three-day cultic journey (v. 8; cf. Exod. 5:1–3), gives the itinerary a religious hue. Some scholars interpret it as a pilgrimage (Smith 1997; Knierim and Coats 2005: 309), which aligns with the analogy seen in Numbers 22 – 24.

This itinerary marks Yahweh's authority over the deities, people groups and topographical challenges at the various locations through which Israel travels so that, at the end of the wilderness journey, Israel has become ready to enter Canaan (vv. 50–56). This conclusion recalls Israel's responsibility to allot the Promised Land justly among the tribes (cf. 26:52–56). This explains the literary position of chapter 33 between the granting of the Transjordan in chapter 32 and the allocation of Canaan in chapter 34. It also addresses Israel's responsibility to destroy Canaanite cultic elements and establish appropriate relationships with its neighbours.

Comment
i. Stages of the itinerary (33:1–49)
1–4. *These* . . . is a sign of an archival document, which is reinforced by the surprising information that this was recorded by Moses, acting like a scribe responsible for the itinerary (cf. Exod. 34:27; Deut. 31:22, 24). However, Moses is not a mere scribe. He is described as military leader, with Aaron, taking Israel out of Egypt 'by their hands' (v. 1, lit.) in a victory parade in the sight of the Egyptians (v. 3). The military feature is also indicated by the

term *ṣābā'* (v. 1), used throughout Numbers 1 – 4 to divide Israel into military units.

However, the religious aspect of Israel's journey is highlighted. First, the starting point for Israel is marked both geographically and chronologically. It happens on *the day after the passover* (v. 3). Following this journey marks participation in Israel's festival calendar as members of God's people. Second, Israel's movements are defined as 'marching points' (*massa'*, vv. 1–2, AT) that would occur, literally, 'by Yahweh's mouth'. This theme recalls chapters 9–10, which determine Israel's marching (10:2, 6, 12, 28). Israel's departures and encampments follow the movement of Yahweh's presence in relation to the tabernacle (9:15–23; Exod. 40:36–38). Thus it is Israel's movements, not Moses' recording of them, that are 'by Yahweh's mouth' (9:20; see Frevel 2020: 34). Israel's 'marching points' map God's movement, presence and action. Third, and most importantly, Israel's initial departure (*They set out from Rameses*, v. 3) is based on Yahweh's presence and action in Egypt as a 'condemnation of their deities' (v. 4, AT; cf. Exod. 12:29; see Levine 2000: 516).

5–8. *Rameses* is an abbreviation of Pi-Rameses, the capital city of Pharaoh Rameses II. *Etham* is probably a variant abbreviation of Pithom (Exod. 1:11), a toponym associated with the temple of the Egyptian solar deity Atum, therefore not geographically determined (see Bietak 2015: 26). The designation of Etham is also used for the wilderness region to which Israel moved south-east of the Nile Delta (v. 8). Both locations are politically and religiously relevant, just like *Baal-zephon* (v. 7). The latter is a reference to a Canaanite deity known from the Ugaritic pantheon who was known and worshipped in Egypt, especially in the Eastern Delta, in the twelfth and eleventh centuries BC (Hoffmeier 1997: 190). Like Pithom, Baal-zephon is not geographically but religiously determined. These three toponyms indicate how Israel's journey is part of Yahweh's condemnation of Egyptian and Canaanite deities.

Some of the other localities situate Israel's movement geographically. *Pi-hahiroth* may be a Hebraized form of Akkadian 'the mouth of the canal' (Levine 2000: 517) with the use of *pi*, 'mouth', as an orienting reference. Variations of this reference, 'facing', Hebrew *pene*, appear three times in verses 7–8, including 'facing' Hahiroth (*pĕnê ḥaḥîrōt*, v. 8). *Marah* literally means 'bitter' (cf. Exod. 15:23), creating a connection to the Bitter Lakes region. With these two geographical markers, and the *three days* reference in verse 8, it is reasonable to locate Israel's crossing of 'the sea' somewhere between the Egyptian Bitter Lakes and the head of the Gulf of Suez. This would put Marah more to the north of the Sinai Peninsula, in today's Bir el-Mura or ʿAyun Musa (Hoffmeier 2005: 162).

9–14. After a reference to Marah, two interruptions occur concerning water, one positive (v. 9) and one negative (v. 14). The *Red* (or 'Reed') *Sea* is mentioned three stations after the crossing *through the sea* in verse 8, suggesting its location should not be rigidly restricted. *Dophkah*, which is unique to Numbers 33, may be the modern Wadi Maghara in south-central Sinai, around 20 km (12 miles) inland from the coast of the Gulf of Suez, part of an Egyptian mining route for copper and turquoise minerals (Hoffmeier 2005: 165–169; cf. Jeon 2022: 44–45). The association of Israel's journey with the mining route accords with the role of the Midianites in the narrative (cf. 10:29–31), who are related to the copper mining on the east side of the Sinai Peninsula, north of Aqaba. The relation between Egyptian and Midianite copper mining in the Aqaba region is especially interesting given the famous archaeological find of the tent-shrine at Timna (see Avner 2014), providing further evidence that locations along this route would be religiously significant.

15–37. Most of the locations here are unidentifiable and unique to Numbers 33, with the exceptions of *Kibroth-hattaavah* and *Hazeroth* (vv. 16–17; see 11:34–35), *Moseroth, Bene-jaakan, Hor-haggidgad* and *Jotbathah* (vv. 30–33; see Deut. 10:6–7), *Ezion-geber* (vv. 35–36; see Deut. 2:8; 1 Kgs 9:26; 22:48; 2 Chr. 8:17; 20:36) and *Kadesh* (vv. 36–37; see, e.g., Gen. 20:1; Num. 13:26; 20:1; 27:14; Deut. 1:2, 19; 32:51; Josh. 14:6). Ezion-geber, located near the head of the Gulf of Aqaba, creates a problem for an itinerary route. From Ezion-geber, Israel moves directly to Kadesh (v. 36). From the flow of Israel's journey in the wilderness narrative, this would have to be Kadesh-barnea in the desert of Paran, south of the Negev, from which the spies were sent out (13:26). However, Numbers 33 does

not associate Kadesh with southern Canaan, but with Edom's
border (v. 37). And the rest of Israel's movements are related
to Transjordan (vv. 42–49). Therefore, Kadesh here might be
identified as Meribath-kadesh, geographically located somewhere
near modern-day Petra (cf. 20:1). In this case, the whole movement
from the Aqaba to the southern Negev is omitted from Numbers
33, which would be surprising given the decisive nature of Israel's
experience there for its wilderness journey (cf. chs. 13–14). The
solution is not to see Numbers 33 as an itinerary following a
geographic logic from beginning to end. Perhaps the mention of
Kadesh here blends both geographical locations to indicate that
all the locations of verses 15–37 belong to the region defined by
the triangle between Sinai in the south, Kadesh-barnea in the
north and Meribath-kadesh in the east (see Milgrom 1990: 281 for
other solutions, and Finkelstein 2015: 46–47 for Israelite historical
familiarity with this region). This interpretation bears similarity
to the grouping of this region, including Moab in Transjordan, in
Assurbanipal's Arabian Wars annals (Tebes 2017: 73).

Although the logic used in Numbers 33 for the sequence of
places listed is indiscernible, the list still appears intentionally
constructed. *Haradah* (v. 24) serves as an exemplary test case.
Juan Tebes connects Haradah with the toponym Ḥiratâqaz/ṣaya
in Assurbanipal's annals and argues for a Semitic etymology of
Aramaic or North Arabian origin, meaning 'cultivated land of
Qos', the Edomite god (Tebes 2017: 74–79). These camp stations,
therefore, are grouped by their location in north Sinai, the
arid steppes from the southern Negev to the Transjordan, with
religious significance. As argued above, Numbers 33 represents
less an itinerary than a mapping of Yahweh's actions in forming
Israel from places previously associated with other groups and
deities, marked by some fluidity in their identities (cf. Finkelstein
2015: 44).

38–40. The longest interruption in the flow of chapter 33
narrates the death of Aaron, the high priest. In verse 40 his death
is connected to the news of the Israelites' arrival in the region
coming to the ears of a Canaanite king who rules the Negev.
The suppression of any military note here (cf. 21:1–3), while
mentioning the Canaanite king ruling crucial territory within the

boundaries of Canaan set out in chapter 34, and the context of the high priest's death, fits the religious and political purpose of chapter 33. The chronological reference to Aaron's death in the *fortieth year* after the exodus is unique to this text (cf. 20:22–29; Deut. 10:6), but Aaron's age of 123 years at his death corroborates his age at the exodus as eighty-three (Exod. 7:7). The toponym *Mount Hor* means 'the mountain top' and might not represent a specific geographic location.

41–49. The general direction of Israel's movement in these verses is from the northern Sinai, cutting through Edomite and Moabite territory to the plains of Moab. *Zalmonah* and *Punon* (vv. 41–43) are unique to Numbers 33. Punon is associated with a centre of copper mining and smelting in Wadi Faynan, north of modern-day Petra. Records from Rameses II attest to its inhabitance by Shasu nomads in the late thirteenth century BC (Levine 2000: 521). The reference to the mountains of *Abarim* facing *Nebo* (v. 47) might indicate the location of all these toponyms along the pass through this mountain range from the east of the southern end of the Dead Sea to the plains of Moab, just east of the northern end of the Dead Sea. Moses ascends Nebo from the plains of Moab to see the land of Canaan (27:12; Deut. 32:49). The composite name *Dibon-gad* is based on Dibon, King Mesha's city (see 32:34–42), and the Israelite tribe, Gad, affirming Gad's possession of Dibon.

Almon-diblathaim (vv. 46–47) may represent a variation of Beth-diblathaim, mentioned in Jeremiah 48:22 and the Mesha Stele (line 30, *COS* 2.138). The variation found here in Numbers 33 might highlight the association of this place with Baal, using a conflation of Baal-meon ('Almon', Milgrom 1990: 282). In the Mesha Stele, the term *beth* stands for 'house' or 'temple', which explains the expression Beth-baal-meon (line 30, *COS* 2.138), which follows Beth-diblaten, a variation of Beth-diblathaim. In this sense, these terms are both toponyms and references to cultic spaces (see Dearman 1997: 207–208). Almon-diblathaim, then, conflates these cultic spaces in the Mesha Stele into one toponym. Similarly, the reference to Baal-peor in 25:5, which is called Beth-peor in Deuteronomy 4:46, concerns the event situated at Shittim, the same region dealt with here in Numbers

33. In that episode, religious and political relations between Israel and Moabites/Midianites function to define Israel's identity in relation to neighbouring groups. By listing these places, Numbers 33 affirms Yahweh's actions in other deities' territories to justify the removal of the identity of these deities and their worshippers attached to these places from Israel's identity. At the same time, such rhetoric establishes these locations and their populations as part of Israel's origins.

ii. Divine instruction for Israel's entrance into Canaan and the consequences of failure (33:50–56)

50. Verses 50–56 conclude the mapping of Yahweh's action in relation to Israel's journey and introduce Canaan's allocation among the tribes in chapter 34. The expression *in the plains of Moab* [across the Jordan from] *Jericho* (vv 48, 50) marks the summary of the book at the location from which the settling generation will enter Canaan (26:3, 63; 31:12; 35:1; 36:13). It creates a hopeful conclusion.

51–54. The strong divine affirmation that Yahweh has already given Canaan to Israel (v. 53) reinforces and anticipates the conclusive aspect of Israel's wilderness journey. God's repeated instruction in summarized form about the division of the Promised Land among the tribes (v. 54; cf. 26:52–56; Josh. 13 – 19) underscores its finality. God's assurance of the gift of the land, however, implies a responsibility for Israel to dispossess the land. This means dispossessing its inhabitants (v. 52) and destroying their cultic objects and spaces so that Israel will *y-š-b* there. The use of this verb in verse 40 recalls the ruling of the Canaanite king of Arad (21:1), hinting that Israel's settlement in Canaan means ruling over the land and its inhabitants, and overcoming their religion. This sovereignty, then, calls for destruction (*'-b-d*) of Canaanite cultural and religious identities. Israel should destroy Canaanite 'figurines', 'molten idols' and *high places*. The first two terms refer to cultic icons, though the precise meaning of the first term, *maśkît*, is elusive (Lev. 26:1; Ps. 73:11; Prov. 18:11; 25:11; Ezek 8:12). The second cultic object is clearly an idol (*ṣelem*) resulting from melting and moulding (see Lev. 19:4; Deut. 9:12; Judg. 17:3–4; 2 Kgs 17:16; Isa. 42:17), which is appropriate given the prevalence of mining in the places mapped in chapter 33.

The third term deserves more attention. Although religious 'high places' (*bāmôt*) are commonly mentioned in the Bible, they are never described. The term appears only here and in Leviticus 26:30 in the Pentateuch. Baruch Levine compares 'the high places' of verse 52 with 'the places where the nations whom you are about to dispossess served their gods' of Deuteronomy 12:2 (Levine 2000: 523), so that the term does not describe any particular feature of it other than its religious use marked by religious items. It can even be used for places of legitimate worship of Yahweh (1 Sam. 9:12–25). Its use here in verse 52, however, is relevant because of the association of many toponyms with cultic activities (cf. vv. 41–49). The Mesha Stele, from which cultic places are conflated in the toponym Almon-diblathaim (see on v. 47), also makes reference to Beth Bamoth, or a temple of Bamoth (line 27 *COS* 2.138; cf. Num. 21:19), suggesting a place with one or more cultic centres (Dearman 1997: 209). Joshua 13:17 even uses the toponym Baal-Bamoth (or Bamoth-baal; cf. Num. 22:41) and associates it with Beth-baal-meon. Israel's responsibility to destroy Canaanite *bāmôt* therefore refers to how Israel must establish or recognize Yahweh's presence and action as a form of rule over Canaanite cultic spaces (see 21:18–19). In doing so, Israel also establishes its allegiance to Yahweh as its identity and a form of rule over Canaanite identity. The outcome is the appropriate relationship between Israel and Canaanite inhabitants and between Yahweh and Canaanite deities, as in Numbers 25. This aligns with the main purpose of Numbers 33 and even with Deuteronomy 12:2–3, where the purpose of destroying such cultic places is to destroy 'the name' of their deities from these places, consequently from Israel's identity, with the implication of establishing Yahweh's 'name' on them.

55–56. These verses describe the consequences of Israel's failure to fulfil such a responsibility. The ultimate consequence would be Israel's expulsion from the land (v. 56): that is, Israel's identity as a people in covenant with Yahweh would not succeed in the land. It is unclear if what Yahweh *thought to do* to the Canaanites has a specific reference. However, the common use of the verb *y-r-š* ('to dispossess') indicates the common notion of the dispossession or expulsion of the previous inhabitants from the land (see Deut. 9:3; cf. Lev. 18:24; 20:22–24), which is among the covenantal curses that might befall Israel (Deut. 28:21, 63).

The penultimate consequence of Israel's failure is described in verse 55 with two obscure images, supplemented by an explanation that the Canaanites might *trouble* Israel. The verb *ṣ-r-r* comes from the substantive *ṣ-r*, 'narrow', which appears in 25:17–18 to describe the relationship between Israel and Midian as a form of oppression by restriction of another's means of life, especially land and produce. Israel's involvement with the Moabite sacrificial cult of Baal in 25:2–3 is described as oppressive service, like that of an animal under a yoke to plough the land. A similar description is also found in 22:24–27.

These textual connections with animal imagery commend a speculative interpretation for the two obscure images: 'pricks in your eyes' (AT) and *thorns in your sides*. The first term, 'prick', occurs only here and has an Akkadian cognate meaning 'pointy tools', such as a knife and nail (see Levine 2000: 525). The second, *thorns*, also occurs in Joshua 23:13, which parallels Numbers 33:51–56 in dealing with the consequences of Israel's failure to dispossess the inhabitants of Canaan. Besides the shared term *thorns*, it uses three other similar terms referring to 'snares' and 'traps' (cf. Exod. 23:33; 34:12; Deut. 7:16; Judg. 2:3). These images in verse 55 may therefore depict tools used to restrict animal movements with the purpose of using them for specific activities, such as with a yoke for ploughing or a saddle for riding. The latter is defined by the verb *ḥ-b-š*, literally 'binding', so also applicable to 'ruling' (Job 34:17; Isa. 3:6–7). Numbers 32:30 already employs the image of an animal trapped and caught as a possession to depict an oppressive hierarchy between people groups. Therefore, the failure to dispossess Canaan by destroying their way of life determined by their deities and establishing Israel's allegiance to Yahweh would eventually lead Israel to become submissive to the Canaanites and their deities and to become Canaanites themselves. That would fracture Israel's relationship with Yahweh and counteract the purpose of Numbers 33, which is to affirm Yahweh's present rule over other deities' territories.

Meaning

When Numbers 33 is compared with other itineraries throughout the Pentateuch, differences abound. Although there is a general geographical logic of Israel's journey from Egypt to the plains of Moab, many parts of chapter 33 exhibit no clear linear spatial or temporal sequence. In this sense, Numbers 33 compares well with *The Sargon Geography*. This is not an itinerary per se, but an outline of the extent of Sargon of Akkad's territory, *c.*2371–2316 BC (see G. I. Davies 1974: 70–71; Roskop 2011: 64). Rather than outlining Israel's territory, Numbers 33 demarcates important places in Israel's origins and formation for the people of God in relation to other groups and their deities prior to its settling in Canaan. However, this purpose presents a crucial message concerning the meaning of Israel's entrance into Canaan and its function there.

Israel's journey is inseparable from the movement of the divine presence, manifested in the cloud and the pillar of fire (chs. 9–10). What was punctual and extraordinary at Sinai becomes routinized and ordinary in the tabernacle in the midst of Israel's camp. This process defines the journey as sacred, even liturgical, while emptying these locations of any future religious value that could lead Israel to take pilgrimages there and attach their identity to them. At points, God's presence is affirmed in the wilderness, in 'no-man's land', but the locations are usually affirmed in someone else's territory. Kings and deities who played any role in oppressing God's people, undermining the divine intentions for it and for the world, are judged and subjugated. Their names and their identities are destroyed, and God's name and presence are established through the movement of Israel's camp. The journey, however, has a destination: Canaan. Israel's entrance into Canaan, therefore, intends to establish God's name and presence there, through Israel's settling or, better, rule in it. Yahweh's settling or ruling in Canaan is attached to Israel's settling and ruling there, because Yahweh's origin is outside Canaan, in the southern desert, following closely on many of the places in Israel's detour (see Deut. 33:2; Judg. 5:4–5; Ps. 68:8–9, 18; Hab. 3:3; R. D. Miller II 2018). According to Numbers 33, Yahweh and Israel's rule in Canaan occurs by the destruction of the identity – cultural, religious, political – of peoples attached to deities other than Yahweh.

Modern communities must consider the ethics of this theological message. One can easily identify reflections of this message in humanity's history, ancient and modern, of imperialism and colonialism, including those acts perpetrated by groups who view these texts as Scripture. It is also reflected in contemporary evangelical supremacism and religious intolerance. In Brazil, for example, evangelicals mock, demonize and destroy Catholic and Afro-Brazilian religions' cultic items. Numbers 33 does not support such a literalist and superficial application of its content (see Pressler 2017: 296).

Whenever this text took shape, the context of Israelite or Judahite priestly scribes behind it is one of a sociopolitical and religious minority. Their vision does not intend to serve the forceful implementation of imperial and colonial purposes, but rather the promotion and reinforcement of Israel's identity as defined by fidelity to Yahweh and the way of life determined by God, in negotiation with its neighbours' identity, similar to what one sees in Numbers 32 (see *Comment* there). Second, and most important, by establishing Yahweh's presence, and Israel's formation in relation to this presence, in places attached to other deities and peoples, from Egypt, through Sinai, the Negev, the Transjordan and into Canaan, Numbers 33 creates ambiguity. On the one hand, the identity of these deities and peoples must be replaced by Yahweh and Israel's rule. On the other hand, the cultic places of these deities and peoples become intrinsic to Yahweh's presence and Israel's origins. This negotiation of identity recognizes the need to differentiate and preserve Yahweh and Israel's uniqueness, while acknowledging some overlap with other groups. This is actually a clash between two ways of life, as will be seen in chapter 34. This is quite different from ancient and modern colonialism and becomes an interesting model for contemporary Christians living in a cultural and religious plural world.

I. Mapping the territory of Canaan (34:1–29)

Context

After mapping the divine movement in the wilderness journey to define the meaning and function of the entrance and settling of

Yahweh and Israel in Canaan (ch. 33), chapter 34 maps Canaan itself. Boundaries are established for the four cardinal directions in the first part of the chapter (vv. 1–15). The second part identifies the tribal leaders responsible for apportioning the land among ancestral households (vv. 16–29).

The fact that the boundaries of Canaan explicitly frame the chapter (vv. 2, 29) is relevant when compared with other biblical traditions. Zecharia Kallai differentiates three territorial concepts: (1) the land promised to the patriarchs; (2) the land of Canaan; and (3) the land of Israel (Kallai 1997: 70). Many mentions of territorial boundaries in the Bible are related to most parts of the land that Israel occupied in its history, summarized in the territorial formula 'from Dan to Beer-sheba' (Judg. 20:1; 1 Sam. 3:20; 2 Sam. 3:10; 17:11; 24:2, 15; 1 Kgs 4:25; 1 Chr. 21:2; 2 Chr. 30:5; cf. 1 Kgs 8:65; 2 Kgs 14:25; Amos 6:14; 8:14). A more theological concept of the Promised Land arises in the divine promise to Abraham in Genesis 15:18 of a more extensive territory reaching from the river of Egypt to the Euphrates (see Deut. 1:7; cf. Exod. 23:31; Deut. 11:24). As a view of the future restoration of Israel, Ezekiel 47:13–23 shares many boundary markers with Numbers 34, but it never describes this territory as Canaan. The notion of Canaan as the Promised Land appears in Genesis 17:8; Joshua 13:2–6; and in the wilderness journey as a whole, especially Numbers 13:2; 21 – 26; and here in chapter 34.

Canaan as a territorial boundary is historically and theologically relevant. After Numbers 32, the omission of the Transjordan in Numbers 34 reveals that Canaan is not being used to define the territory once occupied by Israel, especially because it includes areas that historically never belonged to Israel (Milgrom 1990: 284). The territorial boundaries of Numbers 34 correspond to the Egyptian province of Canaan, both around 1270 BC after the Battle of Kadesh (Grosby 2007: 106–107) and as the territory dominated by Egypt in the last part of the seventh century BC (Levin 2006; Schipper 2011). In both periods, Egypt had a stronghold over Canaan, controlling trade routes and forcing vassal kings to pay tribute.

Both of the interrelated contexts are important for understanding Numbers 34. Geographical concepts based on topographical, political and experiential references, such as Canaan was for Israel, tend to persist through time and even from one society to another. This is true even when some boundary markers of one society are not precisely the same as in another era (Grosby 2007: 99–100). This conceptual persistence, with the heavy Egyptian political dominance, informs the use of Canaan in Numbers 34.

Comment
i. The boundaries of Canaan (34:1–15)

1–2. Rarely in Numbers does Yahweh give Moses a word to command the Israelites (5:1–2; 28:1–2; 30:1; 35:1–2), but these commands all introduce religious, even cultic, instruction. This suggests that establishing the boundaries of Canaan as the land to be occupied by Israel has similar religious features as argued concerning the mapping of the itinerary in chapter 33.

The divine instruction is based on the confirmation that Israel will indeed enter Canaan, which will *fall* to it, implying the apportionment by lot (see v. 13 below) to receive its territories as an inheritance (v. 2). The concept of land inheritance is based on ancestral kinship and attached to indigenous connection to the land. In this sense, Numbers 34 distributes the land according to ancestral households, following the purpose of the second census in chapter 26. It also connects well with chapter 32, where the two-and-a-half tribes receive Transjordanian towns and territories as an inheritance (32:33). The indigenous connection to the land is intriguing considering that the narrative describes Israel entering Canaan as outsiders. Maybe the distance of Israel from Canaan is not geographical but conceptual (see the *Meaning* section below). Although Canaan will be occupied by only nine-and-a-half tribes, and its apportionment will be the responsibility of Eleazar, Joshua and Israel's tribal leaders, Yahweh's command is to all the Israelites. The whole people, and not only its leaders, have a responsibility in receiving and treating Canaan as a divine inheritance, which carries implications for how Israel relates to the land.

3–5. This southern border closely resembles Judah's southern border in Joshua 15:1–4. The Hebrew term for *south* here is *negeb*, meaning 'arid', the same as the desert region of southern Canaan, that is, Negev (33:40). All the cardinal directions in chapter 34 have an indigenous Canaanite orientation – that is, the perspective of the borders is from within Canaan, not from outside it.

The starting point of the southern border is at its eastern corner, the edge of the Dead Sea. From there, the border goes south into the desert of Zin, skirting Edomite territory. Using Edom as a reference for the southern border may imply a seventh-century context when Edom expanded into the Negev highlands (Levin 2006: 67). This part of the border follows 'the Ascent of Scorpions' (AT), perhaps a reference to an Egyptian route found in topographical lists from the Eighteenth Dynasty (*c.*1550–1292 BC; see Levine 2000: 533). The points of reference from here are *Kadesh-barnea*, *Hazar-addar* and *Azmon*. Hazar-addar seems like a conflation of two toponyms, Hezron and Addar (Josh. 15:3). Its precise location, as with that of Azmon, is unknown, but they are probably around the region of Kadesh-barnea, identified with modern-day 'Ain el Qudeirat.

Using Kadesh-barnea as a boundary marker for Canaan is significant. It is the place from which the spies were sent out (13:26), implying that it is outside Canaan. Even as a place outside or on the border of Canaan, Kadesh-barnea was an important place in the Egyptian–Judah political relation in the seventh century BC, having a fortress and serving as an adminis-trative centre. Archaeological evidence from there shows Judahite vassalage to Egypt at the end of the seventh century (Schipper 2011: 279–281). Its use here, then, marks Egyptian dominance over Canaan, unlike Ezekiel 47:19, where the reference is to the 'bitter waters of Kadesh' (AT). The southern border of Canaan ends at the western corner with the 'Brook of Egypt' (AT) reaching the (Mediterranean) Sea (v. 5; cf. Josh. 15:4, 47; 1 Kgs 8:65; 2 Kgs 24:7; Isa. 27:12; Ezek. 47:19; 48:28; 2 Chr. 7:8). This refers to today's Naḥal Besor, a natural boundary between Egypt and Canaan, at the most southern point of Gaza (Levin 2006: 58).

6. This is the simple western border, *the Great Sea*, that is, the Mediterranean Sea. The Hebrew term for 'west' (*yām*) is the same as 'sea', implying an indigenous Canaanite orientation. Using the Mediterranean Sea as the western border implies as part of Canaan the inclusion of Philistine and Phoenician territories that were never occupied by Israel. This definition of Canaanite territory makes sense prior to the invasion of the Sea Peoples at the end of the second millennium BC (Levine 2000: 540), although Egyptian occupation of the Palestine Mediterranean coast in the seventh century BC has archaeological support as well (Schipper 2011: 273–274).

7–9. The northern border shares many similarities with Ezekiel 47:15–17. This is the starting point for Ezekiel's vision of the restored land, as it has a northern perspective, from Babylon. The first point of the northern border is its western corner on a *Mount Hor*. As mentioned at 20:22, this toponym has the general meaning of 'the mountain top'. The Hebrew term for 'north' (*ṣāpón*) is also quite general. It also derives its meaning from an indigenous Canaanite orientation, indicating the mountain ranges extending from the region of Mount Hermon to the Syrian city of Homs (cf. Josh. 13:5). In this sense, the imprecise northern boundary could be somewhere between Damascus and Homs, with Byblos, on the coast, as a central location between the two (see Pressler 2017: 300–301). For this reason, 'Hamath' could be a reference to this whole area, as it can be associated with modern Hama, about 40 km (25 miles) north of Homs, or with *Lebo-hamath* (as in NRSV; cf. Josh. 13:5), for which modern-day Labwe, east of Byblos, fits better as its location (see Ezek. 47:15–17). *Zedad* and *Hazar-enan* are located east of the Damascus–Homs highway, moving inland into Syrian territory on the edge of the Syrian desert (Levine 2000: 534–535; Levin 2006: 60–61).

The northern boundary is imprecise, especially because *Ziphron*, its outer limit, is unidentified. However, Lebo-hamath's relevance as a general region that demarcates the northern boundary of Canaan lies in its historically important role for Egyptian assertion of dominion over Canaan,[1] first in conflict with Hatti[2] and later, in the seventh century BC, in conflict with Assyria (see

---

1   Labwe is mentioned in Amenhotep II's military campaigns in the Levant (*COS* 2.21).
2   In the inscription of Idrimi, an Amorite king of the fourteenth century BC, Hittite advances in this region are mentioned (*COS* 2.479).

Schipper 2011: 269–272). Lebo-hamath is also idealistically used to delineate the extension of David and Solomon's kingdom (1 Kgs 8:65). Theologically, Lebo-hamath is relevant in connecting this demarcation of Canaan and the land surveyed by the spies in Numbers 13. The extent of the land surveyed is said to be *from the wilderness of Zin to Rehob, near Lebo-hamath* (13:21). The land apportioned to the new generation is the one that the exodus generation did not receive.

10–12. Last is the eastern border. The Hebrew term for 'east' (*qēdem*) means 'front, facing', attesting to the eastern orientation of this territory demarcation, although it starts with the southern boundary (see below). Part of the eastern boundary is formed by natural borders: the Sea of Chinnereth, that is, Sea of Galilee, the Jordan River and the Dead Sea (vv. 11–12). The Transjordan, then, is excluded from Canaan. The boundary north of the Sea of Chinnereth is uncertain. *Ain* means 'well, spring', too general to be identified, and *Shepham* is unknown, being mentioned only here.

Most relevant is the appearance of *Riblah* (v. 11). Although the spelling with a definite article and its geographical location to the south-east of Lebo-hamath differs from the biblically and historically known Riblah,[3] this may be a reference to it. This location was crucial in the Egyptian domination of Canaan as the place where the army of Rameses II crossed the Orontes River for the Battle of Kadesh to encounter the Hittite army (Goedicke 1966). In the seventh century BC, Riblah was also crucial for Egyptian domination of Canaan from Judah's perspective and is prominent in the last days of the kingdom of Judah. It was an important military and administrative centre for Necho II's dominion over the whole Levant, being the place where he imprisoned King Jehoahaz on the way to his campaign against Babylon (2 Kgs 23:33). A few years later, when Nebuchadnezzar from Babylon defeated Necho II, Riblah was the place where Judah's king

---

3   This might explain the reading of the LXX, 'Arbela', a toponym in Galilee mentioned in 1 Macc. 9:2 (see Ashley 2022: 519).

Zedekiah was imprisoned and humiliated (2 Kgs 25:6, 20–21; Jer. 39:5–6; 52:9–10, 26–27).

13–15. Canaan, as a territorial concept, is the land nine-and-a-half tribes will receive by lot as an inheritance from Yahweh. The explicit use of the term *lot* as a command from Yahweh clarifies the meaning of verse 2. Although the Transjordan is set apart from Canaan, both lands are apportioned by lot as a divine inheritance through covenant. But comparing the qualifications for their apportionment reveals that Canaan is viewed from an indigenous perspective, while the Transjordan is not. In the current verses, the relationship between the two-and-a-half tribes and the Transjordan is *by their ancestral houses* (v. 14). The qualification of Canaan as a divine inheritance to Israel and its apportionment by lot is *according to . . . their ancestral tribes* (26:55; 33:54, with a slight difference). By including these clarifying verses about Israel's tribes in Transjordan, the mapping of Canaan concludes with an emphasis on the eastern orientation, repeating the term 'to the east' (*qēdem*, v. 15, AT).

ii. Leaders assigned by God to distribute the land among the tribes (34:16–29)

16–29. A second divine speech to Moses names the leaders responsible for giving Israel its territorial inheritance. As with the first speech, this is specified as a divine 'command' (*ṣ-w-ḥ*, vv. 2, 29), framing a cohesive message between mapping Canaan and apportioning it as a divine inheritance. The literary context of the mapping of Canaan, the giving of inheritance by lot, and the heading of the names by the high priest Eleazar indicates that these are not military leaders and this does not depict Israel's entrance into Canaan as a military campaign. Besides Eleazar and Joshua, the land will be apportioned by one chieftain per tribe to receive inheritance in Canaan. The unique order of the tribes follows approximately their geographical position in Canaan, from south to north. The fulfilment of the apportionment of Canaan by lot in Joshua 13 – 19 follows a different order, but it emphasizes Caleb and Judah. The same is true for the current verses. Caleb is named the chieftain of Judah and is listed first. He is the only chieftain from the exodus generation (Joshua is not counted as a chieftain); all other chieftains are new characters in Numbers. This list, then, marks both a break and continuity with Israel's failure to enter Canaan in chapters 13–14, when Caleb was also Judah's representative (13:6). The mapping of Canaan in the first part of the chapter echoes the description of the land surveyed by the spies (13:21), and the list of leaders to apportion the land in the second part of the chapter echoes the list of spies by including two of them, Joshua and Caleb. There is a sense of fulfilment of God's promise in which the new generation has the chance to change the fate of their ancestors.

Meaning

There is a shared meaning in mapping both the route of the wilderness journey and the boundaries of Canaan. They are both about the movement of Yahweh's presence with Israel in other deities' or kings' territories to establish the appropriate relationship between them. This is evidenced in how the mapping of Canaan resembles the organization of the Israelite camp centred on the divine presence in the tabernacle in Numbers 2. The camp is organized following the eastern orientation of the tabernacle, where Judah is positioned (2:2–3). That is why the delineation of Canaan starts on the south, where Judah will be located, but has an eastern starting point (v. 3) and concludes with an emphasis on the east (v. 15). The connection between Canaan and the tabernacle is also recognized by the use of the Hebrew word *pēʾâ* ('side, limit'). It is used to qualify the limits of Canaan (v. 3) and it characterizes the sides of the tabernacle and its dimensions (Exod. 26:18, 20; 27:9, 11–13; 36:23, 25; 38:9, 11–13). The routinization of Sinai in the wilderness journey through Israel's camp (see the *Meaning* for chapter 33) has its climax in Israel's settlement in Canaan.

Numbers 34 is relevant for thinking about the biblical tradition of the 'conquest'. One should recognize how this biblical tradition has been used, in history and still today, to justify the violent and dehumanizing practices of colonialism. The frequent abuse of this tradition took place through the identification of Christian colonial powers with Israel as the people of God, while viewing their indigenous subjects as the Canaanites who opposed God. No wonder, then, that Catholic and Protestant missionary movements were inseparable from colonization (see Crowell 2009). The biblical tradition, then, was part of literary strategies that allowed colonizers to claim foreign lands while securing their innocence, typical of imperial narratives (Mbuwayesango 2021: 132). Also relevant for Numbers 34 is how various claims over Palestine in the last two centuries have tried to minimize the inhabitants' relationship with the land by changing place names and territorial boundaries (Masalha 2015).

At the root of colonizing violence is lust for land and resources, the opposite of what Numbers has been presenting about the responsibility of leadership in relation to the people and of Israel in relation to other peoples. From this perspective one can understand the meaning of Numbers 34 not as imperial and colonizing ideology, but as a strong critique of it. This understanding rests on seeing the delimitations of the land inherited by Israel as the territory of the Egyptian province of Canaan. In this respect, Israel is not the settler-colonizer overcoming the indigenous Canaanites; much to the contrary, Israel is identified as the legitimate, indigenous, successor of Egyptian imperial domination over Canaan. This is true considering the end of the second millennium, when an Israelite identity was emerging in Canaan in the shadow of retreating Egyptian domination. It is also true of the late seventh century BC, when the same territory, the land attached to Israel's and Judah's identity, was subjugated by Egypt (see Grosby 2007: 107–110). However, this is less a struggle for dominance than a conflict about imperial versus indigenous relationships to the land. The conflict is between relating to the land as a commodity to be economically and politically misappropriated by a human king, especially by military force, and relating to the land as divinely given through covenant as an inheritance to sustain a household over generations. Numbers 34, therefore, helps us see the Canaanite polemics as primarily related to Egyptian domination and its vassal kings in Canaan, rather than as a settler-colonialist ideology against indigenous Canaanites (see Hinlicky 2021: 41–46; and Introduction, 'Israel's identity and its neighbours').

As argued here, Numbers 34 expresses the view of the indigenous victims of imperial powers. Therefore, one should not read it from the perspective of imperial military forces and colonizers. By reckoning Christian colonialist ideology based on the biblical tradition of the 'conquest' of Canaan, even more poignant issues arise from chapter 34. For example, Christians can inform their reading by Jesus' indigenous Galilean perspective on the land, following other Jewish traditions and groups in his rejection of violence as a means to remove Roman imperial domination from his people's land (see Horsley 1987; 2003). And Christians must also now read this biblical tradition with the purpose of envisioning restorative justice and historical reparations for the victims of colonization (see Pressler 2017: 302; Mbuwayesango 2021: 137).

J. Special issues concerning the Promised Land (35:1–34)

Context
The final divine speeches in the book of Numbers appear in chapter 35 (vv. 1, 9) to address two related matters: the levitical towns (vv. 1–8) and the *cities* [or 'towns'] *of refuge* (ʿārê miqlāṭ, vv. 9–34). Because the towns of refuge have a function in the broader issue of homicide, from the perspective of justice and impurity, other subdivisions can be established: the divine speech formula (vv. 9–10a), the reason for the need for towns of refuge (vv. 10b–12), the number and distribution of the towns of refuge (vv. 13–15), the definition of intentional homicide (vv. 16–21), the definition of unintentional homicide (vv. 22–23), just requirements for the trial procedures (vv. 24–30), and cultic and theological elements for the trial procedures (vv. 31–34).

These two divine speeches also connect, literarily and thematically, to 33:50–56, another divine speech. That portion concludes the mapping of Yahweh's action in Israel's wilderness journey in chapter 33 and introduces the delineation of Canaan's boundaries in anticipation of its division among the Israelite tribes in chapter 34. The command for the Israelites to provide towns for the Levites is part of the instructions concerning the division of the Promised Land based on the previous divine speech (34:16–29). Therefore, it must be understood in the light of the gift and division of land among the Israelite tribes, beginning in 26:52–56 and traversing prominently through chapters 27–36 (see Frevel 2020: 55).

Although elements of the instructions concerning the towns of refuge appear in other biblical traditions (Gen. 9:5–6; Exod. 21:12–14; Deut. 19:1–13), for which the relation with Numbers 35 is hard to discern, here they have a particular purpose. From different perspectives, the maintenance of the divine presence among Israel marks 33:50–56 and 35:33–34 (see Pressler 2017: 303), and it connects both themes of chapter 35: levitical towns and the towns of refuge. In the light of Yahweh's presence in Israel's camp, one of the most relevant issues in Numbers is how to deal with death in the camp (e.g. 19:11–16). The setting apart of six levitical towns as towns of refuge addresses one specific form of death, that caused by homicide.

Comment

i. Levitical towns (35:1–8)

The divine command to set apart towns for the Levites reaches its fulfilment in Joshua 21 (cf. 1 Chr. 6:54–81), following the distribution of the land to all the other tribes (Josh. 13 – 19). They were probably in part sites of priestly families associated with local sanctuaries, although not all levitical towns necessarily had a sanctuary where Levites performed cultic functions (see Greenberg 1959: 131; Barmash 2005: 85). The levitical towns would most probably be located at tribal boundaries, and the Levites would not have kinship ties to the residents of nearby towns. These features are conceptualized in the placement of the Levites as boundary markers in the organization of the camp (1:53), indicating that Levites were appropriate mediators of religious and legal matters among Israelite tribes as they were not part of the tribal power structure, especially in relation to land (see Hutton 2009: 229–230; 2011: 80–81; Mattison 2018: 249–250).

1–3a. As with 34:1–2, Yahweh gives Moses a word to command Israel, which often introduces religious instruction (5:1–2; 28:1–2; 30:1). The levitical cities are given 'from their [Israelites'] inherited possession' (v. 2, AT; cf. 27:7), but they are not possessions of the Levites, only their place 'to settle' (*y-š-b*, vv. 2–3).

3b–5. The instruction is emphatic concerning the towns' surroundings, defined by the Hebrew term *migrāš* (vv. 2, 3, 4, 5, 7), from the verb *g-r-š*, 'to drive'. As the text makes clear, this area is reserved 'to drive' cattle and livestock to graze (v. 3b; NRSV, *pasture lands*) and would not be used for agriculture (cf. Lev. 25:29–33; see Levine 2000: 569–570). The relation between the thousand cubits of verse 4 and the two thousand cubits of verse 5 is confusing enough that the LXX harmonized them by changing verse 4 to two thousand cubits. However one understands the relation between these measures, they concern an abstraction typical of an idealized plan in which the town is a perfect square or at least quite symmetrical. Such idealism coheres with the camp structure in chapters 1–4 and the Canaanite borders in chapter 34 (cf. Ezek. 40 – 48 for similar idealized plans). As in chapter 34, the territorial limits defined by the term *pē'â*, in verse 5 (4x), link them to the sides and dimensions of the tabernacle (Exod. 26:18, 20; 27:9, 11–13; 36:23, 25; 38:9, 11–13). In this sense, the levitical towns, like the Israelite camp and the land of Canaan, are envisioned as an enclosed container with clear boundaries (see v. 26 below), where the divine presence dwells.

6–8. The total of forty-eight levitical towns also appears in Joshua 21:41–42. Just as in Numbers 26:54, the territorial allocation of levitical towns is proportional to the size of the Israelite tribes (v. 8).

ii. Towns of refuge (35:9–15)

The Hebrew expression for 'towns [or *cities*] of refuge' (*'ārê miqlāt*) literally means 'towns that take in/absorb', from the verb *q-l-t*, a technical term unique to Numbers 35; Joshua 20 – 21; and 1 Chronicles 6. Historically, it is possible to associate the biblical institution of towns of refuge with the evidence for the practice of blood vengeance and sanctuary protection attested in many ancient and contemporary cultures (see Weinfeld 1995: 120–132; Pressler 2017: 307).

Homicide is subject to tribal or kinship revenge against the killer by the hands of the 'blood redeemer' (*gō'ēl haddām*, 35:19, 21, 24, 25, 27; Deut. 19:6, 12; NRSV, *avenger of blood*). The biblical examples of sanctuary protection are unrelated to homicide and

blood vengeance (1 Kgs 1:50; 2:28–34; Neh. 6:10–13). Exodus
21:12–14 mentions an 'altar' (Exod. 21:14), qualifying this place
of protection as a *māqôm* ('place', Exod. 21:13), a term related to
the sanctuary (e.g. Exod. 20:24; Deut. 12:5, 11). Both associations
indicate some relation between a place of protection against blood
vengeance and a sacred space. Numbers 35 does not make the
sanctuary aspect explicit, but the notion of sacredness is apparent
in the levitical character of the towns of refuge and the theological
reasoning behind their institution (see vv. 31–34).

9–10. The typical divine speech formula again introduces
religious or cultic instruction, with a stronger similarity to 34:1–2
than verse 1.

11. The function of the 'towns of refuge' is apparent from the
key verb 'to flee' (*n-w-s*; cf. v. 6; Exod. 21:13; Deut. 19:3, 4, 5, 11;
Josh. 20:3, 4, 6, 9). The one who can find refuge is the 'murderer'
(*rōṣēaḥ*; cf. v. 6; Deut. 4:42; 19:3, 4, 6), pointing to the Decalogue,
'Don't murder' (*lōʾ tirṣāḥ*, Exod. 20:13; Deut. 5:17; AT). In Numbers
35, *rōṣēaḥ* is used for intentional and unintentional killing alike.
Both forms of killing in Numbers 35 input guilt, an important
difference from Deuteronomy 19 that does not consider the
unintentional killer guilty (Mattison 2018: 236). The description of
homicide as 'striking a life' (*makkê-nepeš*) means killing a person
(e.g. Gen. 37:21; Lev. 24:17; Deut. 19:6; 27:25; Josh. 11:11; Jer. 40:14),
but here it has a more technical function (cf. vv. 15, 30). The
relation between homicide and corruption of the land, established
at the end of the chapter (v. 33), is associated with impurity (v.
34) through *nepeš* (cf. ch. 19; see below and Introduction, 'From
impurity to holiness').

12–15. In the towns of refuge the murderer avoids being killed
by the blood redeemer before a just trial (*mišpāṭ*, v. 12) can establish
the possibility of refuge or the death penalty at the hands of
the blood redeemer with the community's approval (v. 21). The
trial will be carried out by *the congregation* [or 'assembly'] (v. 12),
referring to the entirety of the Israelites as an ideal model for local
communities to adjudicate in such cases (Barmash 2005: 88–89).
Of course, the Levites were an important part of the assembly in
these cases. It is relevant that the trial that determines the possibility of refuge must be applicable to both Israelites and foreigners

in Israel (v. 15; cf. Lev. 24:10-23; Num. 15:15). The qualification *among them* determines the concrete experience of the foreigner in relation to the Israelites. The six towns are divided equally between Canaan and Transjordan (v. 14; cf. Deut. 19:7-9; 1 Chr. 6:57-60). These towns are all named in Joshua 20.

iii. Homicide and the corruption of the land (35:16-30)

In chapter 35, every homicide is a murder, inputs guilt and is subject to the death penalty, following the general talionic logic and the sacredness of every life ('life for life'; see Gen. 9:5-6), and the Priestly impurity system (vv. 31-34). However, a murderer can find protection from the 'blood redeemer' by fleeing to the 'towns of refuge' and having the assembly confirm that the act was 'unintentional' (*bišgāgâ*, vv. 11, 15; cf. Lev. 4:2). Intentionality is determined in the current verses by the procedure (actions) and the means (objects) by which the homicide occurred. The cases listed are exemplary rather than exhaustive for determining intentionality (cf. Deut. 19:5). This shows how biblical legislation is not rigid, but intends to promote discernment and wisdom, removing any abstraction of law to deal with real-life experiences that complicate rigid systematization (see Introduction, 'What is "biblical law"?').

16-21. Six cases illustrate intentional homicide. The first three (vv. 16-18) depend on the objects used. If the homicide was caused by an object of iron, stone or wood *that could cause death*, it is evidence of intentional homicide. The second group (vv. 20-21) exemplifies intentional homicides defined by other means. Pushing, tossing (something) and striking with the hand become intentional homicide when characterized by internal motivations: anger, intended action and previous enmity (cf. Exod. 21:13; Deut. 19:4). Therefore, this biblical tradition legislates intention (*mens rea* in legal terms; Strawn 2020: 27).

A form of judicial declaration appears in the repeated formula [*that person*] *is a murderer,* followed by the death-penalty sentence, 'the murderer must be killed' (vv. 16, 17, 18, 21, AT). The assembly takes responsibility for the declaration and sentence in cases where the murderer had fled to a town of refuge. In other Ancient Near Eastern cultures, the execution of the death penalty could be the responsibility of the victim's family (see examples in Bloch 2022), but the king often had the final authority over matters of life and death (see Barmash 2004: 184–193). In Numbers 35 the 'blood redeemer' takes absolute responsibility for executing the death penalty (vv. 19, 21) without depending on centralized political authorization. Such procedures would limit and make the death penalty more unlikely to happen. The submission to a community trial and sentence, and its handling by a common family member of the victim, could eliminate impulsive vengeance and, at the same time, the socially detached and bureaucratic execution by a royal authority. This is reflected in the biblical legislation itself that prioritizes the instructions that restrict, rather than encourage, the death penalty.

22–28. These verses define cases of unintentional homicide. Some of the examples from the previous verses appear here in their unintentional version: pushing someone as a reflex without enmity and tossing something at someone without any ill intention (v. 22). Without ill intention and unintentional harm also characterize death caused by a stone 'that could kill' dropped on someone without the agent 'seeing' (v. 23).

'These judgments' or *ordinances* (v. 24; cf. v. 29) generally denote the trial between the murderer and the victim's family. However, in verse 25, the priority of 'these judgments' is for the assembly to protect the unintentional murderer from the 'blood redeemer'. The introduction of the high priest's death as part of the institution of the towns of refuge (vv. 25, 28) reveals its function beyond the protection of the unintentional murderer. It sets a limit for how long the murderer must stay in the town of refuge, indicating that this is a period of punitive confinement or, better, exile (see m. Makkot; Greenberg 1959: 129). Because the homicide was unintended, the talionic logic applied here is the removal of the murderer from their family and kin group, so that they cannot benefit from and contribute to their livelihood, just as with the victim and their family (see Whitekettle 2018: 350–356). For this reason, the place to which the murderer returns after their exile is 'his possession' (*ăḥuzzātô*, v. 28), a term closely related to kinship property (vv. 2, 8; cf. 27:4, 7; 32:5, 22, 29, 32). The mention of the town's 'boundary' (*gĕbûl*, vv. 26–27) is relevant, as this is not a term used for the limits of towns. It demarcates territory, or land possession, and is a key concept in chapter 34 in the delineation of Canaan (34:3, 6, 7, 9). The towns of refuge, being part of the system of levitical towns, are marked out from the land of Israel and form a territorial boundary. To settle in one of them is to be set apart from 'the land of [Israelite] settling' (AT), which is forbidden for a murderer in verse 32 before the death of the high priest (see Mattison 2018: 249–250).

29–30. Another formulaic break indicates emphasis. Just like 'these judgments' of verse 24, the more complete, even pleonastic, formula 'these are the judicial statutes' (*ʾēllê . . . ḥuqqat mišpāṭ*, v. 29, AT; cf. 27:11) precedes a requirement of protection for the murderer that limits the execution of a death penalty. A murder conviction depends on more than one witness (v. 30), a common requirement in other Ancient Near Eastern cultures. Three elements of verse 29, *ḥuqqat* ('judicial'), *lĕdōrōtêkem* (*throughout your generations*) and *bĕkōl môšĕbōtêkem* ('in all your habitations', *wherever you live*), are typical of Priestly material (see Knohl 1995: 46–55; Stackert 2007: 61–96) and are related to religious instructions and practices (e.g. Exod. 12:20; Lev. 7:26; 10:9; Num. 15:21). Relevant for verses 31–34 are different occurrences of each expression or combinations of them in instructions about atonement (Exod. 30:10; Num. 15:22–26), the use of sacred oil to anoint priests (Exod. 30:31), equal legislation for Israelites and foreigners (Num. 15:15), the prohibition on eating fat and blood (Lev. 3:17; 7:26), the levitical function of 'bearing the sin' of Israelites (Num. 18:23), and the keeping of the Day of Atonement with a threat against the *nepeš* ('life') of those who don't (Lev. 23:31).

iv. Homicide, 'ransom', and the corruption of the land (35:31–34)

The dwelling of Yahweh in the land among the Israelites (v. 34) has serious implications for instructions that deal with death in Numbers, because it contrasts with the life-giving power of Yahweh (Frevel 2020: 377). The relation between death and impurity is described in the Introduction ('From impurity to holiness'), but it is relevant to highlight specific aspects concerning homicide in the context of the Priestly conception of impurity.

First, homicide causes a form of impurity (*ṭāmēʾ*, v. 34) that affects the land but is not contagious (cf. Lev. 12 – 15). Verse 34 concludes a chain of associations of Yahweh's 'dwelling' (*šākan*), from Sinai (Exod. 24:16), to the tabernacle (Exod. 25:8; 40:35), to the Israelite camp (Num. 5:3), to the land where Israel will settle (35:34; cf. Douglas 2001: 148–150; Frevel 2012: 405). Therefore, if homicide affects the land where Yahweh dwells among the Israelites, it certainly affects the camp, the sanctuary and the human agent (cf. Lev. 18:24; 20:3; cf. D. P. Wright 1991: 162; van Wolde 2009: 236).

Second, this form of impurity *pollutes* (*ḥ-n-p*) the land (v. 33). This rendering emphasizes the conceptual metaphor of impurity, though the judicial context supports translating 'corrupts', or even 'incriminates' (see Ps. 106:38; Isa. 24:5; Milgrom 1990: 295; Feder 2021: 163). The corruption of the land results from the association between blood and life (see Gen. 9:5; Lev. 17:11). Blood is a concrete substance of the person's life-force (*nepeš*; see on v. 11; Frevel 2012: 391), which has a polluting effect when out of the body, already entering the realm of the dead (see Frevel 2012: 388–400; Feder 2021: 145–171). In Numbers 19:13–15, the person's life-force outside the body in an enclosed environment pollutes every person and object present, as a form of substance 'in the air'. The same goes for blood, but its material property creates the image of a polluting force that is absorbed by the land. This is described by the image of the homicide victim's blood being shed *in it* [the land] (v. 33). In chapter 34 the land where Israel will settle has been intentionally defined by boundaries, conceptually creating an enclosed container. The victim's life-force outside the body, depicted by its shed blood, is contained in the land and corrupts it all.

Lastly, although unmentioned in chapter 35, the corruption of land leads to agricultural infertility (see 2 Sam. 21; cf. Num. 5:27–28) and exile of the people (see Lev. 18:28). These are forms of 'cutting off' (*kārēt*) the offender(s), that is, exclusion of the guilty from the people (see Num. 15:30–31) to eliminate their lineage (D. P. Wright 1991: 161–163; see 9:7, 13 for a relation between impurity by *nepeš* and the exclusion of a *nepeš* from the community). While the land is intended as a shared living space between Yahweh and Israel to produce resources to sustain Israel's life, it becomes corrupted as an infertile space that expels its inhabitants, human and divine.

31–33. Homicide corrupts the land, and it cannot be overcome through sacrificial rituals as can other forms of impurity (cf. Lev. 4 – 5; Num. 15:22–29; see Klawans 2004: 26). Following the talionic logic, a life for a life is the only way to deal with homicide (vv. 31, 33). In other cultures, such as Hittite, Assyrian and Babylonian, financial compensation for homicide was possible. Even the Hebrew term in verses 31–32 (*kōper*) has a monetary aspect (see Exod. 30:16; Num. 31:50), sometimes with a connotation of bribery (see 1 Sam. 12:3; Prov. 6:35; Amos 5:12; Levine 2000: 559). For this reason, interpreters tend to understand the root *k-p-r* (a substantive, *kōper*, in v. 32; a verb in the *pual*, *kuppar*, in v. 33) here as *ransom*, which can be unrelated to the cultic actions of purgation for pollution as part of the conceptual frame of purity and impurity. Although distinguishing 'ransom' from 'purgation' is important, here they are both part of the broader conceptual metaphor of atonement (see Introduction, 'Atonement and ritual'). In the case of homicide, both are operative. In a Neo-Assyrian document, for example, financial compensation for homicide effected purgation: 'wash the blood away' (Barmash 2004: 188). Jay Sklar rightly affirms that in Numbers 35:32–33, the blood of the murderer is characterized as a suitable 'ransom' (*kōper*) that can effect 'purgation' (*kipper/kuppar*; Sklar 2008: 29–30).

While the corruption of the land can be dealt with only by *the blood of the one who shed it* [the blood] (v. 33), the exile of the unintentional murderer ends with the death of the (high) priest (v. 32). Exile, in this context, separates the agent of death from the land, containing them and their guilt. Just as the enclosed aspect of the land leads to the notion of impurity spreading and corrupting it all, so the enclosed aspect of the towns of refuge physically separates and contains the agent who caused the impurity (see above, vv. 22–28).

The unintentional murderer likely lived as a type of indenture servant for Levites or priests. The fact that the unintentional murderer's freedom is conditioned on the high priest's death recommends this interpretation. First, it resembles the Hellenistic *paramone* relationship in which the indentured servant or adopted slave would be freed upon their master's death (see Whitekettle 2018: 348–349). Second, it follows a similar logic to that of the Year of Jubilee in which indentured service is limited by the cycle of fifty years (Lev. 25:40–41; see Stackert 2007: 88–96). But the anointed (*māšaḥ*, v. 25) character of the high priest actually points in the direction of his function as a representative of the people to atone for their sins and impurity (Lev. 4:3, 5, 16; 16:32). The high priest's death does not atone for the land, but for the unintentional murderer, who can return to their family and possession.

34. Instead of the specific root associated with impurity caused by homicide, *ḥ-n-p*, verse 34 uses the general term for impurity, *ṭāmē'*. The verb follows the expression *wĕlō'*, [*you shall*] *not*, changing from plural, as in verses 31–33, to singular. Now, it is Moses or Israel, not individual Israelites, who is addressed. Also, in verse 34, Yahweh, as the subject of the instruction, becomes emphatic by the double use of the first-person singular pronoun *'ănî* ('I'). The crucial aspect of the verse is also emphasized by repeating that Yahweh 'dwells' (*š-k-n*) among the Israelites in the land where Israel will 'settle' (*y-š-b*). This affirmation serves as the basic and general theological foundation for the entire chapter, even the whole of Numbers. Therefore, failing to observe these instructions about levitical towns, towns of refuge and homicide would cause impurity to negatively affect the relationship between Yahweh and Israel in the land. The whole land, therefore, is associated with the divine presence, even being considered holy (Knohl 1995: 179–180; Seebass 2006), with serious implications for how Israel will live in it.

Meaning

Because Numbers 35 allows, and even demands, the death penalty in the case of intentional murder, it is easy to misinterpret the intention of the instructions. In the biblical context of kinship blood vengeance, Numbers 35, even when allowing or demanding the death penalty, is interested in controlling, discouraging and diminishing bloodshed. Modern contexts are profoundly different. Their social organizations and institutional structures do not require the death penalty to reduce bloodshed.

The reason given in the text for the reduction of bloodshed has a theological basis. The inclusion of internal motivations that result in homicide (vv. 20–23) points to the roots of the problem (see P. D. Miller 2009: 262–268). Another Priestly text, Leviticus 19, considers this aspect: 'You shall not hate in your heart [your brother] . . . You shall not take vengeance . . . you shall love your neighbour as yourself' (Lev. 19:17–18). This movement from the negative to the positive, from internal motivations to practice, is also reflected in Jesus' reconsideration of the commandment against killing in Matthew 5:21–26. Similarly, Calvin derived from this commandment a requirement for duties of love and care to preserve the life of one's neighbour, because God intends it to be dear and precious (Calvin 1960: 2.8.9).

Finally, the distribution of towns throughout the land ties the whole chapter together. They highlight the life-giving power of God in targeted forms of protection of life against the destructive power of death. In the real world, violence will disrupt and threaten life, so Numbers 35 intimates that the divine presence is expanded through communities profoundly committed to the promotion of life. These spaces are marked by the wisdom promoted by the biblical 'law' to the point that it is this 'law', with its concrete visions for the flourishing of life in society, that becomes the means to preserve and expand the divine presence in the land. The 'place' of refuge, where life is protected, promoted and expanded, is the community formed by God's wisdom or Torah (Cocco 2016: 80).

K. Renegotiating land distribution and inheritance outside tribal patrilineage (36:1–12)

Context
This chapter picks up on the case of Zelophehad's daughters addressed earlier in chapter 27. In fact, one Qumran manuscript (4QRP) places 36:1–12 immediately after 27:1–11, which highlights the close connection between these two chapters. The dominant order in the Hebrew and Greek traditions, however, conforms with placing this section at the end of Numbers. As a result, the theme of the inheritance and marriage of Zelophehad's daughters

forms a frame around the final major section of the book, which takes place after the second census (ch. 26) and prepares the Israelites for their transition into the land west of the Jordan River that God had promised them. Their focus on the division of parcels and inheritance *in the land across the Jordan* directs the focus of the narrative beyond both Numbers and Deuteronomy towards Joshua, where this narrative arc comes to fruition in the possession (Josh. 1 – 12) and apportionment of the land among the tribes (Josh. 13 – 21).

The separation of the two narratives raises the question: why did God not provide this complete instruction in Numbers 27, where the topic first arose? This question cannot be resolved completely. However, the combined issues of land inheritance and marriage might suggest a possible interpretation. The identities of Zelophehad's daughters are related to Transjordanian towns in chapters 26 and 27. Their insertion in Israel's genealogies in chapter 26 raises the issue of land and inheritance that is resolved in chapter 27. Nonetheless, their connection within Israel must remain in the same tribe, rather than being transferred from one tribe to another (see 32:34–42 above). Otherwise, land would change from one tribe to another. In the light of how Israel's relationship with other peoples is gendered (Israel should play the role of the husband and other peoples the role of wives; see Introduction, 'Israel's identity and its neighbours'; 5:11–31; and ch. 25), the framing of chapters 27 and 36 for the last section of Numbers offers the ideal relationship for Israel as a people, and even as individuals with regard to intermarriage, for Israel to dwell in the land.

The chapter splits into four parts. Verses 1–6 concern the concrete case of Zelophehad's daughters and therefore the initial division of the land, while verses 7–9 address cases of a daughter's inheritance after the Israelites have settled in their land. Then verses 10–12 narrate the enactment of Yahweh's decision by Zelophehad's daughters, and verse 13 functions as a conclusion to the whole of Numbers.

In addition to Numbers 27, this chapter also assumes familiarity with the Jubilee regulations for returning land to its hereditary owners in Leviticus 25:13. Furthermore, it has in mind the apportioning of the land foreshadowed in Numbers 33:50 – 34:29.

Comment
i. Concerns for land inherited by Zelophehad's daughters
(36:1–6a)

1. The 'heads of the fathers' [households]' play important roles in Exodus 6:14, 25 and Numbers 31:26 (with 7:2) in representing the interests of their families. This term also occurs in 1 Chronicles 7:11; 2 Chronicles 19:8; Ezra 2:68//Nehemiah 7:71. As noted on Numbers 27, Joshua 17 configures the Manassite genealogy differently when reporting the apportioning of land parcels for Zelophehad's daughters. There the Gileadite clans are reported as receiving portions in the Transjordan (also 32:39–40). It is surprising that this counter-claim comes from the Gileadites, who are associated with portions of the land in the Transjordan (32:26–40; Josh. 17:1), while Zelophehad's daughters would receive portions in the Cisjordan, according to Joshua 17:2–6. The Gileadites do not have a direct interest in the judgment. If, however, this case is envisioned more broadly as being about the relationship between Israel and other peoples, the situation in Transjordan is of as much interest as that of Cisjordan.

The *leaders* also appear elsewhere in Numbers, sometimes designated as *heads of the ancestral houses* (7:2; 31:26; 32:28) or alternatively as leaders of the tribes, Israel or the congregation (1:16; 7:2; 27:2; 31:13; 32:2; 34:18). These men take up some judicial responsibilities, helping with the census and being designated to apportion the land, as well as representative roles in worship throughout Numbers. They also pose a potential threat to the leadership of Moses and Aaron in chapters 16–17 (see esp. 16:2; 17:2). Thus, there is always some tension introduced when these figures approach Moses. In any case, the *men* representing Gilead *came forward*, the same term used to describe the action of Zelophehad's daughters in 27:1, indicating the connection between the two narratives.

A striking feature of this verse (cf. below on v. 6 as well) is the implied designation of Manasseh (and thus Ephraim) as the *Josephite clans*. Elsewhere in Numbers, and typically throughout the Bible, these two are considered 'tribes'. Designating them as *clans* (*mišpāḥâ*) in turn constructs a bridge from the typically more 'clan-level' concern of marriage to the broader tribal level under discussion in this text.

2–3. The Gileadites articulate the possible impasse arising from two distinct divine commands: (1) that the land be apportioned by lot (26:55; 34:13) and (2) that Zelophehad's daughters should receive their father's share (27:7). An issue would arise if these women married outside their tribe, for the following reason: the women would be expected to pass on their inherited land to their sons at their death. Because these sons would be considered part of the tribe of their *fathers*, the title of this land would transfer from one tribe (Manasseh – the tribe of their mothers) to whichever tribe their fathers belonged to. Ironically, the Gileadites are Manassite descendants who received their land inheritance through matri-lineage (see 32:34–43). Thus, the focus of the Gileadites' concern shifts from, or perhaps redefines (Johnson 2020: 273), the memory of the *name* of the father (Zelophehad) being *taken away* (27:4; *g-r-*ʾ) to the portion of the *land* being *taken away* (36:3; *g-r-*ʾ). The repeated use of this verbal root strengthens the links between the two chapters. However, the claims contrast the interests of the individual family (ch. 27) with those of the broader social group (ch. 36).

Given that this chapter modifies 27:1–11 such that Zelophehad's grandsons would trace their genealogies through *their* fathers and not back to Zelophehad through their mothers, it is unexpected that the names of three of Zelophehad's daughters (see comment on 27:1–7 above) designate villages or geographical regions found in inscriptions from the area of Manasseh!

4. Maintaining the family (tribal, clan) ownership of a portion of land also features as a major theme in Leviticus 25 (cf. 1 Kgs 21), which addresses means of reacquiring family land that has been sold – with its return to the family of the original Israelite owner at the Jubilee representing the last resort. The argument in this verse confirms that the inheritance that the daughters pass on to their sons would, in the end, be added to the inheritance of their husbands. However, the reference to Jubilee here comes as some surprise and may have in mind such land that would be sold (though this is speculative in that the text does not explicitly articulate this condition). More likely (following Ashley 2022: 531), the reference to the Jubilee could indicate that the ruling here serves as an *extension*, in order to protect the tribal landholdings from a further peril.

5–6a. Moses proclaims that these leaders are right (or 'just'; *kēn*) in their claim, with the same terminology found in 27:7 in God's adjudication of Zelophehad's daughters' argument. An apparent impasse arises – which can often be the case in judicial cases! – as both sides have legitimate claims. By using the subtle expression *according to the word of* [*Yahweh*], it remains unclear, especially when combined with the title *my lord* used for Moses in verses 1–2, whether Moses enquired of Yahweh, or was simply able to adjudicate the case using his own divinely imputed wisdom, thereby being able (in this case) to utter godly judgment on his own. If the latter, then it points to an intriguing pathway to how Scripture itself indicates that it means to be interpreted with creativity and wisdom derived from itself, but not intended to stay the same. Moses affirms the Gileadite leaders' weighing of two separate divine commands in order to reach a solution that respects them both (though, as discussed below, there is no explicit mention of the manner in which the *name* of the deceased man is preserved). As a result, the final chapter of Numbers may offer its audience a divinely ordained *method of interpretation*.

ii. Concerns for land inherited by daughters in the future (36:6b–9)

6b–7. While within the limits of their tribal clans, these daughters receive permission to choose their own husbands, a rare choice in antiquity and in biblical texts. Furthermore, the limitation remains rather opaque for these women through the mention of the *tribe of Joseph* in verse 5. If the 'tribe of Joseph' marks the limit, then it includes the traditional tribes of both Manasseh *and* Ephraim.

The Hebrew term (*d-b-q*) underlying the verb in 'all Israelites *shall retain* their own inheritance' (v. 7, AT) often concerns marriage or worship (e.g. Gen. 2:24; Deut. 13:18), indicating the strong emotional and relational connections of this command.

8–9. The text transitions from the concrete case of the daughters and the parcels of land that would be apportioned to them (after the Israelites take possession of the land in Joshua) to consideration of the regulation of inheritance by daughters thereafter. These verses pick up on the regulations in 27:8. This ruling follows quite closely from verses 1–7: any such woman must marry someone within her father's tribe. This regulation does not explicitly state anything about how this practice would secure the *name* of the father, which was the concern in 27:4. The force of these verses lies in the connection between *each tribe* and its particular land. The parcels must not *be transferred* (lit. 'turn around', *s-b-b*). The defining important feature of the land is not whether it is better or worse than other pieces of land, but one's traditional link to it. It is not bought, sold or inherited simply as a commodity that is passed around (cf. Jer. 6:12), as is often the case in capitalist economic systems.

iii. Enactment of God's decision in the case (36:10–12)

10–12. Unlike in 27:3–4, the women do not speak in this disputation. However, they retain minimal agency in that they appear to have some, now more limited, choice of husbands. These women perform the final actions in Numbers: their willingness to obey the ruling thus provides the final word on faithful human action. They function as an example for all who wish to follow in the path of worshipful living as God's people, which is very significant if they represent other people groups integrated into Israel as discussed in relation to chapter 26. In this case, they also serve as a contrast example to the foreign women of chapter 25. Instead of deceiving Israel, Zelophehad's daughters become a model of Israelite identity. Most striking in their action is their choice of husbands who are much closer in relation than is required by the ruling in verse 6. By choosing their cousins, the allotment of their parcels of land to take place in Joshua establishes a much stronger bond between close clan members, rather than more distant relatives. Furthermore, their action transfers the parcels to those who would have inherited them had Zelophehad not had any daughters, according to 27:9. While speculative, perhaps their submission to this ruling results in their receipt of individual allotments – rather than simply a single allotment for their father that the five daughters would then split – recorded in Joshua 17:5. A similar chain of events takes place in 1 Chronicles 23:22.

L. Conclusion for Numbers (36:13)

13. This verse functions as a subscript for all of Numbers. It bears many similarities to the concluding verse of Leviticus (27:34; also 26:46).

The mention of the *plains of Moab by the Jordan at Jericho* recalls the location in 22:1; 26:3, 63; 31:12; 33:48, 50; and 35:1, indicating some markers for the structure of the latter part of Numbers: especially that chapters 26–36 function as a major section of it, but also to some degree chapters 22–36. *The commandments and the ordinances* commanded by Yahweh at this location applies foremost to the material in chapters 27–36, though the lack of such a statement in, say, chapter 10 indicates that here it functions as the summary for all the legal material of Numbers.

Numbers 33:48–50 had marked the plains of Moab by the Jordan at Jericho as the last station of the exodus from Egypt, thereby providing some closure to the Israelites' journey at that point. Therefore, chapters 34–36 represent an interlude in the people's movement, though all three of these chapters point to future action across the Jordan. This location reappears in Deuteronomy 34:1, thereby connecting the entirety of Deuteronomy with these chapters of Numbers and, with them, leaning forward to the action that will take place in Joshua (see Josh. 1:11; 3:1). In this way, this verse characterizes Numbers as an incomplete narrative on its own, requiring the completion of the narrative arc in Joshua. There is, then, something 'eschatological' at the end of Numbers – that is, an orientation towards the *future* and the fulfilment that lies there.

Meaning
The themes of land, marriage and communal belonging punctuate the conclusion of Numbers. However, there is an important theological insight that comes from concluding it with an addition or revision to God's prior judgment for the division and inheritance of the land promulgated in 27:1–11: God's involvement in Israel's affairs continues to address new situations. The canonical placement of Numbers, just before Moses' last speeches in Deuteronomy, confirms this insight. While Deuteronomy wrestles

with whether there will be another prophet 'like Moses' (cf. Deut. 18:15–22 v. Deut. 34:10–12), Moses' issuance of a *new* ruling according to the command of Yahweh in Numbers 36 confirms the open-ended nature of God's teaching in the Pentateuch. Said differently, the update to God's ruling from chapter 27 in chapter 36 indicates that new situations call both for paying attention to past divine instruction (in this case from 26:55; 27:1–11; 34:13) and attentiveness to a new word from God, however this might be acquired, in the present. This might be especially related to how Israel should enter into relationships with other peoples, which opens up new possibilities for interpreting biblical texts (such as those mentioned in the *Meaning* section of Num. 31).

A second theme emerges from the obedient action of Zelophehad's daughters. Their choice of husbands places a high value on the flourishing of their close community in that they choose to marry closer relatives than those legally required. While the ruling in this chapter limits their freedom, it nonetheless affords them the final action in all of Numbers, indicating the importance of women's initiative, even within the patriarchal hierarchy that the biblical text sets in place.

Finally, the chapter, and Numbers as a whole, points forward to a place of rest across the Jordan. There are many insights that can result with regard to both the hope imagined in the chapter and the importance of a physical location of 'rest' for embodied humans. In general, this invites followers of Christ to consider the physical, social and political features of the kingdom of God that can be desired and enacted in one's present context.

www.ingramcontent.com/pod-product-compliance
Lightning Source LLC
Chambersburg PA
CBHW070931150426
42814CB00024B/97